# Michigan Trail Atlas

## The Guide to
## Cross Country Skiing
## and Hiking Trails

_____

Dennis R. Hansen

with

Danforth Holley

Hansen Publishing Company — Okemos, Michigan

MICHIGAN TRAIL ATLAS—THE GUIDE TO CROSS COUNTRY SKIING AND HIKING TRAILS is published by
Hansen Publishing Company, 1801 Birchwood Drive, Okemos, MI, 48864 in association with
Holley International Company, 131 Kercheval, Grosse Pointe Farms, MI 48236

Printed in the United States of America

Library of Congress Catalog Card Number: 88-091154
ISBN: 0-930098-04-8

Cover art by Kimberly Nickols
Printing by Bookcrafters Inc., Chelsea, MI
Typesetting by Sans Serif Inc., Ann Arbor, MI

*With All My Love,*
*    to my wife Barbara*
*    and daughters Stephanie and Lisa,*

*without who's understanding and support*
*this book would not have been possible.*

# Cross-Country Skiing Etiquette

1. Be courteous and helpful at all times. Don't assume that the other skier is as skilled as you are. If someone else is having some difficulty, ask if you can help. Often they will not ask for assistance but will gladly accept it if asked.

2. Downhill skiers have the right of way. Even on one way trail systems, don't assume that everyone is going the correct direction. The trail ahead could be poorly marked or the on coming skier could be confused. Always look up hill to check for skiers coming down the hill even if you are going the correct direction.

3. The slower skier should yield the track for the faster skier, if there is no space for the faster skier to go around. Judgement should be used here. In crowded trail systems it might be better for the faster skier to ski elsewhere, since they will be inconveniencing many skiers.

4. Keep to the right when meeting on coming skiers.

5. Keep clear of the track when not skiing. Don't stop at the bottom of hills or on blind intersections. Accidents caused by hitting other skiers can be very serious, which is compounded if it occurs some miles from the parking lot.

6. If you must walk, do so at the edge of the ski trail and out of the track.

7. Repair trail damage from falls. This is very important especially on downhill sections. Your sitz mark could cause another fall and/or injury.

8. Carry out all rubbish. Leave the trail cleaner than you found it.

9. Pay the trail fee or make a generous contribution if asked. Many trails are maintained only from the money generated from user contributions. If you liked the trail, show your appreciation. If you don't contribute, don't complain when the trail maintenance disappears.

Even the DNR is not funded to groom pathways. Grooming operations must pay for themselves. Make a generous contribution.

10. Follow the posted rules. They are established so that all skiers can get maximum enjoyment from their outdoor experience.

11. Dogs are not welcome on the ski trail. They bother other skiers and destroy the track. If you wish to take your dog with you, break your own trail rather than using an established system.

# Hiking Etiquette

1. Respect private property rights. Do not use property or facilities that don't belong to you, even if they are not posted to that effect. If you desire to use private property, get permission first.

2. Respect the rights of others, both other hikers and those who depend on the back country for their livelihood.

3. For safety sake, always hike with at least one friend. On the other hand, don't hike in large groups as it adversely impacts the environment and may disturb other hikers who come upon you.

4. Pass through the land without disturbing it. This includes not only growing things but artifacts as well. Remember, someone else did the same so YOU could enjoy them. Do the same for those who follow you. This includes using a self contained stove rather than wood for your back country campfire.

5. Leave your campsite and trail, cleaner than you found it. Pack out everything.

6. Always carry a map and compass.

7. Dispose of human waste and waste water properly.

# Contents

# Important Information

## History of the Atlas

Congratulations on your purchase of the *Michigan Trail Atlas*!! You are now the proud owner of the ONLY comprehensive publication of cross-country skiing and hiking trails in Michigan (and a few selected trails just over the border). This Atlas is the result of many years of collecting material and a lot of skiing which first culminated in 1978 with the publishing of the *Michigan Cross Country Skiing Atlas*. After 3 editions, which included 5 printings and over 22,000 copies, it came time to retire that book. It served its owners, and no doubt many others quite well. But it was time to look to the future with a more comprehensive and current publication.

## The Old and the New

From time to time Dan and I have heard of reports that skiers were using the Atlas as a hiking trail reference book as well. Though we didn't intend it for that purpose, we are glad that they found an additional use for the former Atlas. Realizing that there are many more trails that are suitable only for hiking, we decided to write this new book for that dual purpose. Enter, the *Michigan Trail Atlas—The Guide to Cross Country Skiing and Hiking Trails*. This completely new Atlas now includes all known hiking trails in Michigan whether they are a couple of miles long or the 173 mile network on Isle Royale National Park. Some of you may question our decision to include some rather short trails. We have intentionally done this because the determination as to what is a hiking trail is a personal decision. Who is to say how long a trail has to be to be considered a hiking trail? This Atlas allows you to make that decision.

For those of you who have purchased one or more of the previous editions, be assured that the *Michigan Trail Atlas* is not just a rehash of the information in the previous Atlases.

Every effort has been made to provide you with accurate and up to date trail information. The trail information in this Atlas is completely new from the first trail to the last. Every trail operator has been contacted at least twice and sometimes 3 and 4 times to assure accuracy.

In addition I have made many personal visits (it was a tough job, but someone had to do it) to provide you with accurate information and my personal impressions of those trails. During the winter of 1988 I traveled over 3,700 miles and skied over 80 trails, many of which I have not skied recently. Even with all of this travel I was unable to visit all the trails that I would have liked to ski.

Over a year has gone into compiling the Atlas you are now reading. However, to reduce the possibility of publishing out-of-date information, Dan and I have provided you with a "Revised" date that you will find in the top right corner of the page. If this date is more than three years old, we suggest you may want to call ahead to confirm the information presented. Future editions of the *Michigan Trail Atlas* will show new dates as new information is provided to me or as the current information listed is confirmed to be accurate.

Dan and I are committed to providing you with essential information about the trails depicted, however unlike many other trail books on the market today, we do not intend to provide you with a narrative of each and every mile. We believe that you are entitled to explore the trails as you travel along them. Since we believe that is the only real way to get the most out of your outdoor experience.

You will not find my personal list of the "Best Ski Trails in Michigan". Though I have skied many I have not skied them all. Until that time I would not feel comfortable in giving you that list. Further, what determines a good ski trail is subjective. Obviously there are a few "stand out" trails but beyond that, there are many very good ski trails which would include almost all of them. I would rather have you read the narratives on each trail and make up your own mind.

As in the past, the trail maps have all been redrawn on a common format to make them easy to read and understand. Unfortunately, in some cases it has not been possible to show all the information that was provided to me, but be assured that the important information has been included. A legend can be found at the beginning of the Atlas to explain the meaning of the symbols used. Please take a moment to find this page and review these symbols. Another page has been included that explains the terms and phrases that were used to describe the trails.

For those of you with copies of the earlier *Michigan Cross Country Skiing Atlas*, Dan and I want first to thank you for your purchase. We hope that book met your expectations. In this new Atlas you will be pleased to know that the separate pages for the text and map are gone. Both the text and map are on a single page for easy use. However, to conveniently locate any given trail, this Atlas follows the old book by having the State and this Atlas divided into 4 regions with region maps at the beginning of each section. There is a map following this introductory section, illustrating how we have divided the state into the four regions. Region 1 is the southern half of the lower peninsula, Region 2 is the northern half of the lower peninsula, Region 3 is the eastern half of the upper peninsula and Region 4 is the western half of the upper peninsula.

Another part that you will find missing from this new Atlas is the "Competition Calendar". This has been dropped because the *Great Lakes Skier* has become the primary promoter of ski races in Michigan. They do an excellent job of listing upcoming events and giving results 4 times a year. In addition, the newspaper has many interesting articles about skiing and ski trails. It can be purchased at most ski shops or ordered directly from Great Lakes Sports Publications, Inc, 7990 West Grand River Ave., Suite C, Brighton, MI 48116. Subscription's are $5.00/year.

## Finding Your Way Around Michigan

Since roads and communities depicted in this Atlas in many situations cannot be found on a typical fold out state highway map, it's essential to have a county road atlas to navigate the back roads of Michigan. That is why when using this Atlas to locate a trail, the purchase of a Michigan county road atlas is recommended. There are two map books which I recommend. One is published by the Michigan Natural Resources Magazine called the "Mapbook of Michigan Counties" and the other is published by DeLorne Mapping Company called "Michigan Atlas and Gazetteer". The purchase of both might be a good idea, since the "Gazetteer" is somewhat easier to read and shows vegetation, while the "Mapbook" has more road names, distinguishes state and federal owned land, and some additional detail that is lacking from the former. Both can be purchased at most bookstores.

## Northern Michigan Nordic Ski Council

A recent addition to the cross-country ski scene has been the establishment of the Northern Michigan Nordic Ski Council. Founded by operators of several touring centers in the northern lower peninsula, the Council's purpose is to promote and expand cross-country skiing in Michigan. Initially, it has established two phone numbers (one toll free) for skiers to acquire information on ski areas. An added benefit is that the Council will provide current snow conditions throughout the area of the state covered by the Council. Their numbers are 800-521-0675 and 517-786-2211. If you prefer to write, their address is: Northern Michigan Nordic Ski Council, c/o Garland, Co Rd 489, Lewiston, MI 49756.

## A Word About ATB's (all terrain bicycles)

Since the use of ATB's on public land varies greatly, I have included a line in the data provided to you. This will tell you if ATB's are permitted and if they are, whether soil conditions or other factors make them suitable for use (usually due to extensive soft sand). At this printing Dan and I know of no trails that have been developed solely for the ATB, however many public agencies and private operators are permitting them at this time. Unfortunately all federal agencies prohibit their use on trails designed for hiking, skiing and horseback riding. This means all three national forests, the two national lakeshores and Isle Royale National Park are off limits to ATB's.

## Please Pay Your Own Way

The cost of grooming trails is very high. When you're asked for a donation or requested to pay a daily use fee, don't try to avoid it. Privately operated trails must have that money to stay in business. The publicly operated trails must have that use fee to continue grooming since there is usually no money budgeted by the DNR, national forests or national lakeshores to perform grooming operations on a continuing basis. These public agencies are doing this as a public service and are funding this activity from other established budgets in the hope that the grooming operations will become self-funded. If you like the trails that you ski on, support them generously, otherwise don't complain if they disappear for the lack of money.

## Dan and I Would Appreciate Your Help

Since all the pages of trail data were produced on a computer, revising the Atlas will be easy. Therefore, there will be few reprints but rather new editions to provide you with the most current information possible. We welcome and encourage you to contact me (in writing please) if you find the information presented here, is in error, or if you find a trail that I have missed. My address is 1801 Birchwood Drive, Okemos, MI 48864. Our goal is to provide you with the most accurate and up-to-date publication of Michigan cross-country skiing and hiking trails that is possible.

## You Are Now On Your Own
## (our attorneys made us do it)

This book is intended as an aid for the hiker and cross-country skier. They should understand that hiking and skiing have some inherent danger and they should understand that the use of the trails and areas depicted herein are at their own risk. No one associated with the publication assumes any liability for accidents or injuries through the use of the *Michigan Trail Atlas*.

Dennis R. Hansen
Okemos, Michigan
June, 1988

3

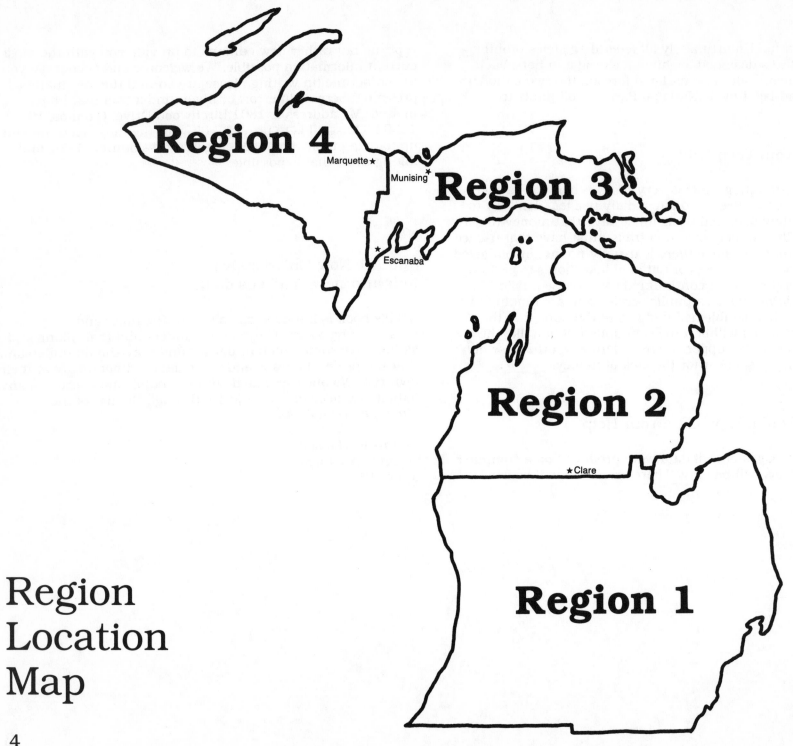

Region 4

Marquette ★

Munising ★

Region 3

★
Escanaba

Region 2

★ Clare

Region 1

Region
Location
Map

# Explanation of Map Information

*Arrow*: The arrow on the maps points to the north

*Scale*: If no scale is stated, it means that the scale of the map was not provided to the author. To my knowledge, the maps are not distorted. They are to some scale, it's just not known.

When the word "SEE" is used, it refers to the listing of another trail found elsewhere in the Atlas.

The HEAVIEST SOLID LINES generally represent plowed roads. However, changes in funding may significantly impact plowing routes. Call ahead to make sure that the route you plan to take is cleared.

The maps don't usually show all the roads that exist in a given area. As suggested in the "Important Information" you should purchase a county map book to reduce the possibility of getting lost, especially in the more remote areas of the state.

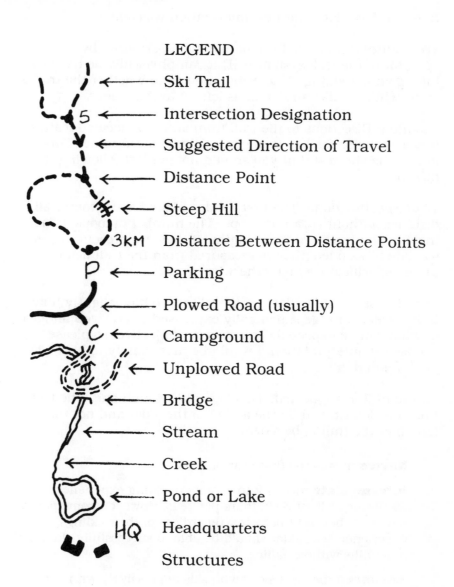

LEGEND

Ski Trail

Intersection Designation

Suggested Direction of Travel

Distance Point

Steep Hill

Distance Between Distance Points

Parking

Plowed Road (usually)

Campground

Unplowed Road

Bridge

Stream

Creek

Pond or Lake

Headquarters

Structures

# Explanation of Text Information

*Revised*: Last date that new information was added

*Trail suitability*: A trail is suitable if it's permitted by the operator of the trail system AND it can physically be used for hiking and/or skiing. A determination as to whether the trail is worthwhile to hike and/or ski is left up to the reader.

*Location*: Directions to the trail from an easily located feature (town or major road(s)) using an easily followed route. This may not be the shortest, but you should not get lost following these directions.

*Trail Specifications*: The first distance listed is the total trail distance without regard to loops. The number of loops do not include point to point trail lengths, if they are present, unless so stated. Loop lengths are measured from the trail head, unless specifically stated otherwise.

*Terrain*: Can include flat, gently rolling, rolling, slightly hilly, hilly, steep. A range is generally expressed to give you an idea of what can be expected. This is very subjective, so please excuse my interpretation. I would be most happy to hear from you, if you don't agree.

*Skiing ability suggested*: This is really a tough one. The factor I used is determined by the ability of the skier and not the length of the trail to be skied.

**Novice** means the first year on skis.

**Intermediate** means 2 to 4 years of skiing experience, assuming at least 6 ski tours per year. However, some people never get beyond this point, regardless of their skiing experience. The skier should be able to successfully ski down most hills without falling.

**Advanced** means a skier who skis aggressively with considerable skill and also includes citizen racers. Must be able to handle all downhill sections without falling and with some reasonable speed.

*Hiking trail difficulty*: This is related to the degree of trail difficulty required to hike the trail. This factor is not related to trail length and location.

*Suitable for all terrain bicycles*: A trail is suitable if the soil on the trail is packed so that a bicycle can travel on it with a minimum of difficulty.

If a trail has been designated as prohibited for use by bicycles, it will be so stated. At this time all federal agencies including the three national forests and two lakeshore's prohibit the use of ATB's on hiking and ski trails. The DNR is presently considering regulating ATB's but at printing time no such law has been passed. I suggest that you check ahead if you intend to use an ATB on hiking or ski trails.

*Grooming method*: A track set trail assumes packing and grooming. Not all of the system may be of the stated type, but a significant amount will be. If variations exist (i.e. skating and/or track set) they will be so stated. Frequency of maintenance may also be stated.

Please keep in mind that grooming is the most tenuous feature of the ski trail. Frequency of grooming will make all the difference for a successful ski outing. If there has been a recent snowfall, a trail listed as track set may not even exist when you arrive. Plan your trip accordingly and call ahead to confirm the grooming schedule, if that requirement is important to you.

Don't expect that every trail that is supposed to be groomed, will be. Funding, community support, equipment breakdown and need for the equipment elsewhere all play a role in changing the schedule or the elimination of the trail grooming altogether.

Plan your trip accordingly and call ahead to confirm the grooming schedule so that your trip will not be less than you had planned.

*Trail use fee*: Fee, if any, will be for skiing only. There may be an additional or separate charge for entering area, independent of the cost to ski the trail. Please don't try to avoid paying the requested fee and if a donation is asked, be generous. Without YOUR money the grooming may stop, something I am sure none of us want.

*Camping*: Facilities limited to the very near proximity of the trail.

*General information*: Information that may be useful to evaluate the trail. This may include facilities, services, who maintains the trail, events held, restrictions if any and locations of nearby lodging and restaurants.

Some abbreviations are used in the text:

| | |
|---|---|
| SF | state forest |
| SFCG | state forest campground |
| NCT | North Country Trail |
| RA | recreation area |
| NF | national forest |
| NFCG | national forest campground |
| SW, NE, SE, etc. | compass directions |
| NA | not applicable |
| Co Rd | county road |
| *, **, *** | refers to other things that are explained further in the general information section at the bottom of the page. |

# Region 1

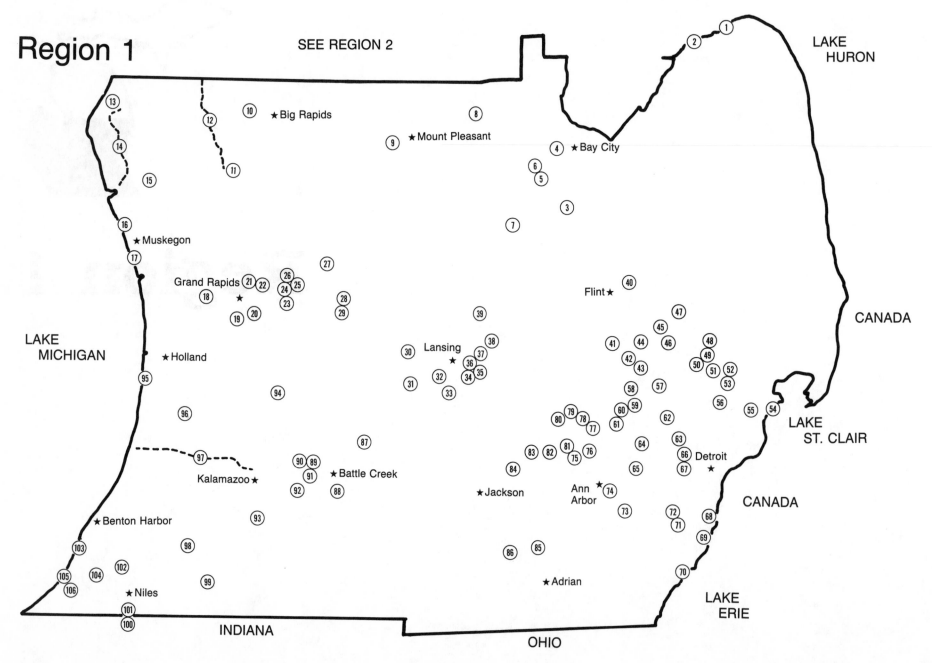

# Region 1

SEE REGION 2

LAKE HURON

LAKE MICHIGAN

CANADA

LAKE ST. CLAIR

CANADA

LAKE ERIE

INDIANA

OHIO

★ Big Rapids

★ Mount Pleasant

★ Bay City

★ Muskegon

Grand Rapids ★

Flint ★

Lansing ★

★ Holland

★ Battle Creek

Kalamazoo ★

★ Jackson

Ann Arbor ★

Detroit ★

★ Benton Harbor

★ Adrian

★ Niles

# Region 1 Contents

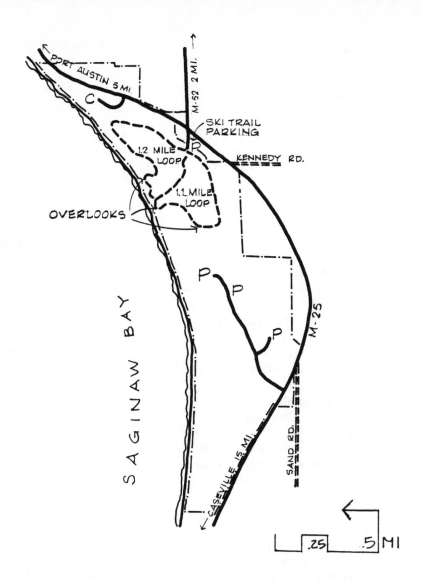

PORT CRESCENT STATE PARK

Port Crescent State Park                    Revised:  8/13/87


Port Crescent State Park
1776 Port Austin Rd.                        517-738-8663
Port Austin, MI  48467

DNR Parks Division Office

                                            517-373-1270

Trail suitable for hiking & skiing

Location:
 On Saginaw Bay, 5 miles west of Port Austin


Trail specifications:
    2.5 mi; 2 loop(s); Loop length(s)-various
Typical terrain: Flat to hilly
Skiing ability suggested: Novice
Hiking trail difficulty: Easy
Nordic trail grooming method: Track set
Suitable for all-terrain bicycle: No
Trail use fee: None, but vehicle entry fee required $2/day, $10/year
Camping: Campground available
Drinking water available at flowing well

General Information:
 Maintained by the DNR Parks Division
 Overlooks of Saginaw Bay from trail
 Candlelight ski tours scheduled throughout the winter
 Ski rentals available locally

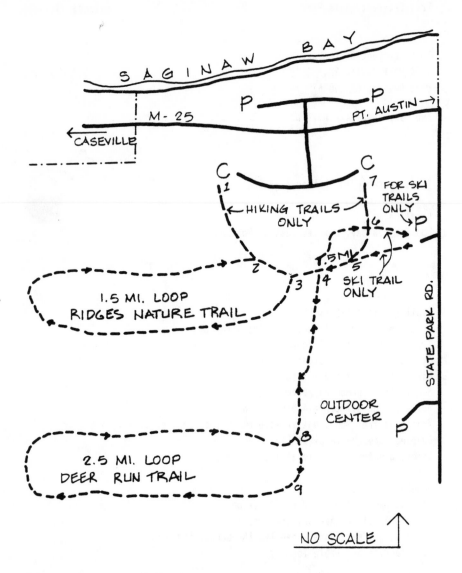

SAGINAW BAY

M-25

P     P
PT. AUSTIN →

← CASEVILLE

C     C
1     7  FOR SKI
         TRAILS
         ONLY
← HIKING TRAILS
      ONLY
              6        P

                1.5 MI.
        2              5
              3  4   SKI TRAIL
                         ONLY

1.5 MI. LOOP
RIDGES NATURE TRAIL

STATE PARK RD.

OUTDOOR
CENTER
              8              P

2.5 MI. LOOP
DEER RUN TRAIL
                      9

NO SCALE

# SLEEPER STATE PARK

Sleeper State Park                    Revised:  3/17/88

Sleeper State Park
6573 State Park Rd.                           517-856-4411
Caseville, MI  48725

Trail suitable for skiing & hiking

Location:
 4 miles east of Caseville on M25 at the north tip of the thumb
 Ski trailhead - Headqarters building on State Park Rd., just east of main
    park entrance
 Hiking trailheads - From campground

Trail specifications:
   4 mi‡; 2 loop(s); Loop length(s)-1.5, 2.5‡
 Typical terrain: Flat
 Skiing ability suggested: Novice
 Hiking trail difficulty: Easy
 Nordic trail grooming method: Track set
 Suitable for all-terrain bicycle: Yes
 Trail use fee: None, but vehicle entry fee required $2/day, $10/year
 Camping: Campground in the park

General Information:
 Maintained by the DNR Parks Division
 ‡ Ski trail distances
 The Ridges Nature Trail has 14 stations that explains various features of
    both natural and historical interest

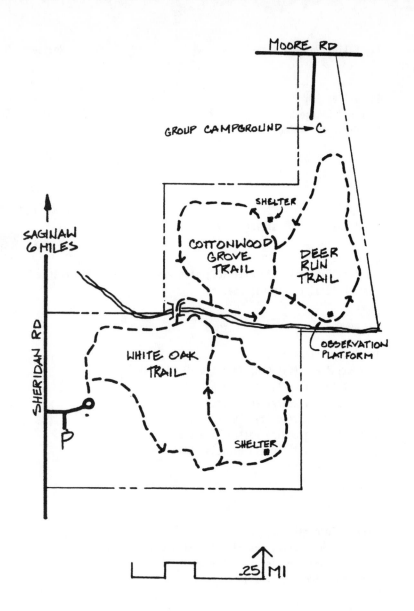

MOORE RD

GROUP CAMPGROUND ——→ C

SHELTER

COTTONWOOD
GROVE
TRAIL

DEER
RUN
TRAIL

SAGINAW
6 MILES

SHERIDAN RD

WHITE OAK
TRAIL

OBSERVATION
PLATFORM

P

SHELTER

.25 MI

# PRICE NATURE CENTER

Price Nature Center                    Revised: 3/19/88

Saginaw County Parks & Recreation Commission
111 S. Michigan Ave                    517-790-5280
Saginaw, MI  48602

Trail suitable for skiing & hiking

Location:
 6 miles south of Saginaw on Sheridan Rd (1 mile east of M13), between
   Moore Rd. and Curtis Rd.

Trail specifications:
   4 mi; 3 loop(s); Loop length(s)-various
Typical terrain: Flat to rolling
Skiing ability suggested: Novice
Hiking trail difficulty: Easy
Nordic trail grooming method: Track set
Suitable for all-terrain bicycle: Not permitted
Trail use fee: None
Camping: Available for organized groups with advance reservation
Drinking water available

General Information:
 Operated by the Saginaw County Parks & Recreation Commission
 Nature programs and ski clinics available with advance notice
 100 year old beech/maple forest
 For information contact Kimberly S. Kinnan, Outdoor Rec. Coordinator

Bay Valley Inn
2470 Old Bridge Rd.                          517-686-3500
Bay City, MI  48706

Trail suitable for skiing only

Location:
 West of Bay City, I75 exit 160, then west on M84 to Old Bridge Road
 Trailhead at the tennis complex

## No Trail Map

Trail specifications:
   4 mi; 4 loop(s); Loop length(s)-2 to 5
Typical terrain: Flat to rolling
Skiing ability suggested: Novice
Hiking trail difficulty: NA
Nordic trail grooming method: Track set
Suitable for all-terrain bicycle: NA
Trail use fee: Yes
Camping: None


General Information:
 A year-round luxury resort hotel with complete facilities
 Ski shop and rentals available
 Covered bridges on trails

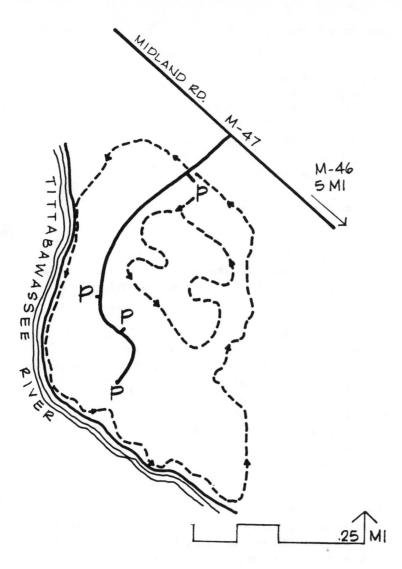

IMERMAN MEMORIAL PARK

Saginaw County Parks & Recreation Commission
111 S. Michigan Ave                        517-790-5280
Saginaw, MI  48602

Trail suitable for skiing & hiking

Location:
 5 miles NW of Saginaw on M47 (Midland Rd.)

Trail specifications:
   2 mi; 1 loop(s); Loop length(s)-.75, 1.25
Typical terrain: Flat to rolling
Skiing ability suggested: Novice
Hiking trail difficulty: Easy
Nordic trail grooming method: Track set
Suitable for all-terrain bicycle: Not permitted
Trail use fee: None
Camping: None
Drinking water is available

General Information:
 Operated by the Saginaw County Parks & Recreation Commission
 Trail follows a scenic section of the Tittabawasse River
 Warming shelter available during clinics
 The long trail is a self guided floodplain nature trail
 Just south of Bintz Apple Mountain Ski Area

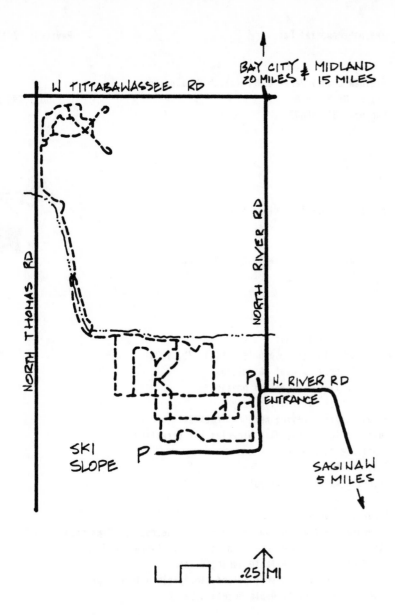

BAY CITY & MIDLAND
20 MILES  15 MILES

W TITTABAWASSEE RD

NORTH THOMAS RD

NORTH RIVER RD

P
N. RIVER RD
ENTRANCE

SKI
SLOPE    P

SAGINAW
5 MILES

.25 MI

BINTZ APPLE MOUNTAIN

Bintz Apple Mountain
4535 North River Rd.                    517-781-2550
Freeland, MI  48623                     517-781-0170

Bintz Apple Farm and Cider Mill
4535 North River Rd.                    517-781-2590
Freeland, MI  48623

Trail suitable for skiing only

Location:
 5 miles south of Freeland and 5 miles NW of Saginaw on North River Rd.
 I75 to I675 and exit at Tittabawassee Rd., then west for 7 miles, across
   Tittabawassee Rd., then first left on River Rd to ski area


Trail specifications:
  7 km; Several loop(s); Loop length(s)-various
 Typical terrain: Flat to slightly rolling in fields and orchards‡
 Skiing ability suggested: Novice
 Hiking trail difficulty: NA
 Nordic trail grooming method: None
 Suitable for all-terrain bicycle: NA
 Trail use fee: $1.00/day
 Camping: None


General Information:
 Privately operated alpine ski area with cross country skiing since 1977
 The first completely mand-made ski hill in the United States (1961)
 Lessons, rentals, ski shop, snack bar, restaurant and lounge
 Lighted trails avaialable
 Trails cover 300 acres of this unique apple orchard and cider mill
 ‡ Use of cross country skis is permitted on the beginners slope
 Lodging nearby

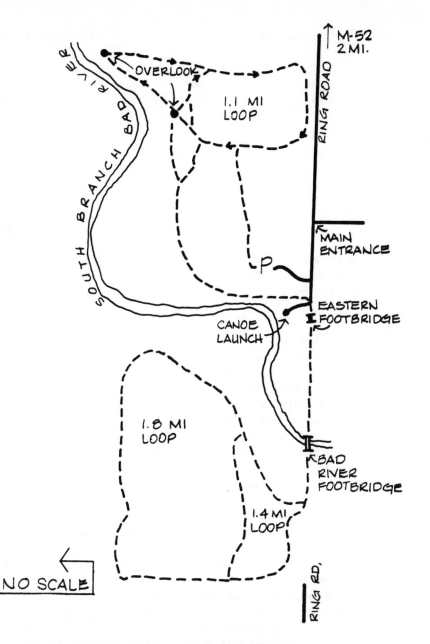

**RINGWOOD FOREST**

M-52
2 MI.

RING ROAD

OVERLOOK

1.1 MI
LOOP

SOUTH BRANCH BAD RIVER

MAIN
ENTRANCE

P

EASTERN
FOOTBRIDGE

CANOE
LAUNCH

1.8 MI
LOOP

1.4 MI
LOOP

BAD
RIVER
FOOTBRIDGE

RING RD.

NO SCALE

Ringwood Forest                              Revised: 12/03/87


Saginaw County Parks & Recreation Commission
111 S. Michgian Ave                          517-790-5280
Saginaw, MI  48602

Trail suitable for skiing & hiking

Location:
  SW of Saginaw near St Charles
  Trailhead - From St Charles south on M52 2 miles to Ring Rd., then west
    2 miles to Fordney Road.  Park entrance at the corner of Ring Rd. and
    Fordney Rd.


Trail specifications:
   3.5 mi; 3 loop(s); Loop length(s)-various
Typical terrain: Flat to rolling
Skiing ability suggested: Novice to intermediate
Hiking trail difficulty: Easy
Nordic trail grooming method: Track set
Suitable for all-terrain bicycle: Not permitted
Trail use fee: None
Camping: None
Drinking water is available


General Information:
  Operated by the Saginaw County Parks & Recreation Commission
  Clinics available
  Park contains the oldest evergreen, a 104 year old spruce.
  For information contact Kimberly S. Kinnan, Outdoor Rec. Coordinator

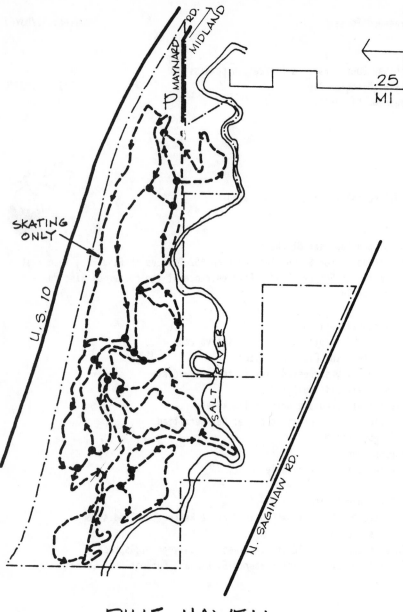

**PINE HAVEN RECREATION AREA**

Midland County Parks & Recreation Commission
1270 James Savage Rd.                                    517-832-6870
Midland, MI 48640-5682

Trail suitable for skiing & hiking

Location:
 NW of Midland and the Village of Sanford, adjacent to and south of US10
 Exit at West River Rd., turn south to Maynard Rd., then west on Maynard
   to the end of the road

Trail specifications:
    16.2 km; 9 loop(s); Loop length(s)-.2 to 3.7
Typical terrain: Flat to rolling
Skiing ability suggested: Novice to advance
Hiking trail difficulty: Easy to moderate
Nordic trail grooming method: Track set
Suitable for all-terrain bicycle: Yes
Trail use fee: None, but donations accepted at trailhead
Camping: None
Drinking water is not available

General Information:
 Maintained by the Midland County Parks and Recreation Commission
 Toilet at trailhead
 Food concession on site during ski season. Food also available in Sanford,
   2 miles from the trail
 Site of cross country ski races throughout the winter
 A very pleasant wooded trail system designed for cross country skiing
 Local ski shops: The Backpacker, 144 E Main St., Midland  517-832-3051
              The Nordic Loft, 6 Ashman Circle, Midland 517-839-0661
 For recorded information on ski trail conditions call 517-687-5700
 Write for brochure

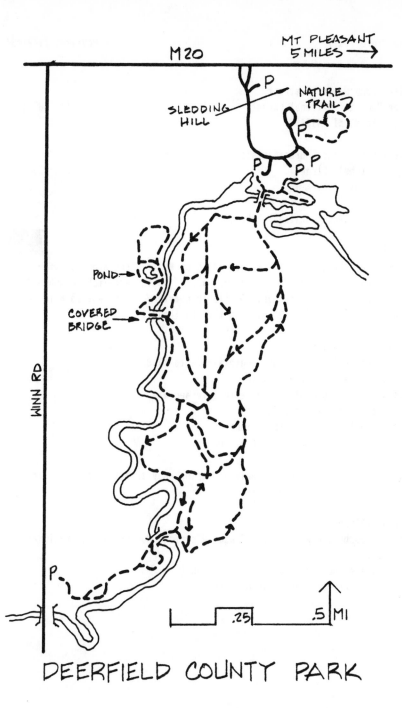

M20

MT PLEASANT
5 MILES →

P

NATURE
TRAIL

SLEDDING
HILL

P

P  P

P

P  P

POND →

COVERED
BRIDGE

WINN RD

P

.25    .5 MI

DEERFIELD COUNTY PARK

Deerfield County Park                                    Revised: 4/08/88

Isabella County Parks Department
200 N. Main St.                                          517-772-0911
Mt Pleasant, MI  48858

Deerfield County Park
2445 W Remus Rd.                                         715-772-2879
Mt Pleasant, MI  48858

Trail suitable for skiing & hiking

Location:
 5.5 miles west of Mt Pleasant on M20

Trail specifications:
   8 mi; Many loop(s); Loop length(s)-various
Typical terrain: Flat to rolling
Skiing ability suggested: Novice to intermediate
Hiking trail difficulty: Easy
Nordic trail grooming method: Track set
Suitable for all-terrain bicycle: Yes
Trail use fee: Entry fee $3.00/vehicle/day when staffed ‡
Camping: Canoe and hike in 10 site campground only
Drinking water available in the park

General Information:
 Operated by the Isabella County Parks Department
 Over 591 acres of all season recreational facilities
 Nature trails, picnic area, ponds for swimming and fishing, sledding, ice
   fishing, tubing and field game areas available
 Two suspension bridges and a wooden covered bridge are in the park
 Trails are always well groomed
 ‡ Also annual permit of $15/vehicle available. Half off all rates for all
   senior citizens
 Ski shop with rentals available at The Stable, 1701 S. Mission,
   Mt. Pleasant  772-1109

21

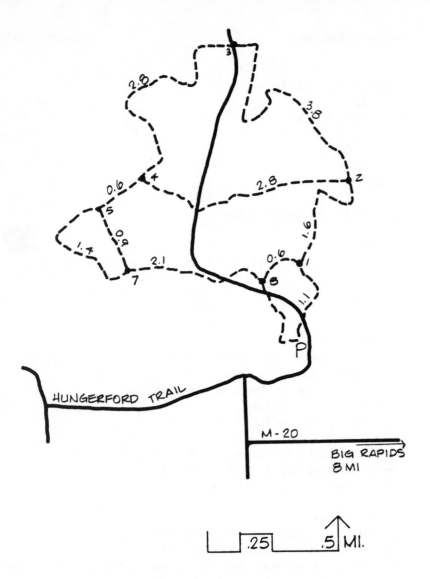

HUNGERFORD TRAIL

Hungerford Trail                              Revised: 11/21/87

White Cloud Ranger District
Huron-Manistee National Forest                616-689-6696
White Cloud, MI  49349

Forest Supervisor, Huron-Manistee National Forest
421 S. Mitchell Street                        616-775-2421
Cadillac, MI  49601

Trail suitable for skiing & hiking

Location:
  West of Big Rapids about 7 miles and NE of White Cloud about 18 miles
  Trailhead - West from Big Rapids 8.5 miles  to the Norwitch Township Hall
    turn north on Cypress Ave. .5 mile to cemetery, then east .5 mile, then
    north on FH5134 for .25 mile to the trailhead

Trail specifications:
  20.8 km; 4 loop(s); Loop length(s)-3.1 to 14.8
Typical terrain: Flat ot rolling
Skiing ability suggested: Novice to intermediate
Hiking trail difficulty: Easy
Nordic trail grooming method: None
Suitable for all-terrain bicycle: Yes
Trail use fee: None
Camping: No campgound but primitive camping away from the trail is permitted
Drinking water is not available

General Information:
  Maintained by the White Cloud Ranger District, Huron-Manistee National
    Forest
  Benches are located at some intersection
  Trail maps are located at intersections

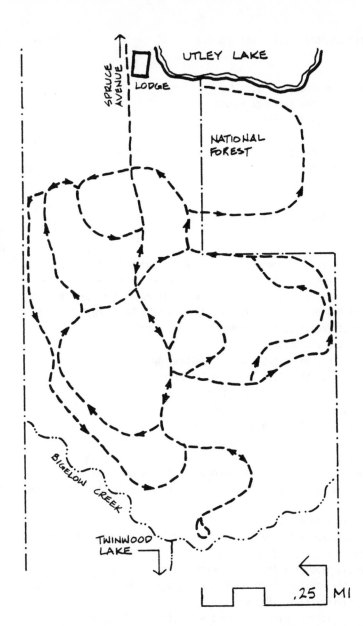

AMERICAN ADVENTURE/
WOODS & WATERS RESORT

Woods & Waters Resort
4495 S. Spruce                                    616-689-6685
White Cloud, MI  49349

Trail suitable for skiing & hiking

Location:
  From Newago north 4.5 miles on M37 to 40th St., then 2 miles east to
     Spruce Ave., then south .25 mile

Trail specifications:
   20 km; Many loop(s); Loop length(s)-various
Typical terrain: Rolling
Skiing ability suggested: Novice
Hiking trail difficulty: Easy
Nordic trail grooming method: None
Suitable for all-terrain bicycle: Yes
Trail use fee: $3/day with rentals $7/day
Camping: Campground on property
Drinking water is available

General Information:
  Privately operated 4 season resort
  Lodging, indoor pool, jacuzzi, snack bar, rentals & lessons
  Deluxe poolside motel rooms
  Trail pass through pine and hardwood forest
  Accomodations for groups and meeting space
  Other facilities include beach, tennis courts, basketball, water slide,
     field sports and country store to name a few

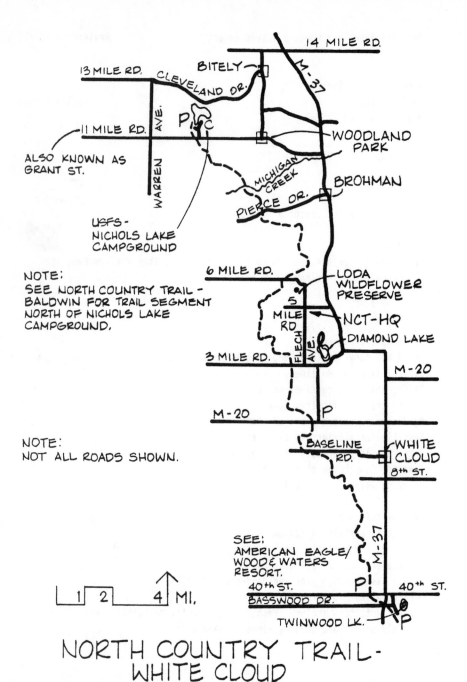

13 MILE RD.
14 MILE RD.
BITELY
CLEVELAND DR.
M-37
11 MILE RD.
WARREN AVE.
P
C
ALSO KNOWN AS GRANT ST.
WOODLAND PARK
MICHIGAN CREEK
BROHMAN
PIERCE DR.
USFS - NICHOLS LAKE CAMPGROUND
NOTE:
SEE NORTH COUNTRY TRAIL - BALDWIN FOR TRAIL SEGMENT NORTH OF NICHOLS LAKE CAMPGROUND.
6 MILE RD.
LODA WILDFLOWER PRESERVE
5 MILE RD.
FLECH AVE.
NCT-HQ
DIAMOND LAKE
3 MILE RD.
M-20
NOTE:
NOT ALL ROADS SHOWN.
M-20
P
BASELINE RD.
WHITE CLOUD
8th ST.
SEE: AMERICAN EAGLE/ WOOD & WATERS RESORT.
M-37
40th ST.
P
40th ST.
BASSWOOD DR.
TWINWOOD LK.
P
1  2    4 MI.

# NORTH COUNTRY TRAIL- WHITE CLOUD

North Country Trail - White Cloud                    Revised: 12/12/87

White Cloud Ranger District
Huron-Manistee National Forest                       616-689-6696
White Cloud, MI  49349

Forest Supervisor, Huron-Manistee National Forest
421 S. Mitchell St.                                  616-775-2421
Cadillac, MI  49601

Trail suitable for hiking & skiing

Location:
 South trailhead-South from White Cloud about 4.5 miles on M37 to 40th St,
    then east .2 mile to Basswood Rd, south on Basswood 1 mile to trailhd.
 North trailhead-North from Brohman 2 miles on M37, then west on 11 Mile
    Rd 4.5 miles to entrance of Nichols Lake Res. Area, then .4 mile to
    boat launch turnoff, then .1 mile to trailhead
Trail specifications:
   26.9 mi; No loop(s); Loop length(s)-NA
Typical terrain: Flat to slightly rolling
Skiing ability suggested: Advanced
Hiking trail difficulty: Easy
Nordic trail grooming method: None
Suitable for all-terrain bicycle: Not permitted
Trail use fee: None
Camping: Nichols Lake Campground and 200' from trail
Drinking water available only in the summer at Nichols Lake Campgound

General Information:
 Maintained by the White Cloud Ranger District, Huron-Manistee NF
 Trail not designed for skiing
 Recommended only for skiers with winter survival skills
 For the additional adjacent section of the North Country Trail see North
    Country Trail - Baldwin
 Varied forest cover and swamp with stream crossings
 For further information about the North Country Trail contact the
  North Country Trail Association, PO Box 311, White Cloud, MI 49349 or
  USDI, Mid West Region, 1709 Jackson St., Omaha, Nebraska 68102
 American Eagle/Woods & Waters Resort near south end trailhead
 Write for more detailed trail map

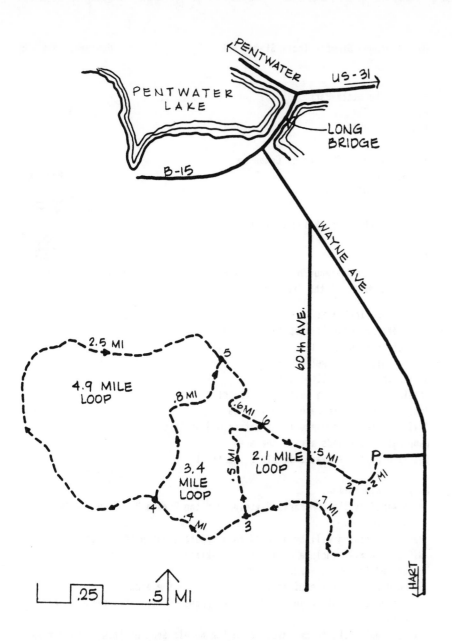

PENTWATER PATHWAY

Pentwater Pathway                                    Revised:  2/03/88

Area Forester, Baldwin Area Forest
Rte 2, Box 2810                                      616-745-4651
Baldwin, MI  49304

District Forest Manager, Pere Marquette State Forest
Rte 1, 8015 South US131                              616-775-9727
Cadillac, MI  49061

Trail suitable for skiing & hiking

Location:
  SE of Pentwater on B15 to Wayne Ave., then south on Wayne Ave. to the
    Pathway.  It is southeast of Pentwater Lake.


Trail specifications:
    7 mi; 4 loop(s); Loop length(s)-1.2, 2, 3.3, 5.5
Typical terrain: Flat to rolling
Skiing ability suggested: Novice
Hiking trail difficulty: Easy
Nordic trail grooming method: None
Suitable for all-terrain bicycle: Yes
Trail use fee: None
Camping: None
Drinking water is not available

General Information:
  Maintained by the DNR Forest Management Division
  Mostly level with one loop that is hilly

Other contacts:
DNR Forest Management Division Office, Lansing, 517-275-1275
DNR Forest Management Region Office, Roscommon, 517-275-5151

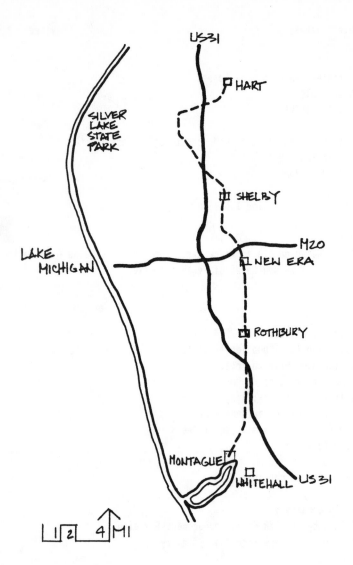

# HART—MONTAGUE BICYCLE TRAIL
# STATE PARK

Hart-Montague Bicycle Trail State Park                    Revised:  4/02/88

Silver Lake State Park
Rte 1, Box 254                                           616-873-3083
Mears, MI  49436

White Lake Area Chamber of Commerce
124 W. Hanson                                            616-893-4585
Whitehall, MI  49461

Trail suitable for skiing & hiking

Location:
 From Hart to Montague parallel to US-31, 60 miles north of Grand Rapids
    with 6 exits of the freeway

Trail specifications:
   21.3‡; No loop(s); Loop length(s)-NA
Typical terrain: Level to slightly rolling
Skiing ability suggested: Novice
Hiking trail difficulty: Easy
Nordic trail grooming method: Track set
Suitable for all-terrain bicycle: Yes
Trail use fee: Yes, amount not determined at this time
Camping: Campgrounds are in the area
Drinking water is available along the trail

General Information:
 Maintained by the DNR Parks Division and the Oceana-Muskegon Trailways
    Commission
 Horseback riding will be allowed on a separate but parallel trail
 Winter use will include cross-country skiing
 Scheduled to open in August, 1988
 Ski and bike rental equipment is available in the area
 Future development includes additional cross-country skiing loops near
    Montague
 If you would like to be envolved in the development of this trail please
    contact the Oceana-Muskegon Trailways Commission, c/o Hart City Hall,
    Hart, MI 49420
 ‡ 100' wide trail right of way
 Other contact:
 DNR Parks Division Office, Lansing, 517-373-1275

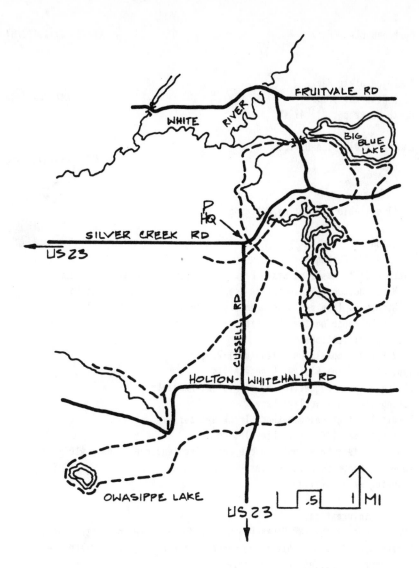

# OWASIPPE SCOUT RESERVATION

Owasippe Scout Reservation
9900 Russell Rd.                                    616-894-4061
Twin Lake, MI   49461                               616-894-8710

Trail suitable for skiing & hiking

Location:
 From US31, Whitehall exit, east 1 mile to Silver Creek Rd., then north
   and east 5 miles to the camp.
 From US31, Russell Rd. exit, north on Russell Rd. (B23), 8 miles to the
   reservation.

Trail specifications:
   20 km; 2 loop(s); Loop length(s)-5, 15
Typical terrain: Rolling to very hilly
Skiing ability suggested: Novice to advanced
Hiking trail difficulty: Moderate to Difficult
Nordic trail grooming method: None
Suitable for all-terrain bicycle: Yes
Trail use fee: $1.00/day
Camping: None
Drinking water available in summer months

General Information:
 Privately operated Boy Scout Reservation that is open to the public
 Open from 9 to 5 daily
 Site of the Muskegon Loppet
 Varied forest cover of oak, pine and maple
 Trail system surrounds two lakes
 Great place for birders
 Area abundant with animals to observe

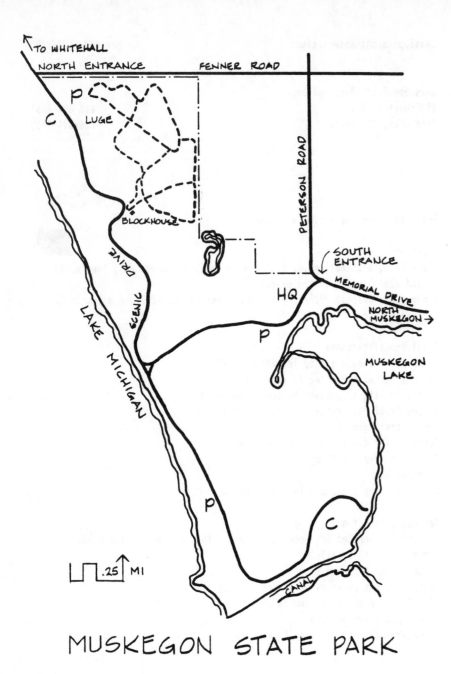

MUSKEGON STATE PARK

Revised: 11/12/87

Muskegon State Park
3560 Memorial Drive
North Muskegon, MI  49445

616-744-3480

DNR Parks Division Office

517-373-1270

Trail suitable for skiing & hiking

Location:
 NW side of Muskegon
 Take US31 to Muskegon State Park exit, then follow signs through
   North Muskegon, then follow Memorial Dr. to Scenic Dr. at Lake
   Michigan, then north on Scenic Dr. about 2 miles to ski/luge
   run entrance on the east side of the road.
Trail specifications:
 7 km; 2 loop(s); Loop length(s)-2.5, 5
Typical terrain: Flat with some hills
Skiing ability suggested: Novice to intermediate
Hiking trail difficulty: Easy
Nordic trail grooming method: Track set daily
Suitable for all-terrain bicycle: No
Trail use fee: None, but vehicle entry fee required $2/day, $10/year
Camping: Campground in the park
Drinking water available

General Information:
 Maintained by the DNR Parks Division and the Muskegon Sports Council
 Snack bar, luge run, biathalon range, ski rentals, lessons and the normal
   summer facilities are available
 This section of the park is the Muskegon Winter Sports Complex
 One of only 4 luge runs in the United States
 For more information about the facility write or call:
        Muskegon Winter Sports Center
        Muskegon State Park
        PO Box 5085
        North Muskegon, Mi 49445    616-774-9629 or 5161

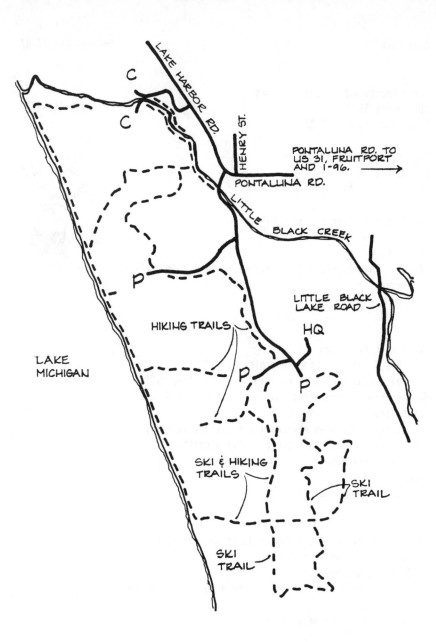

# HOFFMASTER STATE PARK

Hoffmaster State Park
6585 Lake Harbor Rd.                              616-798-3711
Muskegon, MI  49441

DNR Parks Division Office

517-373-1270

Trail suitable for skiing & hiking

Location:
 South of Muskegon on Lake Michigan
 Take US31 south from I69 to Pontaluna Rd., then west 3 miles to the park

Trail specifications:
   10 mi‡; Many loop(s); Loop length(s)-various
Typical terrain: Rolling to hilly
Skiing ability suggested: Novice to advanced
Hiking trail difficulty: Easy to moderate
Nordic trail grooming method: None
Suitable for all-terrain bicycle: No
Trail use fee: None, but vehicle entry fee required $2/day, $10/year
Camping: Campgound in park
Drinking water at campground and picnic areas

General Information:
 Maintained by the DNR Parks Division
 ‡ Ski trails are 3 miles long
 Extensive hiking trail system throughout the park and along the shore
   of Lake Michigan
 The Gillette Nature Center in the park is open Sat-Sun 10-5, T-F 1-5
 Some bridle trails are used for skiing
 For additional information contact the Gillette Nature Center at
   616-798-3573

Grand Rapids Department of Parks
201 Market St SW                                        616-456-3211
Grand Rapids, MI  49503

Community Enrichment Office
201 Market St SW                                        616-456-3361
Grand Rapids, MI  49503

Trail suitable for skiing & hiking

Location:
 On M45 (Lake Michigan Ave) west of Grand Rapids, between 14th and 24th
 Avenues.

Trail specifications:
  8 km; 3 loop(s); Loop length(s)-1.2, 2.4, 3.8
Typical terrain: Flat to rolling with one steep hill
Skiing ability suggested: Novice to intermediate
Hiking trail difficulty: Easy
Nordic trail grooming method: Track set occasionally
Suitable for all-terrain bicycle: Not permitted
Trail use fee: None
Camping: None
Drinking water is not available

General Information:
 Maintained by the Grand Rapids Department of Parks
 Trail follows the Sand Creek
 Mature Beech-Maple forest
 Variety of wildflowers - Please leave for others to enjoy
 Tamarack bog
 Lowland creek with many oxbows
 Small lake with no access
 Site shared with a handicapped children's camp

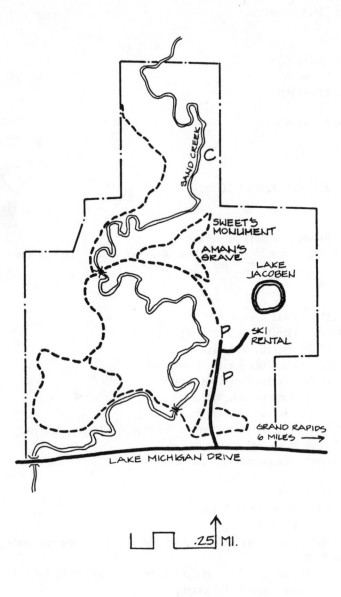

AMAN PARK

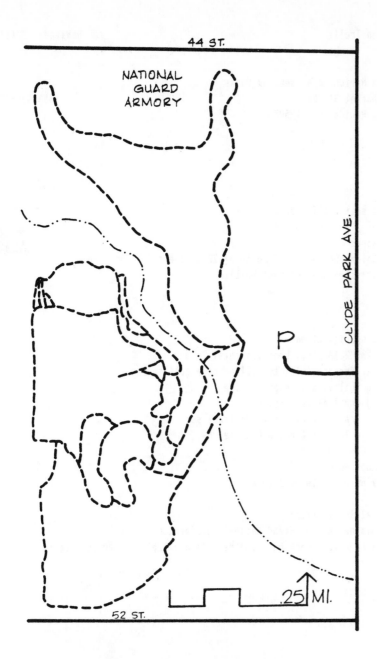

44 ST.

NATIONAL
GUARD
ARMORY

CLYDE PARK AVE.

P

.25 MI.

52 ST.

PALMER PARK

Palmer Park                                      Revised:  9/13/87

Kent County Park Commission
1500 Scribner NW                                 616-774-3697
Grand Rapids, MI  49504

Trail suitable for skiing and hiking

Location:
 In Wyoming (Grand Rapids), at 52nd St and Clyde Park Ave.

Trail specifications:
  5 mi; Several loop(s); Loop length(s)-various
Typical terrain: Flat to rolling
Skiing ability suggested: Novice
Hiking trail difficulty: Easy
Nordic trail grooming method: Track set occasionally
Suitable for all-terrain bicycle: Not permitted
Trail use fee: $1.00/day
Camping: Camping not permitted
Water available in golf course clubhouse

General Information:
 Maintained by the Kent County Park Commission
 Warming building, rentals, snacks and lighted practice area available
 Trails on a golf course

31

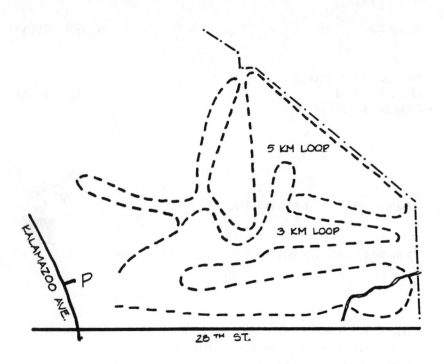

.25 MI.

# INDIAN TRAILS

Grand Rapids Department of Parks
201 Market St. SW
Grand Rapids, MI  49503

616-456-3211

Trail suitable for skiing only

Location:
  On Kalamazoo Ave, just north of 28th Street in Grand Rapids
    2.5 miles west of East Beltline

Trail specifications:
    6 km; 2 loop(s); Loop length(s)-3, 5
  Typical terrain: Flat to rolling on a golf course
  Skiing ability suggested: Novice
  Hiking trail difficulty: NA
  Nordic trail grooming method: Track set
  Suitable for all-terrain bicycle: NA
  Trail use fee: Yes
  Camping: None
  Drinking water is available

General Information:
  Maintained by the Grand Rapids Department of Parks
  Warming area, snack bar, and rentals available in the golf course lodge

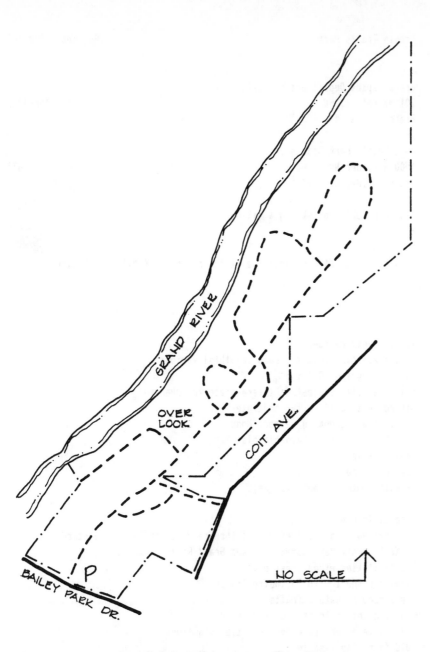

LAMOREAUX PARK

Kent County Park Commission
1500 Scribner NW                                    616-774-3697
Grand Rapids, MI  49504

Trail suitable for hiking & skiing

Location:
  North of the Grand Rapids city limits on Coit Avenue, 1 mile north of
   4 Mile Rd

Trail specifications:
   6 mi; 6 loop(s); Loop length(s)-various
Typical terrain: Flat
Skiing ability suggested: Novice
Hiking trail difficulty: Easy
Nordic trail grooming method: Track set occasionally
Suitable for all-terrain bicycle: No
Trail use fee: None
Camping: None
Pump water available only in the non freezing seasons

General Information:
  Maintained by the Kent County Park Commission
  Parking off Bailey Park Drive and Coit Avenue

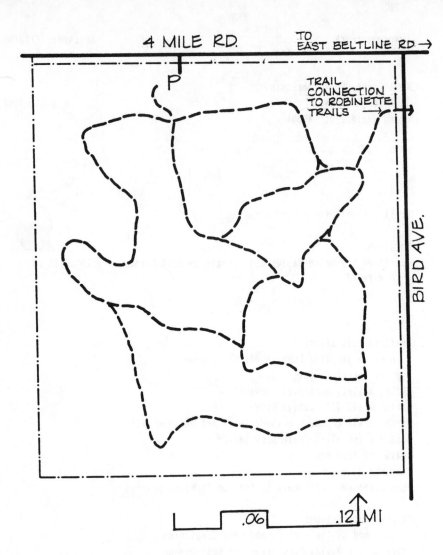

4 MILE RD.

TO EAST BELTLINE RD →

P

TRAIL CONNECTION TO ROBINETTE TRAILS →

BIRD AVE.

.06    .12 MI

PROVIN TRAILS PARK

Provin Trails Park

Revised: 9/01/87

Grand Rapids Department of Parks
201 Market St. SW
Grand Rapids, MI  49503

616-456-3211

Kent County Park Commission
1500 Scribner NW
Grand Rapids, MI  49504

616-774-3697

Trail suitable for skiing & hiking

Location:
 3/4 mile west of East Beltline at the corner of 4 Mile Rd. & Bird Ave

Trail specifications:
   1.7 mi; Many loop(s); Loop length(s)-various
Typical terrain: Rolling
Skiing ability suggested: Intermediate to advanced
Hiking trail difficulty: Moderate
Nordic trail grooming method: None
Suitable for all-terrain bicycle: Yes
Trail use fee: None
Camping: None
Drinking water is not available

General Information:
 Maintained as a joint effort of the Grand Rapids Parks Department,
   Kent County Park Commission and Grand Rapids Township
 No facilities except restrooms
 Trails connect with Robinette Trails
 Developed as nature trails
 Parking lot is located on 4 Mile Rd
 Extensive mature pine reforestation plantings
 Old farm site visable

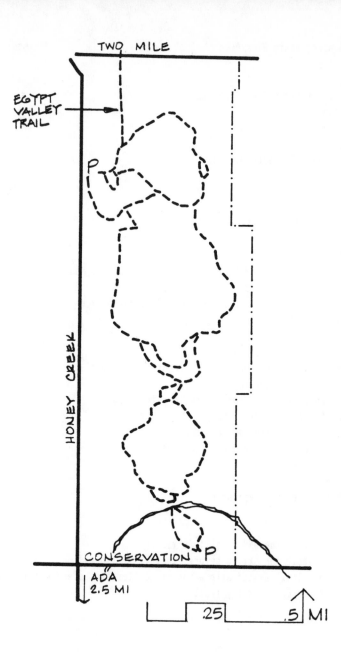

TWO MILE

EGYPT
VALLEY
TRAIL

P

HONEY CREEK

CONSERVATION P

ADA
2.5 MI

.25   .5 MI

SEIDMAN PARK

Seidman Park                          Revised: 3/17/88

Kent County Park Commission
1500 Scribner NW                      616-774-3697
Grand Rapids, MI  49504

Trail suitable for skiing & hiking

Location:
 3 miles north of Ada on Honey Creek Ave, 6 miles east of Grand Rapids

Trail specifications:
   6 mi; 3 loop(s); Loop length(s)-.99, 1.25, 1.26
Typical terrain: Rolling to hilly
Skiing ability suggested: Novice to advanced
Hiking trail difficulty: Easy to moderate
Nordic trail grooming method: Track set occasionally
Suitable for all-terrain bicycle: Not permitted
Trail use fee: None
Camping: None
Drinking water is not available

General Information:
 Maintained by the Kent County Park Commission
 Parking on Honey Creek Ave and Conservation Drive
 Restrooms on Honey Creek Ave and Conservation Drive
 Part of the Egypt Valley Trail
 Waxing area available

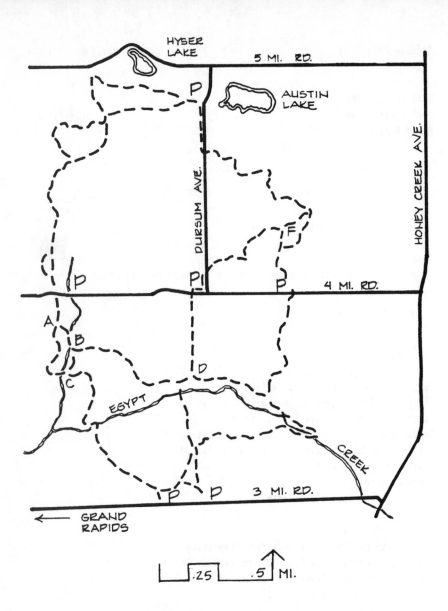

HYSER
LAKE

5 MI. RD.

AUSTIN
LAKE

P

DURSUM AVE.

HONEY CREEK AVE.

F

P      P      P      4 MI. RD.

A

B

D

C

EGYPT

CREEK

P      P      3 MI. RD.

GRAND
RAPIDS

.25      .5 MI.

CANNONSBURG STATE GAME AREA

Cannonsburg State Game Area

Revised: 10/15/87

Cannonsburg State Game Area
350 Ottawa Ave NW
Grand Rapids, MI  49503

616-456-5071

DNR Wildlife Division Office

517-373-1263

Trail suitable for skiing & hiking

Location:
 8 miles east of Grand Rapids between 3 and 5 Mile Rds
 Trailhead – 5 Mile Rd, 1 mile east of Egypt Valley Rd.
 Trailheads – Several locations on 4 Mile Rd. between Egypt Valley Rd. and
    Honey Creek Rd.

Trail specifications:
   15 km; Numerous loop(s); Loop length(s)-various
Typical terrain: Rolling to hilly
Skiing ability suggested: Novice to intermediate
Hiking trail difficulty: Easy
Nordic trail grooming method: None
Suitable for all-terrain bicycle: Yes
Trail use fee: None
Camping: None
Drinking water not available

General Information:
 Maintained by the DNR Wildlife Division
 Not available for skiing before January 1st (sorry)
 Excellent trail system with a variety of terrain, scenery and habitat
 Part of the Egypt Valley Trail

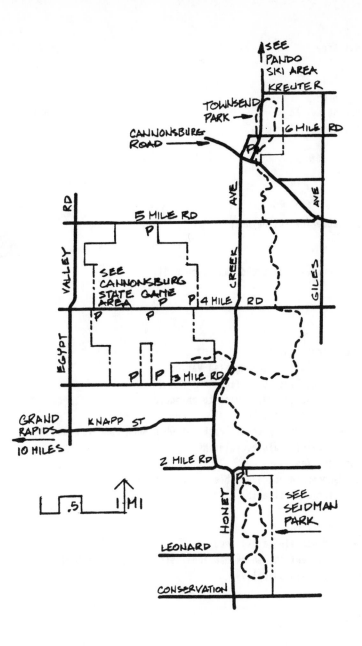

EGYPT VALLEY TRAIL

Egypt Valley Trail                               Revised: 3/13/88

Kent County Park Commission
1500 Scribner NW                                 616-774-3697
Grand Rapids, MI  49504

Trail suitable for hiking & skiing

Location:
 9 miles NE of Grand Rapids
 Trailhead - Cannonsburg State Game Area (see index)
 Trailhead - Seidman Park (see index)
 Trailhead - Townsend Park (see index)

Trail specifications:
 10 mi; Several loop(s); Loop length(s)-various
Typical terrain: Flat to hilly
Skiing ability suggested: Novice to intermediate
Hiking trail difficulty: Moderate to difficult
Nordic trail grooming method: None
Suitable for all-terrain bicycle: Not permitted
Trail use fee: None
Camping: None
No drinking water availble along the trail except at Seidman Park

General Information:
 Maintained by the Kent County Parks and Road Commissions
 Most of the trail is on private property. Please respect the property
   rights of the owners whos land you are using
 Trail open from 12/15 to 4/15 if 2 inches of snow are present
 The state game area section is open for skiing beginning Jan 2nd

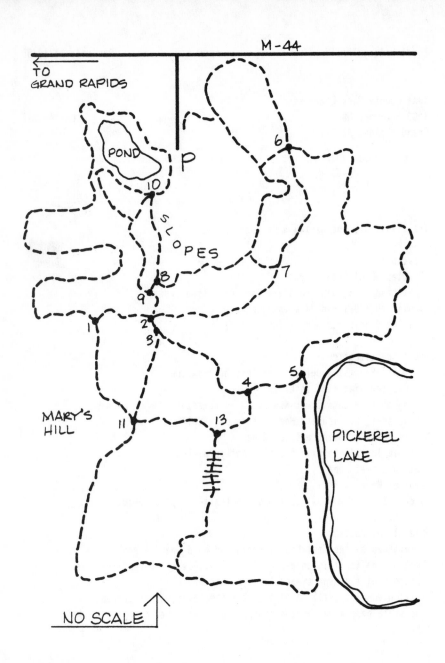

M-44

TO
GRAND RAPIDS

POND

P

SLOPES

6

10

8

9

7

1

2

3

4

5

MARY'S
HILL

11

13

PICKEREL
LAKE

NO SCALE

PANDO SKI AREA

Pando Ski Area                                    Revised: 4/04/87


Pando Ski Area
8076 Belding Rd. NE                               616-874-8343
Rockford, MI  49341

Trail suitable for skiing only

Location:
 12 Miles northeast of Grand Rapids on M-44.


Trail specifications:
   6 mi; 3 loop(s); Loop length(s)-various
 Typical terrain: Flat to rolling
 Skiing ability suggested: Novice to advanced
 Hiking trail difficulty: NA
 Nordic trail grooming method: Track set when snow conditon permits.
 Suitable for all-terrain bicycle: NA
 Trail use fee: Yes
 Camping: Campground not available
 Drinking water is available

General Information:
 Located at Pando alpine ski area
 Warming area, rentals, snack bar and instruction is available
 Site of races held annually

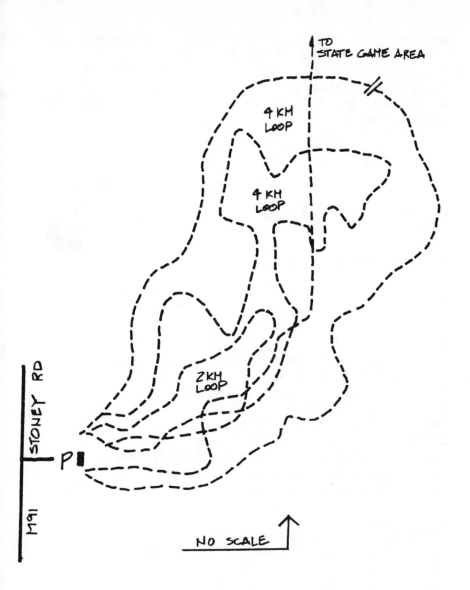

TO
STATE GAME AREA

4 KM
LOOP

4 KM
LOOP

2 KM
LOOP

STONEY RD

M91

P

NO SCALE

CANDLESTONE INN

Candlestone Inn Inc.                              Revised: 11/19/87

Candlestone Inn Inc.
8100 Storey Rd.                                   616-794-1580
Belding, MI  48809                                616-691-7713

Trail suitable for skiing only

Location:
 1 mile north of M44 on M91

Trail specifications:
   10 km; 3 loop(s); Loop length(s)-2, 4, 4
Typical terrain: Flat to gently rolling
Skiing ability suggested: Novice
Hiking trail difficulty: NA
Nordic trail grooming method: Track set as needed
Suitable for all-terrain bicycle: Not permitted
Trail use fee: None
Camping: No camping facilities nearby

General Information:
 Privately operated 4 season resort
 Most trails on golf course
 Trail connect with the Flat River State Game Area
 Lodging and food service available
 Ski packages available
 Horse drawn sleigh rides given on weekends

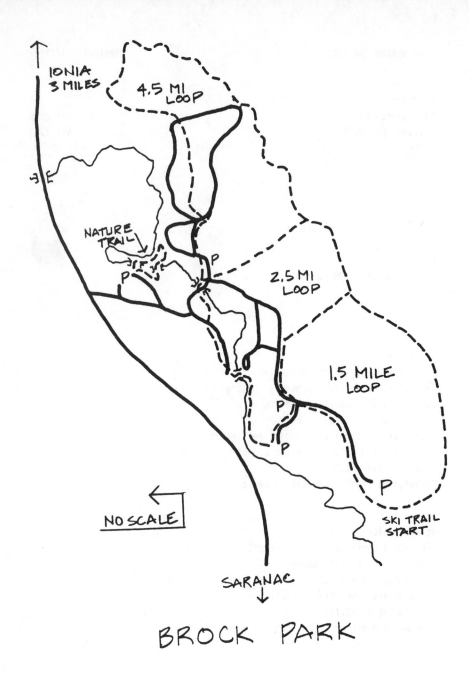

IONIA
3 MILES

4.5 MI
LOOP

NATURE
TRAIL

P

P

2.5 MI
LOOP

1.5 MILE
LOOP

P

P

P

SKI TRAIL
START

NO SCALE

SARANAC

# BROCK PARK

Ionia County Parks Department
2311 W Bluewater Hwy, Rte 3      616-527-0478
Ionia, MI  48846

Trail suitable for skiing & hiking

Location:
 3 miles west of Ionia on M21

Trail specifications:
   9 mi; 4 loop(s); Loop length(s)-1, 1.5, 2.5, 4.5
Typical terrain: Flat to rolling
Skiing ability suggested: Novice to intermediate
Hiking trail difficulty: Easy
Nordic trail grooming method: Track set
Suitable for all-terrain bicycle: Not permitted
Trail use fee: $1/car county residents, $2/car for all others
Camping: Rustic camping available on site
Drinking water is available all year

General Information:
 Operated by the Ionia County Parks Department
 Warming shelter, sledding hill and tubing hill available
 Nature trail not available for skiing
 Tennis courts, ball fields and playground available

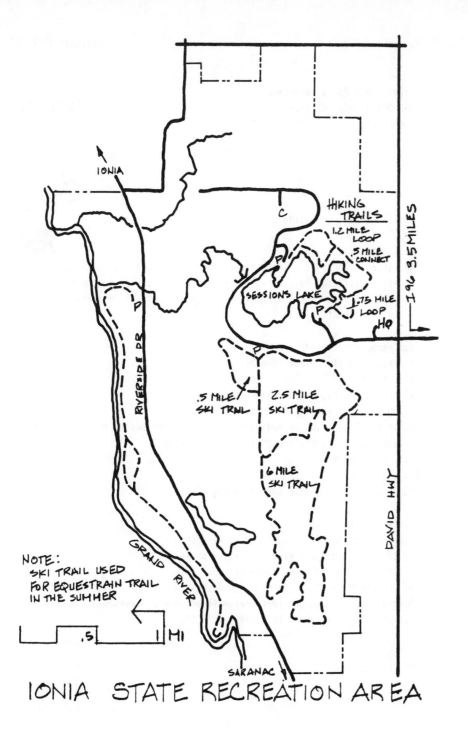

IONIA STATE RECREATION AREA

NOTE:
SKI TRAIL USED
FOR EQUESTRAIN TRAIL
IN THE SUMMER

Ionia State Recreation Area                    Revised: 3/23/88


Ionia Recreation Area
2880 David Highway                             616-527-3750
Ionia, MI  48846

DNR Parks Division Office

                                               517-372-1270

Trail suitable for hiking & skiing

Location:
 South from Ionia 5 miles on M66 to David Hwy, then west 3 miles to
   Recreation Area entrance.
 Trailheads at Beechwood Picnic Area, Point Picnic Area and
   Riverside Picnic Area

Trail specifications:
  13+ mi; 5 loop(s); Loop length(s)-.5 to 6
Typical terrain: Flat to rolling
Skiing ability suggested: Novice to advanced
Hiking trail difficulty: Easy to difficult
Nordic trail grooming method: None
Suitable for all-terrain bicycle: Yes
Trail use fee: None, but vehicle entry fee required $2/day, $10/year
Camping: Rustic campgrounds available
Drinking water available throughout park

General Information:
 Maintained by the DNR Parks Division
 Greatly varied terrain with woods, lakes, fields, streams, rivers
   and numerous scenic views.
 Separate equestrain trails are also in the park

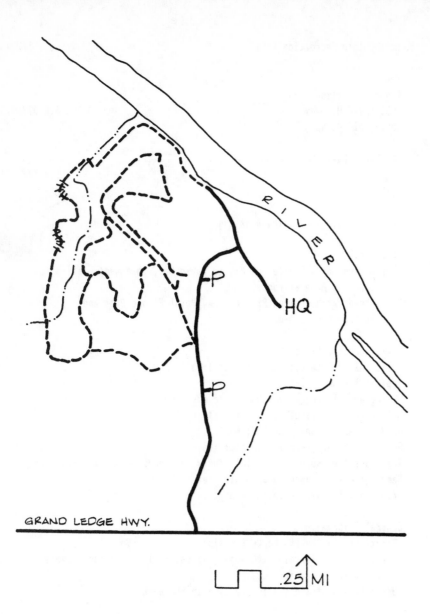

GRAND LEDGE HWY.

.25 MI

FITZGERALD PARK

Revised: 11/21/87

Eaton County Parks Department
3808 Grand Ledge Highway
Grand Ledge, MI  48837

517-627-7351

Trail suitable for skiing & hiking

Location:
  I96 to exit 93A (M43 Saginaw Hwy West). Go approximately 6 miles to Grand
    Ledge Hwy.(Nixon Rd., first blinking light; M100 first stop light: Grand
    Ledge Hwy next to blinking light) and turn right. Park entrance is on
    the left about .5 mile.

Trail specifications:
   3 mi; 5 loop(s); Loop length(s)-various
Typical terrain: Flat to rolling
Skiing ability suggested: Novice to advanced
Hiking trail difficulty: Easy to moderate
Nordic trail grooming method: Track set when snow depth permits
Suitable for all-terrain bicycle: Not permitted
Trail use fee: None
Camping: None
Drinking water available spring through fall

General Information:
 Operated by the Eaton County Parks Department
 Rentals, ski shop and warming shelter on weekends
 Night skiing on selected weekends
 New advanced ski trail through a wooded area along a picturesque brook
 Naturalist programs provided free with advance arrangements
 Picnic facilities and game fields available

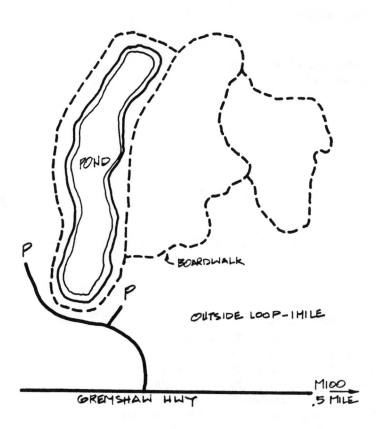

POND

P

P

BOARDWALK

OUTSIDE LOOP-1MILE

M100
.5 MILE

GRESHAW HWY

NO SCALE ↑

# FOX PARK

Eaton County Parks & Recreation Department
3808 Grand Ledge Hwy                                    517-627-7351
Grand Ledge, MI  48837

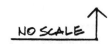

Trail suitable for hiking & skiing

Location:
  I96 to exit 98A (US27/I69) towards Charlotte.  At Potterville, approximately
    5.5 miles, turn (right) north on north M100. Travel 1 mile north to
    Gresham Hwy. Turn left to park entrance which is about .5 mile on the
    right

Trail specifications:
    2 mi; 3 loop(s); Loop length(s)-various
Typical terrain: Flat to gently rolling
Skiing ability suggested: Novice to intermediate
Hiking trail difficulty: Easy
Nordic trail grooming method: Track set
Suitable for all-terrain bicycle: Not permitted
Trail use fee: None
Camping: None
Drinking water only in spring through fall

General Information:
  Operated by the Eaton County Parks and Recreation Department
  Picnic facilities and a warming shelter on weekends
  Trails around several ponds and through wooded areas
  Ski lessons and naturalist programs upon prior arrangements
  Swimming and fishing available
  Ice skating

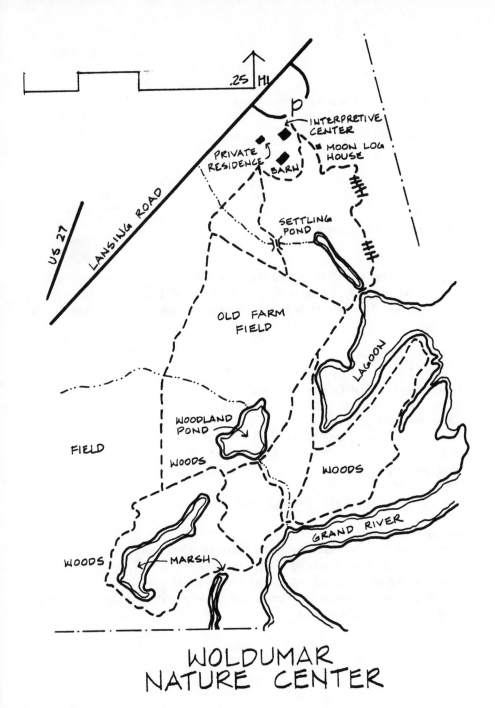

WOLDUMAR
NATURE CENTER

Woldumar Nature Center                                    Revised: 11/15/87


Woldumar Nature Center
5539 Lansing Rd.                                          517-322-0030
Lansing, MI  48917

Trail suitable for hiking & skiing

Location:
 SW of Lansing on Lansing Rd off BR US27, just NE of I96 exit 98B


Trail specifications:
    5+ mi; 3+ loop(s); Loop length(s)-1, 1.5, 2.5
Typical terrain: Flat to very hilly
Skiing ability suggested: Novice to advanced
Hiking trail difficulty: Easy to moderate
Nordic trail grooming method: Skied in by naturalist after each snowfall
Suitable for all-terrain bicycle: Not permitted
Trail use fee: $.50/day, or season ski pass is available
Camping: None
Drinking water available in interpretive building

General Information:
 A non-profit nature center with nature trails
 Some hiking trails may not be suitable for skiing because of steps
 Area borders the Grand River for one mile
 Very scenic area with a wide selection of forest cover
 Warming shelter that serves snacks is open Tuesday - Friday from 9am to
   5pm and weekends from 1 to 5
 Cross country ski workshops are held on most weekends
 Very nice moderate sized trail system
 Write for brochure

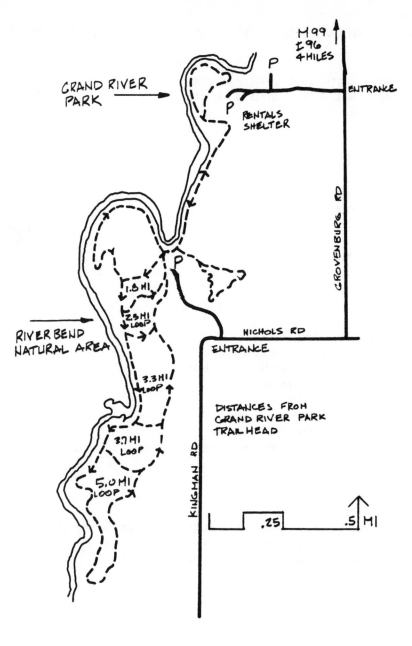

GRAND RIVER PARK

Grand River Park                                    Revised: 3/17/88

Ingham County Parks Department
PO Box 38                                           517-676-2233
Mason, MI  48854

Trail suitable for skiing & hiking

Location:
 SW of Lansing on Grovenburg Rd, just north of Nichols Rd.
 Use Logan St exit south, off I-96, then turn left on Bishop Rd. east
   to Grovenburg Rd., then south to the park.


Trail specifications:
   7 mi; Many loop(s); Loop length(s)-various
Typical terrain: Flat to slightly rolling, with some hills
Skiing ability suggested: Novice
Hiking trail difficulty: Easy
Nordic trail grooming method: Track set as snow condition permits.
Suitable for all-terrain bicycle: Not permitted
Trail use fee: None
Camping: None
Drinking water available in the warming building

General Information:
 Operated by the Ingham County Parks Department
 Ski rentals, snack bar, tobogganing, ice skating, sledding, swimming,
   softball diamond and picnic grounds are provided seasonally
 A trail connects this park and the Riverbend Natural Area
 Moonlight cross-country skiing on alternate weekend evenings. A nominal
   fee is charged
 Cross country ski lessons for beginners are available. A nominal fee is
   charged.
 Snack bar is open on Friday, Saturday and Sunday's during the winter

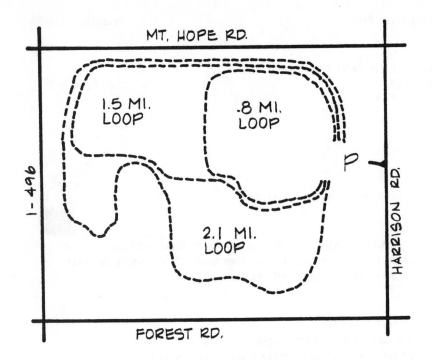

MT. HOPE RD.

I-496

1.5 MI.
LOOP

.8 MI.
LOOP

2.1 MI.
LOOP

P

HARRISON RD.

FOREST RD.

NO SCALE

# M.S.U. CROSS COUNTRY SKI TRAILS

Intramural Sports and Recreative Services
IM Sports West, Michigan State University          517-355-4710
East Lansing, MI  48824                            517-355-1635

Trail suitable for skiing only

Location:
 On the Michigan State University Campus
 Take Harrison Rd just south of Mt Hope Rd to the West Course

Trail specifications:
    4.5 mi; 4 loop(s); Loop length(s)-.8, 1.5, 2.1
Typical terrain: Flat to slightly rolling
Skiing ability suggested: Novice
Hiking trail difficulty: NA
Nordic trail grooming method: None
Suitable for all-terrain bicycle: NA
Trail use fee: Yes, $.50/day for students, $1.00/day for public
Camping: NA

General Information:
 Maintained by the Department of Intramural Sports and Recreative
    Services, Michigan State Universtiy
 Warming shelter, rentals, lessons and snacks available

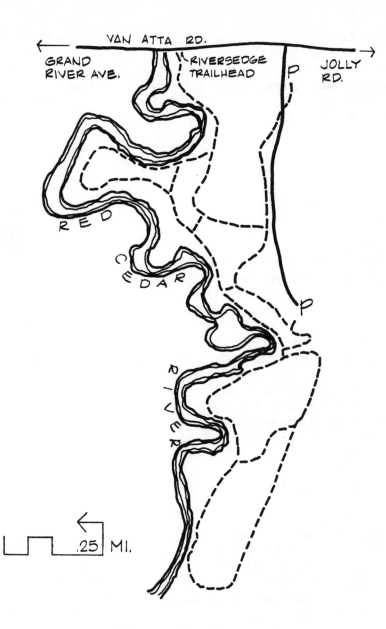

VAN ATTA RD.

GRAND
RIVER AVE.

RIVERSEDGE
TRAILHEAD

JOLLY
RD.

P

R
E
D

C
E
D
A
R

R
I
V
E
R

P

.25 MI.

LEGG PARK

Legg Park                                    Revised: 3/23/88

Parks Department, Charter Township of Meridian
5151 Marsh Rd.                               517-349-1200
Okemos, MI  48864

Trail suitable for hiking and skiing

Location:
  East of Okemos on Grand River Ave to Van Atta Rd., then south 1 mile
    across the Red Cedar River to the park entrance on the right (west) side
    of the road. There is a trailhead on Van Atta Rd. at the Red Cedar River
    at the bridge but parking is very limited.
  The maid parking lot has space for 40 cars
Trail specifications:
  3 mi; 3 loop(s); Loop length(s)-.62, 1.0, 2.6
Typical terrain: Flat with some rolling terrain
Skiing ability suggested: Novice to intermediate
Hiking trail difficulty: Easy
Nordic trail grooming method: Track set twice weekly
Suitable for all-terrain bicycle: Yes
Trail use fee: None
Camping: None
Drinking water available at a hand pump

General Information:
  Maintained by Meridain Charter Township
  Trail along the Red Cedar River
  The area is designated as a riverfront natural area
  Future plans call for expansion of the 70 acre park to 170 acres with an
    additional 4 miles of trails, an interpretive nature center and 3 miles
    of river frontage.
  Portable toilets provided at the trailhead

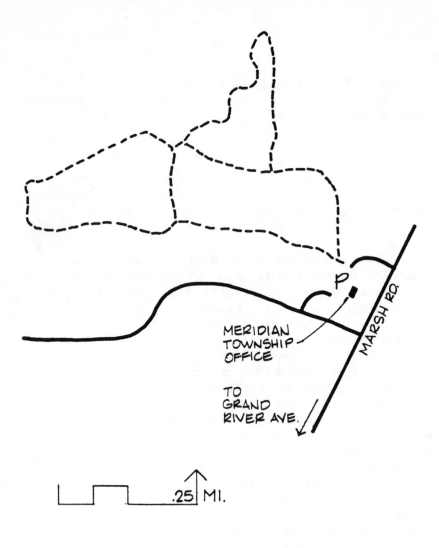

## CENTRAL PARK

Parks Department, Charter Township of Meridian
5151 Marsh Rd.                                              517-349-1200
Okemos, MI  48864

Trail suitable for hiking and skiing

Location:
   .25 mile north of Grand River Ave on the west side of Marsh Rd., behind
     the township offices. Immediately north of Meridian Mall.


Trail specifications:
    2.5 mi; 3 loop(s); Loop length(s)-.5, 1, 2
Typical terrain: Flat to slightly rolling
Skiing ability suggested: Novice
Hiking trail difficulty: Easy
Nordic trail grooming method: Track set twice weekly
Suitable for all-terrain bicycle: Yes
Trail use fee: None
Camping: None
Drinking water avaialble in township offices and Historical Village

General Information:
 Maintained by Meridian Township
 Trails start at the Meridian Historical Village
 The park contains over 230 acres
 Future plans call for the expansion of the trail system an additional 2
    miles, construction of a 4 acre lake, ballfields, picnic area and an
    interpretive nature trail.
 Restrooms available in the township office building and Historical Village

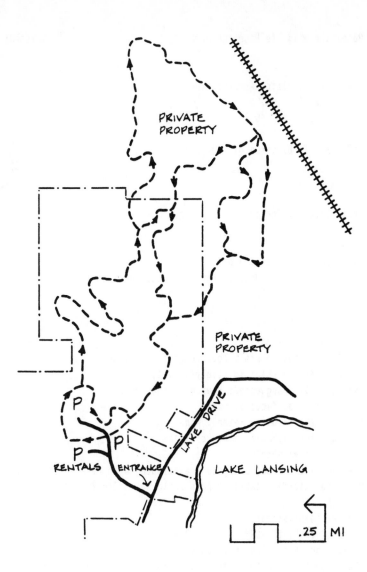

Ingham County Parks Department
PO Box 38                                    517-676-2233
Mason, MI  48854

Trail suitable for skiing & hiking

Location:
 Northeast of Lansing on the north shore of Lake Lansing near Haslett
 Take Saginaw Hwy to Haslett Rd., then left on Marsh Rd. about 1.5 miles
   to North Lake Drive (bear to the right), follow for about 1.5 miles, the
   park is on the left side of the road

Trail specifications:
 9 km; 5 loop(s); Loop length(s)-1.6, 5.3, 3.8, 6.1, 5.1
Typical terrain: Flat to rolling
Skiing ability suggested: Novice to intermediate
Hiking trail difficulty: Easy
Nordic trail grooming method: Track set when snow conditon permits.
Suitable for all-terrain bicycle: Not permitted
Trail use fee: None
Camping: None
Drinking water available

General Information:
 Operated by the Ingham County Parks Department
 Rentals and warming building are available
 Length & number of loops may vary yearly due to adjacent development
 Part of trail crosses wetlands on boardwalks

# NORTH LAKE LANSING PARK

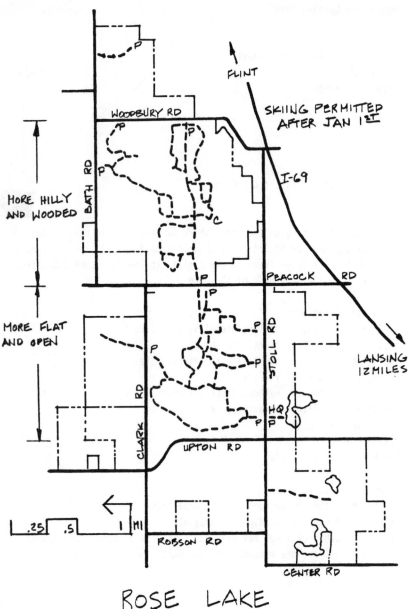

ROSE LAKE
WILDLIFE RESEARCH AREA

Rose Lake Wildlife Research Area                    Revised:  3/17/88

Rose Lake Wildlife Research Area
8562 East Stoll Rd.                                 517-373-9358
East Lansing, MI  48823

DNR Wildlife Division Office

                                                    517-373-1263

Trail suitable for skiing & hiking

Location:
 12 miles NE of Lansing off I69
 From I69 north on Upton, Peacock or Woodbury Rds to parking areas

Trail specifications:
  10+ mi; Many loop(s); Loop length(s)-various
Typical terrain: Flat to slightly hilly
Skiing ability suggested: Novice to intermediate
Hiking trail difficulty: Easy
Nordic trail grooming method: None
Suitable for all-terrain bicycle: Yes
Trail use fee: None
Camping: Youth group campground available, with reservations only‡
Drinking water available at hdqs building on Stoll Rd‡‡

General Information:
 Maintained by the DNR Wildlife Division
 Skiing not permitted until January 2nd
 Very popular area for Lansing area residents and MSU students
 The best terrain with the most wooded trails is between Woodbury and
   Peacock Roads
 This land was purchased with hunting licenses. Please respect the rights
   of the hunters when skiing in this area
 ‡ Limited to small groups of 30 or less
 ‡‡ Open M-F from 8-12 and 1-5

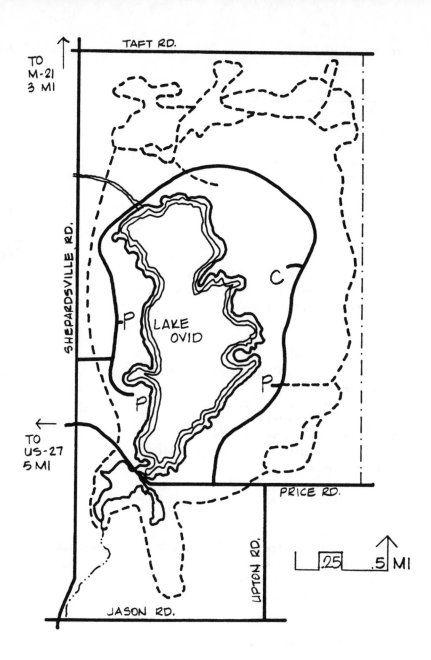

TO
M-21
3 MI

TAFT RD.

SHEPARDSVILLE RD.

LAKE
OVID

P

P

P

C

TO
US-27
5 MI

PRICE RD.

UPTON RD.

.25   .5 MI

JASON RD.

# SLEEPY HOLLOW STATE PARK

Sleepy Hollow State Park                    Revised:  3/28/88


Sleepy Hollow State Park
7835 Price Rd.                              517-651-6217
Lainsburg, MI  48848


DNR Parks Division Office

                                            517-373-1270

Trail suitable for skiing & hiking

Location:
 15 miles NE of Lansing
 From US27 take Price Rd. east 6 miles to park entrance


Trail specifications:
  6 mi*; Several loop(s); Loop length(s)-various
Typical terrain: Flat with some steep hills
Skiing ability suggested: Novice
Hiking trail difficulty: Easy
Nordic trail grooming method: Track set as needed
Suitable for all-terrain bicycle: Yes
Trail use fee: None, but vehicle entry fee required $2/day, $10/year
Camping: Campground in park
Drinking water available

General Information:
 Maintained by the DNR Parks Division
 Ski trail maps available at the headquarters
 Open 7 days a week from 8am to 10pm
 * Trails shown on the map are for hiking.  Ski trails are less extensive
   The trail on the west side of the lake and south of Price Rd. are for
   hiking only.  Check with the Park Manager for a current cross-country
   trail map.

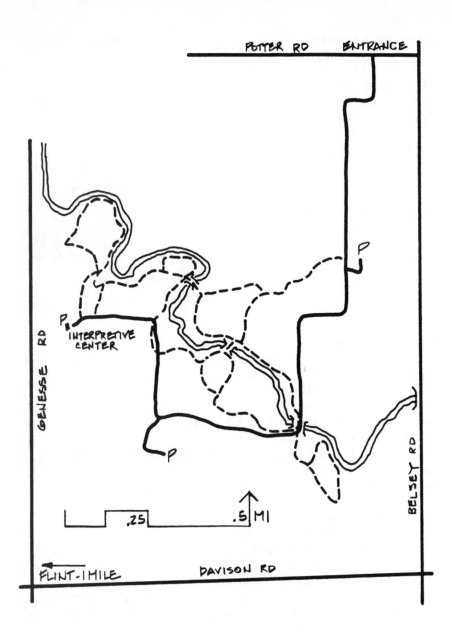

POTTER RD    ENTRANCE

GENESSE RD

INTERPRETIVE
CENTER

P

P

P

BELSEY RD

.25    .5 MI

FLINT-IMILE    DAVISON RD

# FOR-MAR NATURE PRESERVE

For-Mar Nature Preserve                                    Revised: 3/16/88

Genesee County Parks and Recreation Commission
G-5055 Branch Rd.                                          313-736-7100
Flint, MI  48506

For-Mar Nature Preserve
G-2252 N Genesee Rd.                                       313-763-7100
Flint, MI  48506

Trail suitable for skiing & hiking

Location:
  East of Flint 3 miles on I69 to Belsay Rd, north 2 miles to Potter Rd,
    then west .3 mile to preserve entrance
  Trailhead - Interpretive Center

Trail specifications:
  6.7 mi; Many loop(s); Loop length(s)-various
Typical terrain: Flat
Skiing ability suggested: Novice
Hiking trail difficulty: Easy
Nordic trail grooming method: None
Suitable for all-terrain bicycle: Not permitted
Trail use fee: None
Camping: None
Drinking water available at the Interpretive Center

General Information:
  Operated by the Genesee County Parks and Recreation Commission
  Hiking trails may not all be identical
  Trails start at the Interpretive Center
  Open from 9am to 6 pm

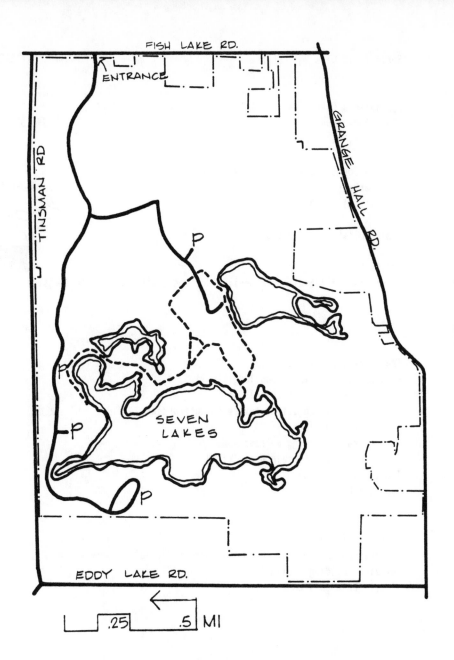

FISH LAKE RD.

ENTRANCE

TINSMAN RD.

GRANGE HALL RD.

P

P

P

SEVEN
LAKES

P

EDDY LAKE RD.

.25    .5 MI

SEVEN LAKES STATE PARK

Seven Lakes State Park                    Revised:  8/12/87


Seven Lakes State Park
2220 Tinsman Rd.                          313-634-7271
Fenton, MI  48430


DNR Parks Division Office

                                         517-373-1270


Trail suitable for hiking & skiing

Location:
 Exit I75 at Grange Hall Rd, then go 6 miles west to Fish Lake Rd.,
   then north on Fish Lake Rd 1 mile to park entrance
 Trailheads at boat launch and north picnic area


Trail specifications:
   3 mi; 1 loop(s); Loop length(s)-3
Typical terrain: Rolling
Skiing ability suggested: Novice
Hiking trail difficulty: Easy
Nordic trail grooming method: None
Suitable for all-terrain bicycle: Yes
Trail use fee: None, but vehicle entry fee required $2/day, $10/year
Camping: No campground available
Drinking water available at HQ and picnic areas (seasonally)

General Information:
 Maintained by the DNR Parks Division
 8 miles west of the Holly Recreation Area
 All 1,400 acres are open for cross-country skiing
 Trails not designed for skiing but are skiable

53

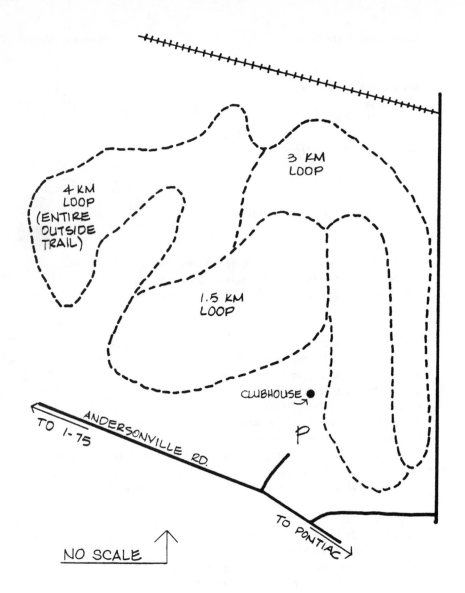

4 KM
LOOP
(ENTIRE
OUTSIDE
TRAIL)

3 KM
LOOP

1.5 KM
LOOP

CLUBHOUSE ●

P

TO I-75

ANDERSONVILLE RD.

TO PONTIAC

NO SCALE

SPRINGFIELD OAKS
GOLF COURSE

Springfield Oaks Golf Course                    Revised:  1/15/88

Springfield Oaks County Park
12450 Andersonville Rd.                          313-625-2540
Davisburg, MI  48019

Oakland County Parks and Recreation Dept
2800 Watkins Lake Rd.                            313-858-0906
Pontiac, MI  48056

Trail suitable for skiing only

Location:
 Just west of I75 at Andersonville Rd. and Davisburg Rd.. in Davisburg

Trail specifications:
   8.5 km; 3 loop(s); Loop length(s)-1.5, 3, 4
Typical terrain: Flat to rolling
Skiing ability suggested: Novice to intermediate
Hiking trail difficulty: NA
Nordic trail grooming method: None
Suitable for all-terrain bicycle: NA
Trail use fee: None
Camping: None

General Information:
 Maintained by the Oakland County Parks & Recreation Commission
 Warming building available
 Trails on a golf course

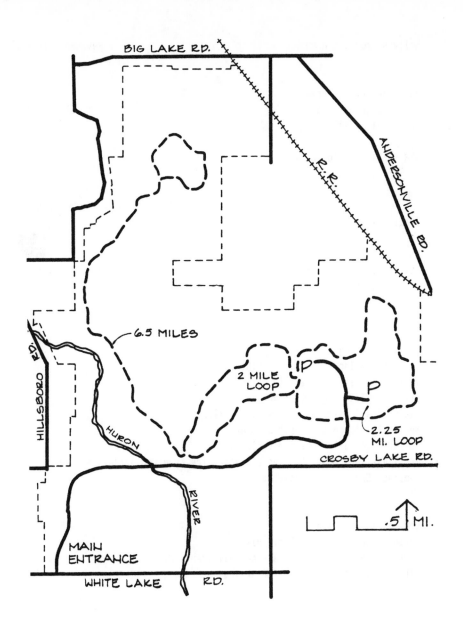

INDIAN SPRINGS METROPARK

6.5 MILES

2 MILE LOOP

P

P

2.25 MI. LOOP

HURON RIVER

HILLSBORO RD.

BIG LAKE RD.

ANDERSONVILLE RD.

R. R.

CROSBY LAKE RD.

MAIN ENTRANCE

WHITE LAKE RD.

.5 MI.

Indian Springs Metropark                    Revised:  4/07/88

Indian Springs Metropark
5200 Indian Trail                           313-685-1561
Clarkston, MI  48016                        800-24-PARKS

Huron-Clinton Metropolitan Authority
13000 High Ridge Drive, PO Box 2001         313-227-2757
Brighton, MI  48116-8001

Trail suitable for skiing & hiking

Location:
 Just north of Pontaic Lake Recreation Area on White Lake Rd,
   between Cuthbert and Teggerdine Roads.


Trail specifications:
   11 mi*; 3 loop(s); Loop length(s)-2, 2.25, 6.5
Typical terrain: Flat to rolling
Skiing ability suggested: Novice
Hiking trail difficulty: Easy
Nordic trail grooming method: Track set
Suitable for all-terrain bicycle: Yes, on established bike/hike trail only**
Trail use fee: None, but vehicle entry fee required $2/day, $10/year
Camping: None
Drinking water is available throughout the park

General Information:
 Operated by the Huron-Clinton Metropolitan Authority
 Ski rentals on weekends only
 Open from 8AM to 8PM October to April and 8AM to 10PM May to September
 Nature Center building is open on a limited schedule during the school
   year weekdays and 10AM to 5PM during the summer.  The weekend
   schedule all year is 10AM to 5PM.
 Pets permitted on a leash only on the bike/hike trail.
 *Trails for skiing, hiking and biking are not identical
 ** ATB's not permitted on nature trails


Call or write for their Metropark Guide, published each year.

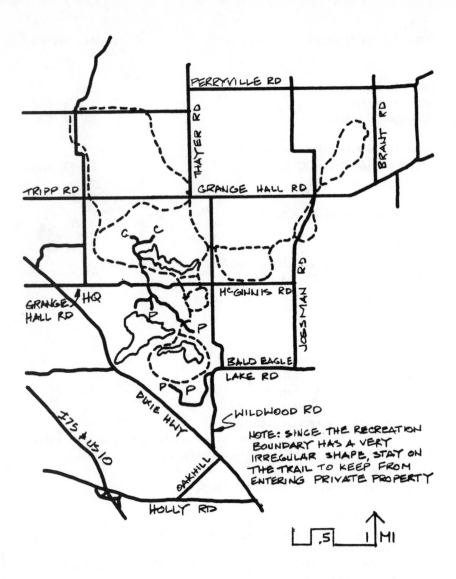

Holly Recreation Area
8100 Grange Hall Rd.                                     313-634-8811
Holly, MI  48442

DNR Parks Division Office

                                                        517-373-1270

Trail suitable for hiking & skiing

Location:
 Exit I75 at Grange Hall Rd. (east of Holly), then east 2.5 miles to the
    recreation area entrance

Trail specifications:
   32 mi; 3 loop(s); Loop length(s)-3.2, 8, 20
Typical terrain: Rolling to hilly
Skiing ability suggested: Novice to advanced
Hiking trail difficulty: Easy to difficult
Nordic trail grooming method: None
Suitable for all-terrain bicycle: Yes
Trail use fee: None, but vehicle entry fee required $2/day, $10/year
Camping: Campground available

General Information:
 Maintained by the DNR Parks Division
 Hiking and skiing trails are not all identical
 The 3 mile trail is best for skiing

NOTE: SINCE THE RECREATION BOUNDARY HAS A VERY IRREGULAR SHAPE, STAY ON THE TRAIL TO KEEP FROM ENTERING PRIVATE PROPERTY

HOLLY  RECREATION  AREA

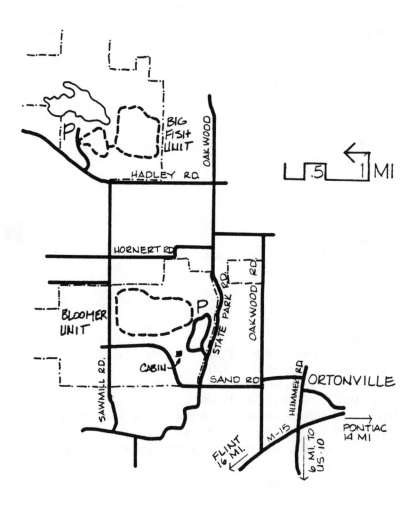

ORTONVILLE RECREATION AREA

Ortonville Recreation Area
5779 Hadley Rd.                               313-627-3828
Ortonville, MI  48462

DNR Parks Division Office

                                              517-373-1270

Trail suitable for skiing & hiking

Location:
 SE of Flint and north of Clarkston, 1.5 miles NE of Ortonville
 1.25 miles north of Oakwood Rd on Hadley Rd. (Big Fish Unit)
 .5 mile east of Sands Rd. on State Park Rd. (Bloomer Unit)


Trail specifications:
   6 mi; 3 loop(s); Loop length(s)-various
Typical terrain: Rolling to hilly
Skiing ability suggested: Novice to intermediate
Hiking trail difficulty: Easy to moderate
Nordic trail grooming method: None
Suitable for all-terrain bicycle: Yes
Trail use fee: None, but vehicle entry fee required $2/day, $10/year
Camping: Group campground available ‡
Drinking water available at Bloomer Unit

General Information:
 Maintained by the DNR Parks Division
 Limited facilities
 Cabin available for rent near Bloomer Unit trail
 ORV's are not allowed in the park
 Near Independence Oaks County Park
 ‡ Family campground available at nearby Holly State Park

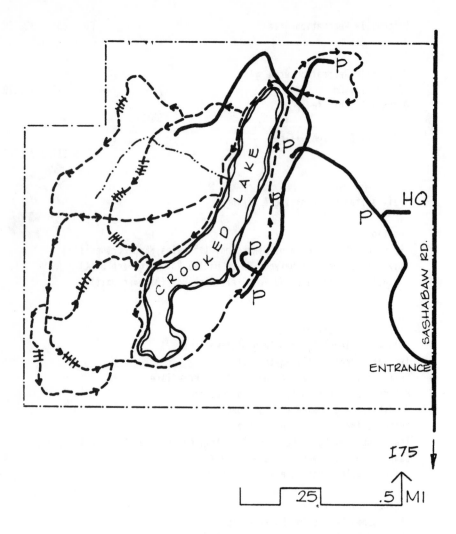

INDEPENDENCE OAKS
COUNTY PARK

I75 ↓

25. .5 MI

Independence Oaks County Park
9501 Sashabaw Rd.                              313-625-0877
Clarkston, MI  48016                           313-625-6473

Oakland County Parks and Recreation Commission
2800 Watkins Lake Rd.                          313-858-0906
Pontiac, MI  48054-1697

Trail suitable for skiing & hiking

Location:
 North of Pontiac off I75 at Sashabaw Rd. exit 89, then north 2.5 miles to
   the park entrance

Trail specifications:
   10 mi‡; 7 loop(s); Loop length(s)-2.4, .66, .39, .37, 2.7, 3.2, .75
Typical terrain: Flat to very hilly
Skiing ability suggested: Novice to advanced
Hiking trail difficulty: Easy to moderate
Nordic trail grooming method: Double track set with Bachler equipment
Suitable for all-terrain bicycle: Not permitted
Trail use fee: None, but vehicle entry fee required $3 and up ‡‡
Camping: None
Drinking water available

General Information:
 Operated by the Oakland County Parks and Recreation Commission
 Rentals, warming area, snack bar, picnic grounds, fishing, boating, nature
   area and center and ice skating
 Some of the best cross country trails in SE Michigan
 Open 8am to sunset daily (Closed Christmas Day)
 Fishing and ice skating available
 ‡ Trail lengths according to skill levels:
    Lakeshore Trail   Novice        2.4 miles
    Rockridge Trail   Intermediate  2.7 miles
    Springlake Trail  Expert        3.2 miles
 ‡‡ Higher on weekends and for non-county residents

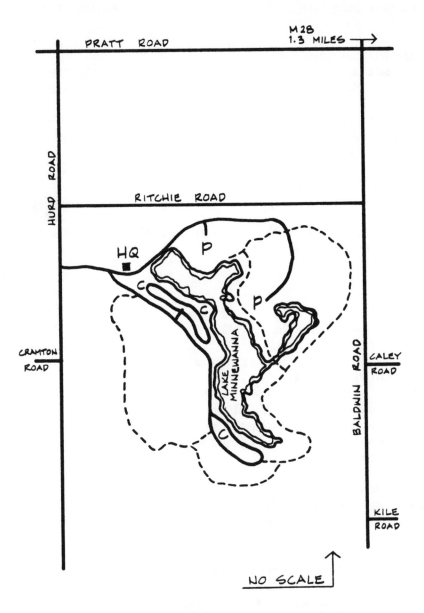

PRATT ROAD

M 28
1.3 MILES →

HURD ROAD

RITCHIE ROAD

HQ

P

P

P

C

C

C

C

LAKE MINNEWANNA

CRAMTON ROAD

BALDWIN ROAD

CALEY ROAD

KILE ROAD

NO SCALE

# METAMORA-HADLEY RECREATION AREA

Metamora-Hadley Recreation Area                    Revised: 3/17/88


Metamora-Hadley Recreation Area
3871 Hurd Rd.                                      313-797-4439
Metamora, MI  48455

DNR Parks Division Office

517-373-1270

Trail suitable for hiking & skiing

Location:
 South from Lapeer on M24 to Pratt Rd., then west 2 miles to Herd Rd., then
   south .7 mile to recreation area entrance.
 Trailheads at campground office and beach area


Trail specifications:
   4.5 mi; 2 loop(s); Loop length(s)-1.75, 2.75
Typical terrain: Rolling
Skiing ability suggested: Novice
Hiking trail difficulty: Easy
Nordic trail grooming method: None
Suitable for all-terrain bicycle: Yes
Trail use fee: None, but vehicle entry fee required $2/day, $10/year
Camping: Campground in recreation area
Drinking water available at HQ and campground(seasonally)

General Information:
 Maintained by the DNR Parks Division
 Skiing may not be suitable if snow depth pemits hiking
 Trails were designed for hiking but are skiable

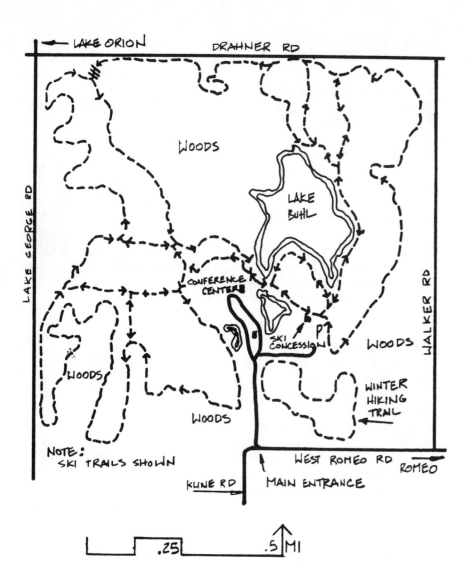

NOTE:
SKI TRAILS SHOWN

|___|‾‾|___|‾‾‾‾‾‾|↑
    .25         .5 MI

# ADDISON OAKS COUNTY PARK

Addison Oaks County Park                    Revised:  4/01/88

Addison Oaks County Park
1480 W Romeo Rd                                          313-693-2432
Oxford, MI  48051                                        313-693-0220*

Oakland County Parks and Recreation Department
2800 Watkins Lake Rd                                     313-858-0906
Pontiac, MI  48056

Trail suitable for skiing & hiking

Location:
 9 miles north of Rochester and 4 miles east of Lake Orion on West Romeo Rd
   (32 Mile Rd) at Kline Rd.

Trail specifications:
   12 mi; 8 loop(s); Loop length(s)-.05 to 5
Typical terrain: Flat to hilly
Skiing ability suggested: Novice to advanced
Hiking trail difficulty: Easy
Nordic trail grooming method: Track set
Suitable for all-terrain bicycle: Not permitted
Trail use fee: None, but vehicle entry fee required $3 and up **
Camping: Modern, primitive and group camping facilities
Drinking water available

General Information:
 Operated by the Oakland County Parks and Recreation Commission
 Year-round recreation area with swimming, picnicking and fishing
 Many nordic races and events held throughout the season
 Lighted trail, lessons, rentals(weekends) available
 Ice skating available as conditions permit
 * Ski rental office
 ** Higher on weekends and for non-county residents
 There is a steep hill available for telemarking
 Foundation Family Fun Day held each winter includes a sled dog race
  fishing contest, snowshoe race and many other events

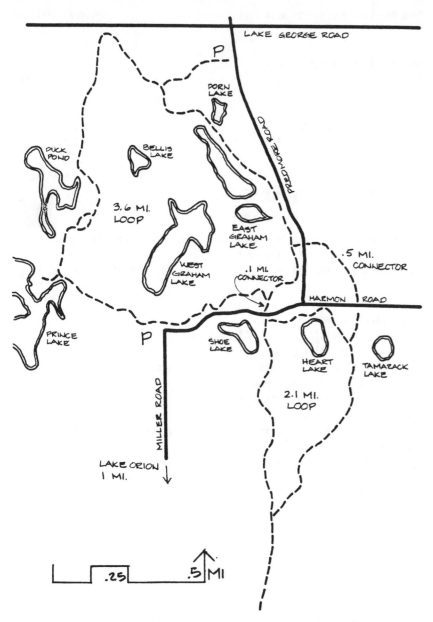

## BALD MOUNTAIN RECREATION AREA
## NORTH UNIT

.25    .5 MI

Bald Mountain Recreation Area-North Unit          Revised:  8/11/87

Bald Mountain Recreation Area
1330 Greenshield Rd., Rte 1                        313-693-6767
Lake Orion, MI  48035

DNR Parks Division Office

                                                  517-373-1270

Trail suitable for skiing & hiking

Location:
 Trailhead-East of Lake Orion at the corner of Miller Rd. and Harmon Rd.
 Trailhead-East of Lake Orion at the corner of Harmon Rd. and Predmore Rd.
 Trailhead-East of Lake Orion just west of Lake George Rd. on Predmore Rd.
 Trailhead-East of Lake Orion 1/2 mile north of Predmore Rd. on
   Lake George Rd  (Watch for signs)
Trail specifications:
   6.5 mi; 2 loop(s); Loop length(s)-2.1,3.6
Typical terrain: Rolling with some steep hills
Skiing ability suggested: Intermediate to advanced
Hiking trail difficulty: Moderate
Nordic trail grooming method: Leveled and scarified lightly
Suitable for all-terrain bicycle: Yes
Trail use fee: None, but vehicle entry fee required $2/day, $10/year
Camping: None, but rustic cabins may be rented
Drinking water available at Tamarack Lake

General Information:
 Maintained by the DNR Parks Division
 Sledding available on Stoney Creek Rd.
 Mostly wooded trails
 Well marked trails with some road crossings
 Paint Creek Trail is south of the recreation area

61

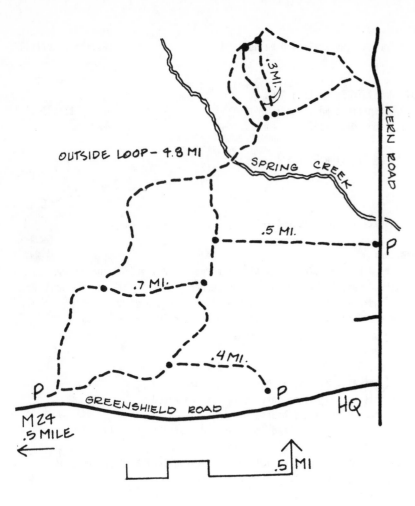

OUTSIDE LOOP - 4.8 MI

SPRING CREEK

KERN ROAD

.3 MI.

.5 MI.

.7 MI.

.4 MI.

P          P          HQ

GREENSHIELD ROAD

M24
.5 MILE

.5 MI

# BALD MOUNTAIN RECREATION AREA - SOUTH UNIT

Bald Mountain Recreation Area-South Unit          Revised:  8/11/87


Bald Mountain Recreation Area
1330 Greenshield Rd., Rte 1                        313-693-6767
Lake Orion, MI  48035

DNR Parks Division Office

517-373-1270

Trail suitable for hiking & skiing

Location:
  Trailhead-South of Lake Orion via M24 to Greenshield Rd., then east .75
    mile or 1.25 miles to parking lots.
  (Park office is located on Greenshield Rd., just east of the east parking
    lot)


Trail specifications:
  7.1 mi; 5 loop(s); Loop length(s)-various to 4.8
Typical terrain: Rolling to hilly
Skiing ability suggested: Intermediate to advanced
Hiking trail difficulty: Moderate
Nordic trail grooming method: None
Suitable for all-terrain bicycle: Yes
Trail use fee: None, but vehicle entry fee required $2/day, $10/year
Camping: None
Water available at the park office & group campground


General Information:
  Maintained by the DNR Parks Division
  Open to hunting and snowmobiles
  Paint Creek Trail is north of the recreation area

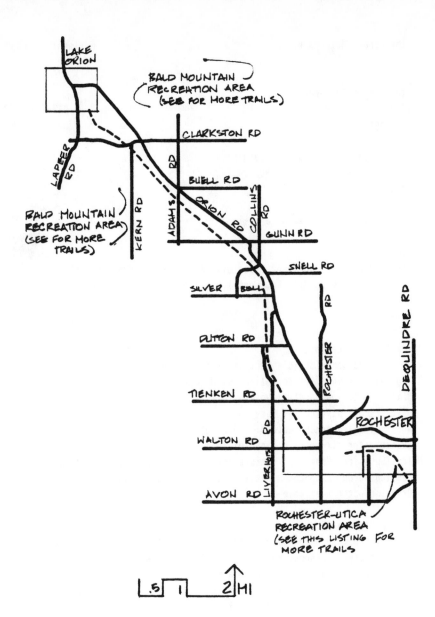

**PAINT CREEK TRAIL**

Paint Creek Trail                                    Revised:  3/23/88

Paint Creek Trailways Commission
4393 Collins Rd.                                     313-651-4440
Rochester, MI  48064

Trail suitable for hiking & skiing

Location:
 Between Lake Orion and Utica along the Paint Creek and the Clinton River

Trail specifications:
   10.5 mi; No * loop(s); Loop length(s)-NA
Typical terrain: Flat
Skiing ability suggested: Novice
Hiking trail difficulty: Easy
Nordic trail grooming method: None
Suitable for all-terrain bicycle: Yes
Trail use fee: None
Camping: None
Drinking water available along the trail

General Information:
 Maintained by the Paint Creek Trailways Commission made up of Oakland
   Township, Rochester Hills, Rochester and Orion Township
 Trail follows the route of a former railroad track
 Development of trail facilities and bike path is continuing
 * A point to point trail
 The trail is also available to horseback riding
 See Rochester-Utica Recreation Area - Bloomer Unit, which is along the
   trail.

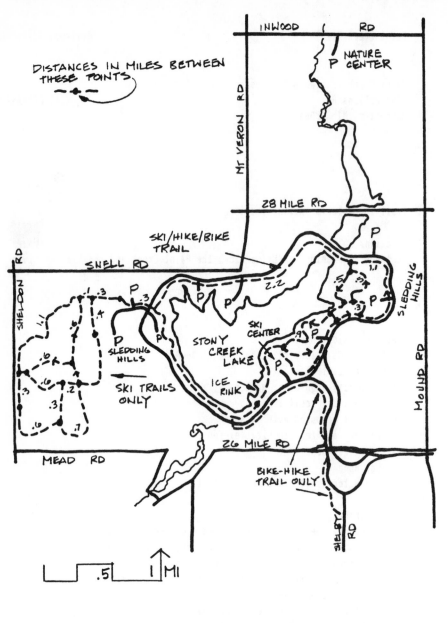

DISTANCES IN MILES BETWEEN THESE POINTS

SKI/HIKE/BIKE TRAIL

SKI TRAILS ONLY

BIKE-HIKE TRAIL ONLY

STONY CREEK METROPARK

.5 1 MI

Stony Creek Metropark                                    Revised: 4/07/88

Stony Creek Metropark
4300 Main Park Rd.                                       313-227-2757
Washington, MI  48094-9763                              800-24-PARKS

Huron-Clinton Metropolitan Authority
1300 High Ridge Drive, PO Box 2001                      313-227-2757
Brighton, MI  48116-8001

Trail suitable for skiing & hiking

Location:
 NE of Rochester, north of Utica off of Van Dyke Expressway (M53)
 From M53, take 26 Mile Rd. west 1.5 miles to park entrance


Trail specifications:
   15+ mi*; Many loop(s); Loop length(s)-various
Typical terrain: Flat to rolling with some steep hills
Skiing ability suggested: Novice to advanced
Hiking trail difficulty: Easy
Nordic trail grooming method: Track set
Suitable for all-terrain bicycle: Yes, on established bike trail only
Trail use fee: None, but vehicle entry fee required $2/day, $10/year
Camping: Group campground available, reservations required **
Drinking water available

General Information:
 Operated by the Huron-Clinton Metropolitan Authority
 Warming area, lessons, rentals, snack bar, ice skating, ice fishing,
   nature study area, sailing, boating, picnic grounds and swimming
*Hike/bike trails overlap on some ski trails.  During the winter the use
   of the trails is limited for skiing only. The hike/bike trails system is
   about 6.2 miles long and is limited to a route around the lake.
** Campground is for organized youth group only.


Call or write for their Metropark Guide, published each year.

64

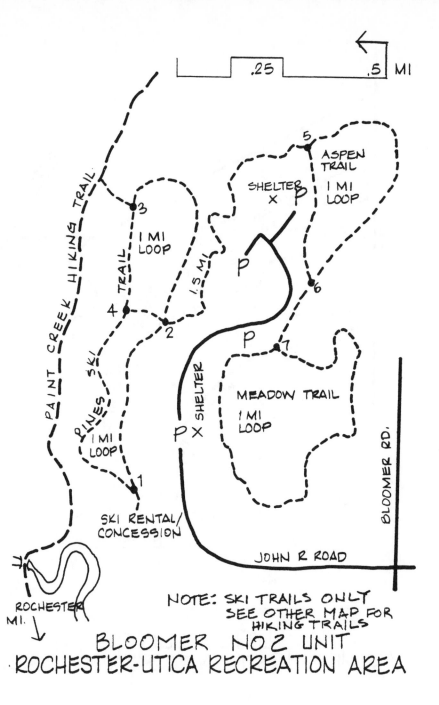

.25 .5 MI

5

ASPEN
TRAIL

SHELTER
X P

I MI
LOOP

3

I MI
LOOP

PAINT CREEK HIKING TRAIL

SKI TRAIL

.5 MI

P

4

2

6

P

7

PINES SKI

I MI
LOOP

P X SHELTER

MEADOW TRAIL

I MI
LOOP

1

SKI RENTAL/
CONCESSION

BLOOMER RD.

JOHN R ROAD

ROCHESTER
MI.

NOTE: SKI TRAILS ONLY
SEE OTHER MAP FOR
HIKING TRAILS

BLOOMER NO 2 UNIT
ROCHESTER-UTICA RECREATION AREA

Rochester-Utica Recreation Area                    Revised: 3/24/88

Rochester-Utica Recreation Area
47511 Woodall                                      313-731-2110
Utica, MI  48087

DNR Parks Division Office

                                                   517-3731270

Trail suitable for skiing & hiking

Location:
  Utica Unit trailhead - 2 miles north of M59 on Ryan Rd., just west of
    Utica, then east on Hamlin to park entrance
  Bloomer Unit trailhead - Take John R north until it ends at the park
    just southeast of Rochester on the south side of the Paint Creek

Trail specifications:
  10+ mi*; 6 loop(s); Loop length(s)-various
Typical terrain: Flat to rolling
Skiing ability suggested: Novice
Hiking trail difficulty: Easy
Nordic trail grooming method: Track set
Suitable for all-terrain bicycle: Yes
Trail use fee: None, but vehicle entry fee required $2/day, $10/year
Camping: None
Drinking water is available

General Information:
 Maintained by the DNR Parks Division
 * Combined distances for both the Bloomer No. 2 and Utica Units
 Warming area, rentals and snack bar available at Bloomer No. 2
 Trail connects to the Paint Creek Trail which is an additional 10.5 miles
   long. See Paint Creek Trail for additional information on the
   noncontiguous section.
 The Bloomer No. 2 Unit has separate trails for hiking and skiing
 The Utica Unit has trails for hiking only
 See three separate maps for the the hiking and ski trails in the
   two separate units.
 A unique swinging bridge is at the SE end of the Bloomer No. 2 Unit
   Trail where it connects with the Yates Unit across from the privately
   owned Yates Cider Mill.

65

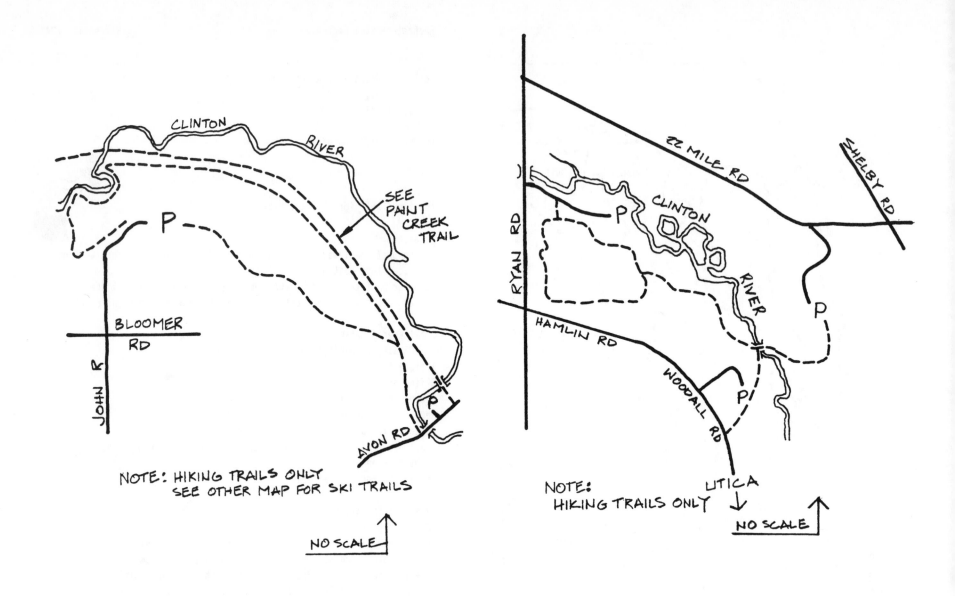

BLOOMER NO. 2 UNIT
ROCHESTER-UTICA RECREATION AREA

UTICA UNIT
ROCHESTER-UTICA RECREATION AREA

66

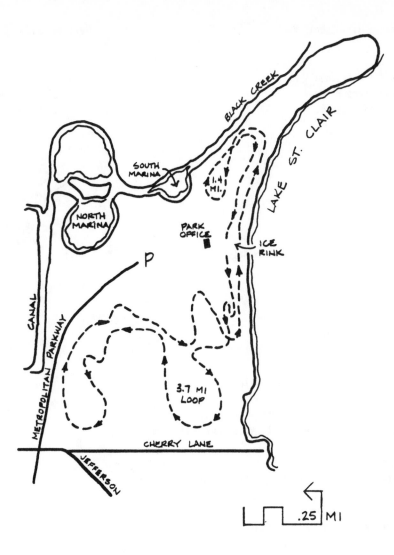

## METRO BEACH METROPARK

Metro Beach Metropark
PO Box 1037                                              313-463-4581
Mt Clemens, MI   48086                                   800-24-PARKS

Huron-Clinton Metropolitan Authority
1300 High Ridge Drive, PO Box 2001                       313-227-2757
Brighton, MI   48116-8001

Trail suitable for skiing only

Location:
 At the east end of the Metro Parkway in Mt Clemens on Lake St. Clair
 Trailhead - At the Center Plaza

Trail specifications:
   5.4 mi; 1 loop(s); Loop length(s)-1
Typical terrain: Flat
Skiing ability suggested: Novice
Hiking trail difficulty: NA
Nordic trail grooming method: Track set
Suitable for all-terrain bicycle: NA
Trail use fee: None, but vehicle entry fee required $2/day, $10/year
Camping: None
Drinking water available

General Information:
 Operated by the Huron-Clinton Metropolitan Authority
 Warming shelter, ski rentals and snack bar available
 Special group rate for ski rentals during the week
 Complete summer recreation center with beach, par 3 golf, tennis, nature
   study area, picnic grounds and much more.

Call or write for their Metropark Guide, published each year.

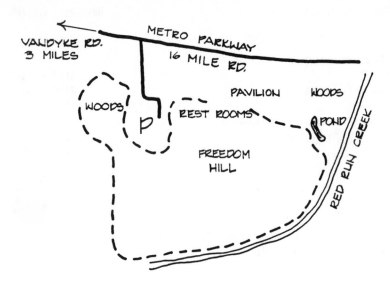

NO SCALE

# FREEDOM HILL COUNTY PARK

Freedom Hill County Park                    Revised: 11/21/87


Freedom Hill County Park
15000 Metro Parkway                         313-979-7010
Sterling Heights, MI   48077                313-979-8750

Trail suitable for skiing & hiking

Location:
 3 miles east of Van Dyke on Metropolitan Parkway (16 Mile Rd.).


Trail specifications:
   2 mi; 1 loop(s); Loop length(s)-2
Typical terrain: Flat
Skiing ability suggested: Novice
Hiking trail difficulty: Easy
Nordic trail grooming method: Track set
Suitable for all-terrain bicycle: Not permitted
Trail use fee: None
Camping: None
Drinking water available at the recreation building

General Information:
 Operated by the Macomb County Park
 Warming area available
 Picnic area and restrooms
 Also tot lot, multi-use building and amphitheater used in summer

Sylvan Glen Municipal Golf Course
5725 Rochester Rd.                                    313-879-0040
Troy, MI   48080

Trail suitable for skiing only

Location:
 On Rochester Rd between Long Lake and Square Lake Rds

# No Trail Map

Trail specifications:
    3 mi; 3 loop(s); Loop length(s)-.75, 1, 2
Typical terrain: Flat to rolling
Skiing ability suggested: Novice to intermediate
Hiking trail difficulty: NA
Nordic trail grooming method: Track set
Suitable for all-terrain bicycle: NA
Trail use fee: $2/day residents, $3/day non-residents
Camping: None
Drinking water available

General Information:
 Maintained by the Troy Park and Recreation Department
 Ski shop, warming shelter and rentals are available
 Trails marked by traffic cones. No map available

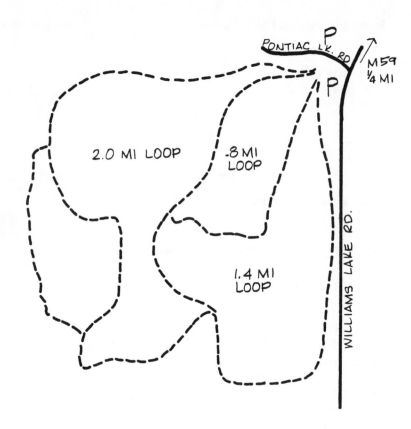

PONTIAC LK. RD.

P

P

M59
¼ MI

2.0 MI LOOP

.8 MI
LOOP

1.4 MI
LOOP

WILLIAMS LAKE RD.

## WHITE LAKE OAKS GOLF COURSE

White Lake Oaks Golf Course                    Revised: 1/15/88

White Lake Oaks County Park
991 S. Williams Lake Rd.                        313-698-2700
Pontiac, MI 48054

Oakland County Parks & Recreation Commission
2800 Watkins Lake Rd.                           313-858-0906
Pontiac, MI 48054-1697

Trail suitable for skiing only

Location:
  On Williams Lake Rd., just south of Highland Rd. (M59)
    and Pontiac Lake Rd.

Trail specifications:
    6.6 km; 3 loop(s); Loop length(s)-1.2, 2.2, 3.2
Typical terrain: Flat to rolling
Skiing ability suggested: Novice
Hiking trail difficulty: NA
Nordic trail grooming method: Packed
Suitable for all-terrain bicycle: NA
Trail use fee: None
Camping: None

General Information:
  Maintained by the Oakland County Parks & Recreation Commission
  Warming area, snack bar, lessons and rentals available
  Trails are on a golf course

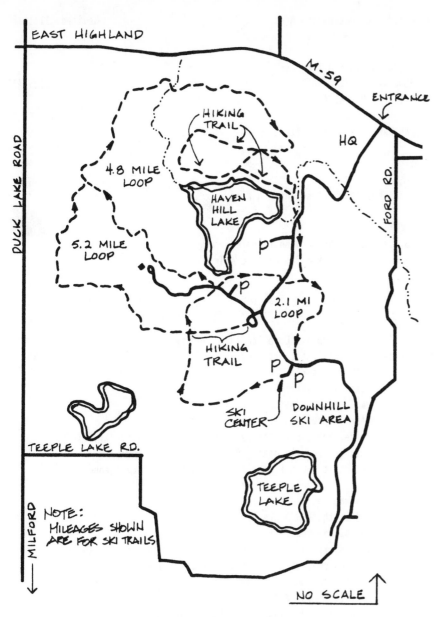

EAST HIGHLAND

DUCK LAKE ROAD

M-59

ENTRANCE

HQ

FORD RD.

HIKING TRAIL

4.8 MILE LOOP

HAVEN HILL LAKE

5.2 MILE LOOP

P

P

2.1 MI LOOP

HIKING TRAIL

P

P

SKI CENTER

DOWNHILL SKI AREA

TEEPLE LAKE RD.

MILFORD

TEEPLE LAKE

NOTE: MILEAGES SHOWN ARE FOR SKI TRAILS

NO SCALE

# HIGHLAND RECREATION AREA

Highland Recreation Area                    Revised:  1/06/88

Highland Recreation Area
5200 East Highland Rd.                       313-887-5135
Milford, MI  48042

DNR Parks Division Office

                                             517-373-1270

Trail suitable for skiing & hiking

Location:
 NE of Milford off M59 1 mile east of Duck Lake Rd.

Trail specifications:
   12.2 mi; 3 loop(s); Loop length(s)-2, 4.8, 5.2
Typical terrain: Rolling to hilly
Skiing ability suggested: Novice to intermediate
Hiking trail difficulty: Easy to moderate
Nordic trail grooming method: Track set
Suitable for all-terrain bicycle: Yes
Trail use fee: None, but vehicle entry fee required $2/day, $10/year
Camping: Campground within the recreation area
Drinking water available

General Information:
 Maintained by the DNR Parks Division
 Warming area, downhill slopes, rentals and snack bar on weekends
 Hiking trails are not identical to those listed above
 Near many other trail systems in the area
 Some ski trails used as equestrian trails in the snowless months

Proud Lake Recreation Area
3500 Wixom Rd., Rte 3                          313-685-2433
Milford, MI  48042

DNR Parks Division Office

                                               517-373-1270

Trail suitable for skiing & hiking

Location:
 3 miles SE of Milford on Wixom Rd. or
 From I96 take Wixom Rd. north 6 miles

Trail specifications:
   20 km; 8+* loop(s); Loop length(s)-various
Typical terrain: Flat to rolling
Skiing ability suggested: Novice
Hiking trail difficulty: East
Nordic trail grooming method: 10 km track set
Suitable for all-terrain bicycle: Yes
Trail use fee: None, but vehicle entry fee required $2/day, $10/year
Camping: Campground with heated restroom open all year
Drinking water at the ski center, headquarters and campground

General Information:
 Maintained by the DNR Parks Division
 Nature and hiking trails provided
 Ski center located at trailhead, operated by Heavner Concessions.
   Rentals, lessons, ski shop, refreshments and warming shelter
   For information phone 685-2379
 Lodging available for groups
 * Also connector and point to point trails

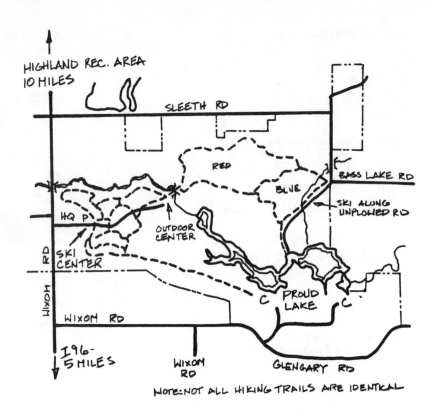

HIGHLAND REC. AREA
10 MILES

SLEETH RD

RED

BLUE

BASS LAKE RD

SKI ALONG
UNPLOWED RD

HQ P

OUTDOOR
CENTER

SKI
CENTER

WIXOM RD

PROUD
LAKE

C        C

WIXOM RD

I96-
5 MILES

WIXOM
RD

GLENGARY RD

NOTE: NOT ALL HIKING TRAILS ARE IDENTICAL

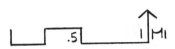

.5        1 MI

# PROUD LAKE RECREATION AREA

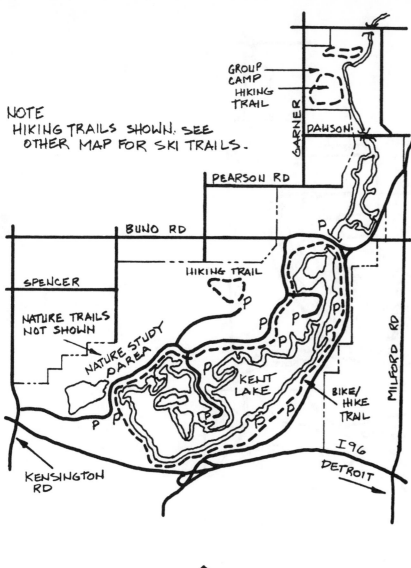

NOTE
HIKING TRAILS SHOWN. SEE
OTHER MAP FOR SKI TRAILS.

GROUP
CAMP
HIKING
TRAIL

GARNER

DAWSON

PEARSON RD

BUNO RD

HIKING TRAIL

SPENCER

NATURE TRAILS
NOT SHOWN

NATURE STUDY
AREA

KENT
LAKE

BIKE/
HIKE
TRAIL

MILFORD RD

I 96

DETROIT

KENSINGTON
RD

.5    1         2 MI

KENSINGTON METROPARK

Kensington Metropark                    Revised:  4/07/88


Kensington Metropark
2240 West Buno Rd.                                 313-685-1561
Milford, MI  48042-9725                            800-24-PARKS

Huron-Clinton Metropolitan Authority
1300 High Ridge Drive, PO Box 2001                 313-227-2757
Brighton, MI  48116-8001

Trail suitable for skiing & hiking

Location:
 SW of Milford toward Brighton, just north of I96
 Exit I96 at Milford Rd., Kent Lake Rd. (exit153) or Kensington Rd.
   (exit 151) and turn north toward park


Trail specifications:
   12 mi #; Many loop(s); Loop length(s)-various
Typical terrain: Flat to rolling
Skiing ability suggested: Novice to intermediate
Hiking trail difficulty: Easy
Nordic trail grooming method: Track set as needed
Suitable for all-terrain bicycle: Yes ##
Trail use fee: None, but vehicle entry fee required $2/day, $10/year
Camping: Youth group campground only, reservations required
Drinking water available

General Information:
 Operated by the Huron-Clinton Metropolitan Authority
 Warming area, rentals, lessons, snack bar, fishing, ice skating, boating
   golf, nature center with trails, group camping and sledding
 Some ski trails for beginners are on the golf course
 # Mileage for ski trails.   Includes round trip distances on point to
   point ski trails.  Bike/hike trail distance is 8.2 miles and nature
   trails (hiking only) are about 5 miles long.  Bike/hike and
   ski trails overlap.
 ## No special mountain bike trails.  Must use regular bike trails and
   only in non-skiing months

   Call or write for their Metropark Guide, published each year.

73

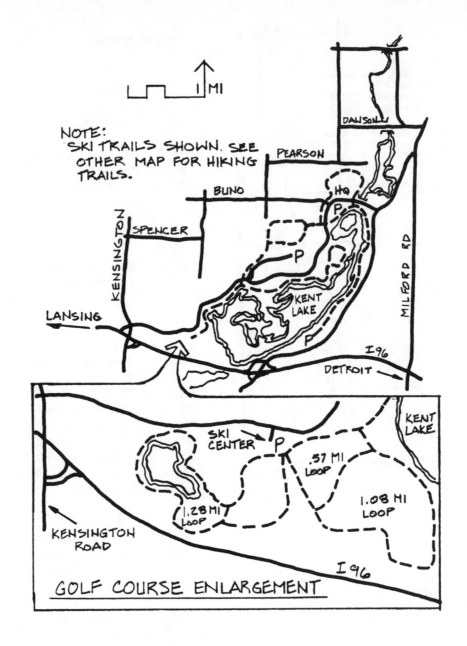

NOTE:
SKI TRAILS SHOWN. SEE
OTHER MAP FOR HIKING
TRAILS.

DAWSON

PEARSON

BUNO

HQ

P

KENSINGTON

SPENCER

P

MILFORD RD

LANSING

KENT LAKE

P

I 96

DETROIT

SKI CENTER

P

KENT LAKE

.57 MI LOOP

1.08 MI LOOP

1.28 MI LOOP

KENSINGTON ROAD

I 96

GOLF COURSE ENLARGEMENT

KENSINGTON METROPARK

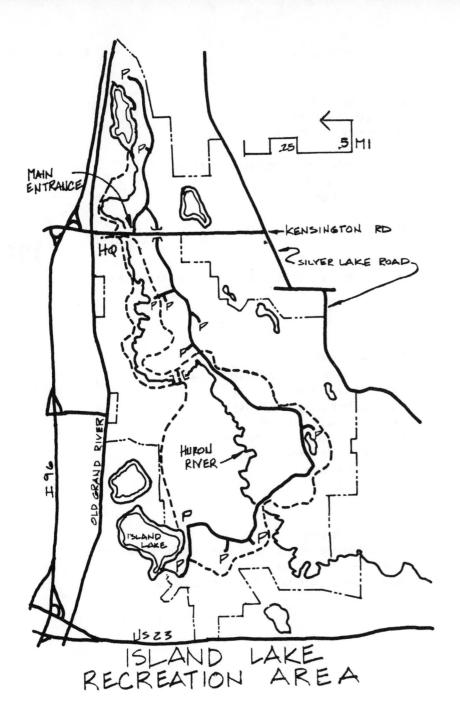

ISLAND LAKE
RECREATION AREA

Island Lake Recreation Area                          Revised:  4/09/88


Island Lake Recreation Area
12950 East Grand River                          313-229-7067
Brighton, MI  48116

DNR Parks Division Office

                                                517-373-1270

Trail suitable for hiking & skiing

Location:
 West of Brighton on Grand River Ave to Kensington Rd., then south to
   park entrance
 Exit I96 at Kensington Rd., then south to park entrance
 Trailheads at picnic areas and the park headquarters

Trail specifications:
   12 mi; 1 loop(s); Loop length(s)-12
Typical terrain: Rolling to hilly
Skiing ability suggested: Novice to intermediate
Hiking trail difficulty: Easy
Nordic trail grooming method: None
Suitable for all-terrain bicycle: Yes
Trail use fee: None, but vehicle entry fee required $2/day, $10/year
Camping: Rustic, semi modern and organized campgrounds avaiable
Drinking water available at campgrounds

General Information:
 Maintained by the DNR Parks Division
 The 7 miles of the Huron River within the park boundary is designated as
   " country scenic", under the Natural Rivers Act
 Adjacent to Kensington Metropark on the north

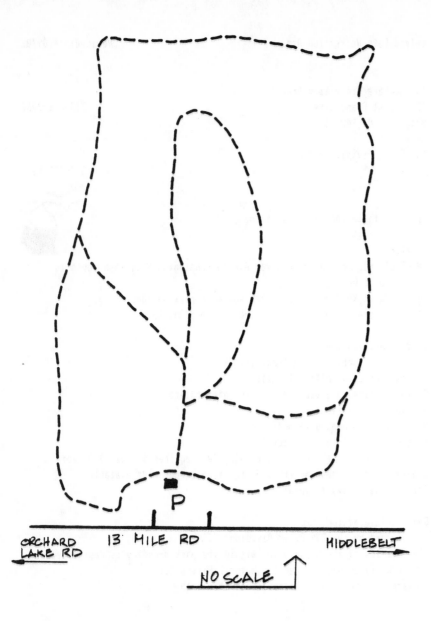

GLEN OAKS GOLF COURSE

Glen Oaks Golf Course                    Revised: 1/15/88

Glen Oaks County Park
30500 West 13 Mile Rd.                        313-851-8356
Farmington Hills, MI  48018                   313-626-2600

Oakland County Parks & Recreation Commission
2800 Watkins Lake Rd.                         313-858-0906
Pontiac, MI  48054-1697

Trail suitable for skiing only

Location:
 Between Orchard Lake and Middlebelt Rds on 13 Mile Rd.

Trail specifications:
   5.7 km; 3 loop(s); Loop length(s)-1.2, 2, 2.5
Typical terrain: Flat to rolling
Skiing ability suggested: Novice
Hiking trail difficulty: NA
Nordic trail grooming method: Packed
Suitable for all-terrain bicycle: NA
Trail use fee: None
Camping: None

General Information:
 Operated by the Oakland County Parks and Recreation Commission
 Trails on a golf course
 Warming area, snack bar and ski rental available

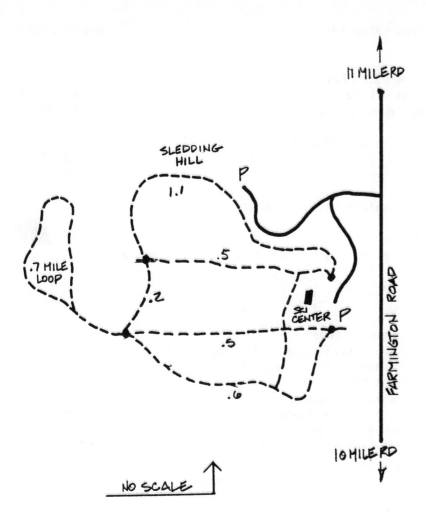

SLEDDING HILL

P

1.1

.7 MILE LOOP

.5

.2

SKI CENTER P

.5

.6

11 MILE RD

10 MILE RD

FARMINGTON ROAD

NO SCALE

Heritage Park

Revised: 1/09/88

City of Farmington Hills
31555 11 Mile Rd.
Farmington Hills, MI  48018

313-473-9570

Trail suitable for hiking & skiing

Location:
 Located on Farmington Rd between 10 and 11 Mile Rds in Farmington Hills

Trail specifications:
   3.3 mi; 5 loop(s); Loop length(s)-.2 to 2.6
Typical terrain: Flat to gently rolling
Skiing ability suggested: Novice to intermediate
Hiking trail difficulty: Easy to moderate
Nordic trail grooming method: Track set as needed
Suitable for all-terrain bicycle: Not permitted
Trail use fee: None
Camping: None
Drinking water available

General Information:
 Maintained by the City of Farmington Hills
 Ski rental, warming area, sledding hill and ice skating available

# HERITAGE PARK

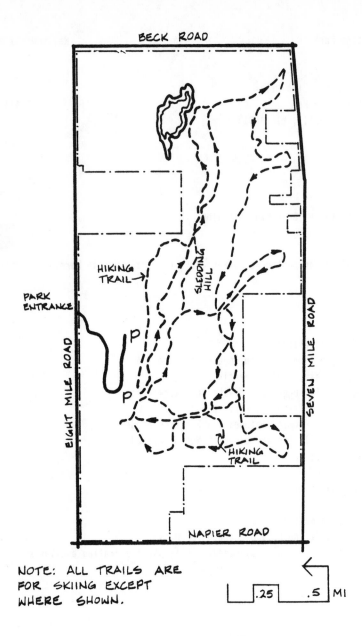

BECK ROAD

PARK
ENTRANCE

EIGHT MILE ROAD

HIKING
TRAIL →

SLEDDING
HILL

P

P

SEVEN MILE ROAD

HIKING
TRAIL

NAPIER ROAD

NOTE: ALL TRAILS ARE
FOR SKIING EXCEPT
WHERE SHOWN.

.25   .5   MI

# MAYBURY STATE PARK

Maybury State Park                                    Revised: 11/20/87


Maybury State Park
20145 Beck Rd.                                        313-349-8390
Northville, MI  48167                                 313-348-1190

DNR Parks Regional Office

                                                      517-322-1300


Trail suitable for skiing & hiking

Location:
 5 miles west of I275 on 8 Mile Rd., betweem Napier and Beck Rds


Trail specifications:
   8 mi‡; 3 loop(s); Loop length(s)-2.5, 4, 8.5
Typical terrain: Flat to slightly rolling
Skiing ability suggested: Novice to intermediate
Hiking trail difficulty: Easy
Nordic trail grooming method: Track set 2 to 3 times weekly by volunteers
Suitable for all-terrain bicycle: Yes ‡
Trail use fee: None, but vehicle entry fee required $2/day, $10/year
Camping: None
Drinking water available at concession

General Information:
 Maintained by the DNR Parks Division
 Warming area, rentals, snack bar, lighted ski trail on weekends,
   picnic grounds and sledding hill
 Hiking and ski trails are not all identical
 ‡ 4 miles of paved bicycle trails

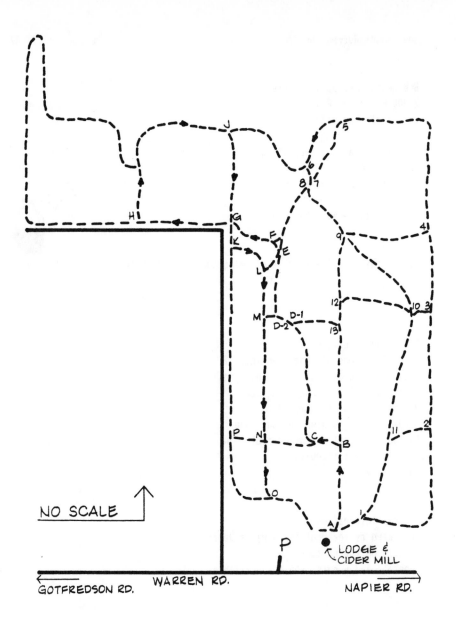

NO SCALE

GOTFREDSON RD.  WARREN RD.  NAPIER RD.

LODGE &
CIDER MILL

# PLYMOUTH ORCHARDS & CIDER MILL

Plymouth Orchards and Cider Mill                    Revised:  1/31/88

Plymouth Orchards and Cider Mill
10685 Warren Rd.                                    313-455-2290
Plymouth, MI   48170

Trail suitable for skiing only

Location:
  On Warren Rd., 1.5 miles south of M14 between Napier Rd. and Gotfreson Rd.

Trail specifications:
    10 km; Several loop(s); Loop length(s)-various
Typical terrain: Flat to rolling
Skiing ability suggested: Novice
Hiking trail difficulty: NA
Nordic trail grooming method: Track set when snow conditions permit
Suitable for all-terrain bicycle: NA
Trail use fee: $2.00/day/adults, $1.50/day/child, passes available ‡
Camping: None

General Information:
  Privately operated orchard with ski trails
  3 km of lighted trails open until 10PM
  Snack bar, warming area and rentals available
  ‡ Group, family and senior citizen discounts available
  Some trails in wooded area in addition to orchard trails

Beechwoods Recreation Center
26000 Evergreen Rd.                                    313-354-4786
Southfield, MI  48076

Southfield Parks & Recreation
26000 Evergreen Rd.                                    313-354-9603
Southfield, MI  48076

Trail suitable for skiing only

Location:
 In Southfield, 1 mile east of Telegraph Rd. at 9 Mile Rd and Beech Daly

## No Trail Map

Trail specifications:
   2 mi; 1 loop(s); Loop length(s)-2
Typical terrain: Flat to slightly rolling
Skiing ability suggested: Novice
Hiking trail difficulty: NA
Nordic trail grooming method: None
Suitable for all-terrain bicycle: NA
Trail use fee: $1.00/day
Camping: None


General Information:
 Operated by the Southfield Parks Department
 Trails on the golf course
 Rentals and warming shelter available

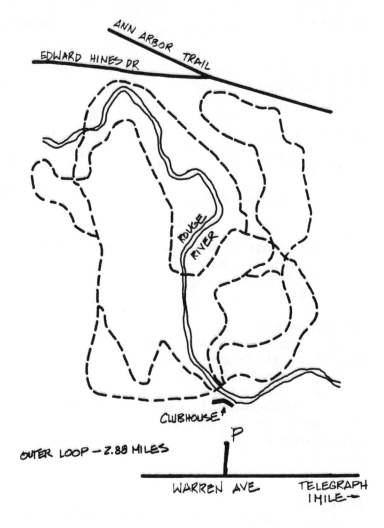

ANN ARBOR TRAIL

EDWARD HINES DR

ROUGE RIVER

CLUBHOUSE

P

OUTER LOOP — 2.88 MILES

WARREN AVE

TELEGRAPH 1 MILE →

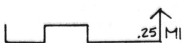

.25 MI

Warren Valley Golf Course                    Revised: 11/29/87

Wayne County Department of Parks and Recreation
33175 Ann Arbor Trail                         313-261-1990
Westland, MI  48135

Warren Valley Golf Course
26116 West Warren                             313-561-1040
Dearborn, MI  48127

Trail suitable for skiing only

Location:
  In Dearborn Heights on Warren Rd. just east of Beech Daly Rd.

Trail specifications:
   7 km; 5 loop(s); Loop length(s)-various
Typical terrain: Flat to rolling
Skiing ability suggested: Novice
Hiking trail difficulty: NA
Nordic trail grooming method: Track set
Suitable for all-terrain bicycle: NA
Trail use fee: None
Camping: None

General Information:
  Operated by the Wayne County Department of Parks and Recreation
  Warming area, rentals, restaurant, lounge and  snack bar
  All trails are on a golf course

# WARREN VALLEY GOLF COURSE

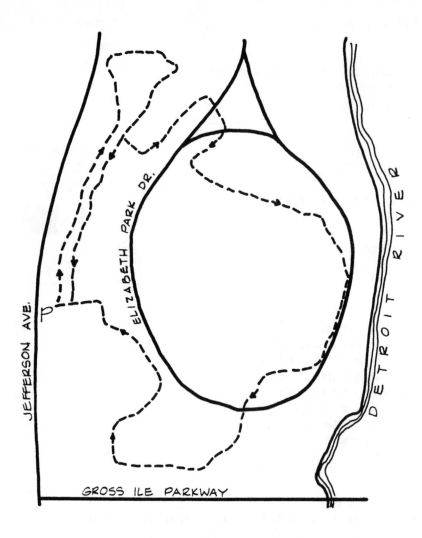

JEFFERSON AVE.

ELIZABETH PARK DR.

P

GROSS ILE PARKWAY

DETROIT RIVER

NO SCALE

ELIZABETH PARK

Elizabeth Park                                          Revised: 2/20/88


Wayne County Dept of Parks and Recreation
33175 Ann Arbor Trail                                   313-261-1990
Westland, MI  48135


Elizabeth Park Office
4250 Elizabeth Park Drive                               313-675-8037
Trenton, MI  48183

Trail suitable for skiing & hiking

Location:
  I75 to eastbound West Rd., then 3.5 miles to southbound Jefferson, then to
    3873 W. Jefferson.  Trailhead is at the first recreation building on the
    left side past Solcum St.


Trail specifications:
    2 mi*; 2 loop(s); Loop length(s)-various
  Typical terrain: Flat to gently rolling
  Skiing ability suggested: Novice
  Hiking trail difficulty: Easy
  Nordic trail grooming method: Track set daily as needed
  Suitable for all-terrain bicycle: Yes
  Trail use fee: None
  Camping: None


General Information:
  Operated by the Wayne County Department of Parks and Recreation
  Scenic views of the Detroit River from along the trail
  Comfort station is open form M-F from 7:30 to 4:00
  * Hiking trail distances are longer

82

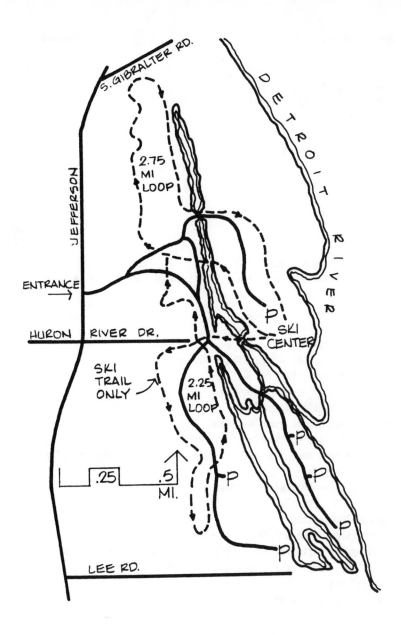

LAKE ERIE METROPARK

Lake Erie Metropark
32481 West Jefferson, PO Box 120          313-379-5020
Rockwood, MI  48173                       800-24-PARKS

Huron-Clinton Metropolitan Authority
13000 High Ridge Drive                    313-227-2757
Brighton, MI  48116-8001

Trail suitable for skiing only

Location:
 South of Gibraltar on Jefferson Ave along the shore of Lake Erie
 Just north of Huron River Drive on Jefferson Ave

Trail specifications:
  5 mi; 2 loop(s); Loop length(s)-2.25, 2.75
Typical terrain: Flat
Skiing ability suggested: Novice
Hiking trail difficulty: NA
Nordic trail grooming method: Track set daily if needed
Suitable for all-terrain bicycle: NA
Trail use fee: None, but vehicle entry fee required $2/day, $10/year
Camping: None
Drinking water available

General Information:
 Operated by the Huron-Clinton Metropolitan Authority
 Rentals and snack bar available
 Great Wave Pool, picnic area and marina available

Call or write for their Metropark Guide, published each year.

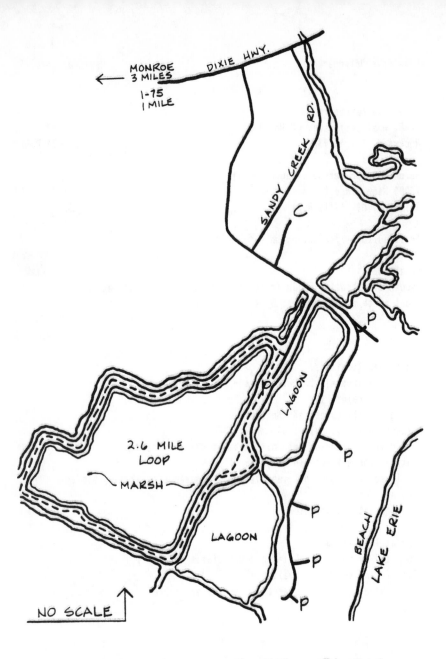

MONROE
3 MILES

DIXIE HWY.

I-75
1 MILE

SANDY CREEK RD.

C

P

LAGOON

2.6 MILE
LOOP

MARSH

LAGOON

P

P

P

P

BEACH

LAKE ERIE

NO SCALE

STERLING STATE PARK

Sterling State Park                                     Revised:  3/28/88


Sterling State Park
2800 State Park Rd., Rte 5                              313-289-2715
Monroe, MI  48161

DNR Parks Division Office

                                                       517-373-1270


Trail suitable for hiking & skiing

Location:
 East of Monroe on Lake Erie
 Take Dixie Hwy east from the I75 exit about 1 mile to park entrance


Trail specifications:
    2.6 mi; 1 loop(s); Loop length(s)-2.6
Typical terrain: Flat
Skiing ability suggested: Novice
Hiking trail difficulty: Easy
Nordic trail grooming method: None
Suitable for all-terrain bicycle: Yes
Trail use fee: None, but vehicle permit required $2/day, $10/season
Camping: Campgound in park
Drinking water available in campground

General Information:
 Maintained by the DNR Parks Division
 Trail along backwater marsh of Lake Erie, and includes a small open air
    shelter and several displays with an observation tower to overlook the
    marsh area
 Swimming available at beach area

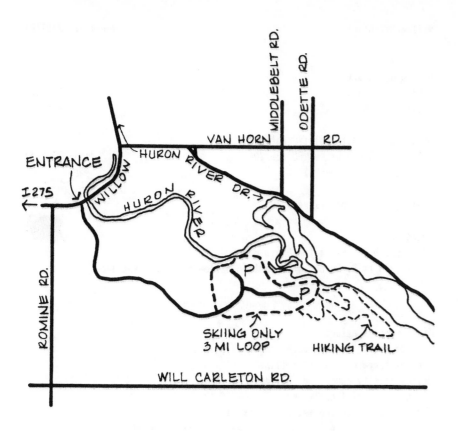

 .5 MI.

ENTRANCE

I275

VAN HORN RD.

MIDDLEBELT RD.

ODETTE RD.

HURON RIVER DR.→

WILLOW

HURON RIVER

ROMINE RD.

P

P

SKIING ONLY
3 MI LOOP

HIKING TRAIL

WILL CARLETON RD.

OAKWOODS METROPARK

Oakwoods Metropark
PO Box 332                                              313-697-9181
Flat Rock, MI   48134                                   800-24-PARKS

Huron-Clinton Metropolitan Authority
13000 High Ridge Drive, PO Box 2001                     313-227-2757
Brighton, MI  48116-8001

Trail suitable for  skiing & hiking

Location:
 From I275 exit 11 at S. Huron, west to Bell Rd., south to Willow, east on
  Willow Rd .75 mile to the park (past the entrance to Willow Metropark)


Trail specifications:
  3 mi ⚹; 1 loop(s); Loop length(s)-3
Typical terrain: Flat
Skiing ability suggested: Novice
Hiking trail difficulty: Easy
Nordic trail grooming method: Track set when necessary
Suitable for all-terrain bicycle: Not permitted on trails
Trail use fee: None, but vehicle entry fee required $2/day, $10/year
Camping: None
Drinking water in building

General Information:
 Operated by the Huron-Clinton Metropolitan Authority
 Warming area, picnic grounds, nature center and nature study area
  available.
 ⚹ Hiking trail (nature trail) is different then the ski trail.
 Adjacent to Willow Metropark


Call or write for their Metropark Guide, published each year.

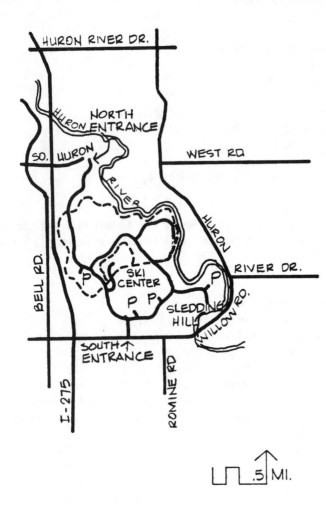

WILLOW METROPARK

Willow Metropark
17845 Savage Rd.                                    313-697-9181
Belleville, MI  48111                               800-24-PARKS

Huron-Clinton Metropolitan Authority
13000 High Ridge Drive, PO Box 2001                 313-227-2757
Brighton, MI  48116-8001

Trail suitable for skiing only

Location:
 Just south of I94 at the South Huron exit 11
 Exit I275 at S. Huron, then east to Willow Metropark entrance


Trail specifications:
   4.25 mi; 2 loop(s); Loop length(s)-1, 3.5
Typical terrain: Flat to rolling
Skiing ability suggested: Novice
Hiking trail difficulty: NA
Nordic trail grooming method: Track set
Suitable for all-terrain bicycle: Yes, on park roads only
Trail use fee: None, but vehicle entry fee required $2/day, $10/year
Camping: None
Drinking water available at Activity Building

General Information:
 Operated by the Huron-Clinton Metropolitan Authority
 Warming area, nature trails and picnic grounds
 Rentals, snack bar and established trails only at Willow
 Sledding hill
 Adjacent to Oakwoods Metropark on the south and Lower Huron Metropark
   to the north


Call or write for their Metropark Guide, published each year.

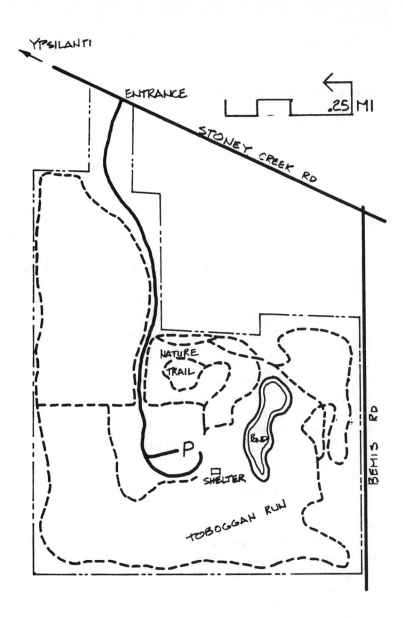

YPSILANTI

ENTRANCE

STONEY CREEK RD

.25 MI

BEMIS RD

NATURE TRAIL

P

POND

SHELTER

TOBOGGAN RUN

ROLLING HILLS COUNTY PARK

Rolling Hills County Park                    Revised: 3/17/88

Rolling Hills County Park
7660 Stony Creek Rd.                         313-484-3870
Ypsilanti, MI  48197

Washtenaw County Parks and Recreation Commission
PO Box 8645                                  313-971-6337
Ann Arbor, MI  48107

Trail suitable for skiing & hiking

Location:
 From I94, use the Huron Street exit and proceed south to Stony Creek Rd.,
   then turn right and go 5 miles on Stony Creek Road.  The park
   entrance is on the right side of the road.  The entrance is .5 mile
   north of Bemis Road.

Trail specifications:
   3.5 mi; Several loop(s); Loop length(s)-various
Typical terrain: Flat to rolling
Skiing ability suggested: Novice to intermediate
Hiking trail difficulty: Easy
Nordic trail grooming method: Track set‡
Suitable for all-terrain bicycle: Not permitted
Trail use fee: None, but entrance fee required $2.50/day to $25/year ‡‡
Camping: None
Drinking water is available at the recreation building

General Information:
 Maintained by the Washtenaw County Parks and Recreation Commission
 Rentals, toboggan run, lighted ski trails, ice skating, warming shelter,
   picnic area restrooms make for a complete year-round recreational
   facility
 ‡ Skiing permitted on all trails except the nature trail (.5 mile)
 ‡‡ Fee varies between county and non-county residents

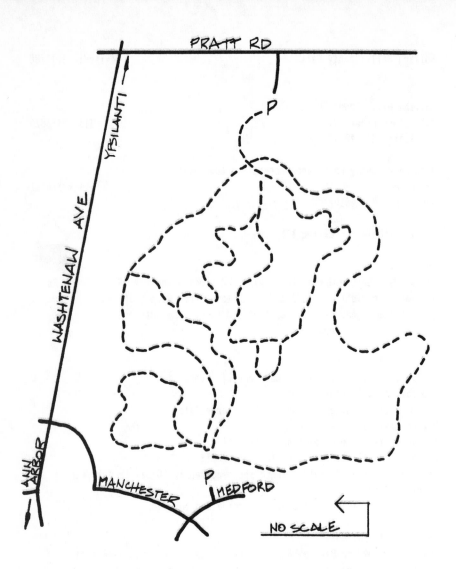

PRATT RD

P

YPSILANTI

WASHTENAW AVE.

ANN ARBOR

MANCHESTER      P MEDFORD

NO SCALE

COUNTY FARM PARK

Washtenaw County Parks & Recreation Commission
PO Box 8645                                          313-971-6337
Ann Arbor, MI   48107

Trail suitable for skiing & hiking

Location:
  Between Ann Arbor and Ypsilanti on Washtenaw Ave, just east of the
     Washtenaw East Stadium Blvd intersection
  West trailhead-Take Pratt Rd. south from Washtenaw Ave to parking lot
  East trailhead-Take Manchester south from Washenaw Ave past a water
     tower to the first intersection, then east(left) on Medford to lot
Trail specifications:
  4 mi*; 4* loop(s); Loop length(s)-.25, .75, 1.5, 1.5
Typical terrain: Flat to rolling
Skiing ability suggested: Novice to intermediate
Hiking trail difficulty: Easy
Nordic trail grooming method: None
Suitable for all-terrain bicycle: Not permitted
Trail use fee: None
Camping: None
Drinking water is available at the shelter building

General Information:
  Maintained by the Washtenaw County Parks and Recreation Commission
  Open and wooded landscape in the heart of the Ann Arbor metro area
  * One ski trail loop 1.5 miles long
  Shelter with restrooms
  Par course along one trail
  Perennial demonstrations garden with native shrub plantings

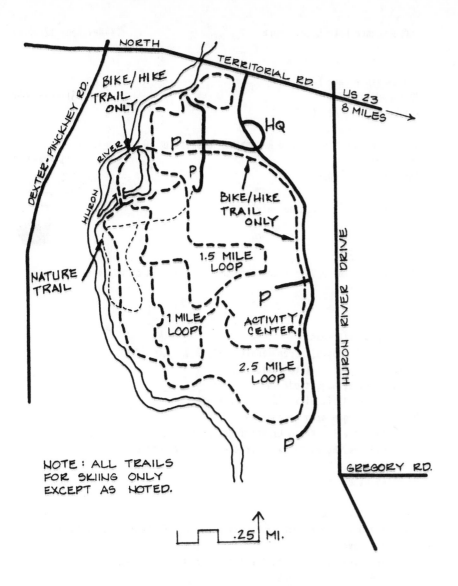

NOTE: ALL TRAILS FOR SKIING ONLY EXCEPT AS NOTED.

⊏⊓_ .25 MI.

# HUDSON MILLS METROPARK

Hudson-Mills Metropark
880 N. Territorial Rd.                     313-426-8211
Dexter, MI  48130                         800-24-PARKS

Huron-Clinton Metropolitan Authority
13000 High Ridge Drive, PO Box 2001       313-227-2757
Brighton, MI  48116-8001

Trail suitable for skiing & hiking

Location:
 NW of Ann Arbor on the Huron River
 On North Territorial Rd just west of Huron River Drive, 8 miles west of
  US23

Trail specifications:
  7.5 mi‡; Several loop(s); Loop length(s)-various‡‡
Typical terrain: Flat to rolling
Skiing ability suggested: Novice to intermediate
Hiking trail difficulty: Easy to moderate
Nordic trail grooming method: Track set as needed
Suitable for all-terrain bicycle: Yes, on the established bike/hike trail only
Trail use fee: None, but vehicle entry fee required $2/day, $10/year
Camping: Group campground only, reservations required
Drinking water available

General Information:
 Operated by the Huron-Clinton Metropolitan Authority
 Ski rentals, snack bar, picnic grounds and bike rentals
 ‡ Separate skiing, bike/hike and nature trails.
 ‡‡ Ski trail loops are 1, 1.5, 2.5 and 2.5 miles
 The bike/hike trail is paved.
 Ice skating when weather permits

Call or write for their Metropark Guide, published each year.

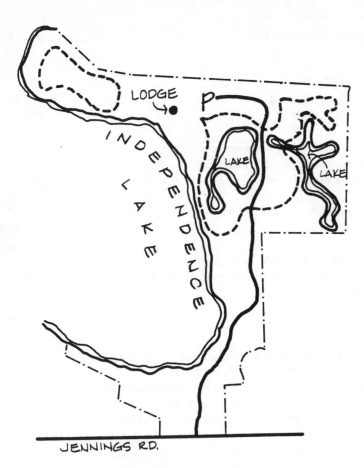

LODGE

INDEPENDENCE LAKE

LAKE

LAKE

JENNINGS RD.

NO SCALE ↑

# INDEPENDENCE LAKE COUNTY PARK

Independence Lake Park
3200 Jennings Rd.                            313-449-8998
Whitmore Lake, MI  48189

Washtenaw County Parks and Recreation Commission
PO Box 8645                                  313-994-2575
Ann Arbor, MI  48107

Trail suitable for hiking only

Location:
 NW of Ann Arbor
 2 miles west of US23 off Jennings Rd., 3 miles SW of Whitmore Lake

Trail specifications:
   4.5 mi; 2 loop(s); Loop length(s)-1, 3.5
Typical terrain: Flat to rolling
Skiing ability suggested: NA
Hiking trail difficulty: Easy to moderate
Nordic trail grooming method: NA
Suitable for all-terrain bicycle: Not permitted
Trail use fee: None, but an entrance fee is required
Camping: None
Drinking water is available

General Information:
 Maintained by the Washtenaw County Parks and Recreation Commission
 Restrooms available
 A nature area open only in the spring through fall seasons
 Call ahead for park hours

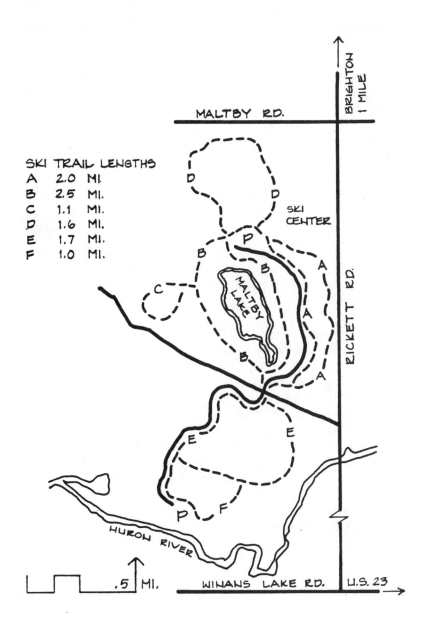

SKI TRAIL LENGTHS
A   2.0  MI.
B   2.5  MI.
C   1.1  MI.
D   1.6  MI.
E   1.7  MI.
F   1.0  MI.

.5 MI.

HURON MEADOWS METROPARK

Huron Meadows Metropark                                    Revised:  4/07/88


Huron Meadows Metropark
8765 Hammel Rd.                                            313-227-2757
Brighton, MI  48130                                       800-24-PARKS

Huron-Clinton Metropolitan Authority
13000 High Ridge Drive                                    313-227-2757
Brighton, MI  48116-8001

Trail suitable for skiing only

Location:
  South of Brighton on US23, exit Silver Lake Rd. west, then south on
     Whitmore Lake Rd. 500 ft to Winans Lake Rd., then west .5 mile to
     Rickett Rd., then north on Rickett Rd. 1 mile to Hammel Rd., then west
     to park entrance

Trail specifications:
   9 mi; 6 loop(s); Loop length(s)-1, 1.1, 1.6, 1.7, 2.0, 2.5
Typical terrain: Rolling
Skiing ability suggested: Novice to intermediate
Hiking trail difficulty: NA
Nordic trail grooming method: Track set as needed
Suitable for all-terrain bicycle: Yes, on park roads only
Trail use fee: None, but vehicle entry fee required $2/day, $10/year
Camping: None
Drinking water available

General Information:
  Operated by the Huron-Clinton Metropolitan Authority
  Warming area, ski rentals and snack bar available
  Just east of the Brighton Recreation Area
  Summer recreation includes golf course and picnic grounds


Call or write for their Metropark Guide, published each year.

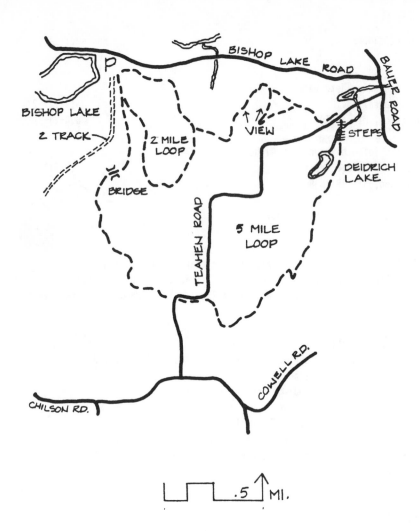

BRIGHTON RECREATION AREA

Brighton Recreation Area                                    Revised:  9/14/87


Brighton Recreation Area
6360 Chilson Rd., Rte 3                                      313-229-6566
Howell, MI  48843

DNR Parks Division Office

                                                            517-373-1270

Trail suitable for hiking & skiing

Location:
  West from Brighton on Brighton Rd. to Chilson Rd., then west 1.5 miles to
    Bishop Lake Rd., then east 1.5 miles to Bishop Lake picnic area.
  The Penosha and Kahchin trailheads start at the parking lot


Trail specifications:
   7 mi; 2 loop(s); Loop length(s)-2, 5
Typical terrain: Rolling
Skiing ability suggested: Novice
Hiking trail difficulty: Easy
Nordic trail grooming method: None
Suitable for all-terrain bicycle: Yes
Trail use fee: None, but vehicle entry fee required $2/day, $10/year
Camping: Campground available at Bishop Lake, just west of trailhead
Drinking water is available at campground and headquarters

General Information:
 Maintained by the DNR Parks Division
 Trails not specifically designed for skiing but are skiable

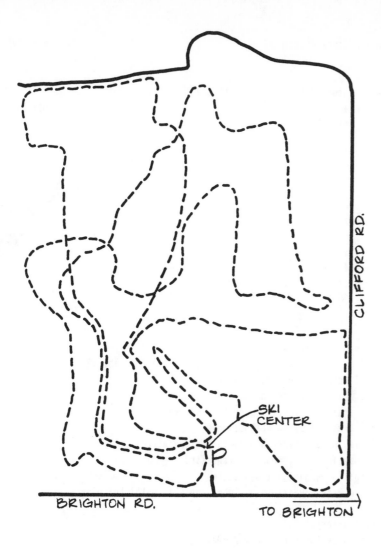

CLIFFORD RD.

SKI
CENTER

P

BRIGHTON RD.

TO BRIGHTON

NO SCALE

OAK POINTE GOLF COURSE

Oak Pointe Golf Course                    Revised:  3/13/88

Oak Pointe Golf Course
5341 Brighton Rd.                         313-227-1381
Brighton, MI  48116

Trail suitable for skiing & hiking

Location:
 3 Miles west of Brighton on Brighton Rd.

Trail specifications:
    9 mi; 4 loop(s); Loop length(s)-1, 3, 3.5
Typical terrain: Flat to rolling
Skiing ability suggested: Novice
Hiking trail difficulty: NA
Nordic trail grooming method: Track set
Suitable for all-terrain bicycle: NA
Trail use fee: Yes, $3/day
Camping: None

General Information:
 A privately operated nordic ski area
 Rentals, snack bar and dining room available
 1.75 mile lighted trail is available on Friday and Saturday
 Skiing and hiking trails may not be identical

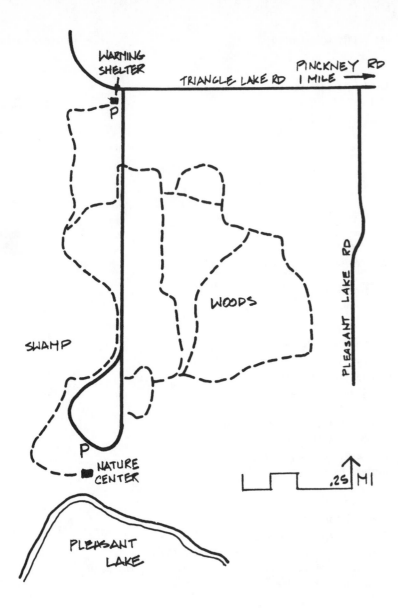

Howell Nature Center   Attn. Dick Grant
1005 Triangle Rd.                                   517-546-0249
Howell, MI  48843


Trail suitable for hiking & skiing

Location:
 South of Howell, 4.5 miles on Pinckney Rd., then west on Triangle Rd. for
   about 1.5 miles to the nature center entrance


Trail specifications:
   4.5 mi; 6 loop(s); Loop length(s)-.5, 1.5, 3, .75, .25, .5
Typical terrain: Rolling to hilly
Skiing ability suggested: Novice to advanced
Hiking trail difficulty: Easy to moderate
Nordic trail grooming method: None
Suitable for all-terrain bicycle: Not permitted
Trail use fee: Yes, donation requested
Camping: Campground not available
Drinking water available at lodge and ski rental building

General Information:
 Operated by the Presbytery of Detroit
 Available to any organized group for day or overnight use
 Ski rentals and warming building available
 Lodge available for groups with advance reservations

# HOWELL NATURE CENTER

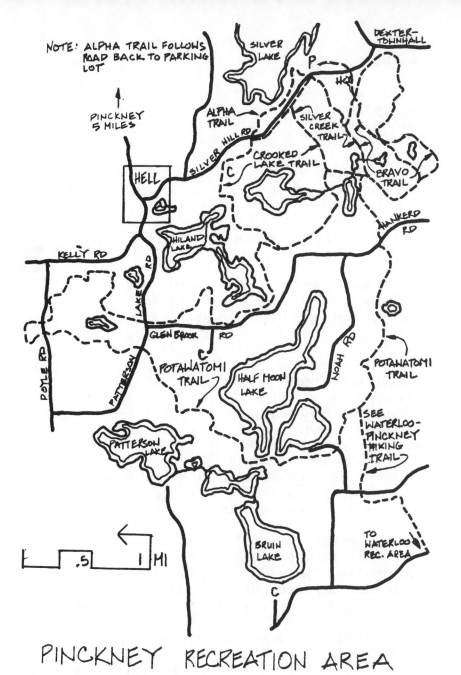

NOTE: ALPHA TRAIL FOLLOWS ROAD BACK TO PARKING LOT

PINCKNEY 5 MILES

SILVER LAKE

DEXTER-TOWNHALL

P
HQ

ALPHA TRAIL

SILVER CREEK TRAIL

SILVER HILL RD

CROOKED LAKE TRAIL

C

BRAVO TRAIL

HELL

HANKERD RD

HILAND LAKE

KELLY RD

LAKE RD

GLEN BROOK RD

POTAWATOMI TRAIL

HALF MOON LAKE

NOAH RD

POTAWATOMI TRAIL

POTTER RD

PATTERSON

SEE WATERLOO-PINCKNEY HIKING TRAIL

PATTERSON LAKE

.5    1 MI

BRUIN LAKE

TO WATERLOO REC. AREA

C

PINCKNEY RECREATION AREA

Pinckney Recreation Area                    Revised: 3/17/88

Pinckney Recreation Area
8555 Silver Hill Rd., Rte 1                    313-426-4913
Pinckney, MI  48169

DNR Parks Division Office

517-373-1270

Trail suitable for hiking & skiing

Location:
 15 miles NW of Ann Arbor at the Washtenaw County line
 Trail head - From US23 west on N. Territorial Rd. about 10 miles to
   Dexter-Townhall Rd., turn north for 1.2 miles to Silver Hill Rd., bear
   west to parking lot at Silver Lake Beach

Trail specifications:
   20+ mi; 5‡ loop(s); Loop length(s)-various‡‡
Typical terrain: Rolling to hilly
Skiing ability suggested: Intermediate
Hiking trail difficulty: Easy to moderate
Nordic trail grooming method: None
Suitable for all-terrain bicycle: Yes
Trail use fee: None, but vehicle entry fee required $2/day, $10/year
Camping: Campgrounds available all year ‡‡
Drinking water only at campgrounds and at the beach (seasonally)

General Information:
 Maintained by the DNR Parks Division
 ‡‡ 2 rustic campgrounds open in the snowless months. The Bruin Lake
    Campground is open all year.
 The east end of the Pinckney-Waterloo Hiking Trail(46 mi)
 ‡ The Alpha (2 mile loop) and the Bravo (4 mile loop) trails are the only
    trails designated for skiing.
    Silver Creek, Crooked Lake and Potawatomi Trail(17 mi) are designated
    for hiking only.  See Park HQ for detailed maps of each trail
 Horse back riding and snowmobiles are allowed in some parts of the
    recreation area.  ORV's are prohibited from the entire park
 There is a good possibility that ATB's may be restricted in this
    recreation area in the future.  Call ahead so you will not be
    disappointed.

95

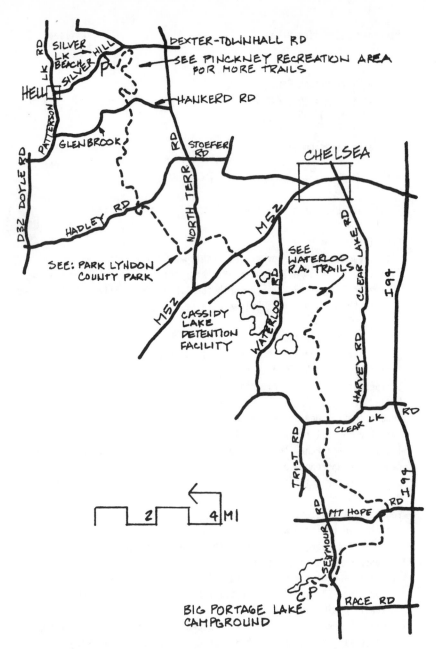

WATERLOO-PINCKNEY HIKING TRAIL

Waterloo-Pinckney Hiking Trail                    Revised: 5/15/88

Waterloo Recreation Area
16345 McClure Rd., Rte 1                           313-457-8307
Chelsea, MI  48118

Pinckney Recreation Area
8555 Silver Hill Rd., Rte 1                        313-426-4913
Pinckney, MI  48169

Trail suitable for hiking & skiing

Location:
 Between Waterloo and Pinckney Recreation Areas, NW of Ann Arbor
 North trailhead-Silver Lake Beach in Pinckney Recreation Area
 South trailhead-Big Portage Lake Campground in Waterloo Recreation Area


Trail specifications:
   25 mi; No loop(s); Loop length(s)-NA
Typical terrain: Flat to hilly
Skiing ability suggested: Advanced
Hiking trail difficulty: Moderate
Nordic trail grooming method: None
Suitable for all-terrain bicycle: Yes
Trail use fee: None, but vehicle entry fee required $2/day, $10/year
Camping: Campgrounds available at both recreation areas
Drinking water is available along the trail

General Information:
 Maintained by the DNR Parks Division
 This trail was not designed for skiing, but portions can be skied
 Trail is connected to the Waterloo Recreation Area ski trail at the Cedar
   Lake Outdoor Center on Pierce Rd and the Potawatomi Trail system in the
   Pinckney Recreation Area
 Cedar Lake Lodge in the Waterloo Recreation Area is open on weekends in
   the winter with limited refreshments
 Trail marking is not complete is some sections.  Be prepared by taking
   a compass along with you.  Call to confirm adequacy of trail markings.
 The trail section between McClure Rd west of the Hq's and Katz Rd is
   used by horseback riders. Because of extensive loose sand and severe
   erosion, this section is not recommended for ATB's or hiking.  It's
   unfortunate because Pond Lily Lookout has a spectacular view.
 Many side trails are not shown on the trail map.

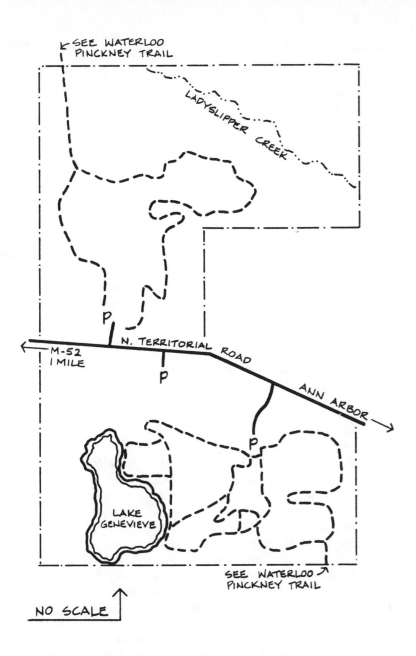

SEE WATERLOO
PINCKNEY TRAIL

LADYSLIPPER CREEK

P

M-52
1 MILE

N. TERRITORIAL ROAD

P

ANN ARBOR →

P

LAKE
GENEVIEVE

SEE WATERLOO
PINCKNEY TRAIL

NO SCALE

# PARK LYNDON

Park Lyndon                                    Revised: 12/23/87


Washtenaw County Parks and Recreation Commission
PO Box 8645
Ann Arbor, MI  48107                           313-971-6337

Trail suitable for skiing & hiking

Location:
 5 miles north of Chelsea and northwest of Ann Arbor
 1 mile east of M52 on North Territorial Rd.


Trail specifications:
   2.75 mi; 3 loop(s); Loop length(s)-1, 1, .75
Typical terrain: Rolling to very hilly
Skiing ability suggested: Intermediate to advanced‡
Hiking trail difficulty: Easy to moderate
Nordic trail grooming method: None
Suitable for all-terrain bicycle: Not permitted
Trail use fee: None
Camping: Limited camping available
Drinking water available

General Information:
 Maintained by the Washtenaw County Parks and Recreation Commission
 ‡ Skiing permitted in Park Lyndon North only, South park trails are too
   hazardous
 Restrooms available
 The 47 mile Waterloo-Pinckney Trail passes through this park
 Open from 8am to dusk
 A very fine scenic nature preserve

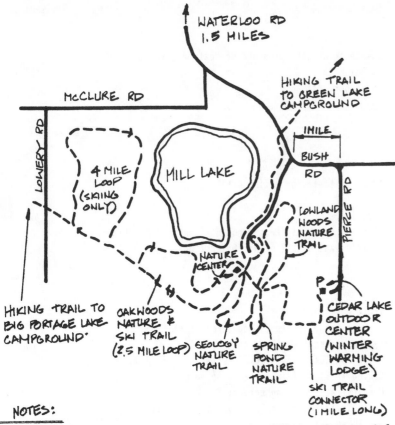

HIKING TRAIL TO GREEN LAKE CAMPGROUND

WATERLOO RD 1.5 MILES

McCLURE RD

LOWERY RD

1 MILE

BUSH RD

PIERCE RD

4 MILE LOOP (SKIING ONLY)

MILL LAKE

LOWLAND WOODS NATURE TRAIL

NATURE CENTER

HIKING TRAIL TO BIG PORTAGE LAKE CAMPGROUND

OAKWOODS NATURE & SKI TRAIL (2.5 MILE LOOP)

GEOLOGY NATURE TRAIL

SPRING POND NATURE TRAIL

CEDAR LAKE OUTDOOR CENTER (WINTER WARMING LODGE)

SKI TRAIL CONNECTOR (1 MILE LONG)

**NOTES:**

HIKING TRAIL IS PART OF THE WATERLOO-PINCKNEY TRAIL SYSTEM. SEE OTHER SYSTEM FOR MORE INFORMATION

NATURE CENTER CLOSED IN WINTER. USE CEDAR LAKE OUTDOOR CENTER FOR SKIING TRAILHEAD

NO SCALE

# WATERLOO RECREATION AREA

Waterloo Recreation Area                                    Revised: 5/23/88

Waterloo Recreation Area
16345 McClure Rd, Rte 1                                     313-475-8307
Chelsea, MI  48118

DNR Parks Division Office

                                                           517-373-1270

Trail suitable for hiking & skiing

Location:
 Adjacent to and NW of I94 and M52 and the city of Chelsea
 Winter trailhead-From Chelsea east on Cavanaugh Lake Rd. to Pierce Rd.,
   then north .5 mile to the Cedar Lake Outdoor Center
 Summer trailhead-Mill Lake Outdoor Center or Geology Interpretive Center

Trail specifications:
   20+ mi‡; 2‡‡ loop(s); Loop length(s)-2.5, 4‡‡
 Typical terrain: Flat to hilly
 Skiing ability suggested: Novice
 Hiking trail difficulty: Easy
 Nordic trail grooming method: None
 Suitable for all-terrain bicycle: Yes ‡‡‡
 Trail use fee: None, but vehicle entry fee required $2/day, $10/year
 Camping: Campgrounds available in the recreation area
 Drinking water available at the headquarters and campgrounds

General Information:
 Maintained by the DNR Parks Division
 Warming shelter & snack bar open winter weekends at Cedar Lake Lodge
 Ski trail uses a portion of the Waterloo-Pinckney Hiking Trail, known as
   the Oakwoods Nature Trail in the recreation area
 ‡ Total trails within the Waterloo Recreation Area.  Includes both
   hiking and skiing.  Also this distance includes that portion of the
   Waterloo-Pinckney Trail (listed elsewhere) in the Waterloo Recreation
   Area.  Other nature trails not shown are located at the Crooked Lake
   Picnic Area, Portage Lake and Sugarloaf Lake
 ‡‡  Hiking trails more numerous (shown on map)
 In recent years trail maintenance and signing has been neglected for lack of
   funding but efforts are currently underway to improve the trail system.
 ‡‡‡ See the Pinckney-Waterloo Hiking Trail for the best ATB trails

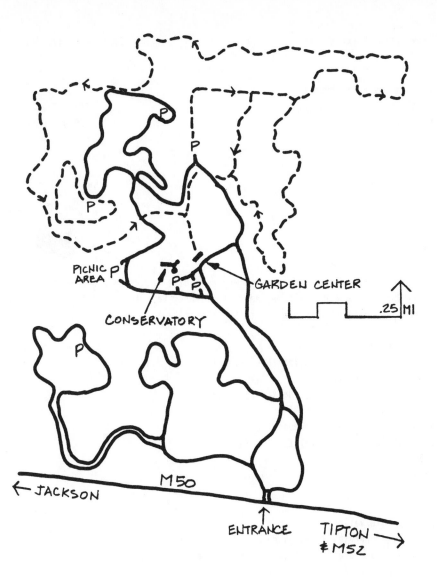

PICNIC AREA P

CONSERVATORY

GARDEN CENTER

.25 MI

← JACKSON     M50

ENTRANCE     TIPTON → & M52

# HIDDEN LAKE GARDENS

Hidden Lake Gardens                           Revised:  4/06/88


Director
Hidden Lake Gardens                           517-431-2060
Tipton, MI  49287


Division Of Campus Park & Planning
412 Olds Hall, Michigan State University       517-355-9582
East Lansing, MI  48824

Trail suitable for hiking only

Location:
 SE of Jackson on M50 just west of Tipton


Trail specifications:
   5 mi; Many loop(s); Loop length(s)-various
Typical terrain: Flat to hilly
Skiing ability suggested: NA
Hiking trail difficulty: Easy to moderate
Nordic trail grooming method: NA
Suitable for all-terrain bicycle: Not permitted
Trail use fee: None, but entry fee required
Camping: None
Drinking water available


General Information:
 Maintained by Michigan State University and administered by the
   Division of Campus Park & Planning
 This facility is a landscape arboretum
 The gardens include 670 acres on which is a Plant Conservatory that
   contains a tropical dome, arid dome and greenhouse; a Visitor Center
   with informative exhibits, auditorium, meeting rooms, library and
   gift shop; a picnic area; and over 6 miles of one way roads.
 The Gardens are set in the scenic Irish Hills which provides many scenic
   vistas along the various trails
 Open 365 days from 8AM to dusk during April through October and
   8AM to 4PM during November to March

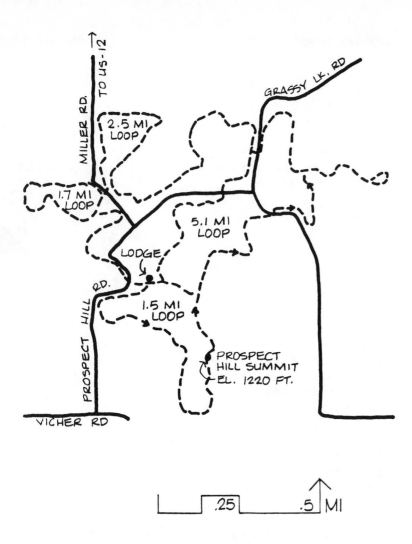

Sauk Valley Farms Resort
10750 Prospect Hill Rd.
Brooklyn, MI  49230

517-467-2061
800-USA-SALK

Trail suitable for skiing only

Location:
 20 miles SE of Jackson on US12
 From US12, take Miller Rd south to Prospect Hill Rd., then right to resort
 From US23, take Round Lake Hwy north to Vischer Rd., then east to
   Prospect Hill Rd., then north to the resort

Trail specifications:
   6 mi; 4 loop(s); Loop length(s)-1.5, 1.7, 2.5, 5.1
Typical terrain: Rolling
Skiing ability suggested: Novice to advanced
Hiking trail difficulty: NA
Nordic trail grooming method: Track set
Suitable for all-terrain bicycle: Yes
Trail use fee: $3/day
Camping: None

General Information:
 Privately operated 4 season resort
 Lodging, restaurant, rentals, snack bar, lessons, ski shop
 Accomodations in cabins or the lodge
 In the heart of the Irish Hills

# SAUK VALLEY FARMS RESORT

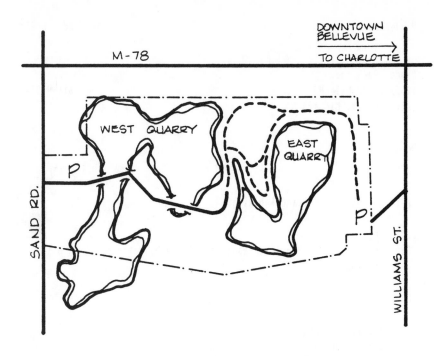

M-78

DOWNTOWN BELLEVUE →

TO CHARLOTTE

WEST QUARRY

EAST QUARRY

P

P

SAND RD.

WILLIAMS ST.

NO SCALE

# KEEHNE ENVIRONMENTAL AREA

Keehne Environmental Area                    Revised: 11/21/87

Eaton County Parks and Recreation Area
3808 Grand Ledge Hwy                         517-627-7351
Grand Ledge, MI  48837

Trail suitable for skiing & hiking

Location:
  I96 to exit 98A (27/I69 south) towards Charlotte.  Travel 23 miles to exit
    48(Bellevue exit M78 west)  Turn right on west M78 to park

Trail specifications:
  .75 mi; 1 loop(s); Loop length(s)-.75
Typical terrain: Flat
Skiing ability suggested: Novice
Hiking trail difficulty: Easy
Nordic trail grooming method: Track set
Suitable for all-terrain bicycle: Not permitted
Trail use fee: None
Camping: None
Drinking water in spring through fall

General Information:
 Operated by the Eaton County Parks and Recreation Department
 Picnic area
 Ski lessons, naturalist programs available with prior notice
 Fishing and ice skating available

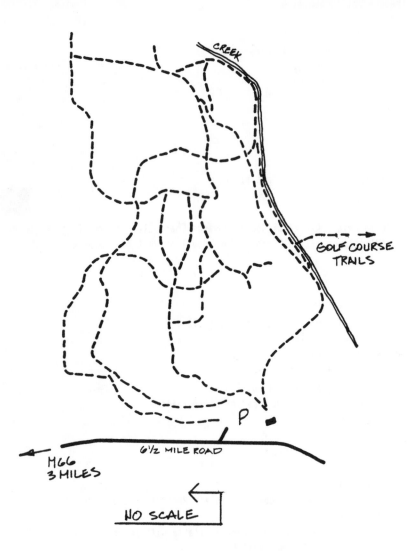

CREEK

GOLF COURSE
TRAILS

P

6½ MILE ROAD

M66
3 MILES

NO SCALE

BINDER PARK

Binder Park Inc.                                    Revised: 8/23/87


Binder Park Inc.
11632 6 1/2 Mile Rd                                 616-979-4233
Battle Creek, MI  49015

Trail suitable for skiing & hiking

Location:
 South of I94 via on M66, then east on B Drive N., then south on 6 1/2 Mile
   Rd. to the park.


Trail specifications:
   15 mi; 7 loop(s); Loop length(s)-various
Typical terrain: Rolling to hilly
Skiing ability suggested: Novice to advanced
Hiking trail difficulty: Easy
Nordic trail grooming method: Double track set when snow condition permits
Suitable for all-terrain bicycle: Yes
Trail use fee: $2.50/day
Camping: None
Drinking water is available

General Information:
 Operated by Binder Park Inc., a non-profit corporation
 Rentals, snack bar, instruction and sledding available
 Picnic area and playground available in the summer

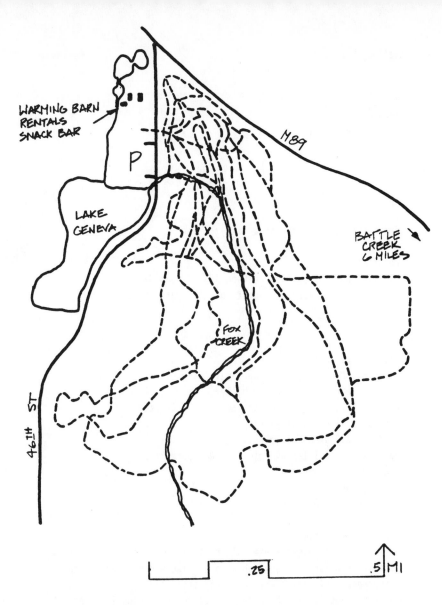

## TUR-SKI-REE TRAILS

Tur-Ski-Ree Trails                                    Revised: 1/04/88

Tur-Ski-Ree Trails
7801 North 46th St.                                   616-731-5266
Augusta, MI  49012

Trail suitable for skiing only

Location:
  About 6 miles west of Battle Creek on M89 at 46th St.  Turn south on
    46th St., parking lot .2 mile on right. WATCH OUT FOR SKIERS CROSSING
    46th STREET!

Trail specifications:
    15 mi; Many loop(s); Loop length(s)-various
Typical terrain: Flat to very hilly
Skiing ability suggested: Novice to advanced
Hiking trail difficulty: NA
Nordic trail grooming method: Track set*
Suitable for all-terrain bicycle: NA
Trail use fee: $4.00/day or $25.00/season
Camping: None
Drinking water available

General Information:
 Privately operated touring center owned by Hugh & Dorothy Acton
 A very fine touring center that should not be overlooked
 Expertly groomed trails, warming barn with rentals and a snack bar of all
   homemade food makes this area a great touring center.
 Open weekends, Christmas and New Years holidays
 Ski parties at other times by prior arrangement
 Lighted 2 km trail on Wednesays only
 *  5 miles of skating trails
 Trails pass through all types of terrain and forest cover with open
   fields.  The trail system is set in the Fox River Valley and
   surrounding upland.
 Most trails are in wooded areas.  The few open field trails can be
   avoided when windy conditions exist
 Call ahead for snow conditions and further information

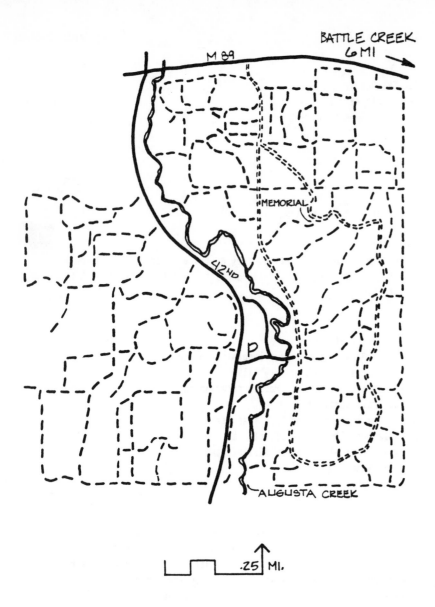

BATTLE CREEK
6 MI.

M 89

MEMORIAL

42ND

P

AUGUSTA CREEK

.25 MI.

# KELLOGG FOREST

Kellogg Forest
42nd Street
Augusta, MI  49012

616-731-4597

Trail suitable for skiing & hiking

Location:
 9 miles west of Battle Creek on M89 at 42nd St
 Parking lot on 42nd St. about .5 mile south of M89

Trail specifications:
   10 mi; Many loop(s); Loop length(s)-various
Typical terrain: Rolling to hilly
Skiing ability suggested: Novice to intermediate
Hiking trail difficulty: Easy
Nordic trail grooming method: None
Suitable for all-terrain bicycle: Not permitted
Trail use fee: None
Camping: None
Drinking water available

General Information:
 Operated by Michigan State University as a forestry research station
 Trails used for skiing and hiking are lanes developed for research
   purposes; off trail skiing is not permitted.
 Some snowmobiles in the general area but they usually do not use the lanes
   that are used for hiking and skiing
 Open 8am to 5pm everyday except holidays

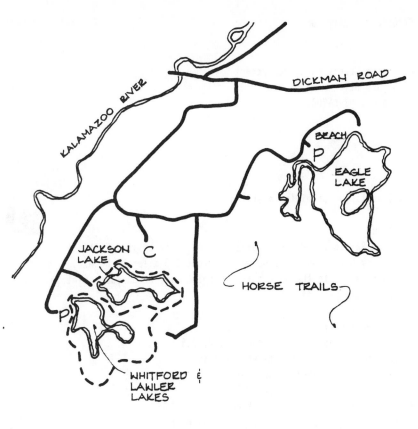

## FORT CUSTER
## RECREATION AREA

NO SCALE

Labels on map: DICKMAN ROAD, KALAMAZOO RIVER, BEACH, P, EAGLE LAKE, JACKSON LAKE, C, HORSE TRAILS, P, WHITFORD & LAWLER LAKES

Fort Custer Recreation Area
5163 W. Fort Custer Drive
Augusta, MI 49012

616-731-4200

DNR Parks Division Office

517-373-1270

Trail suitable for skiing & hiking

Location:
  5 miles west of Battle Creek and .25 mile east of Augusta on M96 (Dickman Rd.)
  Trailhead - At Whitford and Lawler Lakes picnic area
  Trailhead - Jackson Lake boat ramp

Trail specifications:
  3.5 mi; 2 loop(s); Loop length(s)-1.5, 1.5
Typical terrain: Flat to rolling
Skiing ability suggested: Novice
Hiking trail difficulty: Easy
Nordic trail grooming method: None
Suitable for all-terrain bicycle: Yes
Trail use fee: None, but vehicle entry fee required $2/day, $10/year
Camping: Campground available in the recreation area
Drinking water available

General Information:
  Maintained by the DNR Parks Division
  Ski and hiking trail area is closed to snowmobiles but some find their way into the area during the winter
  Cabins can be rented on the lake. The trail passes next to the cabins
  Many other trails are in the general area including Tur-Ski-Ree on M89, just west of Battle Creek

105

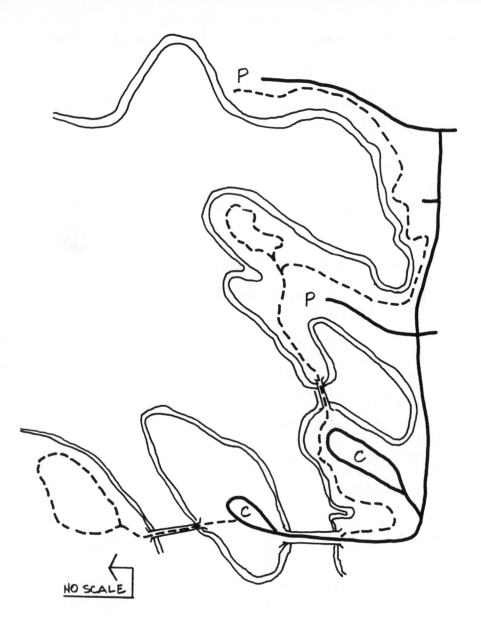

# COLDBROOK COUNTY PARK

Coldbrook County Park                    Revised: 4/25/88

Kalamazoo County Parks Department
2900 Lake St.                            616-383-8778
Kalamazoo, MI  49001

Trail suitable for hiking & skiing

Location:
  Between Battle Creek and Kalamazoo, just south of I64. Exit I64 at
  Mercury Drive southwest bound for about 2.5 miles to MN Ave.  Then turn
  right (west) to the park entrance which will be on your right about 1
  mile, just past 44th St.

Trail specifications:
  4.5 mi; 2 loop(s); Loop length(s)-2, 2.5
Typical terrain: Flat to slightly rolling
Skiing ability suggested: Novice
Hiking trail difficulty: Easy
Nordic trail grooming method: None
Suitable for all-terrain bicycle: Not permitted
Trail use fee: None but summer vehicle entry fee required $2/vehicle
Camping: Camping with both rustic and improved sites available
Drinking water avaiable

General Information:
  Maintained by the Kalamazoo County Parks Department
  This is complete recreation area with swimming, boat rentals, camping
   picnic grounds with shelters, ice fishing, ice skating, boat ramp and
   access to three lakes.
  The park contains about 275 acres

NO SCALE

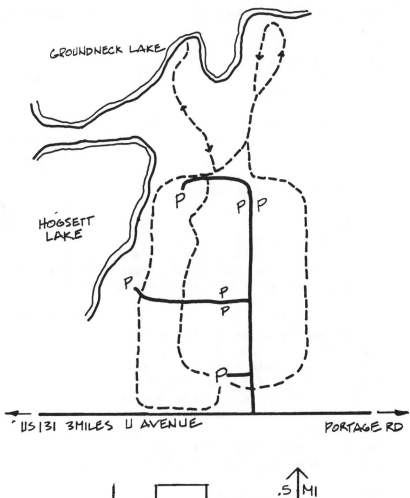

GROUNDNECK LAKE

HOGSETT
LAKE

P  P P
P

P
P
P

P

US131 3MILES  U AVENUE                    PORTAGE RD

.5 MI

# PRAIRIE VIEW PARK

Prairie View Park                          Revised:  4/25/88

Kalamazoo County Parks Department
2900 Lake St.                              616-383-8778
Kalamazoo, MI  49001

Trail suitable for skiing & hiking

Location:
 South of Kalamazoo about 9 miles on US131, then east on U Ave 3 miles
   to park entrance

Trail specifications:
   5 km; 1 loop(s); Loop length(s)-5
Typical terrain: Flat to very gently rolling
Skiing ability suggested: Novice
Hiking trail difficulty: Easy
Nordic trail grooming method: Track set
Suitable for all-terrain bicycle: Not permitted
Trail use fee: None, but vehicle entry fee required $2/day
Camping: None
Drinking water available

General Information:
 Operated by the Kalamazoo County Parks Department
 Sledding hill, warming shelter, beach, concessions, picnic shelters and
   play fields.
 Park is about 210 acres
 Rentals available in Schoolcraft and Kalamazoo.

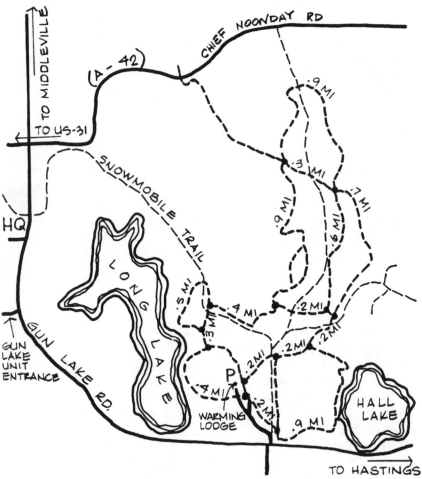

TO MIDDLEVILLE

CHIEF NOONDAY RD

(A-42)

TO US-31

SNOWMOBILE TRAIL

HQ

.9 MI

.3 MI

.7 MI

.9 MI

.9 MI

.9 MI

LONG LAKE

GUN LAKE

.5 MI

.4 MI

.2 MI

.3 MI

.2 MI

GUN LAKE UNIT ENTRANCE

GUN LAKE RD.

.2 MI

.2 MI

.2 MI

.4 MI

P

.2 MI

WARMING LODGE

.9 MI

HALL LAKE

TO HASTINGS

NOTE: SKI TRAILS ONLY. SEE
OTHER MAP FOR HIKING TRAILS

.5 MI

YANKEE SPRINGS
RECREATION AREA

Yankee Springs Recreation Area                    Revised: 3/08/88


Yankee Springs Recreation Area
2140 Gun Lake Rd.                                  616-795-9081
Middleville, MI  49333


DNR Parks Division Office

                                                   517-373-1270


Trail suitable for skiing & hiking

Location:
 9 miles west of Hastings on Co Rd A42
 Winter trailhead - Long Lake Outdoor Center on Gun Lake Rd.
 Hiking trailheads - Park Hdqs, Long Lake Outdoor Center, near Chief
   Noonday Outdoor Center, Deep Lake Campground and Beach Campground

Trail specifications:
  20 mi; Many loop(s); Loop length(s)-various
 Typical terrain: Rolling to hilly
 Skiing ability suggested: Novice to advanced *
 Hiking trail difficulty: Easy to moderate *
 Nordic trail grooming method: Track set as needed
 Suitable for all-terrain bicycle: Yes
 Trail use fee: None
 Camping: Campgrounds in the recreation area
 Drinking water available at warming shelter and campgrounds

General Information:
 Maintained by the DNR Parks Division
 Hiking and cross-country ski trails are separate systems
 The cross-country ski trail system has 6 loops with loops ranging from 1.5
   5 miles to 5.3 miles long
 Hiking trail system has 5 trails ranging in length from .5 mile to
   5 miles.
 * There are two separate maps for the hiking and ski trails
 Rustic cabin rentals available
 Winter weekend events on 3rd and 4th weekends of January
 Warming shelter provided at the Long Lake Outdoor Center.  Open weekends
   and holidays with a self serve snack bar

108

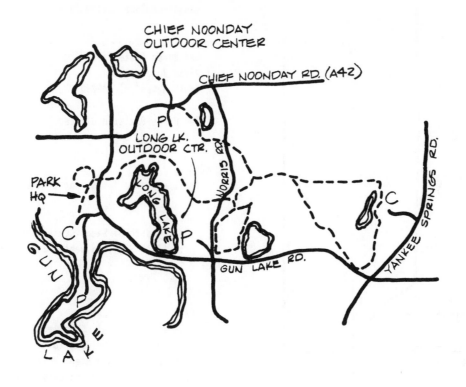

CHIEF NOONDAY
OUTDOOR CENTER

CHIEF NOONDAY RD. (A42)

P

LONG LK.
OUTDOOR CTR.

NORRIS RD.

YANKEE SPRINGS RD.

PARK
HQ

LONG LAKE

C

P

C

GUN

LAKE

P

GUN LAKE RD.

NOTE: HIKING TRAILS
SHOWN. SEE OTHER
MAP FOR SKI TRAILS

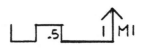

.5     1 MI

# YANKEE SPRINGS
# RECREATION AREA

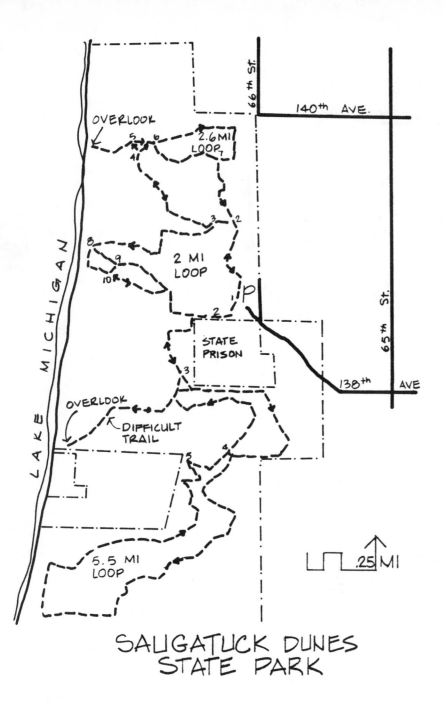

OVERLOOK

2.6 MI LOOP

2 MI LOOP

P

STATE PRISON

OVERLOOK

DIFFICULT TRAIL

5.5 MI LOOP

LAKE MICHIGAN

66th St.

140th AVE.

65th St.

138th AVE

.25 MI

SAUGATUCK DUNES
STATE PARK

Saugatuck Dunes State Park                    Revised: 3/20/88

Van Buren State Park
23960 Ruggles Rd.                             616-637-2788
South Haven, MI  49090

DNR Parks Division Office

                                              517-373-1270

Trail suitable for skiing & hiking

Location:
 1 mile north of Saugatuck via north on A2 to 64th St., then north 1 mile
   to 138th St, then west 1 mile to the park entrance

Trail specifications:
  14 mi; 7 loop(s); Loop length(s)-2.0 to 5.5
Typical terrain: Rolling to hilly
Skiing ability suggested: Novice (limited) & advanced
Hiking trail difficulty: Easy to moderate
Nordic trail grooming method: Track set
Suitable for all-terrain bicycle: Limited use because of loose sand
Trail use fee: None, but vehicle entry fee required $2/day, $10/year
Camping: None
Drinking water is available

General Information:
 Maintained by the DNR Parks Division
 Scenic view of Lake Michigan and the dunes
 Over 1000 acres of hardwoods, pine forests and sand dunes
 Sand dunes raise up to 180 feet above Lake Michigan
 Complete picnic grounds are provided

110

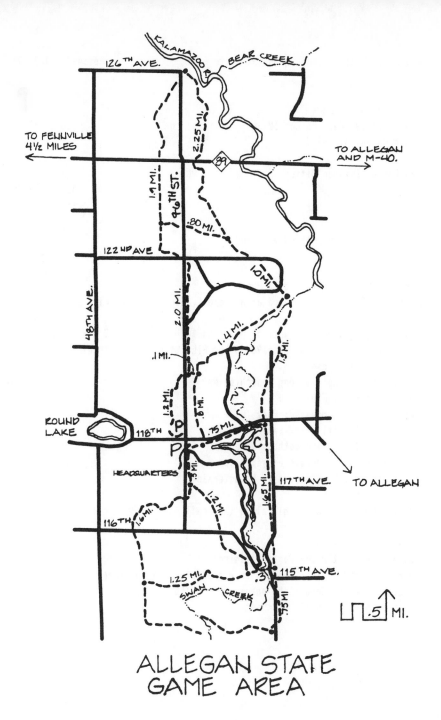

ALLEGAN STATE
GAME AREA

Allegan State Game Area                    Revised:  3/18/88


Allegan State Game Area
4590 118th Ave                             616-673-2430
Allegan, MI  49010

DNR Wildlife Division Office

                                           517-373-1263

Trail suitable for skiing & hiking

Location:
 8 miles west of Allegan
 Take M40/89 out of Allegan to Monroe Rd, then turn left to 118th Ave
 Trailhead - A game area office on 118th Ave and 46th St
 Trailhead - North on 46th St, then east on 121st Place to Swan Creek
    Highbanks unit office
Trail specifications:
   23 mi; 9 loop(s); Loop length(s)-2.5, 7.5, 7.5, 10.5, 4.5, 6.5, 8, 13.5
Typical terrain: Flat to rolling with a few steep hills
Skiing ability suggested: Novice to intermediate
Hiking trail difficulty: Easy
Nordic trail grooming method: None but usually skied in well
Suitable for all-terrain bicycle: Yes
Trail use fee: None
Camping: Campground available in the game area
Drinking water available. Limited in winter


General Information:
 Maintained by the DNR Wildlife Division
 Skiing not permitted until January 1st
 Ski trails and hiking trails may not all be identical
 The trail is very well marked with direction change arrows and confidence
    markers between intersections
 Pit toilets are available south of 122nd Ave.  None are provided in the
    north 1/3 of the game area.
 Sign in at the headquarters when you arrive.  They welcome comments and
    suggestions.

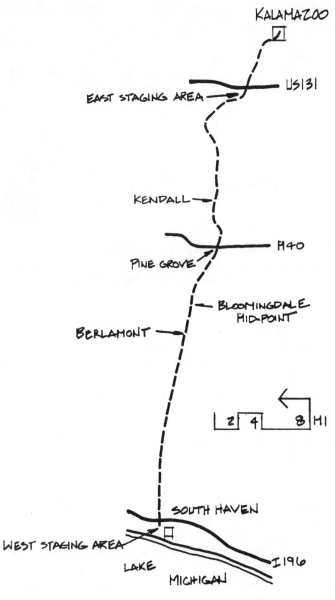

KALAMAZOO

US131

EAST STAGING AREA

KENDALL

M40

PINE GROVE

BLOOMINGDALE
MID-POINT

BERLAMONT

2 4 8 MI

SOUTH HAVEN

WEST STAGING AREA

LAKE
MICHIGAN

I196

KAL-HAVEN TRAIL
SESQUICENTENNIAL STATE PARK

Kal-Haven Trail Sesquicentennial State Park          Revised:  4/02/88


Van Buren State Park
23960 Ruggles Rd., PO Box 122-B                      616-637-2788
South Haven, MI  49090


DNR Parks Division Office

517-373-1270

Trail suitable for hiking & skiing

Location:
 Between Kalamazoo and South Haven
 "Station Sites" are located at Berlamont, Bloomingdale, Pine Grove and
   Kendall.
 East staging area-Just west of US131 on 10th St between G & H Avenues
 West staging area-West of I196 on the Blue Star Hwy, north of South Haven
Trail specifications:
   36 mi; No loop(s); Loop length(s)-NA
Typical terrain: Flat
Skiing ability suggested: Easy
Hiking trail difficulty: Easy
Nordic trail grooming method: None
Suitable for all-terrain bicycle: Yes
Trail use fee: Yes, amount to be determined
Camping: None
Drinking water is available along the trail


General Information:
 Maintained by the DNR Parks Division
 Horseback riding is permitted on a separate parallel trail
 Sections are planned to be opened during 1988
 Further development is planned

Cass County Parks Department
340 N. O'Keefe St.                                   616-445-8611
Cassopolis, MI  49031

Trail suitable for skiing & hiking

Location:
  Between Dowagiac and Marcellus on Marcellus Highway about 8 miles west of
    Marecllus, just outside of the Village of Volinia

**No Trail Map**

Trail specifications:
   3 mi; 3 loop(s); Loop length(s)-1, 1, 2
Typical terrain: Flat to gently rolling
Skiing ability suggested: Novice
Hiking trail difficulty: Easy
Nordic trail grooming method: None
Suitable for all-terrain bicycle: Yes
Trail use fee: None
Camping: None
Drinking water available

General Information:
 Operated by the Cass County Parks Department
 Part of the 640 acre Michigan State University Research Forest
 Picnic area with shelter and toilets
 A Class A trout stream runs through the park

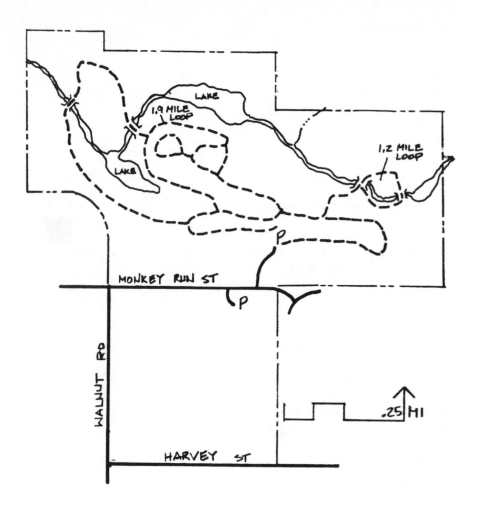

MONKEY RUN ST

WALNUT RD

HARVEY ST

.25 MI

DR. T.K. LAWLESS PARK

Cass County Parks Department
340 N. O'Keefe St.                        616-445-8611
Cassopolis, MI  49031

Dr T.K. Lawless Park
15122 Monkey Run St.                      616-476-2730
Vandalia, MI  49095

Trail suitable for skiing & hiking

Location:
 Between Cassopolis and Three Rivers off of M60
 12 miles east of Cassopolis and about 3 miles southeast of Vandalia
 Take Lewis Lake St. south off of M60 about 1 mile, then east on Monkey Run
   Street to the park entrance

Trail specifications:
   4 mi; 6 loop(s); Loop length(s)-.5 to 2
Typical terrain: Flat to hilly
Skiing ability suggested: Novice to advanced
Hiking trail difficulty: Easy to difficult
Nordic trail grooming method: Track set as needed
Suitable for all-terrain bicycle: Not permitted
Trail use fee: None, but vehicle entry fee required $1/vehicle/day
Camping: None
Drinking water available

General Information:
 Operated by the Cass County Parks Department
 Tubing hill, warming shelter with fireplace and picnic area
 Special event held the first Saturday in February

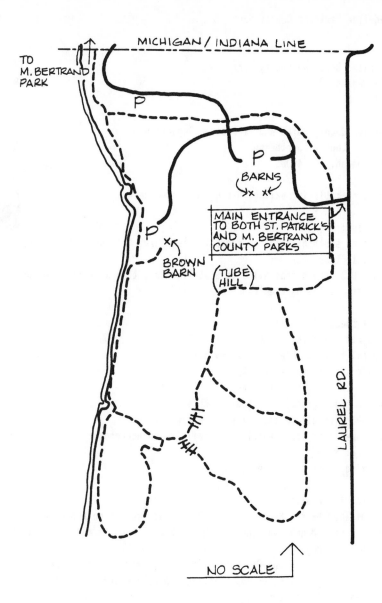

MICHIGAN / INDIANA LINE

TO M. BERTRAND PARK

P

P

P
BARNS
x  x

MAIN ENTRANCE
TO BOTH ST. PATRICK'S
AND M. BERTRAND
COUNTY PARKS

P
x

BROWN
BARN

(TUBE)
HILL

LAUREL RD.

NO SCALE

# ST. PATRICK'S PARK

St. Patrick's County Park

St. Patrick's County Park
50651 Laurel Rd.
South Bend, IN  46637

219-277-4828

Trail suitable for skiing and hiking

Location:
 On the Michigan/Indiana border just south of Niles and west of US33/31
  Take US33/31.(between the state line and I90 in Indiana) west on Auten Rd.
   to Laurel Rd., then north 1 mile to park entrance

Trail specifications:
  2 mi; 3 loop(s); Loop length(s)-.3, .5, 1.1
Typical terrain: Flat to hilly
Skiing ability suggested: Novice
Hiking trail difficulty: Easy
Nordic trail grooming method: Track set
Suitable for all-terrain bicycle: Not permitted
Trail use fee: $1/day
Camping: None
Drinking water available

General Information:
 Operated by the St. Joseph County Parks Department
 Adjacent to the Madeline Bertrand County Park with connecting trails for
  added hiking and skiing trail distance
 Tubing hill and picnic area
 Swimming lake in season

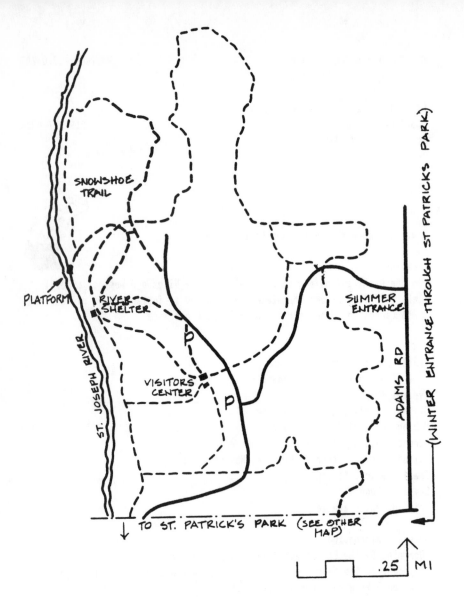

SNOWSHOE TRAIL

PLATFORM

ST. JOSEPH RIVER

RIVER SHELTER

VISITORS CENTER

P

P

P

SUMMER ENTRANCE

ADAMS RD

(WINTER ENTRANCE THROUGH ST PATRICK'S PARK)

TO ST. PATRICK'S PARK (SEE OTHER MAP)

.25 MI

MADELINE BERTRAND PARK

Madeline Bertrand County Park                    Revised:  3/23/88


Madeline Bertrand County Park
3038 Adams Rd.                                   616-683-8280
Niles, MI  49120


Berrien County Parks and Recreation Department
Berrien County Courthouse                        616-983-7111
St. Joseph, MI  49085

Trail suitable for skiing, hiking and snowshoeing


Location:
 4 miles south of Niles on the St. Joseph River at the Michigan/Indiana
    state line
 Take US31 south from Niles to Stateline Rd., then west to Adams Rd., then
    north to the park entrance


Trail specifications:
   3 mi; 2 loop(s); Loop length(s)-1, 2
 Typical terrain: Flat with a few hills
 Skiing ability suggested: Novice
 Hiking trail difficulty: Easy
 Nordic trail grooming method: Track set
 Suitable for all-terrain bicycle: Not permitted
 Trail use fee: Yes, vehicle and trail fee on weekends
 Camping: None
 Drinking water available


General Information:
 Maintained by the Berrien County Parks and Recreation Department
 Park closed Monday and Tuesday. Hours W-F 12 noon to sunset, weekends
    10am to sunset
 Park is adjoining the St. Patrick's County Park in Indiana, with
    connecting trails for added skiing and hiking trail distance
 Heated visitor center
 Picnicing/resting area in Bertrand Lodge. The lodge is dominated by a
    large stone fireplace
 Trails wind through a stately evergreen forest
 Torch-lighted skiing is available on most weekends
 Snowshoe rental available. Ski rentals are available at adjoining St.
    Patrick's Park. Separate snowshoe trails provided.
 Scheduled naturalist activities throughout the year
 Facilities available for rent and/or private torch-light skiing

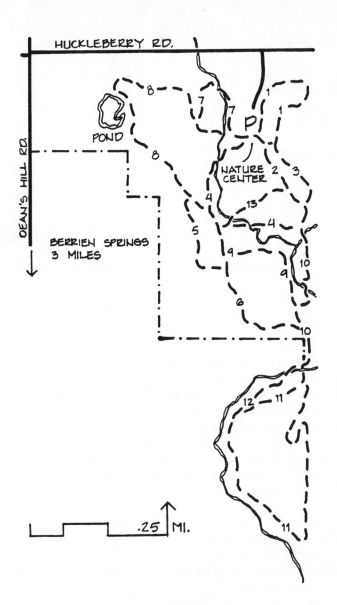

HUCKLEBERRY RD.

DEAN'S HILL RD.

POND

8

7

7

P

8

NATURE
CENTER

2  3

4

13

5

4

4

10

9

8

10

12  11

11

BERRIEN SPRINGS
3 MILES

.25 MI.

LOVE CREEK COUNTY
PARK & NATURE CENTER

Love Creek County Park & Nature Center          Revised:  4/01/08

Love Creek Nature Center
9228 Huckleberry Rd.                                              616-471-2617
Berrien Springs, MI  49102

Berrien County Parks and Recreation Department
Berrien County Courthouse                            ext 435  616-983-7111
St Joesph, MI  49085

Trail suitable for skiing, hiking & snowshoeing

Location:
 From Berrien Springs, take US31 south about .75 mile to Deans Hill Rd.,
    then turn left, then turn immediately right on Pokagon Rd. for 2 miles
    to Huckleberry Rd., then north 1 mile to the park entrance


Trail specifications:
  10+ km; 13+ loop(s); Loop length(s)-various
Typical terrain: Moderately hilly
Skiing ability suggested: Intermediate to advanced
Hiking trail difficulty: Moderate
Nordic trail grooming method: Track set as needed
Suitable for all-terrain bicycle: Not permitted
Trail use fee: Yes for skiing, no for hiking
Camping: None
Drinking water is available

General Information:
 Operated by the Berrien County Parks and Recreation Department
 Rentals and ski instruction available
 Special activities throughout the year
 Lake effect snow provides excellent conditions throughout season
 Addition trails available for hiking during the rest of the year
 Call for hours of operation
 Separate winter hiking and snowshoeing trails are provided
 Some trails are different for summer hiking
 Spectacular spring woodland wildflower show in late April & early May
 Write for their brochure

117

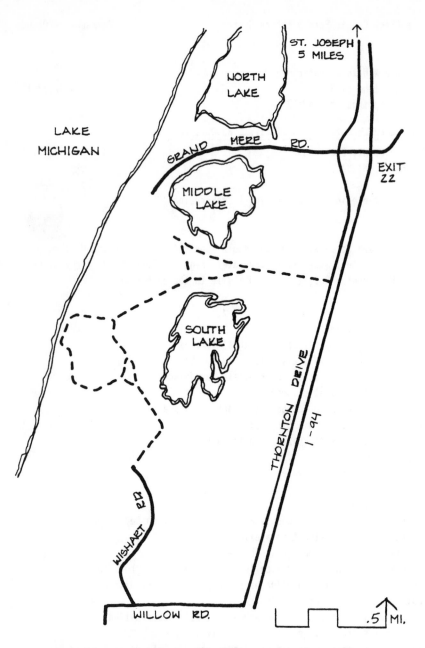

GRAND MERE STATE PARK

Grand Mere State Park                                    Revised: 9/22/87


Warren Dunes State Park
Red Arrow Highway                                        616-426-4013
Sawyer, MI  49125


DNR Parks Division Office

                                                         517-373-1270


Trail suitable for hiking & skiing

Location:
 5 miles south of St Joesph on I94 at exit 22, then west to the park



Trail specifications:
   4+ mi; None loop(s); Loop length(s)-NA
Typical terrain: Rolling to hilly
Skiing ability suggested: Novice to intermediate
Hiking trail difficulty: Easy to moderate
Nordic trail grooming method: None
Suitable for all-terrain bicycle: Some trails
Trail use fee: Yes, DNR permit
Camping: Campgound available at Warren Dunes SP, 10 miles south
Drinking water not available

General Information:
 Maintained by the DNR Parks Division
 Many trails on primary dune
 In the beginning stages of development with all trails not maintained
 Use trails at your own risk

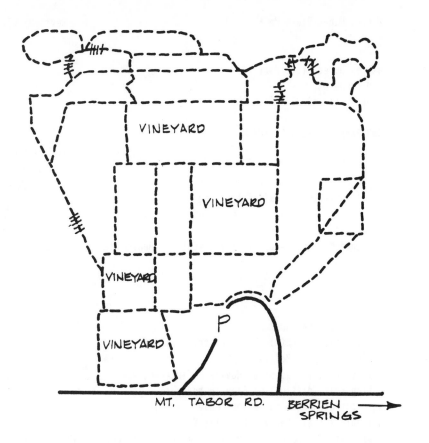

## TABOR HILL VINEYARD

Tabor Hill Vineyard                                          Revised: 11/20/87

Tabor Hill Vineyard
185 Mt Tabor Rd.                                             616-422-1161
Buchanan, MI  49107

Trail suitable for skiing & hiking

Location:
 7 miles east of Bridgeman and 6 miles west of Berrien Springs, just south
   of Snow Rd on Mt Tabor Rd

Trail specifications:
   15 km; 5 loop(s); Loop length(s)-3, 4, 5, 6, 8
Typical terrain: Flat to rolling
Skiing ability suggested: Novice to intermediate
Hiking trail difficulty: NA
Nordic trail grooming method: Packed only
Suitable for all-terrain bicycle: NA
Trail use fee: $5.00/day
Camping: None

General Information:
 Privately operated vineyard with groomed trails
 Warming shelter, wine tasting and tours, snack bar, lessons and rentals
   with prior arrangement
 Panoramic views of Lake Michigan dunes

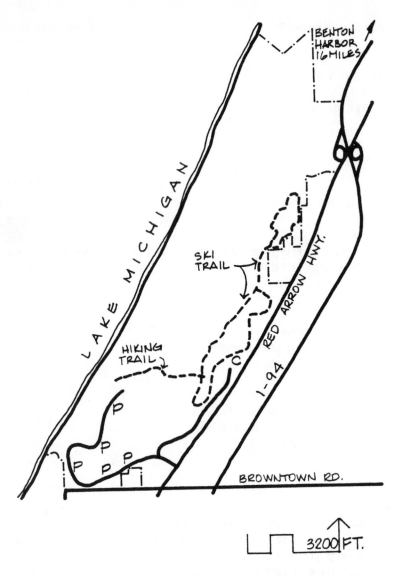

BENTON
HARBOR
16 MILES

LAKE MICHIGAN

SKI
TRAIL

HIKING
TRAIL

RED ARROW HWY.

I-94

P P P P P

BROWNTOWN RD.

3200 FT.

# WARREN DUNES STATE PARK

Warren Dunes State Park                    Revised:  3/28/88


Warren Dunes State Park
Red Arrow Hwy                              616-426-4013
Sawyer, MI  49125


DNR Parks Divison Office


                                          517-373-1270

Trail suitable for skiing & hiking

Location:
 On Lake Michigan about 16 miles south of Benton Harbor at exit 16


Trail specifications:
    4.5 mi‡; 2 loop(s); Loop length(s)-2.5, 4
 Typical terrain: Rolling
 Skiing ability suggested: Novice to intermediate
 Hiking trail difficulty: Easy to Moderate
 Nordic trail grooming method: None
 Suitable for all-terrain bicycle: Yes
 Trail use fee: None, but DNR vehicle permit is required $2/day, $10/year
 Camping: Available on site
 Drinking water is available

General Information:
 Maintained by the DNR Parks Division
 ‡ Ski trail is .5 mile shorter
 Beach and dune climb are available in the park along with the campground.

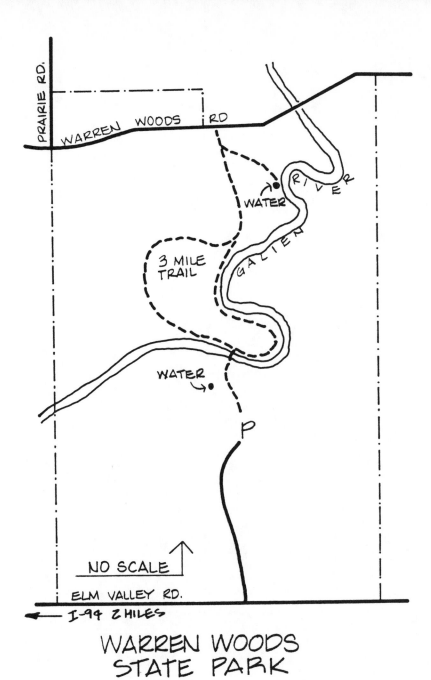

PRAIRIE RD.

WARREN WOODS RD

GALIEN RIVER

WATER

3 MILE TRAIL

WATER

P

NO SCALE

ELM VALLEY RD.

← I-94 2 MILES

## WARREN WOODS STATE PARK

Warren Woods State Park                    Revised: 3/28/88

Warren Dunes State Park
Red Arrow Hwy                              906-492-3415
Sawyer, MI  49125

DNR Parks Division Office

                                           517-373-1270

Trail suitable for skiing & hiking

Location:
 3 miles from Lake Michigan and 5 miles from Indiana state line
 Exit I94 at Union Pier Rd., then west 2.5 miles on Elm Valley Rd. to
    the park, which is on the north side of the road
 Warren Woods State Park is about 7 miles north

Trail specifications:
   3 mi; 1 loop(s); Loop length(s)-3
Typical terrain: Rolling
Skiing ability suggested: Novice
Hiking trail difficulty: Easy
Nordic trail grooming method: None
Suitable for all-terrain bicycle: Yes
Trail use fee: None, but vehicle permit required $2/day, $10/year
Camping: None
Drinking water available

General Information:
 Maintained by the DNR Parks Division
 A primeval forest preserve which is substantially undeveloped except for a
    picnic area, toilets and of course the trail.

# Trail Notes

# Region 2

# Region 2

LAKE MICHIGAN

LAKE HURON

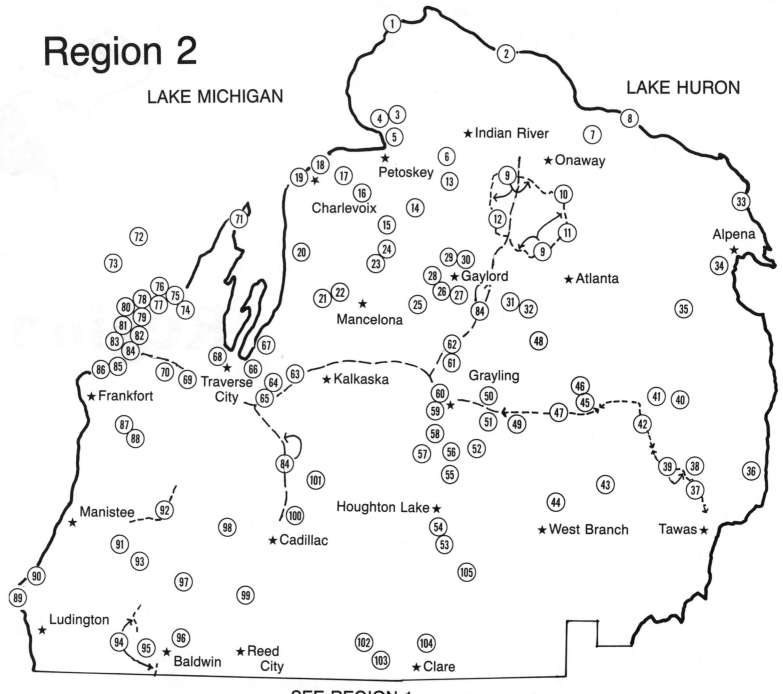

★ Indian River

★ Onaway

★ Petoskey

Charlevoix

★ Atlanta

Alpena
★

★ Gaylord

★ Mancelona

Grayling

★ Kalkaska

Traverse
City

★ Frankfort

Houghton Lake ★

Manistee
★

★ West Branch

Tawas ★

★ Cadillac

Ludington
★

★ Reed
City

★ Baldwin

★ Clare

SEE REGION 1

124

# Region 2 Contents

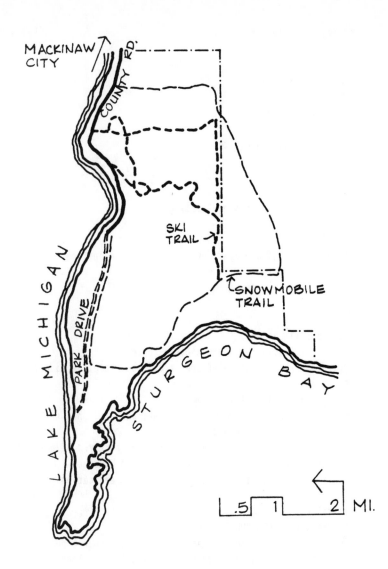

MACKINAW CITY

COUNTY RD.

LAKE MICHIGAN

PARK DRIVE

SKI TRAIL

SNOWMOBILE TRAIL

STURGEON BAY

.5  1  2 MI.

WILDERNESS STATE PARK

Wilderness State Park                                    Revised: 11/05/87

Wilderness State Park
Wilderness Park Drive                                   616-436-5381
Carp Lake, MI  49718

DNR Parks Division Office

517-373-1270

Trail suitable for skiing & hiking

Location:
 West of Mackinaw City on C81 and Wilderness Park Drive on Lake Michigan

Trail specifications:
   35 mi; Many loop(s); Loop length(s)-various
Typical terrain: Flat to rolling
Skiing ability suggested: Novice to intermediate
Hiking trail difficulty: Easy to moderate
Nordic trail grooming method: None
Suitable for all-terrain bicycle: Yes
Trail use fee: None, but vehicle entry fee required $2/day, $10/year
Camping: Available in park
Drinking water is available

General Information:
 Maintained by the DNR Parks Division
 Ski in cabins available for rent on a reservations only basis (bookings
   for weekends should be made well in advance)
 Great back country skiing can be found here

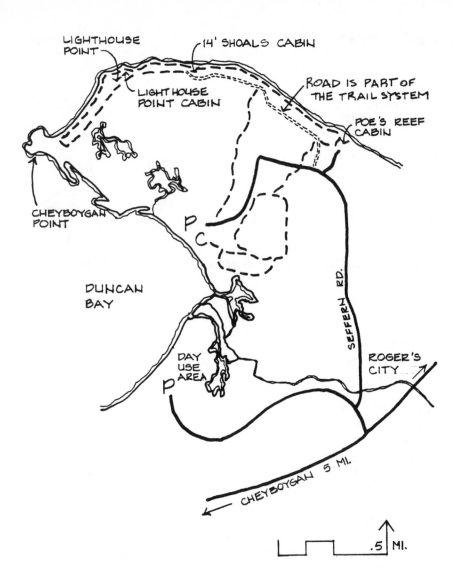

## CHEYBOYGAN STATE PARK

Labels on map:
- LIGHTHOUSE POINT
- 14' SHOALS CABIN
- LIGHTHOUSE POINT CABIN
- ROAD IS PART OF THE TRAIL SYSTEM
- POE'S REEF CABIN
- CHEYBOYGAN POINT
- P C
- DUNCAN BAY
- DAY USE AREA
- P
- SEFFERN RD.
- ROGER'S CITY
- CHEYBOYGAN 5 MI.
- .5 MI.

Cheboygan State Park                     Revised: 4/01/88

Cheboygan State Park
4490 Beach Rd.                                    616-627-2811
Cheboygan, MI  49721

DNR Parks Division Office

517-373-1270

Trail suitable for hiking & skiing

Location:
 5 miles east of Cheboygan on US23, then turn left on Seffern Rd and
   follow the signs

Trail specifications:
   3 mi; 4 loop(s); Loop length(s)-1.5 to 3
Typical terrain: Flat, with some trails on shoreline ridges
Skiing ability suggested: Novice
Hiking trail difficulty: Easy
Nordic trail grooming method: Track set when 12" snow depth is reached
Suitable for all-terrain bicycle: Yes
Trail use fee: None, but vehicle entry fee required $2/day, $10/year
Camping: Camping on site from April through November
Drinking  water available at campground, HQ and cabins

General Information:
 Maintained by the DNR Parks Division
 Two rustic cabins are available for rent all year around.  In the
   winter cabins can only be reached by skiing to them.  Contact the
   park manager to make reservations, which are required.
 Park covers over 1,200 acres
 The first lighthouse, the Cheboygan Light, was built in 1857. It was
   later relocated to the shore and operated until 1930

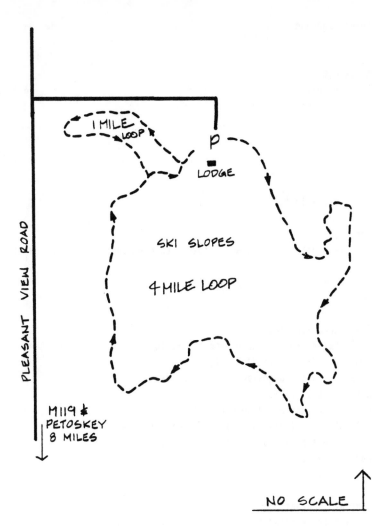

PLEASANT VIEW ROAD

1 MILE LOOP

P

LODGE

SKI SLOPES

4 MILE LOOP

M119 &
PETOSKEY
8 MILES

NO SCALE

NUBS NOB

Nub's Nob                                    Revised: 11/13/87

Nub's Nob
4021 Nubs Nob Rd.                            616-526-2131
Harbor Springs, MI  49740

Trail suitable for skiing only

Location:
 NE of Harbor Springs on C81

Trail specifications:
   5 mi; 2 loop(s); Loop length(s)-1, 4
Typical terrain: Flat to hilly
Skiing ability suggested: Novice and advanced
Hiking trail difficulty: NA
Nordic trail grooming method: None
Suitable for all-terrain bicycle: NA
Trail use fee: None
Camping: None

General Information:
 Privately operated downhill ski resort
 Restaurant, lodge, and rentals
 Thought not groomed the trail is usually skied in well
 The 4 mile loop should only be attemped by advanced skiers since there is
   a 400 foot elevation change in the trail
 Follow the blue markers since the trail intersects logging roads often
 Just east of Boyne Highlands

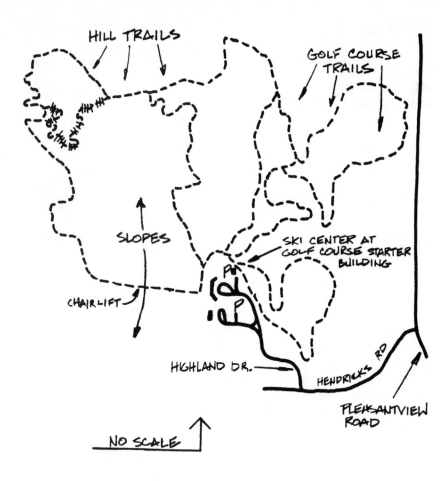

HILL TRAILS

GOLF COURSE TRAILS

SLOPES

SKI CENTER AT GOLF COURSE STARTER BUILDING

CHAIRLIFT

HIGHLAND DR.

HENDRICKS RD

PLEASANTVIEW ROAD

NO SCALE

BOYNE HIGHLANDS

Boyne Highlands

Revised: 4/05/88

Mr John McGregor
Boyne Highlands
Harbor Springs, MI  49740

616-526-2171
800-562-3899

Trail suitable for skiing & hiking

Location:
 Between Harbor Springs and Petoskey on Pleasantview Rd (follow signs).

Trail specifications:
  28 km; 4 loop(s); Loop length(s)-3 to 10
Typical terrain: Flat to hilly
Skiing ability suggested: Novice to advanced
Hiking trail difficulty: NA
Nordic trail grooming method: Track set
Suitable for all-terrain bicycle: Not permitted
Trail use fee: $3.00/day or free with lift ticket *
Camping: None

General Information:
 Privately operated 4 seasons resort with all facilities
 Scenic veiws of the surrounding area from some trails
 Access to trails may be gained by use of the chair lift
 Some trails on the golf course but many miles are in the wooded hills
   behind the downhill slopes
 * Additional $3.00 charge if the chair lift is used
 Trail maintenance and grooming has been rather inconsistant over the
   past several seasons. Boyne management has assured me that regular
   track setting and trail maintenance will occour in the future.  Since
   the trails in the hills north of the slopes are well designed, the
   hopefully increased emphasis on grooming should improve trail
   conditions significantly.

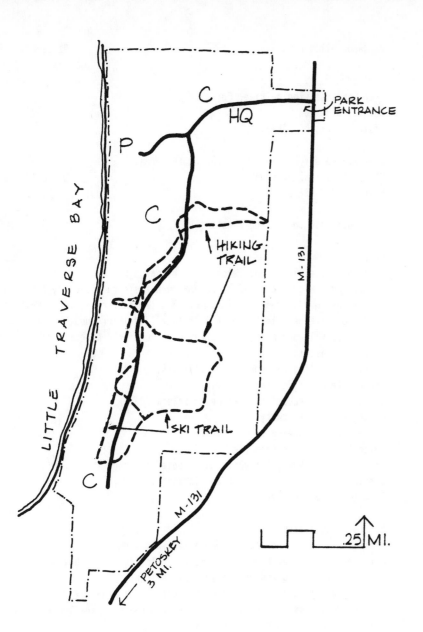

Little Traverse Bay

C
P
HQ
PARK ENTRANCE

C

HIKING TRAIL

M-131

SKI TRAIL

C

M-131

PETOSKEY 3 MI.

.25 MI.

PETOSKEY STATE PARK

Petoskey State Park                                    Revised:  3/28/88

Petoskey State Park
2475 Harbor-Petoskey Rd.                              616-347-2311
Petoskey, MI  49770

DNR Parks Division Office

                                                      517-373-1270

Trail suitable for skiing & hiking

Location:
  West of Petoskey via US31, then north on M119 (Harbor-Petoskey Rd.) to the
   park which will be on your left

Trail specifications:
   3.5 mi; 2 loop(s); Loop length(s)-.5, 2
Typical terrain: Rolling to hilly
Skiing ability suggested: Novice
Hiking trail difficulty: Moderate
Nordic trail grooming method: Track set
Suitable for all-terrain bicycle: Yes
Trail use fee: None, but vehicle entry fee required $2/day, $10/year
Camping: Campground available in park
Drinking water available in spring through fall

General Information:
 Maintained by the DNR Parks Division

131

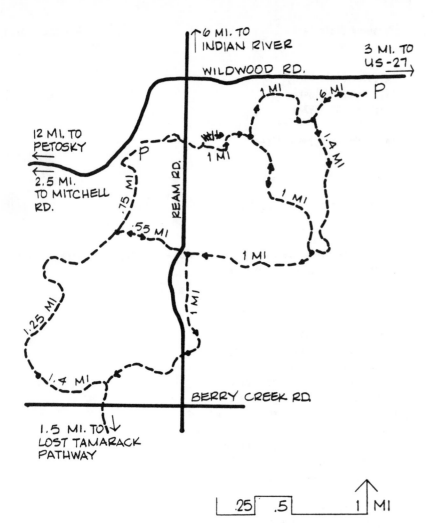

6 MI. TO
INDIAN RIVER

3 MI. TO
US-27

WILDWOOD RD.

1 MI

.6 MI

P

12 MI. TO
PETOSKY

P

1 MI

.4 MI

2.5 MI.
TO MITCHELL
RD.

REAM RD.

.75 MI

1 MI

.55 MI

1 MI

1.25 MI

1 MI

1.4 MI

BERRY CREEK RD.

1.5 MI. TO
LOST TAMARACK
PATHWAY

.25  .5       1 MI

# WILDWOOD HILLS PATHWAY

132

Wildwood Hills Pathway                    Revised:  3/06/88

Area Forester, Indian River Forest Area
Box 10, 6984 M68                                      616-238-9313
Indian River, MI  49749

District Forest Manager, Mackinaw State Forest
PO Box 667, 1732 West M32                             517-732-3541
Gaylord, MI  49735

Trail suitable for skiing & hiking

Location:
 Between Indian River and Petoskey on Wildwood Rd.
 Trailhead - From Indian River on M68 turn south on old US27, then south
   2 miles to Wildwood Rd., then west 3 miles to parking lot (south side)
 Trailhead - From Petoskey on C58 (Mitchell Rd.) for about 9.5 miles, then
   pick up Wildwood Rd. (left fork), continue for 3 miles to parking lot
Trail specifications:
 9.3 mi; 3 loop(s); Loop length(s)-4, 4.5, 5.75
Typical terrain: Rolling to hilly
Skiing ability suggested: Novice to intermediate
Hiking trail difficulty: Easy
Nordic trail grooming method: Track set
Suitable for all-terrain bicycle: Yes
Trail use fee: None, but donation accepted to groom trail
Camping: Available in Alanson and Indian River
Drinking water not available


General Information:
 Maintained by the DNR Forest Management Division
 Ski rentals available in Indian River, Petoskey and Cheboygan
 A very interesting and enjoyable trail system
 Some snowmobiles are in the area but because of the heavy use this trail
   receives, they seldom if ever cause problems with the trails
 All difficult hills can be by passed
 One of the better trails developed by the DNR
 Toilets available at the parking lots
 A point to point trail (not groomed) connects to the Lost Tamarack Pathway
   located south of Wildwood Hills Pathway

Other contacts:
 DNR Forest Management Division Office, Lansing, 517-373-1275
 DNR Forest Management Region Office, Roscommon, 517-275-5151

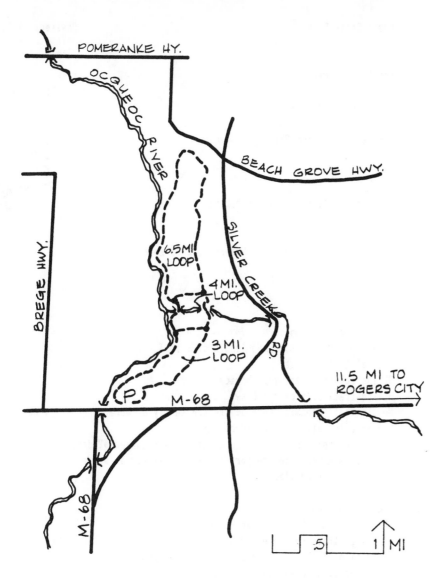

POMERANKE HY.

OCQUEOC RIVER

BEACH GROVE HWY.

BREGE HWY.

SILVER CREEK RD.

6.5 MI. LOOP

4 MI. LOOP

3 MI. LOOP

P.

M-68

M-68

11.5 MI TO ROGERS CITY

.5   1 MI

# OCQUEOC FALLS BICENTENNIAL PATHWAY

Ocqueoc Falls Bicentennial Pathway          Revised:  3/06/88

Area Forester, Atlanta Forest Area
Rte 1, Box 30                                517-785-4251
Atlanta, MI  49709

District Forest Manager, Mackinaw State Forest
Box 667, 1732 West M32                       517-732-3541
Gaylord, MI  49735

Trail suitable for skiing & hiking

Location:
 On M68, 12 miles west of Rogers City at Ocqueoc Falls Rd. where M68 turns
   south
 11 miles east of Onaway on M68

Trail specifications:
   11 km; 3 loop(s); Loop length(s)-4.8, 6.4, 10.5
Typical terrain: Flat to slightly rolling with one steep hill
Skiing ability suggested: Novice to intermediate
Hiking trail difficulty: Moderate
Nordic trail grooming method: Track set
Suitable for all-terrain bicycle: Yes
Trail use fee: Donation accepted for trail grooming
Camping: SF campground at trailhead
Drinking water at trailhead

General Information:
 Maintained by the DNR Forest Management Division
 Falls are at the trailhead
 Rolling hills in area with scenic overlooks

Other contacts:
DNR Forest Management Division Office, Lansing, 517-373-1275
DNR Forest Management Onaway Field Office, Onaway, 517-733-8775
DNR Forest Management Region Office, Roscommon, 517-275-5151

133

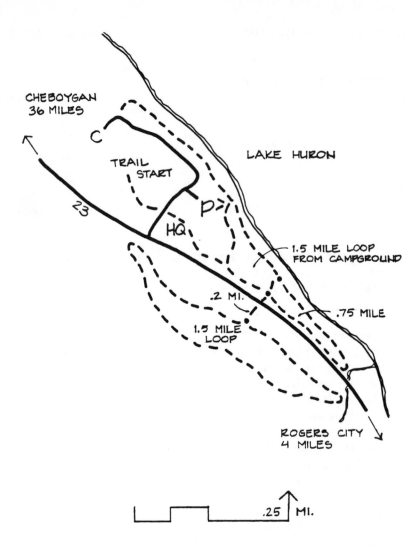

CHEBOYGAN
36 MILES

C

TRAIL START

LAKE HURON

23

P>

HQ

1.5 MILE LOOP
FROM CAMPGROUND

.2 MI.

.75 MILE

1.5 MILE
LOOP

ROGERS CITY
4 MILES

.25 MI.

# HOEFT STATE PARK

Hoeft State Park
US23                                                517-734-2543
Rogers City, MI  49779

DNR Parks Division Office

                                                    517-373-1270

Trail suitable for skiing & hiking

Location:
 On US23, 5 miles north of Rogers City on Lake Huron

Trail specifications:
   4.5 mi; 2 loop(s); Loop length(s)-1.5, 3
Typical terrain: Flat
Skiing ability suggested: Novice
Hiking trail difficulty: Easy
Nordic trail grooming method: Tracked weekly or more frequent if needed
Suitable for all-terrain bicycle: Yes
Trail use fee: None, but vehicle entry fee required $2/day, $10/year
Camping: Available in the park (plowed in winter as needed)
Drinking water available

General Information:
 Maintained by the DNR Parks Division
 Trail in the Huron Dunes area
 A portion of the trail passes along Lake Huron
 Food and lodging available in Rogers City
 Ski rental available in Rogers City at the following places:
    Peacock's Sporting Goods  734-3465
    Lake Shore Sporting Goods  734-4150
    Adrians Sport Shop  734-2303
    Tour America Bike Shop  734-3946
 Near Ocqueoc Falls Bicentennial Pathway

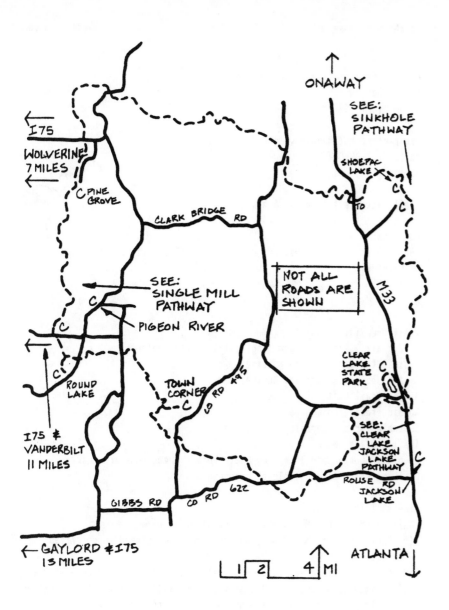

HIGH COUNTRY PATHWAY

High Country Pathway                                    Revised: 4/15/88

Area Forester, Pigeon River Country Forest Area
9966 Twin Lakes Rd.                                     517-983-4101
Vanderbilt, MI  49795

District Forest Manager, Mackinaw State Forest
Box 667, 1732 West M32                                  517-732-3541
Gaylord, MI  49735

Trail suitable for hiking only

Location:
  Northeast of Gaylord and southwest of Onaway
  Trailheads — West from Vanderbilt about 9 & 12 miles on Sturgeon Valley Rd
  Trailhead — Clear Lake State Park on M33 south of Onaway
  Trailhead — Sinkhole Pathway, 10 miles south of Onaway via M33 and east
    on Tomahawk Lake Hwy
Trail specifications:
  80+ mi; 1 loop(s); Loop length(s)-80
Typical terrain: Flat to very hilly
Skiing ability suggested: NA
Hiking trail difficulty: Moderate
Nordic trail grooming method: NA
Suitable for all-terrain bicycle: Yes
Trail use fee: None
Camping: Numerous campgrounds along the trail
Drinking water available only at campgrounds

General Information:
  Maintained by the DNR Forest Management Division
  Not designed or recommended for skiing.  The trail is difficult to find
    in the winter.
  The High Country Pathway is part of the Shingle Mill Pathway and the
    Clear Lake-Jackson Lake Pathway.  It also passes through the Sinkhole
    Pathway area.  See those trails for more detail.
  There is as much variety in terrain and habitat as can be found anywhere
    in the lower peninsula.

Other contacts:
DNR Forest Management Division Office, Lansing, 517-373-1275
DNR Forest Management Region Office, Roscommon, 517-275-5151

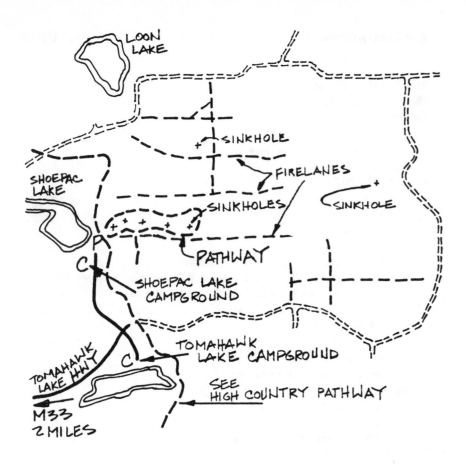

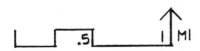

# SINKHOLE PATHWAY

Sinkhole Pathway                    Revised: 3/06/88

Area Forester, Atlanta Forest Area
Rte 1, Box 30                                          517-785-4251
Atlanta, MI  49709

District Forest Manager, Mackinaw State Forest
Box 667, 1732 M32                                      517-732-3541
Gaylord,

Trail suitable for skiing & hiking

Location:
 Between Onaway (8 miles) and Atlanta (16 miles) off M33 via Tomahawk
   Lake Hwy

Trail specifications:
   2.5 mi; 2 loop(s); Loop length(s)-1, 2 (see below)
Typical terrain: Flat to rolling
Skiing ability suggested: Novice
Hiking trail difficulty: Easy
Nordic trail grooming method: None
Suitable for all-terrain bicycle: Yes
Trail use fee: None
Camping: Shoepac and Thomahawk State Forest Campgounds are nearby
Drinking water is available at campgrounds

General Information:
 Maintained by the DNR Forest Management Division
 The Sinkhole Area contains 2,600 acres that are closed to motorized
   vehicles
 There are many miles of fire lines within this area that area suitable
   for skiing & hiking beyond that which is listed above.  It's recommended
   that the user take along a compass since there are no maps or trail
   makings on the interior of this area
 This area has a unique geological formation from the result of dissolving
   bedrocklimestone.
 Shoepac Lake is a result of this dissolving limestone

Other contacts:
DNR Forest Management Division Office, Lansing, 517-373-1275
DNR Forest Management Region Office, Roscommon, 517-275-5151

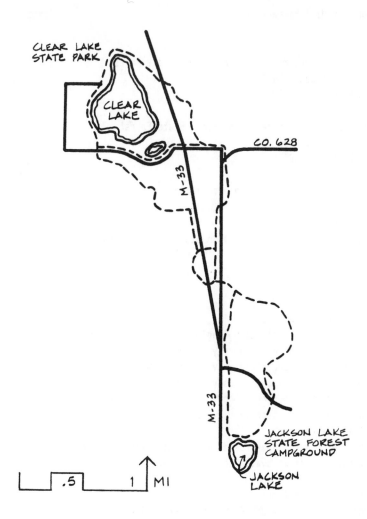

CLEAR LAKE
STATE PARK

CLEAR
LAKE

M-33

CO. 628

M-33

JACKSON LAKE
STATE FOREST
CAMPGROUND

JACKSON
LAKE

.5          1   MI

# CLEAR LAKE –
# JACKSON LAKE PATHWAY

Clear Lake - Jackson Lake Pathway                    Revised:  4/15/88

Clear Lake State Park
Rte 1                                                517-785-4388
Atlanta, MI  49709

Area Forester, Mackinaw State Forest
Rte 1, Box 30                                        517-785-4251
Atlanta, MI  49709

Trail suitable for hiking only

Location:
 10 miles north of Atlanta on M33 at the Clear Lake State Park
 Trailhead also at Jackson Lake State Forest Campground, 3 miles south


Trail specifications:
  7.5 mi; 3 loop(s); Loop length(s)-various
Typical terrain: Rolling to hilly
Skiing ability suggested: Intermediate
Hiking trail difficulty: Moderate
Nordic trail grooming method:
Suitable for all-terrain bicycle: Yes
Trail use fee: None, but vehicle entry permit required $2/day, $10/year
Camping: Campgrounds available ⚹
Drinking water available at campgrounds

General Information:
 Maintained by DNR Parks and Forest Management Divisons
 Part of the High Country Pathway
 ⚹ At Clear Lake State Park and at Jackson Lake State Forest Campground


Other contacts:
DNR Parks Division Office, Lansing, 517-373-1270
DNR Forest Management Region Office, Roscommon, 517-275-5151
DNR Forest Management Division Office, Lansing, 517-373-1275

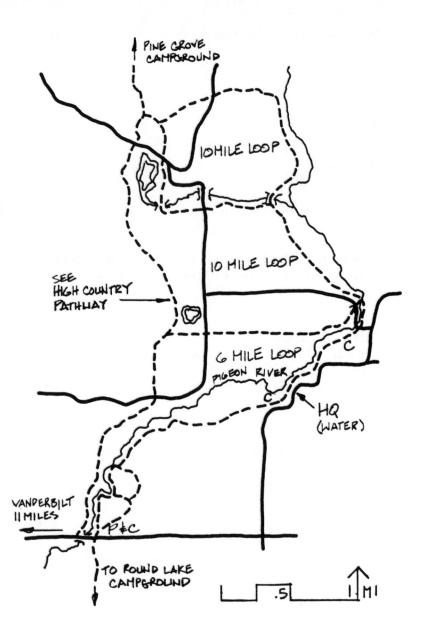

PINE GROVE CAMPGROUND

10 MILE LOOP

10 MILE LOOP

SEE HIGH COUNTRY PATHWAY

6 MILE LOOP

PIGEON RIVER

C

C

HQ (WATER)

VANDERBILT 11 MILES

P & C

TO ROUND LAKE CAMPGROUND

.5        1 MI

## SHINGLE MILL PATHWAY

Shingle Mill Pathway                          Revised:  3/05/88

Area Forester, Pigeon River Country State Forest
9966 Twin Lakes Rd.                                    517-983-4101
Vanderbilt, MI  49759

District Forest Manager, Mackinaw State Forest
Box 667, 1732 West M32                                 517-732-3541
Gaylord, MI  48735

Trail suitable for skiing and hiking

Location:
 9 miles east of Vanderbilt on Sturgeon Valley Rd.

Trail specifications:
   18 mi; 5 loop(s); Loop length(s)-.75, 1.25, 6, 10, 10
Typical terrain: Flat to very hilly
Skiing ability suggested: Novice to advanced
Hiking trail difficulty: Easy to moderate
Nordic trail grooming method: Track set on occasion
Suitable for all-terrain bicycle: Yes
Trail use fee: None
Camping: Several campgrounds are located along the trail
Drinking water is available (see below)

General Information:
 Maintained by the DNR Forest Management Division
 A very popular trail system that can absorb many users without becoming
    too crowded because of its size
 Pigeon River Country Forest Area HQ with its resident Area Forester, is
    located along the trail
 A scenic overlook is along the 10 mile loop
 Part of the North Country Pathway
 Drinking water is available all year at the headquarters bldg and
    seasonally at the campgrounds

Other contacts:
DNR Forest Management Division Office, Lansing, 517-373-1275
DNR Forest Management Region Office, Roscommon, 517-275-5151

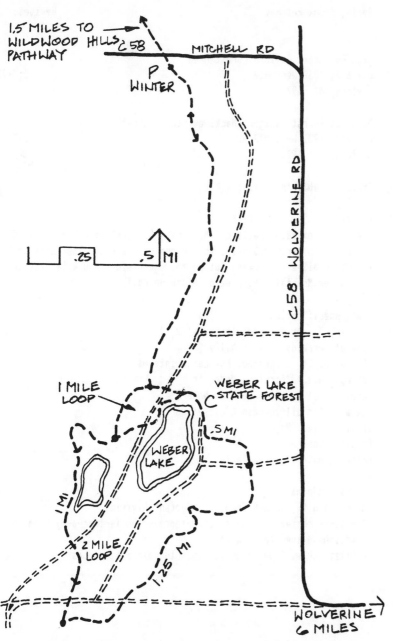

## LOST TAMARACK PATHWAY

1.5 MILES TO WILDWOOD HILLS PATHWAY
C58
MITCHELL RD
P WINTER
C58 WOLVERINE RD
.25 .5 MI
1 MILE LOOP
WEBER LAKE STATE FOREST
WEBER LAKE
.5 MI
1 MI
2 MILE LOOP
1.25 MI
WOLVERINE 6 MILES

Lost Tamarack Pathway

Revised: 4/16/88

Area Forester, Indian River Forest Area
Box 10, 6984 M68                                616-238-9313
Indian River, MI  49749

District Forest Manager, Mackinaw State Forest
Box 667, 1732 West M32                          517-732-3541
Gaylord, MI  49735

Trail suitable for hiking only

Location:
 6.5 miles west of Wolverine in C58 at Weber Lake State Forest Campground

Trail specifications:
    4.75 mi*; 2 loop(s); Loop length(s)-1, 3
Typical terrain: Rolling
Skiing ability suggested: NA
Hiking trail difficulty: Easy to moderate
Nordic trail grooming method: NA
Suitable for all-terrain bicycle: Yes
Trail use fee:
Camping: Campground at trailhead
Drinking water at trailhead

General Information:
 Maintained by the DNR Forest Management Division
 * Includes a 1.25 mile point to point trail
 The point to point trial is connected to a 1.5 mile trail that connects to
    to the Wildwood Hills Pathway

Other contacts:
DNR Forest Management Division Office, Lansing, 517-373-1275
DNR Forest Management Region Office, Roscommon, 517-275-5151

139

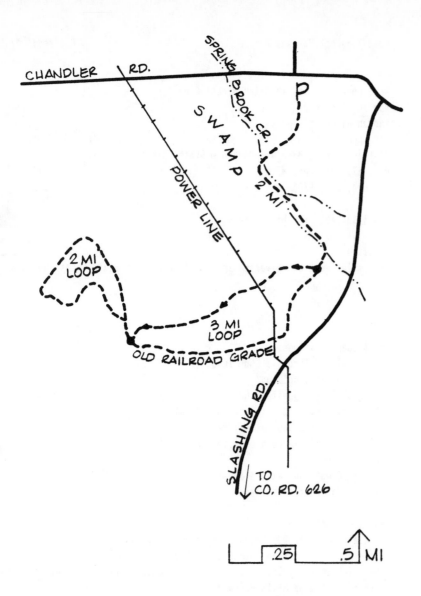

CHANDLER RD.

SPRING BROOK CR.

SWAMP

POWER LINE

2 MI

2 MI LOOP

3 MI LOOP

OLD RAILROAD GRADE

SLASHING RD.

TO CO. RD. 626

P

.25    .5 MI

SPRING BROOK PATHWAY

Spring Brook Pathway                    Revised: 3/05/88

Area Forester, Gaylord Forest Area
Box 667, 1732 West M32                    517-732-3541
Gaylord, MI  49735

District Forest Manager, Mackinaw State Forest
Box 667, 1732 West M32                    517-732-3541
Gaylord, MI  49735

Trail suitable for skiing & hiking

Location:
 Just east of Boyne Falls on Thumb Lake Rd. (C48) for 5 miles to Slashing
    Rd., then north 2.5 miles to the end of the road, then west on Chandler
    Rd. .4 miles to parking lot on the south side (you will pass the old
    Thunder Mountain ski area on Slashing Rd.)

Trail specifications:
   5 mi; 3 loop(s); Loop length(s)-2, 4, 5
Typical terrain: Flat to hilly
Skiing ability suggested: Novice to intermediate
Hiking trail difficulty: Moderate
Nordic trail grooming method: None
Suitable for all-terrain bicycle: No
Trail use fee: None
Camping: None
Drinking water not available

General Information:
 Maintained by the DNR Forest Management Division
 The loops contain more difficult terrain the farther away from the
    trailhead the user travels
 Habitat varies from cedar lowlands to upland hardwoods

Other contacts:
DNR Forest Management Division Office, Lansing, 517-373-1275
DNR Forest Management Region Office, Roscommon, 517-275-5151

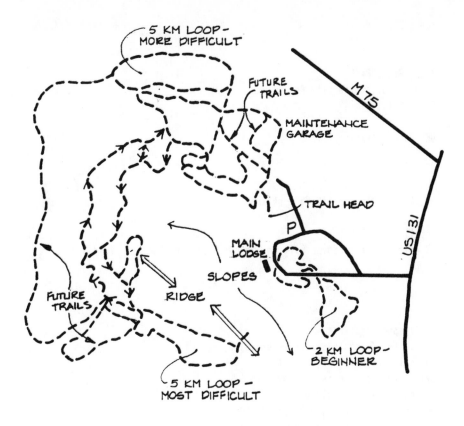

## 5 KM LOOP - MORE DIFFICULT

FUTURE TRAILS

MAINTENANCE GARAGE

M 75

TRAIL HEAD

US 131

P

MAIN LODGE

SLOPES

FUTURE TRAILS

RIDGE

2 KM LOOP - BEGINNER

5 KM LOOP - MOST DIFFICULT

NO SCALE

# BOYNE MOUNTAIN

Boyne Mountain                                      Revised:  4/05/88

Bill Winchester
Boyne Mountain                                      616-549-2441
Boyne Falls, MI  49713                              800-632-7174

Lou Awodey, Cross Country Director
Boyne Mountain                                      same as above
Boyne Falls, MI  49713

Trail suitable for skiing & hiking

Location:
  15 miles south of Petoskey at Boyne Falls, just SW of US131 amd M75
     intersection at the south edge of Boyne Falls


Trail specifications:
   15 km; 3‡ loop(s); Loop length(s)-various
Typical terrain: Rolling to very hilly
Skiing ability suggested: Novice to advanced
Hiking trail difficulty: Moderate
Nordic trail grooming method: Track set with skating lanes‡‡
Suitable for all-terrain bicycle: Not permitted
Trail use fee: $3.00/day or free with lift ticket
Camping: None


General Information:
 Privately operated 4 season resort
 Lodging, restaurant, snack bar, lessons, rentals, pool and shops
 One trail is very challenging
 One trail goes to the top of the mountain
 ‡ Three main trails with several loops within each trail
 Special events are planned throughout the winter season, including
    a 10km race in January, guided picnic tours, nordic demo-days,
    hot dog roasts and wine & cheeze tours.
 ‡‡ Call ahead to check on the grooming schedule
 Cross country skiing/lodging packages available. Packages include lodging
    food, lessons, trail passes, and apres' ski activities
 Telemark equipment is available for rent.
 Trail expansion is planned for 1988/89

141

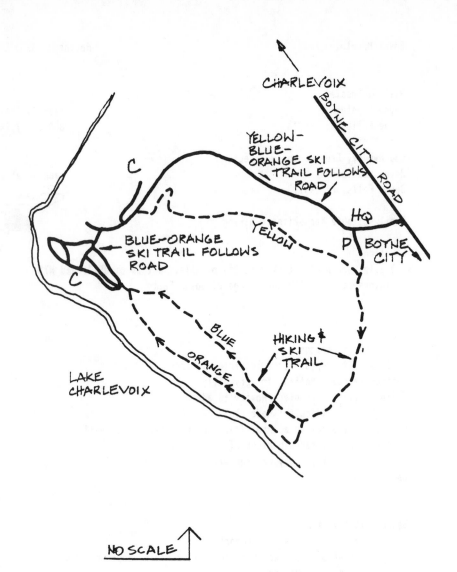

CHARLEVOIX

BOYNE CITY ROAD

YELLOW-
BLUE-
ORANGE SKI
TRAIL FOLLOWS
ROAD

C

BLUE-ORANGE
SKI TRAIL FOLLOWS
ROAD

C

YELLOW

HQ

P

BOYNE
CITY

LAKE
CHARLEVOIX

BLUE

ORANGE

HIKING &
SKI
TRAIL

NO SCALE

YOUNG STATE PARK

Young State Park                                    Revised: 11/16/87


Young State Park
PO Box 3651, Boyne City Rd.                        616-582-7523
Boyne City, Mi  49712


DNR Parks Division Office

                                                   517-373-1270


Trail suitable for hiking & skiing

Location:
 3 miles north of Boyne City on the north side of Lake Charlevoix on
   Boyne City Rd.



Trail specifications:
   4.5 km; 3 loop(s); Loop length(s)-3, 4, 4.5
Typical terrain: Flat to rolling
Skiing ability suggested: Novice
Hiking trail difficulty: Easy
Nordic trail grooming method: Packed
Suitable for all-terrain bicycle: Yes
Trail use fee: None, but vehicle entry fee required $2/day, $10/year
Camping: Campground available in park
Drinking water available in park


General Information:
 Maintained by the DNR Parks Division

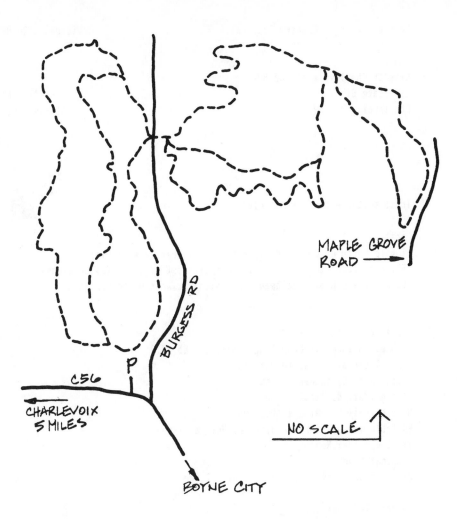

CHARLEVOIX
5 MILES

C56

P

BURGESS RD

BOYNE CITY

MAPLE GROVE
ROAD →

NO SCALE ↑

WINDMILL FARMS

Windmill Farms
Rte 3, Box 234                                    616-547-2746
Charlevoix, MI  49720                             616-547-2077

Trail suitable for skiing & hiking

Location:
  5 miles SW of Charlevoix on the north side of Lake Charlevoix on
    Boyne City Rd. (C-56)

Trail specifications:
    16 mi; 3 loop(s); Loop length(s)-2.5, 5, 10
Typical terrain: Rolling to hilly
Skiing ability suggested: Novice to advanced
Hiking trail difficulty: Easy
Nordic trail grooming method: Track set‡
Suitable for all-terrain bicycle: Not permitted
Trail use fee: $2/day
Camping: Campground on the property

General Information:
 Privately operated touring center
 Restaurant, warming area and rentals
 Lighted 2.5 km trail
 Very fine touring center with well groomed trails and interesting and
    scenic views of the area and Lake Charlevoix
 ‡ Call ahead to check on the extent of track set trails available

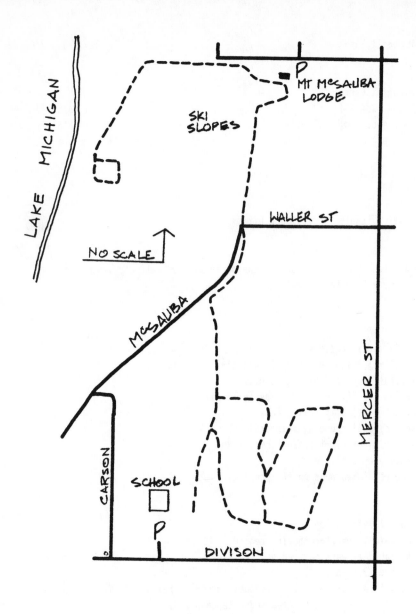

LAKE MICHIGAN

MT MeSAUBA LODGE

SKI SLOPES

NO SCALE

WALLER ST

MeSAUBA

MERCER ST

CARSON

SCHOOL

DIVISON

CHARLEVOIX
CROSS COUNTRY SKI TRAIL

Charlevoix Cross Country Ski Trail          Revised: 2/28/88

City of Charlevoix c/o Bo Boss
210 State St.                               616-547-3267
Charlevoix, MI  49720                       616-547-9098


Trail suitable for skiing only

Location:
 1 mile north of Charlevoix, west of US31 near Lake Michigan
 Ski area lodge trailhead - Pleasant St. west of US31 (follow signs)
 Elementary school trailhead - Division St. west of Mercer St.


Trail specifications:
  5 mi; 3 loop(s); Loop length(s)-.75, .85, 3.8
Typical terrain: Flat to rolling
Skiing ability suggested: Novice
Hiking trail difficulty: NA
Nordic trail grooming method: None
Suitable for all-terrain bicycle: Not permitted
Trail use fee: None
Camping: None
Drinking water available at ski hill lodge

General Information:
 Downhill ski hill operated by the City of Charlevoix
 Warming area and snack bar

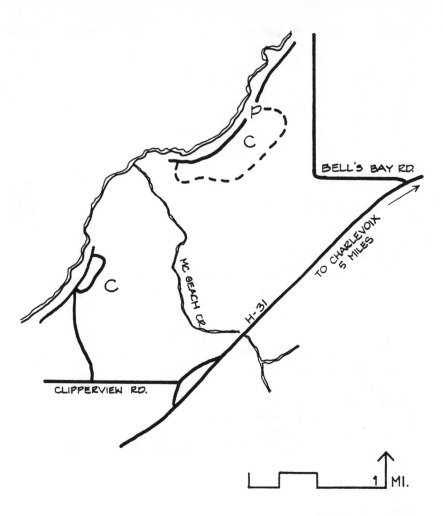

FISHERMAN'S ISLAND
STATE PARK

BELL'S BAY RD.

TO CHARLEVOIX
5 MILES

MC BEACH CR.

H-31

CLIPPERVIEW RD.

1 MI.

Fisherman's Island State Park                    Revised: 3/28/88


Fisherman's Island State Park
PO Box 456                                        616-547-6641
Charlevoix, MI  49720

DNR Parks Division Office

                                                  517-373-1270


Trail suitable for hiking & skiing

Location:
 5 miles SW of Charlevoix on US31, turn west on Bell's Bay Rd.


Trail specifications:
   2 mi; 1 loop(s); Loop length(s)-2
Typical terrain: Rolling
Skiing ability suggested: Novice to intermediate
Hiking trail difficulty: Easy
Nordic trail grooming method:
Suitable for all-terrain bicycle: Yes
Trail use fee: None, but vehicle entry fee required $2/day, $10/year
Camping: Rustic campground available in park
Drinking water available in the park

General Information:
 Maintained by the DNR Parks Division
 On the shore of Lake Michigan

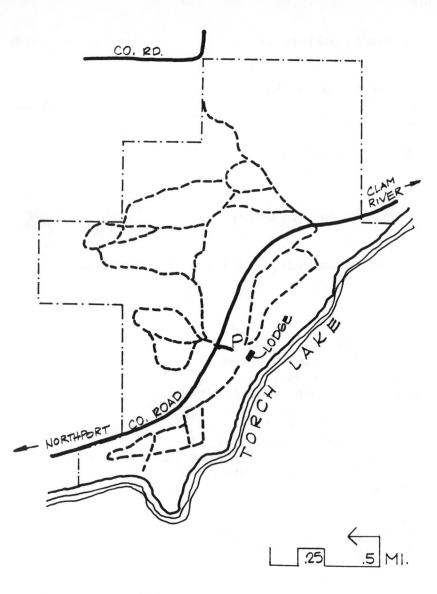

# HAYO-WENT-HA
# NORDIC SKI CENTER

Hayo-Went-Ha
RR1 Box 30                                          616-544-5915
Central Lake, MI  49622

Trail suitable for skiing only

Location:
 5 miles south of Eastport on East Torch Lake Drive
 or 5 miles west of Central Lake on East Torch Lake Drive

Trail specifications:
    12 km; 4 loop(s); Loop length(s)-1 to 4
Typical terrain: Flat to hilly
Skiing ability suggested: Novice to advanced
Hiking trail difficulty: NA
Nordic trail grooming method: Track set
Suitable for all-terrain bicycle: NA
Trail use fee: $2.50/day for adults and $2.00/day for children‡
Camping: None

General Information:
 State YMCA camp lodge available for groups of 25 or more during the
    fall, winter and spring seasons
 Rentals, warming area and instruction available
 Scenic views of Torch Lake from the trail
 Available to individuals on a day use basis
 ‡ Season passes are $7.50 for adults and $5.00 for children. Family and
    senior rates available

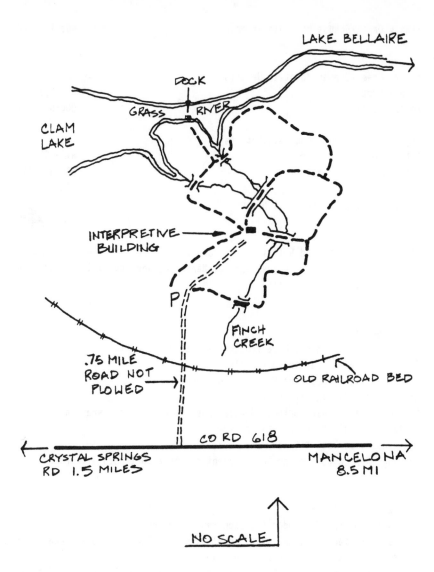

LAKE BELLAIRE

DOCK

GRASS RIVER

CLAM LAKE

INTERPRETIVE BUILDING

P

FINCH CREEK

.75 MILE ROAD NOT PLOWED

OLD RAILROAD BED

CO RD 618

CRYSTAL SPRINGS RD 1.5 MILES

MANCELONA 8.5 MI

NO SCALE

# GRASS RIVER NATURAL AREA

Grass Lake Natural Area                                    Revised: 4/01/88

Grass River Natural Area, Inc
PO Box 231                                                 616-533-8607
Bellaire, MI  49615-0231                                   616-533-8576*

Antrim Co. Soil Conservation District
PO Box 312                                                 616-533-8709
Bellaire, MI  49615-0312

Trail suitable for hiking & skiing

Location:
 Between Lake Bellaire and Clam Lake, 8.5 miles west of Mancelona
    via M88 and Co Rd 618 (Alden Hwy)
 1.5 miles east of Crystal Springs Rd. and .5 mile west of Comfort Rd. on
    Co Rd 618 (Alden Hwy).

Trail specifications:
   2 mi; 3 loop(s); Loop length(s)-.5, .5, 1
Typical terrain: Flat
Skiing ability suggested: Novice**
Hiking trail difficulty: Easy
Nordic trail grooming method: None**
Suitable for all-terrain bicycle: Not permitted
Trail use fee: None, donations accepted (tax deductible)
Camping: Not permitted
Drinking water available in summer only

General Information:
 Maintained by Grass Lake Natural Area, Inc a non profit corporation
 The Natural Area covers over 1,000 acres
 * Interpretive Center phone answered in the summer only
 ** Limited skiing because of narrow boardwalks.  Additional 5 miles of
    old railroad right-of-way from Crystal Springs Rd to Brake Rd. is
    available for skiing and hiking (closed to motorized vehicles)
 A .75 mile long access road from Co Rd 618 is not plowed
 Please leave your smoking, pets and food at home when visiting this
    natural area

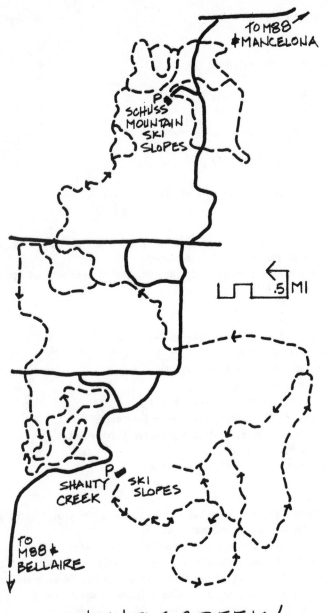

SHANTY CREEK/
SCHUSS MOUNTAIN RESORTS

Shanty Creek/Schuss Mountain Resorts          Revised: 11/29/87

Shanty Creek/Schuss Mountain Resorts
Shanty Creek Office                           616-533-8621
Bellaire, MI  49615                           800-632-7118

Shanty Creek/Schuss Mountain Resorts
Schuss Mountain Office                        616-587-9162
Mancelona, MI  49659                          800-632-7170

Trail suitable for skiing & hiking

Location:
 Between Mancelona and Bellaire north and east of M88 (follow signs)
 Shuss Mountain Resort is just west of Mancelona and Shanty Creek Lodge is
    just southeast of Bellaire

Trail specifications:
   50 km; Many loop(s); Loop length(s)-various
 Typical terrain: Flat to very hilly
 Skiing ability suggested: Novice to advanced
 Hiking trail difficulty: Easy to difficult
 Nordic trail grooming method: Single track with space for skating
 Suitable for all-terrain bicycle: Yes
 Trail use fee: Yes, $10/day
 Camping: KOA campground on M88 adjacent to the resort open all year

General Information:
 Privately operated 2 lodge 4 season resort system
 Lodging, restaurants, ski shops, pools(indoor/outdoor), saunas, snack bars
    rentals, lessons and everything else
 Site of the annual White Pine Stampede held the first Saturday of February
    each year
 This unique 2 lodge trail system allows for some very unique skiing
    opportunities with an interconnecting trail between the lodges for a
    full day of skiing
 Lighted 14.5 km trail

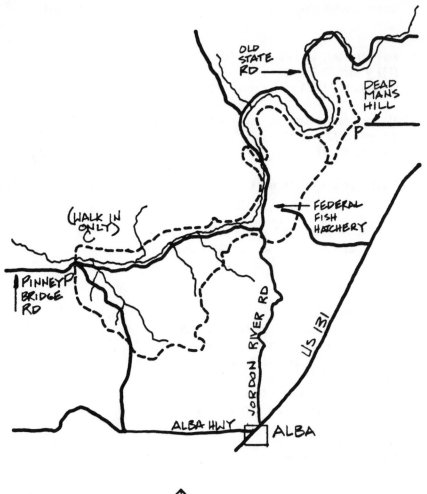

## JORDAN VALLEY PATHWAY

Jordan Valley Pathway                                    Revised: 4/15/88

Area Forester, Gaylord Forest Area
1732 West M32, PO Box 667                                517-732-3541
Gaylord, MI  49735

District Forest Manager, Mackinaw State Forest
Box 667, 1732 West M32                                   517-732-3541
Gaylord, MI  49735

Trail suitable for hiking only

Location:
  6 miles north of Mancelona and west of US131
  9 miles south of Boyne Falls
  Trailhead - 1.5 miles south of the intersection of M32 and US131, turn
      west on Deadmans Hill Rd. to overlook
  Trailhead - 2 miles west from M66 on Pinney Bridge Rd. to SF campground
Trail specifications:
    18 mi; 1 loop(s); Loop length(s)-18
Typical terrain: Very hilly
Skiing ability suggested: NOT DESIGNED FOR SKIING-VERY DANGEROUS
Hiking trail difficulty: Moderate to difficult
Nordic trail grooming method: NA
Suitable for all-terrain bicycle: Yes, most of trail
Trail use fee: None
Camping: At Pinney Bridge hike in campsite only
Drinking water available at campgrounds and fish hatchery

General Information:
 Maintained by the DNR Forest Management Division
 NOT SUITABLE FOR SKIING - TRAIL VERY STEEP WITH NO OUTRUNS
 One of the most scenic river valley's in the state
 The loop is most rewarding with an overnight stay at the hike-in
    campground.

Other contacts:
DNR Forest Management Division Office, Lansing, 517-373-1275
DNR Forest Management Region Office, Roscommon, 517-275-5151

149

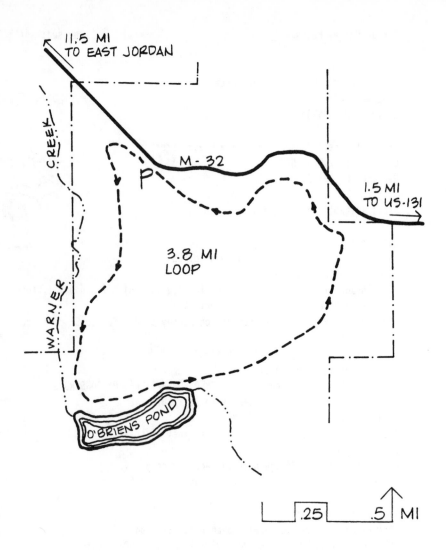

11.5 MI
TO EAST JORDAN

CREEK

M - 32

1.5 MI
TO US-131

3.8 MI
LOOP

WARNER

P

O'BRIENS POND

.25     .5 MI

# WARNER CREEK PATHWAY

Warner Creek Pathway                    Revised:  3/08/88

Area Forester, Gaylord Forest Area
1732 W M32, PO Box 667                   517-732-3541
Gaylord, MI  49735

District Forest Manager, Mackinaw State Forest
Box 667, 1732 West M32                   517-732-3541
Gaylord, MI  49735

Trail suitable for skiing & hiking

Location:
 Between US131 and East Jordan on M32
 Trailhead - 1.5 miles west of US131 on M32

Trail specifications:
   3.8 mi; 1 loop(s); Loop length(s)-3.8
Typical terrain: Flat to rolling hills
Skiing ability suggested: Novice to intermediate
Hiking trail difficulty: Easy
Nordic trail grooming method: Track set
Suitable for all-terrain bicycle: Yes
Trail use fee: None
Camping: None
Drinking water not available

General Information:
 Maintained by the DNR Forest Management Division
 Developed for skiers because the nearby Jordan Valley Pathway is not
   available for skiing

Other contacts:
 DNR Forest Management Division Office, Lansing, 517-373-1275
 DNR Forest Management Region Office, Roscommon, 517-275-5151

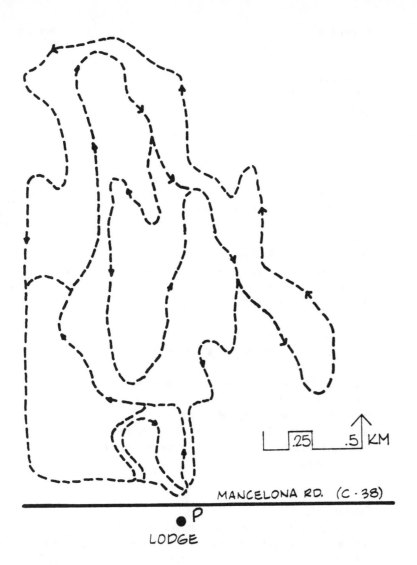

WILDERNESS VALLEY

MANCELONA RD. (C-38)

P

LODGE

.25    .5 KM

Wilderness Valley    Attn. Dave Smith
7519 Mancelona Rd.
Gaylord, MI  49735                    616-585-7141

Trail suitable for skiing only

Location:
  10 miles SW of Gaylord via Old US27 to the south end of Otsego Lake, then
      west on C-38(Mancelona Rd) 7 miles to the touring center
  Trailhead is on the north side of the road from the touring center

Trail specifications:
  40 km; 6 loop(s); Loop length(s)-1.6 to 20
Typical terrain: Rolling to very hilly
Skiing ability suggested: Novice to expert
Hiking trail difficulty: Easy to moderate
Nordic trail grooming method: Double track set daily with skating lane
Suitable for all-terrain bicycle: Yes
Trail use fee: $5.00/day with season passes available
Camping: None

General Information:
 Privately operated ski touring center
 Warming lodge, rentals, ski shop, restaurant and lodging is available
 A lighted 1.6 km trail is available on weekends
 The entire 2000 acre hardwood and pine forest is devoted exclusively to
  cross-country skiing
 Trails for skiers and bikers of all abilities on wooded trails
 Chalet rentals available
 Picnic area with stoves provided along the trail
 The well groomed trails were widened for the 88/89 season
 Hours 9am to dusk weekdays and 10pm on Friday and Saturday
 Host of the annual Winterstart race held the 2nd weekend of December
 Host of the annual Gaylord Winterfest races held the 2nd weekend
  in February

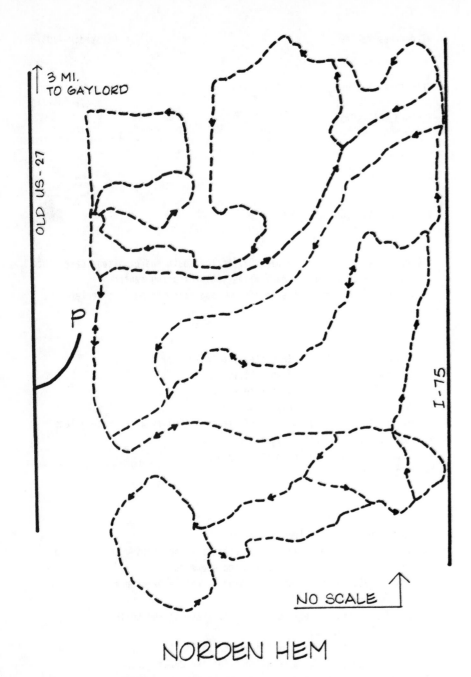

↑ 3 MI.
TO GAYLORD

OLD US - 27

P

I-75

NO SCALE ↑

NORDEN HEM

Norden Hem
4815 Historic 27, PO Box 623                          800-624-7518
Gaylord, MI  49735                                    517-732-6794

Trail suitable for hiking & skiing‡

Location:
 5 miles south of Gaylord
 I75 to exit 279, then south on Old 27 about 1.5 miles to the entrance on
    the east side of the road
 Formerly known as Ken Mar on the Hill

Trail specifications:
   28 km‡‡; Many loop(s); Loop length(s)-various
Typical terrain: Hilly
Skiing ability suggested: Novice to advanced
Hiking trail difficulty: Easy
Nordic trail grooming method: Track set
Suitable for all-terrain bicycle: Not permitted
Trail use fee: None, but limited to guests only ‡
Camping: None

General Information:
 Privately operated resort and conference center
 Extensively remodeled and expanded from the original Ken-Mar on the Hill
 Facilities include 32 jacuzzi suites, pool, sauna, whirlpool,
  exerise and tanning facilities. 8 double jacuzzi theme suites available.
 This trail system is a delight ski.  All trails are well groomed
    with 3.5 km are lighted.
 ‡ Trails are available only for overnight quests
 ‡‡ Expansion of the trail system is planned
 Lodges are elaborately decorated with theme decorating
 Four Diamond and AAA rated
 Breakfast included with each room
 Golf and ski packages available as well as group rates

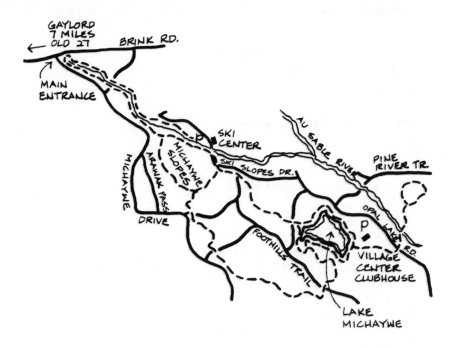

GAYLORD
7 MILES
OLD 27

BRINK RD.

MAIN
ENTRANCE

MICHAYWE DRIVE

ARAWIAK PASS

MICHAYWE SLOPES

P SKI CENTER

SKI SLOPES DR.

AU SABLE RIVER

PINE RIVER TR.

FOOTHILLS TRAIL

OPAL LAKE RD.

P

VILLAGE CENTER CLUBHOUSE

LAKE MICHAYWE

NO SCALE

# MICHAYWE SLOPES

Michaywe Slopes                    Revised:  2/03/88


Michaywe Slopes    Attn. Stan Stock
1535 Opal Lake Rd.                          517-939-8919
Gaylord, MI  49735                          517-939-8800

Trail suitable for skiing only

Location:
  7 miles south of Gaylord on old US27, then east on Charles Brink Rd
    to Michaywe main entrance, then follow signs to Ski Center at the
    base of the alpine slopes


Trail specifications:
  16.5 km; 6 loop(s); Loop length(s)-various
Typical terrain: Flat to very hilly
Skiing ability suggested: Novice to intermediate
Hiking trail difficulty: NA
Nordic trail grooming method: Double track set
Suitable for all-terrain bicycle: NA
Trail use fee: $3.00/day
Camping: Available on site and at a nearby KOA
Drinking water available

General Information:
  Privately operated alpine and nordic resort
  Lessons, rentals, lodging, restaurant, snack bar, entertainment and bar
  Telemark area with lifts and lessons available
  Very nice well groomed trail system
  Light trail on weekends

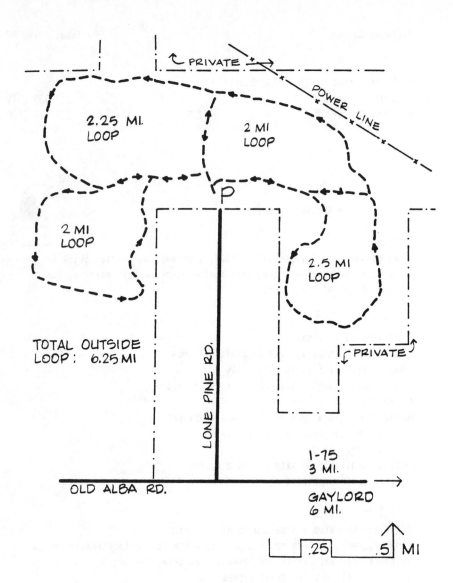

TOTAL OUTSIDE
LOOP: 6.25 MI.

2.25 MI. LOOP

2 MI LOOP

2 MI LOOP

2.5 MI LOOP

P

LONE PINE RD.

PRIVATE

POWER LINE

PRIVATE

I-75
3 MI.

GAYLORD
6 MI.

OLD ALBA RD.

.25    .5 MI

# PINE BARON PATHWAY

Pine Baron Pathway                                    Revised: 3/06/88

Area Forester, Gaylord Forest Area
PO Box 667, 1732 West M32                              517-732-3541
Gaylord, MI  49735

District Forest Manager, Mackinaw State Forest
Box 667, 1732 West M32                                517-732-3541
Gaylord, MI  49735

Trail suitable for skiing & hiking

Location:
 West of Gaylord and south of M32
 Trailhead - West from I75 at the south Gaylord exit 279 on Alba Rd. 2.4
   miles to Lone Pine Rd., then right (north) to the end of the road

Trail specifications:
  8.75 mi; 4 loop(s); Loop length(s)-2, 2, 2.25, 2.5
Typical terrain: Flat
Skiing ability suggested: Novice only
Hiking trail difficulty: Easy
Nordic trail grooming method: Double track set
Suitable for all-terrain bicycle: Yes
Trail use fee: None
Camping: Camground available at Otsego Lake State Park and private campgrounds
Drinking water not available

General Information:
 Maintained by the DNR Forest Management Division
 Forested trail system of second growth trees
 No steep hills on the trail.  Good for the beginning skier
 Pit toilet at parking lot

Other contacts:
DNR Forest Management Division Office, Lansing, 517-373-1275
DNR Forest Management Region Office, Roscommon, 517-275-5151

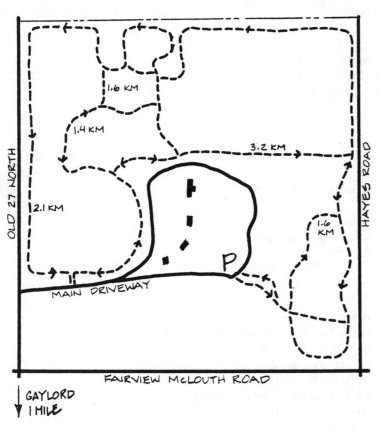

OLD 27 NORTH

1.6 KM

1.4 KM

3.2 KM

HAYES ROAD

2.1 KM

1.6 KM

P

MAIN DRIVEWAY

FAIRVIEW McLOUTH ROAD

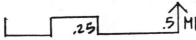

GAYLORD
1 MILE

.25 | .5 MI

# ALPINE CENTER TRAILS

Alpine Center Trails

Revised: 4/01/88

Otsego County Parks and Recreation Commission
225 W. Main St.
Gaylord, MI  49735

517-732-6484

Trail suitable for skiing & hiking

Location:
 1 mile north of Gaylord on Old US23

Trail specifications:
   10 km; 4 loop(s); Loop length(s)-various
Typical terrain: Flat to rolling
Skiing ability suggested: Novice to intermediate
Hiking trail difficulty: Easy
Nordic trail grooming method: Packed 2 to 3 times/week
Suitable for all-terrain bicycle: Yes
Trail use fee: None
Camping: None
Drinking water not available

General Information:
 Maintained by the Otsego County Parks and Recreation Department
 Signs designating tree species of northern hardwoods are along the
   trails
 Benches provided along the trail

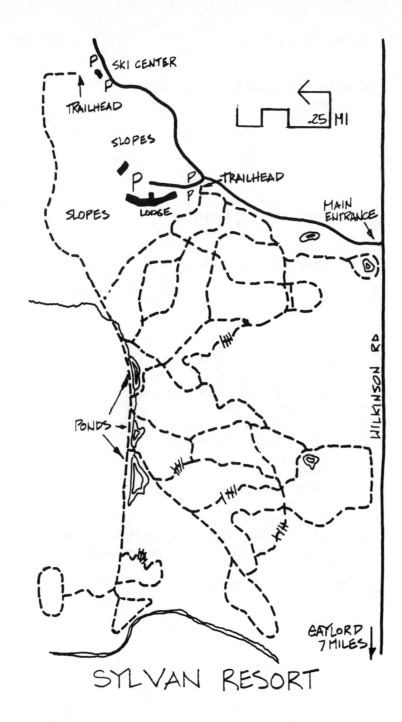

SYLVAN RESORT

Sylvan Resort
3962 Wilkinson Rd.                              800-368-4133
Gaylord, MI  49735

Trail suitable for skiing & hiking

Location:
 7 miles east of Gaylord via M32 and Wilkinson Rd (follow signs).

Trail specifications:
   15 km; Many loop(s); Loop length(s)-various
Typical terrain: Flat to hilly
Skiing ability suggested: Novice to advanced
Hiking trail difficulty: Easy to moderate
Nordic trail grooming method: Double track set
Suitable for all-terrain bicycle: Not permitted
Trail use fee: Yes
Camping: None

General Information:
 Privately operated full service alpine ski area
 All services available including instruction, rentals, ski shop,
   128 room hotel, entertainment and complete food service
 2.5 km lighted trail available
 Most of the trails are on golf course fairways but the terrain is very
   hilly and protected from the wind. The open very steep slopes of the
   fairways are excellent for telemarking
 There are several hilly wooded trails between the fairways and around the
   golf course that make for a very interesting trail system
 A different kind of trail system that allows for a full variety of
   techniques including telemarking, classic and skating.  A great place
   to spend a day on well groomed trails.
 A very complete 4 color trail map is provided.

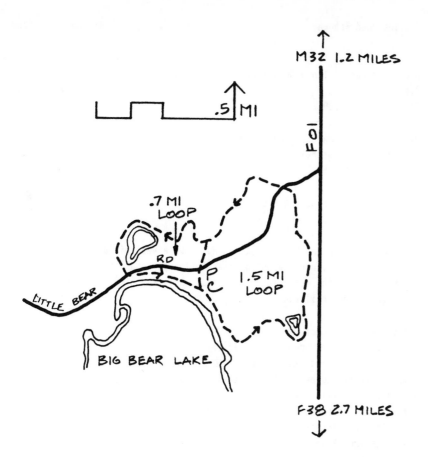

M32 1.2 MILES

.5 MI

.7 MI
LOOP

F 0 1

1.5 MI
LOOP

LITTLE BEAR

R
RD

P
C

BIG BEAR LAKE

F38 2.7 MILES

BIG BEAR LAKE NATURE PATHWAY

Big Bear Lake Nature Pathway                    Revised: 4/15/88

Area Forester, Gaylord Forest Area
Box 667, 1732 West M32                          517-732-3541
Gaylord, MI  49735

District Forest Manager, Mackinaw State Forest
Box 667, 1732 West M32                          517-732-3541
Gaylord, MI  49735

Trail suitable for hiking only

Location:
 Take M32 east from Gaylord to Co Rd 495 (Meridian Line Rd.), then south
   about 1.5 miles to the state forest campground

Trail specifications:
   2.2 mi; 2 loop(s); Loop length(s)-1.1, 1.5
Typical terrain: Flat to rolling
Skiing ability suggested: NA
Hiking trail difficulty: Novice
Nordic trail grooming method: NA
Suitable for all-terrain bicycle: Yes
Trail use fee: None
Camping: Campground at trailhead
Drinking water available

General Information:
 Maintainted by the DNR Forest Management Division
 Trail follows the shore of Big Bear Lake and through the Big Bear Lake
   State Forest Campground
 A beaver lodge is visable along the trail

Other contacts:
DNR Forest Management Division Office, Lansing, 517-373-1275
DNR Forest Management Region Office, Roscommon, 517-275-5151

157

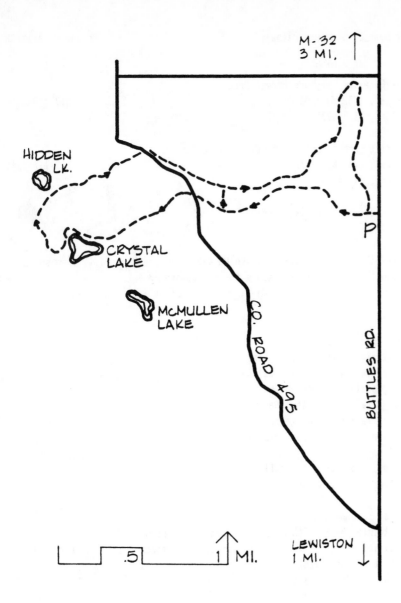

HIDDEN LK.

CRYSTAL LAKE

McMULLEN LAKE

CO. ROAD 495

BUTTLES RD.

M-32
3 MI.

P

LEWISTON
1 MI.

.5    1 MI.

# BUTTLES ROAD PATHWAY

Buttles Road Pathway                         Revised: 4/15/88

Area Forester, Atlanta Area Forest
Rte 1, Box 30                                517-785-4251
Atlanta, MI  49709

District Forest Manager, Mackinaw State Forest
Box 667, 1732 West M32                       517-732-3541
Gaylord, MI  49735

Trail suitable for hiking & skiing

Location:
 Between Lewiston and M32 on Buttles Rd.(1 mile west of Co Rd 491)
 Take Buttles Rd., north about 3 miles to the parking lot at the
   trailhead on the west side of the road.  Ellsworth Rd. is about 1 mile
   north of the trailhead

Trail specifications:
   7 mi; 2 loop(s); Loop length(s)-3.5, 7
Typical terrain: Flat to rolling
Skiing ability suggested: Novice to intermediate
Hiking trail difficulty: Easy
Nordic trail grooming method: Track set
Suitable for all-terrain bicycle: Yes
Trail use fee: None
Camping: None
Drinking water not available

General Information:
 Maintained by the DNR Forest Management Division

Other contacts:
DNR Forest Management Division Office, Lansing, 517-373-1275
DNR Forest Management Region Office, Roscommon, 517-275-5151

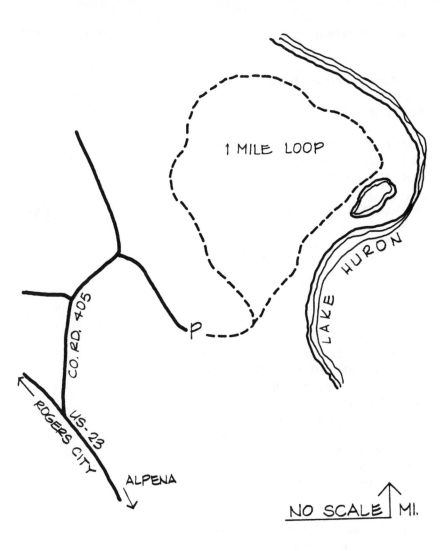

1 MILE LOOP

LAKE HURON

CO. RD. 405

US-23

ROGERS CITY

ALPENA

P

NO SCALE ↑ MI.

BESSER BELL PATHWAY

Area Forester, Atlanta Forest Area
Rte 1, Box 30                                    517-785-4251
Atlanta, MI  49709

District Forest Manager, Mackinaw State Forest
Box 667, 1732 West M32                           517-732-3541
Gaylord, MI  49735

Trail suitable for hiking only

Location:
 Between Alpena and Rogers City
 From US23, about 8 miles north of Alpena to Co Rd 405 (Grand Lake Rd.)
   near Lakewood, then north on Co Rd 405 to parking lot


Trail specifications:
   1 mi; 1 loop(s); Loop length(s)-1
Typical terrain: Flat to slightly rolling
Skiing ability suggested: NA
Hiking trail difficulty: Easy
Nordic trail grooming method: None
Suitable for all-terrain bicycle: Yes
Trail use fee: None
Camping: None
Drinking water availalble

General Information:
 Maintained by the DNR Forest Management Division
 This is a nature with several points of interest
 Trail passes near the site of the former village of Bell that once
   was a logging town of about 100 people

Other contacts:
DNR Forest Management Division Office, Lansing, 517-373-1275
DNR Forest Management Region Office, Roscommon, 517-275-5151

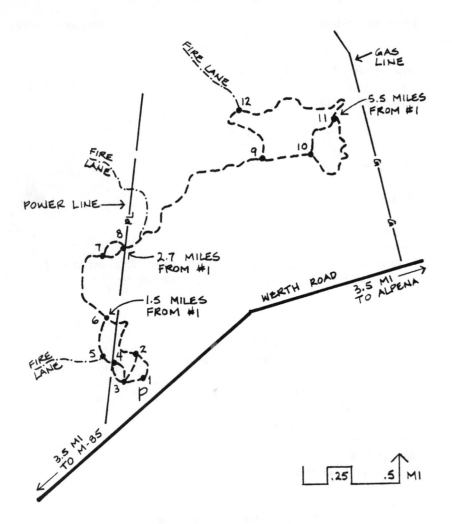

FIRE LANE

GAS LINE

12

5.5 MILES FROM #1

11

FIRE LANE

9    10

POWER LINE →

8

7

2.7 MILES FROM #1

1.5 MILES FROM #1

6

WERTH ROAD

3.5 MI TO ALPENA

FIRE LANE

5    4    2

3    1

P

3.5 MI TO M-85

| .25 | .5 | MI

NORWAY RIDGE PATHWAY

Area Forester, Atlanta Forest Area
Rte 1, Box 30                                    517-785-4251
Atlanta, MI  49709

District Forest Manager, Mackinaw State Forest
PO Box 667, 1732 West M32                         517-732-3541
Gaylord, MI  49735

Trail suitable for skiing & hiking

Location:
 4.5 miles SW of Alpena on Werth Road

Trail specifications:
   7 mi; 3 loop(s); Loop length(s)-various
Typical terrain: Flat to slightly rolling
Skiing ability suggested: Novice
Hiking trail difficulty: Easy
Nordic trail grooming method: Track set
Suitable for all-terrain bicycle: Yes
Trail use fee: None
Camping: None
Drinking water is not available

General Information:
 Maintained by the DNR Forest Management Division
 Very popular with the local skiers

Other contacts:
 DNR Forest Management Division Office, Lansing, 517-373-1275
 DNR Forest Management Region Office, Roscommon, 517-275-5151

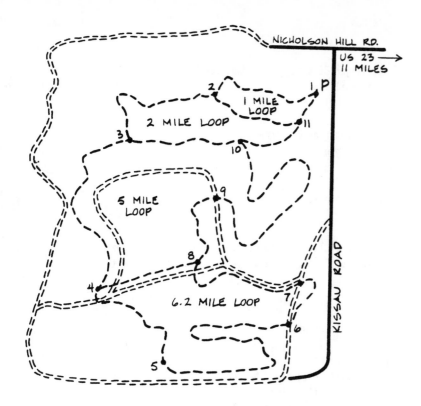

NICHOLSON HILL RD.

US 23 →
11 MILES

1 P

2

1 MILE LOOP

11

2 MILE LOOP

3

10

9

5 MILE LOOP

8

KISSAU ROAD

4

7

6.2 MILE LOOP

6

5

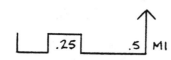

.25    .5 MI

# CHIPPEWA HILLS PATHWAY

Chippewa Hills Pathway                    Revised:  3/05/88

Fire Officer, Mackinaw State Forest
4343 M32 West                             517-354-2209
Alpena, MI  49707

District Forest Manager, Mackinaw State Forest
Box 667, 1732 West M32                    517-732-3541
Gaylord, MI  49735

Trail suitable for skiing & hiking

Location:
 Between Harrisville and Alpena, 11 miles west of Ossineke (US23) on
   Nicholson Hill Rd.
 Trailhead - Just south of Nicholson Hill Rd. on Kissau Rd. Overflow
   parking available on Nicholson Hill Rd., just west of Kissau Rd.

Trail specifications:
  6.6 mi; 4 loop(s); Loop length(s)-1, 2, 5, 6.2
Typical terrain: Flat to hilly
Skiing ability suggested: Novice to intermediate
Hiking trail difficulty: Easy
Nordic trail grooming method: Track set with a double track
Suitable for all-terrain bicycle: Yes
Trail use fee: None
Camping: None
Drinking water is not available

General Information:
 Maintained by the DNR Forest Management Division
 Deer often seen along trail
 Waxing and sitting benches provided along trail
 Trail maps and directional arrows at all intersections
 Scenic overlook along trail

Other contacts:
 DNR Forest Management Division Office, Lansing, 517-373-1275
 DNR Forest Management Region Office, Roscommon, 517-275-5151

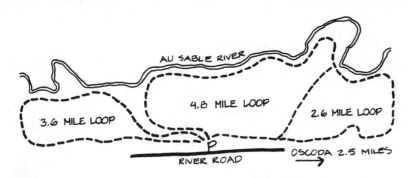

AU SABLE RIVER

3.6 MILE LOOP

4.8 MILE LOOP

2.6 MILE LOOP

RIVER ROAD

OSCODA 2.5 MILES

NO SCALE

EAGLE RUN

Eagle Run                                        Revised:  5/23/88

Tawas Ranger Distict, Huron-Manistee National Forest
Federal Building                                 517-362-4477
East Tawas, MI  48730

Oscoda Chamber of Commerce
100 W Michigan                                   800-235-4625
Oscoda, MI  48750

Trail suitable for skiing & hiking

Location:
 NW from East Tawas on Monument Rd. to River Rd., then east 13 miles, or
    west from Oscoda 2 1/2 miles on River Rd. to the trail


Trail specifications:
   10.5 mi; 3 loop(s); Loop length(s)-2.6, 3.6, 4.8
Typical terrain: Flat
Skiing ability suggested: Novice
Hiking trail difficulty: Easy
Nordic trail grooming method: Track set
Suitable for all-terrain bicycle: Not permitted
Trail use fee: None
Camping: None
Drinking water is not available

General Information:
 Maintained by the Huron-Manistee National Forest with community support
 Scenic views of the Au Sable River from the trail
 Nordic Sports Ski Shop, 218 West Bay St., East Tawas,  362-2001
 For information contact the Oscoda Chamber of Commerce (see above)

162

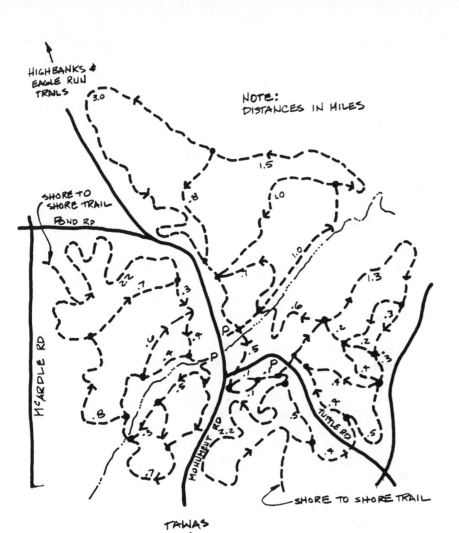

HIGHBANKS &
EAGLE RUN
TRAILS

3.0

1.5

NOTE:
DISTANCES IN MILES

SHORE TO
SHORE TRAIL
FOND RD

.8

1.0

1.0

1.0

1.3

.7

.2.2

.7

.3

.6

.3

.9

.5

.2

.3

.5

.8

.3

.3

.4

.8

MCARDLE RD

MONUMENT RD
2.2

TUTTLE RD

.5

.5

.7

.5

.4

SHORE TO SHORE TRAIL

TAWAS

.25 .5 1 MI

CORSAIR TRAILS

Corsair Ski Council
PO Box 608                                          800-55TAWAS
Tawas City, MI  48763                               517-362-8643

Tawas Ranger District, Huron-Manistee National Forest
Federal Building                                    517-362-4477
East Tawas, MI  48730

Trail suitable for skiing & hiking

Location:
 From M55 & US23 intersection take M55 west about .8 mile to Wilbur Rd,
   then north on Wilbur Rd to 1.2 miles to Monument Rd, then NW on
   Monument Rd about 7 miles to trails
 Trailheads on both sides of the road for the 3 systems, Corsair,
   Wright's Lake and Silver Valley
Trail specifications:
   26+ mi; Many loop(s); Loop length(s)-various
Typical terrain: Flat to very hilly
Skiing ability suggested: Novice to advanced
Hiking trail difficulty: Easy to moderate
Nordic trail grooming method: Track set with skating space on some sections
Suitable for all-terrain bicycle: Yes, excellent area
Trail use fee: None
Camping: Check with the tourist bureau
Drinking water available

General Information:
 Developed by the local community in cooperation with the Huron-Manistee
   National Forest
 An excellent trail system for all skill levels
 The Silver Valley section is the site of an old toboggan and alpine ski
   area of the 1940's
 Site of the annual Silver Creek Challenge citizen race held the last
   Saturday of January each year
 Excellent lodging packages are available from the local motels
 Rentals and ski equipment are available from Nordic Sports in East Tawas
   at 218 West Bay St., 517-362-2001
 Just south of the Highbanks Trail overlooking the Au Sable River
 Write or call the tourist bureau for lodging information and
   reservations

163

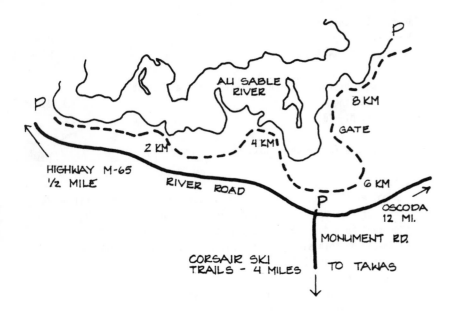

P

P

AU SABLE
RIVER

8 KM

GATE

2 KM

4 KM

HIGHWAY M-65
½ MILE

RIVER ROAD

6 KM

P

OSCODA
12 MI.

MONUMENT RD.

CORSAIR SKI
TRAILS - 4 MILES

TO TAWAS

NO SCALE

## HIGHBANKS TRAIL

Corsair Ski Council
PO Box 608                                          800-55TAWAS
Tawas City, MI  48763

Tawas Ranger District, Huron-Manistee National Forest
Federal Building                                    517-362-4477
East Tawas, MI  48730

Trail suitable for skiing & hiking

Location:
 Take Monument Rd. past the Corsair Trails✷ north until it ends at River Rd

  The trailhead is in the parking lot directly across from that
  intersection.

Trail specifications:
 10 km; No✷✷ loop(s); Loop length(s)-NA
Typical terrain: Flat
Skiing ability suggested: Novice to intermediate
Hiking trail difficulty: Easy to moderate
Nordic trail grooming method: Track set
Suitable for all-terrain bicycle: NA
Trail use fee: None
Camping: None
Drinking water not available

General Information:
 Developed by the local community in cooperation with the Huron-Manistee
  National Forest
 The trail is rather flat but the scenery of the Au Sable River is
  outstanding
 The Lumbermans Monument is located at he trailhead
 ✷ See Corsair Trails listing
 ✷✷  A point to point trail

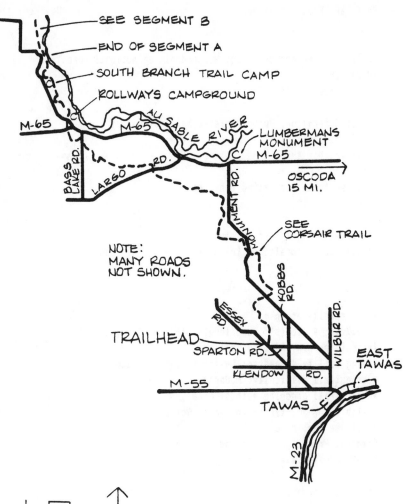

SEE SEGMENT B
END OF SEGMENT A
SOUTH BRANCH TRAIL CAMP
ROLLWAYS CAMPGROUND

M-65
M-65
AU SABLE RIVER
LUMBERMANS MONUMENT
M-65
OSCODA 15 MI.

BASS LAKE RD.
LARGO RD.
MONUMENT RD.

SEE CORSAIR TRAIL

NOTE:
MANY ROADS
NOT SHOWN.

KOBBS RD.

ESSEX RD.
WILBUR RD.

TRAILHEAD
SPARTON RD.
KLENDOW RD.

EAST TAWAS

M-55

TAWAS

M-23

2   4 MI

SHORE TO SHORE TRAIL
SEGMENT A

Tawas Ranger District
Huron-Manistee National Forest                517-362-4477
East Tawas, MI  48730

Forest Supervisor, Huron-Manistee National Forest
421 S. Mitchell St.                          616-775-2421
Cadillac, MI  49601

Trail suitable for hiking & skiing

Location:
 From Tawas to a point near the Au Sable River at the South Branch Trail
   Camp
 Trail also passes through the Corsair Trail system

Trail specifications:
   25 mi; No loop(s); Loop length(s)-NA
 Typical terrain: Flat to rolling
 Skiing ability suggested: Advanced
 Hiking trail difficulty: Easy to moderate
 Nordic trail grooming method: None
 Suitable for all-terrain bicycle: Yes, some sections
 Trail use fee: None
 Camping: Campgrounds along the trail *
 Drinking water available along the trail **

General Information:
 Maintained by the Tawas Ranger District, Huron-Manistee National Forest
 * Campgrounds at Rollways and South Branch with wilderness camping
   pemitted more than 200' from the trail
 ** Drinking water available at the campgrounds and at Corsair and
   Rollways Picnic Areas
 For maps of the entire trail contact: Michigan Trail Riders Association
  Chamber of Commerce, Traverse City, MI 49684   616-947-5075
 The trail is also used as a horseback riding trail
 Can be used for backcountry skiing for experienced skiers with winter
   survival skills

165

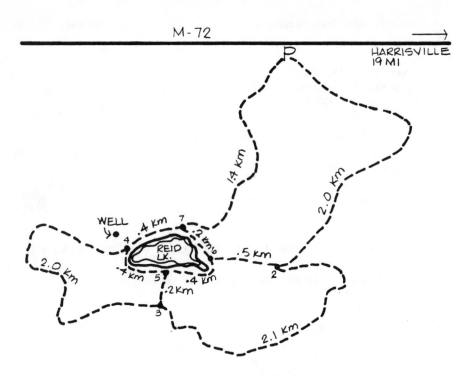

M-72

HARRISVILLE
19 MI

P

WELL

.4 Km   7
.2 km
4
REID LK.
1.4 km
2.0 Km
2.0 Km
.5 km
.4 Km   5
2
.4 km
.2 Km
3
2.1 Km

.25    .5    1 MI

# REID LAKE FOOT TRAVEL AREA

Reid Lake Foot Travel Area                    Revised: 11/21/87

Harrisville Ranger District, Huron-Manistee National Forest
PO Box 289                                    517-724-6471
Harrisville, MI  48740

Forest Supervisor, Huron-Manistee National Forest
421 S. Mitchell St.                           616-775-2421
Cadillac, MI  49601

Trail suitable for skiing & hiking

Location:
 19 miles west of Harrisville on M72
 Trailhead is located on the south side of the road

Trail specifications:
   9.7 km; 4 loop(s); Loop length(s)-2.25, 3.25, 5, 4.5
Typical terrain: Flat to rolling
Skiing ability suggested: Novice to intermediate
Hiking trail difficulty: Moderate
Nordic trail grooming method: None
Suitable for all-terrain bicycle: Not permitted
Trail use fee: None
Camping: Primitive campground available
Drinking water available

General Information:
 Maintained by the Harrisville Ranger District, Huron-Manistee
   National Forest
 Pleasant area for back country skiing and hiking
 Near the Hoist Lakes Foot Travel Area

## Map

**F32 (FR 4516)**

2¼ MI.

2¼ MI.

1¾ MI.

4

3

M 72/65

5

¼ MI.

¼ MI.

½ MI.

6

P

8

½ MI.

WATER

1 MI.

NO NAME LK.

11

½ MI.

12

PENOYER LK.

¾ MI.

2

WATER

¾ MI.

M 72

9 10

1¾ MI.

BYRON LAKE

1 MI.

W. HOIST LK.

14

1½ MI.

1

2½ MI.

13

S HOIST LK.

W. HOIST LK.

HARRISVILLE 22 MILES ON M72

FR 4119

GLENNIE 7 MILES

1 MI

# HOIST LAKE
# FOOT TRAVEL AREA

Harrisville Ranger District, Huron-Manistee National Forest
PO Box 289                                               517-724-6471
Harrisville, MI  48740

Forest Supervisor, Huron-Manistee National Forest
421 S. Mitchell St.                                      616-775-2421
Cadillac, MI  49601

Trail suitable for skiing & hiking

Location:
  22 miles west of Harrisville on M72 at M65 Jct.
  East trailhead - .25 mile south of Jct on M65
  West trailhead - On F32(FR4516) just north of the Au Sable Rd
    intersection

Trail specifications:
  32.3 km; Many loop(s); Loop length(s)-various
Typical terrain: Rolling to hilly
Skiing ability suggested: Intermediate to advanced
Hiking trail difficulty: Moderate to difficult
Nordic trail grooming method: None
Suitable for all-terrain bicycle: Not permitted
Trail use fee: None
Camping: Off trail camping permitted
Drinking water is available in the area at points 2 & 8

General Information:
  Maintained by the Harrisville Ranger District, Huron-Manistee NF
  An extensive area of 10,600 acres restricted for use by hikers, skiers
    and snowshoers only
  Write for brochure

167

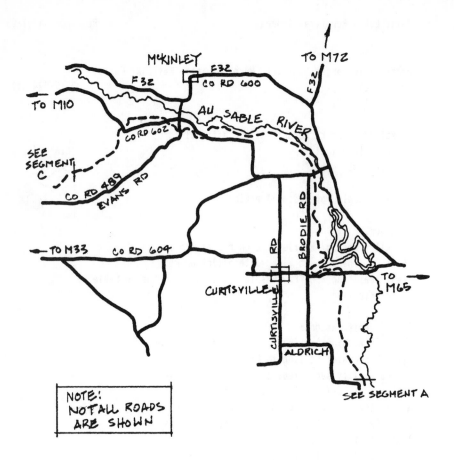

NOTE:
NOT ALL ROADS
ARE SHOWN

2  4 MI

SHORE TO SHORE TRAIL
SEGMENT B

Harrisville Ranger District, Huron-Manistee National Forest
PO Box 289                                        517-724-6471
Harrisville, MI  48740

Forest Supervisor, Huron-Manistee National Forest
421 S. Mitchell St.                               616-775-2421
Cadillac, MI  49601

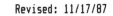

Trail suitable for hiking & skiing

Location:
 From the Iosco Co line near the Au Sable River west to a point about
   4 miles SW of McKinley near Co Rd 602
 McKinley Trail Camp-From Mio east on Co Rd 602 for 9 miles to the camp
 Trail access-From M65 in Glennie take Bamfield Rd west 6 miles to the
   Curtisville Store.  The trail is across the road from the store
Trail specifications:
   22 mi; No loop(s); Loop length(s)-NA
Typical terrain: Rolling
Skiing ability suggested: Advanced
Hiking trail difficulty: Moderate
Nordic trail grooming method: None
Suitable for all-terrain bicycle: No
Trail use fee: None
Camping: McKinley Trail Camp and wilderness camping permitted
Drinking water not available along this section

General Information:
 Maintained by the Harrisville Ranger District, Huron-Manistee National
   Forest and the Michigan Trail Riders Association
 Can be used for backcountry skiing for experienced skiers with good
   winter survival skills
 A significant section of the trail follows the ridge along the Au Sable
   River
 Several wood bridges cross streams along the trail
 For maps of the entire trail contact: Michigan Trail Riders Association,
   Chamber of Commerce, Traverse City, MI 49684   616-947-5075
 Used for horseback riding

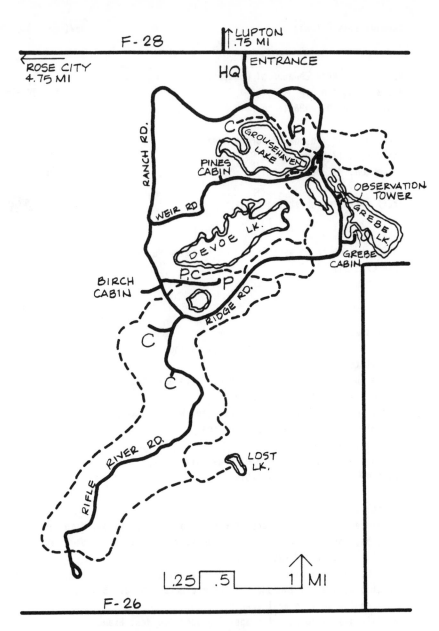

F-28

LUPTON
.75 MI

ROSE CITY
4.75 MI

ENTRANCE

HQ

RANCH RD.

GROUSEHAVEN LAKE

C

PINES CABIN

OBSERVATION TOWER

WEIR RD.

GREBE LK.

DEVOE LK.

GREBE CABIN

BIRCH CABIN

P.C.

P

RIDGE RD.

C

C

RIFLE RIVER RD.

LOST LK.

.25  .5    1 MI

F-26

RIFLE RIVER
RECREATION AREA

Rifle River Recreation Area

Revised: 11/21/87

Rifle River Recreation Area
2550 East Rose City Rd
Lupton, MI  48635

517-437-2258

DNR Parks Division Office

517-373-1270

Trail suitable for hiking only‡

Location:
 4.75 miles east of Rose City on F28 (Rose City Rd)

Trail specifications:
    11 mi; Several loop(s); Loop length(s)-various
Typical terrain: Flat to very hilly
Skiing ability suggested: NA
Hiking trail difficulty: Easy to moderate
Nordic trail grooming method: NA
Suitable for all-terrain bicycle: Yes
Trail use fee: None, but vehicle entry fee required $2/day, $10/year
Camping: Campground in recreation area
Drinking water available

General Information:
 Maintained by the DNR Parks Division
 Extensive trail system
 Excellent for wildlife observations
 ‡ Because of the very steep hills and sharp corners that were
   constructed only for hiking these trails are not available suitabler
   cross country skiing

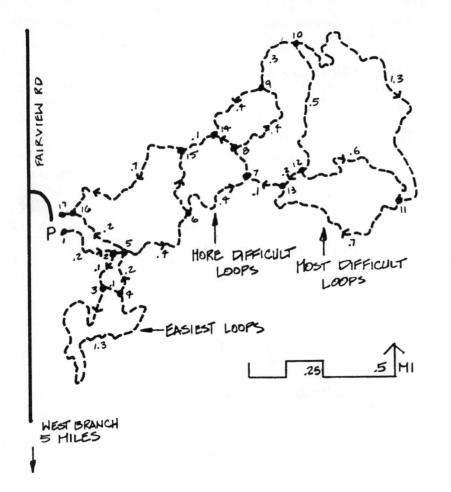

FAIRVIEW RD

P

MORE DIFFICULT LOOPS

MOST DIFFICULT LOOPS

EASIEST LOOPS

.25      .5 MI

WEST BRANCH
5 MILES

# OGEMAW HILLS PATHWAY

Ogemaw Hills Pathway                    Revised:  3/05/88

West Branch Area Chamber of Commerce
422 W. Houghton Ave                     517-345-2821
West Branch, MI  48661

Area Forester, Roscommon Forest Area
Box 218, 8717 N. Roscommon Rd.         517-275-5151
Roscommon, MI  48653

Trail suitable for skiing only

Location:
 5.5 miles north of West Branch on Fairview Rd. (F7)
 Use exit 212 off I75

Trail specifications:
   9.2 mi; 7 loop(s); Loop length(s)-various
Typical terrain: Hilly
Skiing ability suggested: Intermediate to advanced
Hiking trail difficulty: Moderate
Nordic trail grooming method: Track set weekly
Suitable for all-terrain bicycle: Yes
Trail use fee: None
Camping: Available in the area seasonally
Drinking water is not available

General Information:
 Developed by the West Branch Kiwanis and Optimist Clubs, Michigan Youth
   Corps, DNR, Ogemaw Ski Council and many local volunteers
 Maintained by the Ogemaw Ski Council
 Well designed, marked and groomed trail system
 Lodging at Quality Inn and Tri Terrace Motel in West Branch
 Many restaurants in West Branch
 Rentals available at J & P Sporting Goods in West Branch

 DNR Forest Management Division Office, Lansing, 518-373-1275
 DNR Forest Management District Office, Mio, 517-826-3211
 DNR Forest Management Region Office, Roscommon, 517-275-5151

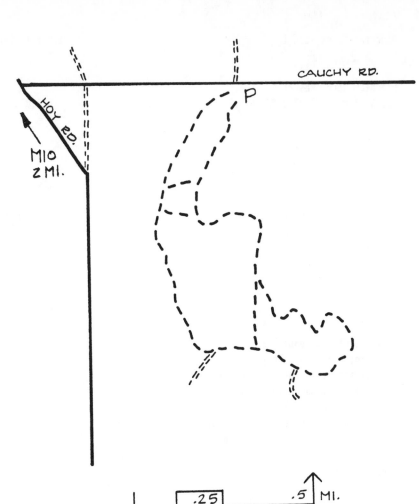

## LOUD CREEK
## CROSS COUNTRY SKI TRAIL

CAUCHY RD.

HOY RD.

MIO
2 MI.

P

.25     .5 MI.

Mio Ranger District, Huron-Manistee National Forest
401 Court St.                                          517-826-3252
Mio, MI  48647

Forest Supervisor, Huron-Manistee National Forest
421 S. Mitchell St.                                    616-775-2421
Cadillac, MI  49601

Trail suitable for skiing & hiking

Location:
 From East 14th St. in Mio, south 1 mile on Hoy Rd., then east .5 mile on
   Cauchy Rd. to parking lot

Trail specifications:
   3 mi; 4 loop(s); Loop length(s)-.6, .7, 1.7, 2.2
Typical terrain: Rolling to hilly
Skiing ability suggested: Intermediate
Hiking trail difficulty: Easy
Nordic trail grooming method: Packed
Suitable for all-terrain bicycle: No
Trail use fee: None
Camping: Backcountry camping permitted
Drinking water not available

General Information:
 Maintained by the Mio Ranger District, Huron-Manistee National Forest
 A total of 12 miles of ski loops are planned for this system in coming
   years
 The trail system will be designed for the intermediate to advanced skier
 These original loops have been built by labor from the Camp Lehman
   Correctional Facility.  Additional mils will be added through
   volunteer efforts.

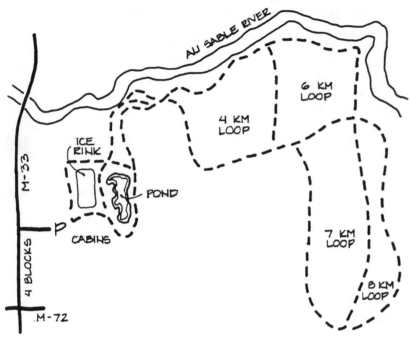

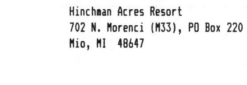

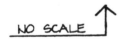

HINCHMAN ACRES RESORT

NO SCALE

Hinchman Acres Resort
702 N. Morenci (M33), PO Box 220                    517-826-3267
Mio, MI  48647

Trail suitable for skiing & hiking

Location:
 North end of Mio, just south of the Au Sable River on the east side
  of M33

Trail specifications:
   20 km; 6 loop(s); Loop length(s)-1 to 8
Typical terrain: Flat to slightly rolling
Skiing ability suggested: Novice
Hiking trail difficulty: Easy
Nordic trail grooming method: Double track set
Suitable for all-terrain bicycle: Not permitted
Trail use fee: $3.00/day, free if staying at the resort
Camping: None

General Information:
 Privately operated 4 season resort
 Warming area, snack bar, lodging, rentals, ski shop and night skiing
 Ice skating rink on the property
 Lodging available - 13 cottages, 6 with fireplaces
 Scenic trails in the Huron National Forest with spectacular views of
   the Au Sable River.
 Free rental, no trail fee and free instruction when staying at the resort.
   Call for more information on these "special packages"
 AAA approved resort
 Operated since 1933

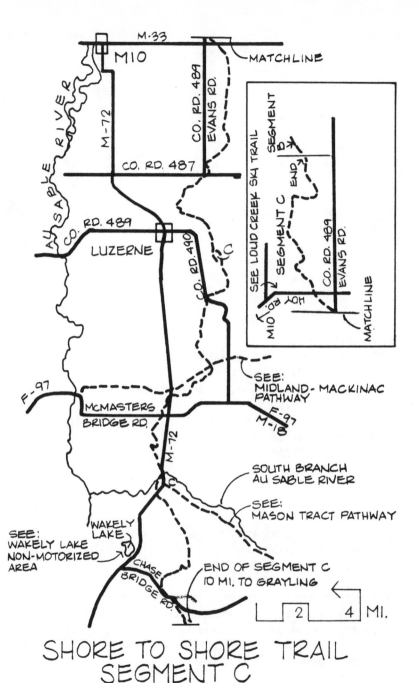

SHORE TO SHORE TRAIL
SEGMENT C

Mio Ranger District, Huron-Manistee National Forest
401 Court St.                                      517-826-3252
Mio, MI  48647

Forest Supervisor, Huron-Manistee National Forest
421 S. Mitchell St.                               616-775-2421
Cadillac, MI  49601

Trail suitable for hiking & skiing

Location:
  From a point 6 miles SE of Mio to about 8 miles SE of Grayling
  Luzerne Trail Camp-Mio west on M72 8 miles to Luzerne, then south on
    Co Rd 490 for 2 miles, then continue on FR 4153 for 1 mile to the camp


Trail specifications:
  41 mi; No loop(s); Loop length(s)-NA
Typical terrain: Rolling
Skiing ability suggested: Advanced
Hiking trail difficulty: Moderate
Nordic trail grooming method: None
Suitable for all-terrain bicycle: No
Trail use fee: None
Camping: Campground at Luzerne Trail Camp and backcountry camping permitted
Drinking water is available at the Luzerne Trail Camp

General Information:
  Maintained by the Mio Ranger District, Huron-Manistee National Forest
    and the Michigan Trail Riders Association
  For maps of the entire Trail contact: Michigan Trail Riders Association,
    Chamber of Commerce, Traverse City, MI 49684
  Trail used for horseback riding
  Can be used for backcountry skiing for experienced skiers only with good
    winter survival skills
  Trail crosses several creeks and the South Branch of the AuSable River

173

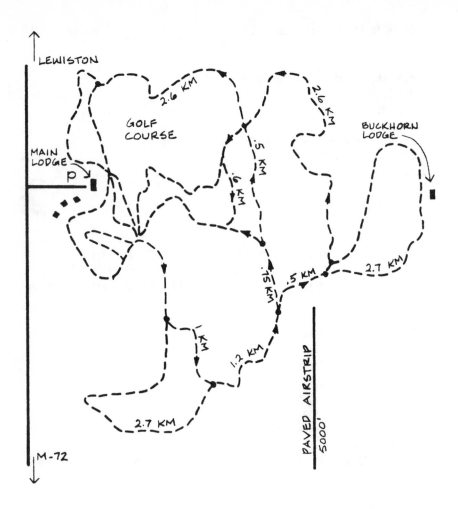

↑ LEWISTON

GOLF COURSE

MAIN LODGE

P

BUCKHORN LODGE

2.6 KM

2.6 KM

.5 KM

.6 KM

.75 KM

.5 KM

2.7 KM

.75 KM

1 KM

1.2 KM

2.7 KM

PAVED AIRSTRIP 5000'

M-72

NO SCALE ↑

GARLAND

Garland                                          Revised: 4/05/88

Garland
Co Rd 489                                        517-786-2211
Lewiston, MI  49756

Trail suitable for skiing only

Location:
 4.5 miles south of Lewiston on Co Rd 489
 12 miles north of Luzerne on Co Rd 489

Trail specifications:
   54 km; 7 loop(s); Loop length(s)-2.2, 2.5 ,4.5, 8.5, 10, 12, 15
Typical terrain: Flat to rolling
Skiing ability suggested: Novice to intermediate
Hiking trail difficulty: NA
Nordic trail grooming method: Track set
Suitable for all-terrain bicycle: Not permitted
Trail use fee: $5.00/day
Camping: None

General Information:
 Privately operated 3,000 acre, four seasons resort
 Ski shop, rentals, lodging, lessons, skating rink, restaurant, sauna, pool
   and jacuzzi are available
 Some trails are on a golf course
 5000 foot airstrip is on the property with charter air service available
 Very elegant lodge and duplex accomodations are available
 Future expansion of the trail system is planned for next year
 Trail system improvements are planned for the 1988/89 season but nothing
   has been finalized as of this date

174

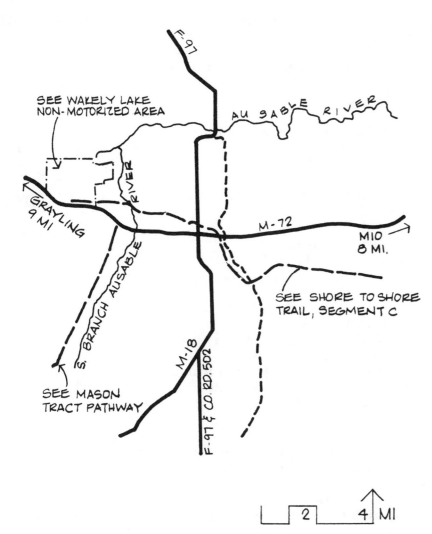

# MIDLAND TO MACKINAC PATHWAY

Mio Ranger District, Huron-Manistee National Forest
401 Court St.                                      517-826-3252
Mio, MI  48647

Forest Supervisor, Huron-Manistee National Forest
421 S. Mitchell St.                               616-775-2421
Cadillac, MI  49601

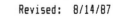

Trail suitable for hiking & skiing

Location:
 On M72, 14 miles west of Mio or 16 miles east of Grayling at FR 4027
 Parking available on FR 4027, just east of the pathway

Trail specifications:
   12 mi; No* loop(s); Loop length(s)-NA
Typical terrain: Varied
Skiing ability suggested: Advanced
Hiking trail difficulty: Easy to moderate
Nordic trail grooming method: None
Suitable for all-terrain bicycle: Not permitted
Trail use fee: None
Camping: Camping is permitted but there are no established campgrounds
Drinking water has not been provided along the trail

General Information:
 Maintained by the Mio Ranger District, Huron-Manistee National Forest
 Trail is marked with blue paint
 Recommended only for skiers with winter survival skills
 Contact the Boy Scouts of America, Council 265 for information on other
   segments of the trail system. 5001 South 11 Mile Rd., Auburn, Mi 43611
   Phones 313-662-4964 or 313-695-5593 (repeated attempts to contact the
   Scouts were not successful)
 * This is a point to point trail

175

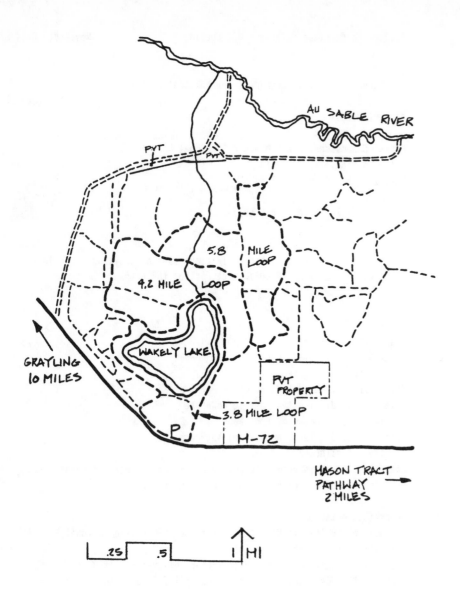

GRAYLING
10 MILES

AU SABLE RIVER

PVT

PVT

5.8 MILE LOOP

4.2 MILE LOOP

WAKELY LAKE

PVT PROPERTY

3.8 MILE LOOP

P

M-72

MASON TRACT PATHWAY 2 MILES

.25   .5   1   MI

WAKELY LAKE NON-MOTORIZED AREA

Mio Ranger District, Huron-Manistee National Forest
401 Court St.                                        517-826-3252
Mio, MI  48647

Forest Supervisor, Huron-Manistee National Forest
421 S. Mitchell St.                                 616-775-2421
Cadillac, MI  49601

Trail suitable for skiing & hiking

Location:
  10 miles east Grayling on M72
  22 miles west of Mio on M72

Trail specifications:
    14.5 mi; 3 loop(s); Loop length(s)-4, 4.5, 6
Typical terrain: Rolling to hilly
Skiing ability suggested: Novice to advanced
Hiking trail difficulty: Easy to moderate
Nordic trail grooming method: None
Suitable for all-terrain bicycle: Yes
Trail use fee: None
Camping: Permitted but no developed campgrounds in area
Drinking water is not available

General Information:
 Maintained by the Mio Ranger District, Huron-Manistee National Forest
 A new, non-motorized area that is currently under development

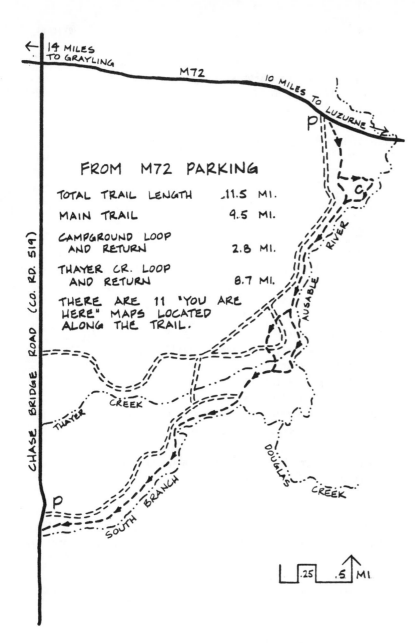

FROM M72 PARKING

| | |
|---|---|
| TOTAL TRAIL LENGTH | .11.5 MI. |
| MAIN TRAIL | 9.5 MI. |
| CAMPGROUND LOOP AND RETURN | 2.8 MI. |
| THAYER CR. LOOP AND RETURN | 8.7 MI. |

THERE ARE 11 "YOU ARE
HERE" MAPS LOCATED
ALONG THE TRAIL.

14 MILES
TO GRAYLING

M72

10 MILES TO LUZURNE

P

C

AUSABLE RIVER

CHASE BRIDGE ROAD (CO. RD. 519)

THAYER CREEK

DOUGLAS CREEK

P

SOUTH BRANCH

.25 .5 MI

MASON TRACT PATHWAY

Mason Tract Pathway                    Revised:  3/06/88

Area Forester, Roscommon Forest Area
Box 218, 8717 N. Roscommon Rd                    517-275-5151
Roscommon, MI  48635

District Forest Manager, Au Sable State Forest
191 S. Mt. Tom Rd.                               517-826-3211
Mio, MI  48647

Trail suitable for skiing & hiking

Location:
  15 miles east of Grayling on M72
  North trailhead - On M72 about 15 miles east of Grayling
  South trailhead - 12 miles east of Grayling turn south on Chase Bridge Rd.
    then continue about 10 miles to South Branch Au Sable River bridge.
    Trailhead is on the north side of the bridge
Trail specifications:
  11.5 mi‡; No loop(s); Loop length(s)-NA
Typical terrain: Rolling to slightly hilly
Skiing ability suggested: Novice to intermediate
Hiking trail difficulty: Easy
Nordic trail grooming method: Track set weekly
Suitable for all-terrain bicycle: Yes
Trail use fee: None
Camping: Campground on AuSable River along trail at Canoe Harbor
Drinking water available at campground

General Information:
  Maintained by the DNR Forest Mananagment Division
  ‡ This is a point to point trail
  Lodging available in Grayling or at Bear Paw Cabins on M72, about 8 miles
    east of the trail  517-826-3313

Other contacts:
DNR Forest Management Division Office, Lansing, 517-373-1275
DNR Forest Management Region Office, Roscommon, 517-275-5151

**TISDALE TRIANGLE PATHWAY**

Area Forester, Roscommon Forest Area
Box 218, 8717 N. Roscommon Rd.                    517-275-5151
Roscommon, MI 48635

District Forest Manager, Au Sable State Forest
191 S. Mt. Tom Rd.                               517-826-3211
Mio, MI 48647

Trail suitable for skiing & hiking

Location:
 Trailhead - Off M76, 1 mile south of Roscommon
 Trailhead - At the east end of Tisdale Rd. .5 mile east of Roscommon on
  M18

Trail specifications:
    10.1 mi; 4 loop(s); Loop length(s)-2.4, 4, 6.1, 3.6
Typical terrain: Flat
Skiing ability suggested: Novice
Hiking trail difficulty: Easy
Nordic trail grooming method: Track set regularly
Suitable for all-terrain bicycle: Yes
Trail use fee: None
Camping: Public and private campgrounds in the area
Drinking water is not available

General Information:
 Maintained by the DNR Forest Management Division
 Used mainly by local residents of Roscommon and the surrounding area

Other contacts:
DNR Forest Management Division Office, Lansing, 517-373-1275
DNR Forest Management Region Office, Roscommon, 517-275-5151

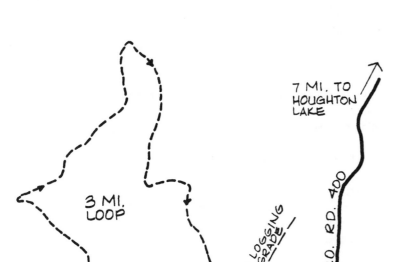

7 MI. TO
HOUGHTON
LAKE

3 MI.
LOOP

OLD LOGGING
R.R. GRADE

CO. RD. 400

P

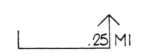

.25 MI

# LOST TWIN LAKES PATHWAY

Area Forester, Roscommon Forest Area
Box 158                                          517-422-5522
Houghton Lake Heights, MI   48630

District Forest Manager, Au Sable State Forest
1919 S. Mt. Tom Rd.                              517-826-3211
Mio, MI   48647

Trail suitable for skiing & hiking

Location:
  7 miles south of M55 (Houghton Lake) on Reserve Rd. (Co Rd 400)
    (McDonalds's is on the corner of M55 and Reserve Rd.)
  Trailhead is not well marked


Trail specifications:
   3 mi; 1 loop(s); Loop length(s)-3
Typical terrain: Very hilly
Skiing ability suggested: Intermediate to advanced
Hiking trail difficulty: Moderate to difficult
Nordic trail grooming method: None
Suitable for all-terrain bicycle: Yes, for advanced only
Trail use fee: None
Camping: None
Drinking water not available

General Information:
 Maintained by the DNR Forest Management Division
 Just south of the Nokomis Pathway
 Very wild and challenging trail

Other contacts:
 DNR Forest Manggement Division Office, Lansing, 517-373-1275
 DNR Forest Management Region Office, Roscommon, 517-275-5151

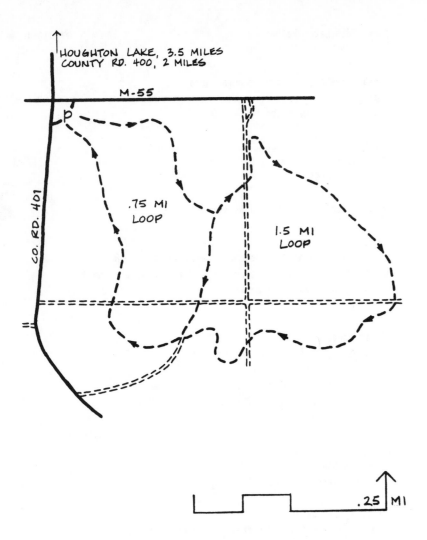

HOUGHTON LAKE, 3.5 MILES
COUNTY RD. 400, 2 MILES

M-55

CO. RD. 401

P

.75 MI
LOOP

1.5 MI
LOOP

.25 MI

# NOKOMIS PATHWAY

Area Forester, Roscommon Forest Area
Box 158                                                        517-422-5522
Houghton Lake Heights, MI  48630

District Forest Manager, Au Sable State Forest
191 S. Mt. Tom Rd.                                             517-826-3211
Mio, MI  48647

Trail suitable for skiing & hiking

Location:
 Between Houghton Lake and Prudenville
 Trailhead - 3.5 miles south of M55 on Reserve Rd. (Co Rd 400/401) at
   Waco Rd.

Trail specifications:
   2.8 mi; 2 loop(s); Loop length(s)-1.2, 1.5
Typical terrain: Rolling
Skiing ability suggested: Novice
Hiking trail difficulty: Easy
Nordic trail grooming method: None
Suitable for all-terrain bicycle: Yes
Trail use fee: None
Camping: Campgrounds at Higgins Lake State Park and private campgrounds
Drinking water not available

General Information:
 Maintained by the DNR Forest Management Division
 Part of the trail is through a beautiful pine plantation

Other contacts:
 DNR Forest Management Division Office, Lansing, 517-373-1275
 DNR Forest Management Region Office, Roscommon, 517-275-5151

180

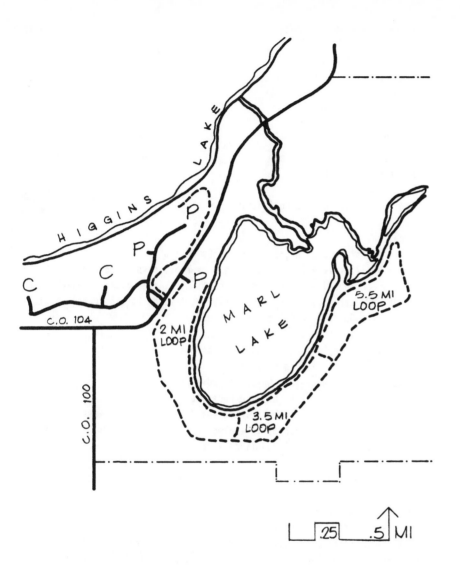

C.O. 104

C.O. 100

HIGGINS LAKE

MARL LAKE

5.5 MI LOOP

2 MI LOOP

3.5 MI LOOP

.25 .5 MI

SOUTH HIGGINS LAKE
STATE PARK

South Higgins Lake State Park                    Revised: 10/09/87

South Higgins Lake State Park
106 State Park Drive                             517-821-6374
Roscommon, MI  48653

DNR Parks Division Office

517-373-1270

Trail suitable for skiing & hiking

Location:
 On the south end of Higgins Lake on Co Rd 100

Trail specifications:
    5.8 mi; 3 loop(s); Loop length(s)-2, 3.5, 5.5
Typical terrain: Flat to rolling
Skiing ability suggested: Novice to intermediate
Hiking trail difficulty: Easy
Nordic trail grooming method: Track set
Suitable for all-terrain bicycle: Yes
Trail use fee: None, but vehicle entry fee required $2/day, $10/year
Camping: Campground in the park open throughout the year
Drinking water available

General Information:
 Maintained by the DNR Parks Division
 Trails designed for skiing
 Rentals available from nearby private ski shops

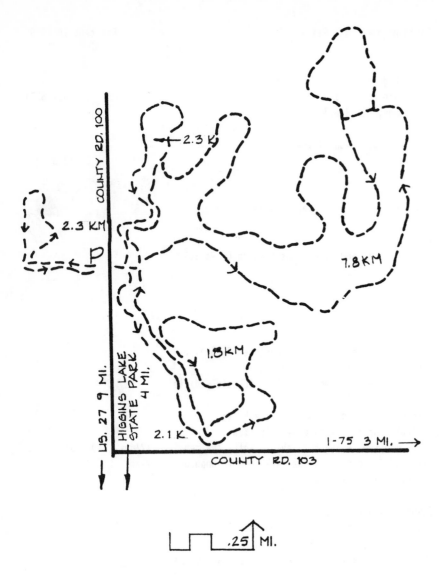

COUNTY RD. 100

2.3 k

2.3 KM

7.8KM

US. 27 9 MI.

HIGGINS LAKE STATE PARK 4 MI.

1.8KM

2.1 K.

I-75 3 MI. →

COUNTY RD. 103

.25 MI.

CROSS COUNTRY
SKI HEADQUARTERS

Cross Country Ski Headquarters
9435 Co Rd 100, Higgins Lake                517-821-6661
Roscommon, MI  48653

R & L Frye
943 Co Rd 100, Higgins Lake
Roscommon, MI  48653                        517-821-6661

Trail suitable for skiing & hiking

Location:
 On the east side of Higgins Lake on Co Rd 100
 From NB I75 take exit 239, turn left over overpass, then right on Co Rd
  103. Continue 3.5 miles to stop and blinker, then right .5 mile to shop
 From US27 take Higgins Lake Rd. exit, go towards Higgins Lake 3.5 miles
  past the South Park(9.1 miles from US27)
Trail specifications:
   18 km; 5 loop(s); Loop length(s)-various
Typical terrain: Flat to rolling
Skiing ability suggested: Novice to advanced
Hiking trail difficulty: Easy to moderate
Nordic trail grooming method: Track set 3 to 7 times per week
Suitable for all-terrain bicycle: Yes
Trail use fee: None, but donations accepted*
Camping: None
Drinking water available at day lodge, picnic area and sundeck

General Information:
 Privately operated touring center
 Ski shop, warming shelter with sundeck,snack bar and restrooms
 Owners, Bob and Lynne Frye are very knowledgeable in the proper selection
   of ski equipment for every level of skier.  Extensive
   selection of performance ski equipment is available.
 Trails are very good considering limited terrain variety available
 2.3 km lighted trail
 Races and events held throughout the ski season
 *Sponsorships available at $10/person or $20/family
 Convenient large parking lot at trailhead
 Accomodations available adjacent to the trail at the
   Northwinds Motor Lodge 821-6972
 New trails developed for the 1988/89 season

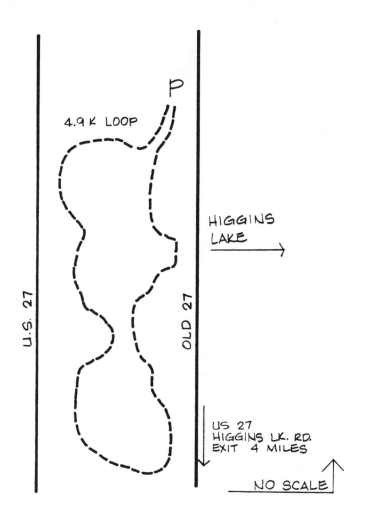

**4.9 K LOOP**

U.S. 27

OLD 27

HIGGINS LAKE →

US 27
HIGGINS LK. RD.
EXIT 4 MILES

NO SCALE

WEST HIGGINS LAKE TRAIL

West Higgins Lake Trail                          Revised: 12/03/87

Au Sable Valley Nordic Ski Club
PO Box 385
Roscommon, MI  48653

Cross Country Ski Headquarters
9435 Co Rd 100, Higgins Lake                          517-821-6661
Roscommon, MI  48653

Trail suitable for skiing & hiking

Location:
  Exit US27 northbound at Higgins Lake Rd. (South Higgins Lake State Park),
    then east .25 mile to Old 27, then north about 4 miles to a parking lot
    on the west side of the road


Trail specifications:
  4.9 km; 1 loop(s); Loop length(s)-4.9
Typical terrain: Flat to rolling
Skiing ability suggested: Novice to intermediate
Hiking trail difficulty: Easy
Nordic trail grooming method: Track set as needed
Suitable for all-terrain bicycle: Yes
Trail use fee:
Camping: None
No drinking water available

General Information:
  Developed and maintained by the Au Sable Valley Nordic Ski Club

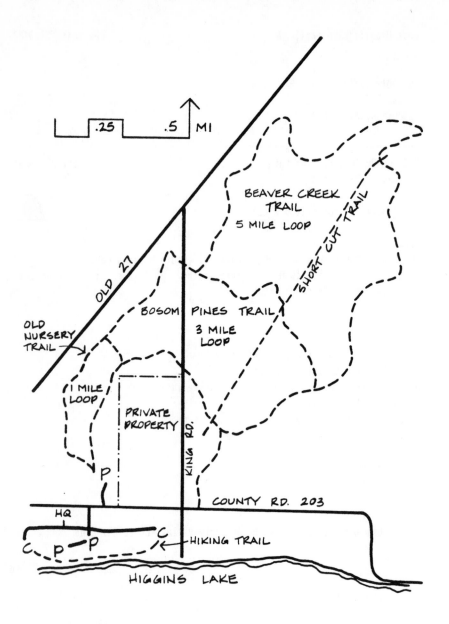

# NORTH HIGGINS LAKE
## STATE PARK

North Higgins Lake State Park
11511 W. Higgins Lake Drive                    517-821-6125
Roscommon, MI  48653

DNR Parks Division Office

517-373-1270

Trail suitable for skiing & hiking

Location:
   1.5 miles east of US27 or 4.5 miles west of I75 on Co Rd 200
      (Roscommon Rd.) at the north end of Higgins Lake

Trail specifications:
   7.5 mi; 3 loop(s); Loop length(s)-1, 3, 5
Typical terrain: Flat to rolling with some hills
Skiing ability suggested: Novice to intermediate
Hiking trail difficulty: Easy
Nordic trail grooming method: Track set‡
Suitable for all-terrain bicycle: Yes
Trail use fee: None, but vehicle entry fee required $2/day, $10/year
Camping: Available in the park
Drinking water available

General Information:
 Maintained by the DNR Parks Division
 Site of the Beaver Creek Challenge held in February
 Hanson Hill, Cross Country Ski Headquarters and Tisdale Triangle are other
    trails nearby
 ‡ Most trails are double width. Some are single with a skating lane
 The 1 and 3 mile loops have the most hills
 A nature and fitness trail are also part of the system

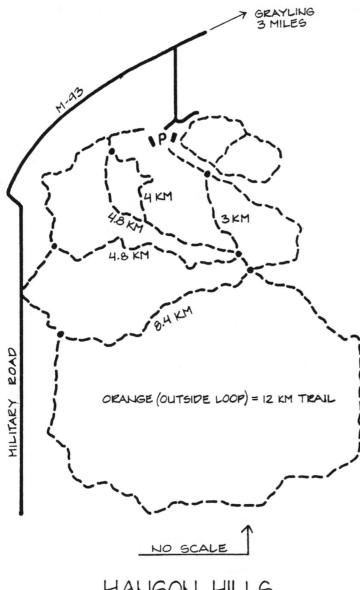

## HANSON HILLS RECREATIONAL PARK

GRAYLING 3 MILES

M-93

P

4 KM

4.8 KM

4.8 KM

3 KM

8.4 KM

ORANGE (OUTSIDE LOOP) = 12 KM TRAIL

MILITARY ROAD

NO SCALE

Hanson Hills Recreational Park                    Revised: 11/01/87

Hanson Hills Recreational Park
PO Box 361                                        517-348-9266
Grayling, MI  49738

Trail suitable for skiing only

Location:
  Take  M72/M93 west 1.5 miles to the M93 cutoff, then south on M93 to
    the park
  1.5 miles west of Grayling


Trail specifications:
   35 km; Many loop(s); Loop length(s)-various
Typical terrain: Flat to very hilly
Skiing ability suggested: Novice to advanced
Hiking trail difficulty: Easy to moderate
Nordic trail grooming method: Track set *
Suitable for all-terrain bicycle: Yes, but some sandy sections exist
Trail use fee: $4/day for adults, $3/day for children
Camping: None


General Information:
  Maintained by a local community group on the Hanson State Game Refuge
  Rentals, snack bar, warming area and alpine skiing
  Orginally developed in the 1940's for cross-country skiing.  Some of the
    original trail signs are still visable
  All trails completely redone in 1986
  Site of races held annually
  * Skating trail available
  Write for brochure which includes a motel directory

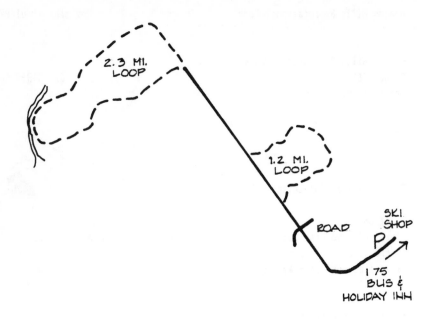

2.3 MI. LOOP

1.2 MI. LOOP

SKI SHOP

ROAD

P

I 75 BUS & HOLIDAY INN

NO SCALE

# CROSS COUNTRY SKI SHOP

Cross Country Ski Shop                    Revised:  4/01/88

Cross Country Ski Shop
PO Box 745                                        517-348-8558
Grayling, MI  49738                               517-821-6559

Trail suitable for skiing only

Location:
  On I75 Business Loop behind the Holiday Inn on the south side of Grayling

Trail specifications:
    2.5 mi; 2 loop(s); Loop length(s)-1.2, 2.3
Typical terrain: Flat
Skiing ability suggested: Novice
Hiking trail difficulty: NA
Nordic trail grooming method: Track set with space for skating*
Suitable for all-terrain bicycle: NA
Trail use fee: None
Camping: None

General Information:
  Complete ski shop with rentals operated by skiers
  Excellent place to try out equipment before purchasing
  Accomodations available at the adjacent Holiday Inn
  Childrens equipment exchange program available
  * Skating lane is up to 30' wide

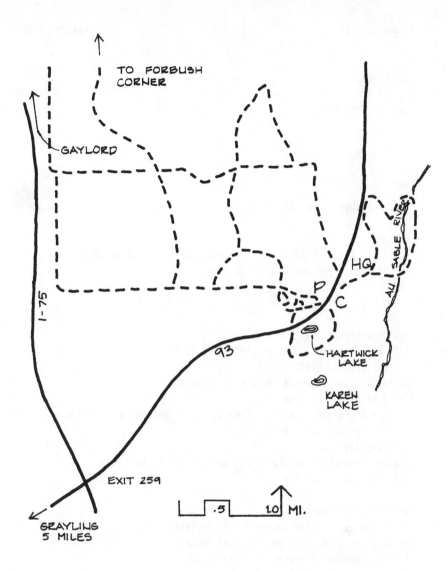

HARTWICK PINES STATE PARK

Hartwick Pines State Park
Rte 3, Box 3840                              517-348-7068
Grayling, MI  49738

DNR Park Division Office

                                             517-373-1270

Trail suitable for skiing & hiking

Location:
 7.5 miles NE of Grayling on M93 just east of I75 about 3 miles

Trail specifications:
   18 mi; 6 loop(s); Loop length(s)-3 to 9
Typical terrain: Flat to hilly
Skiing ability suggested: Novice to intermediate
Hiking trail difficulty: Easy to moderate
Nordic trail grooming method: Designated ski trails are track set
Suitable for all-terrain bicycle: Yes
Trail use fee: None, but vehicle entry fee required $2/day, $10/year
Camping: Campground in park year open all year
Drinking water available in the park

General Information:
 Maintained by the DNR Parks Division
 A unique state park with a stand of virgin White Pine, one over 300 years
   old.
 Site of the Logging Museum
 Trails are enjoyable, and they connect with Forbush Corner cross
   country ski area on the north
 One trail crosses the Au Sable River twice (not track set) with a
   spectacular view of the Au Sable River valley

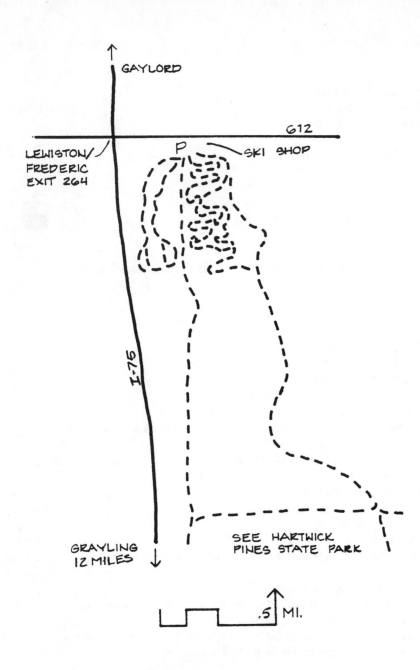

GAYLORD

612

LEWISTON/
FREDERIC
EXIT 264

P

SKI SHOP

I-76

GRAYLING
12 MILES

SEE HARTWICK
PINES STATE PARK

.5 MI.

# FORBUSH CORNER

Dave Forbush
Box 327                          517-348-5989
Frederic, MI  49733

Trail suitable for skiing only

Location:
  9 miles north of Grayling on I75, then .25 mile east of exit 264
    (Lewiston/Frederic) to the ski area

Trail specifications:
   20 km; 4 loop(s); Loop length(s)-3.5 to 11
Typical terrain: Flat to hilly
Skiing ability suggested: Novice to advanced
Hiking trail difficulty: NA
Nordic trail grooming method: Expertly track set and groomed space for skating
Suitable for all-terrain bicycle: NA
Trail use fee: Yes
Camping: Campground available at Hartwick Pines State Park
Drinking water available

General Information:
 A touring center privately operated by Dave Forbush
 Warming area, lessons, lodging(bunk house), ski shop with rentals
 Clinics throughout season-write for information
 Lighted trail available
 Trails connect with Hartwick Pines State Park
 Home of the Michigan High School Cross-Country Ski Championships and the
    Fredric Loppet
 Organized tours planned to Hartwick Pines
 Write for a free brochure

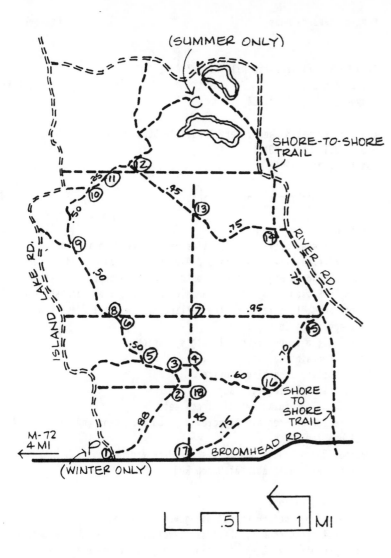

(SUMMER ONLY)

C

SHORE-TO-SHORE TRAIL

RIVER RD.

ISLAND LAKE RD.

SHORE TO SHORE TRAIL

M-72 4 MI

P

(WINTER ONLY)

BROOMHEAD RD.

.5    1 MI

SAND LAKES
QUIET AREA

Sand Lakes Quiet Area                                    Revised: 10/17/87

Area Forester, Pere Marquette State Forest
404 W. 14th St.                                          616-946-4920
Traverse City, MI  49684

DNR Forest Management Division Office

517-373-1275

Trail suitable for skiing & hiking

Location:
 Between Kalkaska and Traverse City, south of M72
 Trailhead - (For skiers) 1.5 miles east of Williamsburg on M72 take
   Broomhead Rd. south for about 4 miles to parking lot on the left
 Trailhead -(For hikers) Take Island Lake Rd. west from Kalkaska for about
   9 miles to Guernsey Lake State Forest Campground (follow signs)
Trail specifications:
 10+ mi; Many loop(s); Loop length(s)-various
Typical terrain: Flat to very hilly
Skiing ability suggested: Novice
Hiking trail difficulty: Easy to moderate
Nordic trail grooming method: None, but well skied all of the time
Suitable for all-terrain bicycle: Yes
Trail use fee: None
Camping: Campground in the quiet area is open during snowless months
Drinking water available when campground is open

General Information:
 Maintained by the DNR Forest Management Division
 This 2,800 acre quiet area is colsed to motorized vehicles, making it a
   very delightful ski, hiking and ATB trail area
 The shore to shore trail passes through the area
 The cicular route around the quiet area is best for skiing since the
   EW and NS trails are on section lines and disregard the difficult
   terrain that is very difficult to ski
 A hike-in camping site is provided on the interior of the area with pit
   toilets and a water well
 This area is a favorite of the local skiers

189

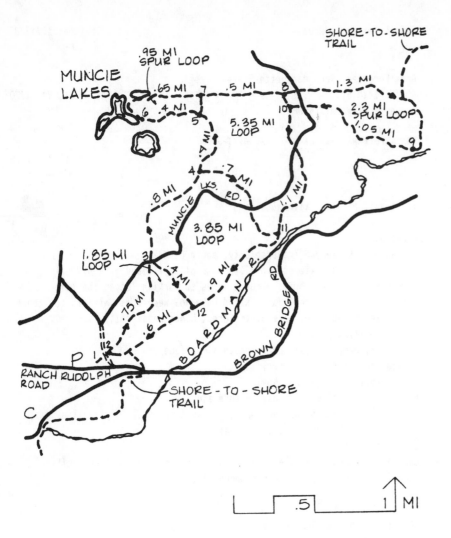

SHORE-TO-SHORE
TRAIL

.95 MI
SPUR LOOP

MUNCIE
LAKES

.65 MI  7  .5 MI  8  1.3 MI

.6  .4 MI
5  10  2.3 MI
SPUR LOOP
1.05 MI
.4 MI
5.35 MI
LOOP
9

4  .7 MI

.8 MI  MUNCIE LKS. RD.  1.1 MI

3.85 MI
LOOP  11

1.85 MI
LOOP  3

.9 MI

.75 MI  .6 MI  12

P 1
RANCH RUDOLPH
ROAD

SHORE-TO-SHORE
TRAIL

C

BOARDMAN R.  RD.
BROWN BRIDGE

.5  1 MI

MUNCIE LAKES PATHWAY

190

Muncie Lakes Pathway                                   Revised: 3/06/88

Area Forester, Traverse City Forest Area
404 W 14th St.                                          616-946-4920
Traverse City, MI  49684

District Forest Manager, Pere Marquette State Forest
Rte 1, 8015 South US131                                 616-775-9727
Cadillac, MI  49601

Trail suitable for skiing & hiking

Location:
 SE of Traverse City about 13 miles near Ranch Rudolf resort
 From Traverse City take Garfield Ave south to Hammond Rd., then east on
   Hammond Rd to High Lake Rd, south .5 mile to Supply Rd., then east on
   Supply Rd. about 3 miles to Rennie Lake Rd., then turn south until it
   dead ends, turn left and the parking lot is about 2 miles away
Trail specifications:
 11.5 mi; 5 loop(s); Loop length(s)-various
Typical terrain: Rolling to hilly
Skiing ability suggested: Novice
Hiking trail difficulty: Easy
Nordic trail grooming method: Track set
Suitable for all-terrain bicycle: No, too much sand and ruts from horses
Trail use fee: None
Camping: Ranch Rudolf and Jellystone Park are nearby
Drinking water available at Ranch Rudolf

General Information:
 Maintained by the DNR Forest Management Division
 The first cross country ski trail developed by the DNR.  Numerous
   refinements have been made since that time to make this a
   delightful trail that passes by the beautiful Boardman River
 A trail connects to Ranch Rudolf with its food and lodging facilities
 Many hills throughout the system makes for a very popular trail for local
   skiers
 Sand Lakes Quiet Area is only a few miles to the east

Other contacts:
DNR Forest Management Division Office, Lansing, 517-373-1275
DNR Forest Management Region Office, Roscommon, 517-275-5151

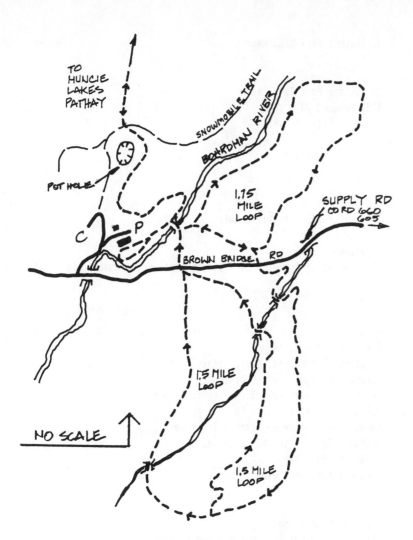

TO
MUNCIE
LAKES
PATHAY

SNOWMOBILE TRAIL

BOARDMAN RIVER

POT HOLE

1.75
MILE
LOOP

SUPPLY RD
CO RD 660
605

C
P

BROWN BRIDGE RD

1.5 MILE
LOOP

NO SCALE

1.5 MILE
LOOP

RANCH RUDOLF

Ranch Rudolf                                    Revised:  1/13/88


Ranch Rudolf
6841 Brownbridge Rd., PO Box 1729                616-947-9529
Traverse City, MI  49684

Trail suitable for skiing & hiking

Location:
 SW of Traverse City on Brownbridge Rd. on the Boardman River between
   Co Rd 605/660 and Co Rd 661


Trail specifications:
   15 km; 3 loop(s); Loop length(s)-various
Typical terrain: Flat to hilly
Skiing ability suggested: Novice to intermediate
Hiking trail difficulty: Easy
Nordic trail grooming method: Track set
Suitable for all-terrain bicycle: Some trails are suitable
Trail use fee: Donation requested
Camping: Campground on property
Drinking water available at lodge

General Information:
 Privately operated resort with lodging, restaurant, pool(summer),ski shop,
   horse back riding, entertainment, lessons and rentals
 Connecting trail to the Muncie Lake Pathway and near Sand Lakes Quiet Area

 These trails are somewhat limited but with the connection to the Muncie
   Lakes Pathway, it makes for an extensive trail system

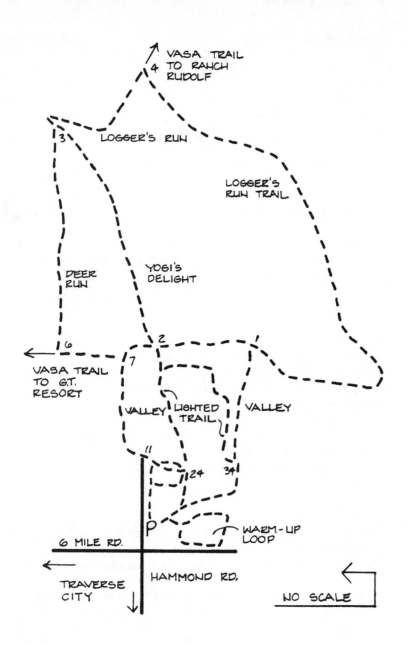

VASA TRAIL
TO RAHCH
RUDOLF

4

3   LOGGER'S RUN

LOGGER'S
RUN TRAIL

DEER
RUN

YOGI'S
DELIGHT

6        2

7

VASA TRAIL
TO G.T.
RESORT

VALLEY  LIGHTED
TRAIL    VALLEY

11

24    34

P

WARM-UP
LOOP

6 MILE RD.

HAMMOND RD.

TRAVERSE
CITY

NO SCALE

## JELLYSTONE PARK CAMP RESORT

Jellystone Park Camp Resort                    Revised:  6/09/87

Jellystone Park Camp Resort
4050 Hammond Rd.                               616-947-2770
Traverse City, MI  49684

Trail suitable for skiing only

Location:
  7 miles SE of Traverse City at the east end of Hammond Rd. at 6 Mile Rd

Trail specifications:
  15 km; 5 loop(s); Loop length(s)-.75, 1.7, 5.6, 6.5
Typical terrain: Flat to hilly
Skiing ability suggested: Novice to Intermediate
Hiking trail difficulty: NA
Nordic trail grooming method: Track set
Suitable for all-terrain bicycle: NA
Trail use fee: Yes
Camping: Yes, see below

General Information:
  Privately operated 4 season campground
  Snack bar, lessons, rentals and warming area is available
  Heated restrooms and showers available in winter
  A lighted 2 km trail is available
  The site of many races throughout the season

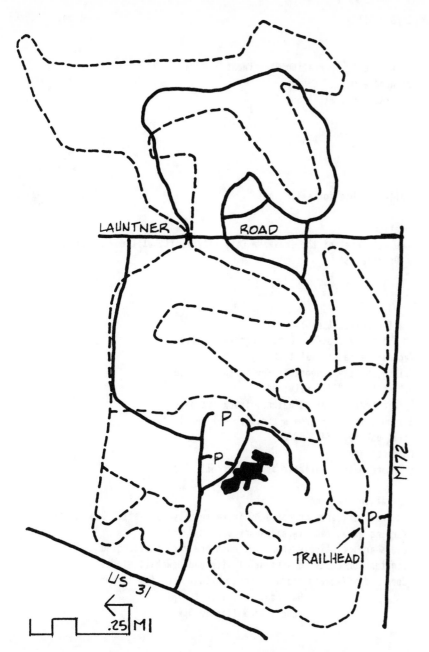

LAUNTNER ROAD

P
P
P
TRAILHEAD

US 31

.25 MI

GRAND TRAVERSE RESORT VILLAGE

M72

Grand Traverse Resort Village

Revised: 3/24/88

Grand Traverse Resort Village

Grand Traverse Village, MI  49610-0404

800-678-1308
800-72-SKITC

Trail suitable for skiing only

Location:
 About .5 mile west of the M72 and US31 intersection
 6 miles NE of Traverse City

Trail specifications:
   16 km; 6 loop(s); Loop length(s)-1, 1.1, 2, 2, 2.3, 7.6
 Typical terrain: Flat to rolling on a golf course
 Skiing ability suggested: Novice to intermediate
 Hiking trail difficulty: NA
 Nordic trail grooming method: Track set
 Suitable for all-terrain bicycle: NA
 Trail use fee: Yes
 Camping: Campground available at Traverse City State Park

General Information:
 A complete 4 seasons resort, rated Four Star by Mobil and Four Diamond
   by AAA
 Start and finish of the North American Vasa citizen cross country ski
   race
 6 km lighted trail
 750 luxury rooms, suites and condominum villas.  Some condos along the
   ski trails
 10 restaurants and lounges
 Complete health and racquet club with swimming pools and shopping gallery

Revised:  2/09/88

Traverse City Recreation Department
625 Woodmere St.
Traverse City, MI  49684

616-947-8566

Trail suitable for skiing only

Location:
 One mile west of the Traverse City city limit, at the west end of
   Randolph St.

Trail specifications:
   3.5 mi; 2 loop(s); Loop length(s)-1, 1.5
Typical terrain: Flat to hilly
Skiing ability suggested: Novice to advanced
Hiking trail difficulty: NA
Nordic trail grooming method: Track set daily
Suitable for all-terrain bicycle: Not permitted
Trail use fee: Yes, $2/day
Camping: None
Drinking water available at the ski hill lodge

General Information:
 Downhill ski area operated by Traverse City Recreation Department
 Warming area, rentals and snack bar
 Loops are relatively short but most are very challenging
 Lighted for cross country ski trails and downhill slopes
 Open 7 days/week:  Monday through Friday from 4pm to 9pm
                    Saturday from 11am to 9pm
                    Sunday from 11am to 5pm

# No Trail Map

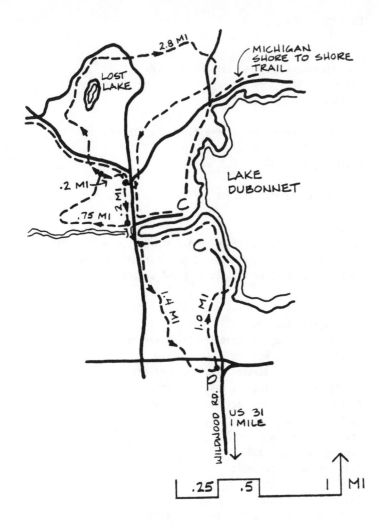

**LOST LAKE PATHWAY**

Lost Lake Nature Pathway                    Revised: 3/05/88

Area Forester, Traverse City Area Forest
404 14th St.                                            616-946-4920
Traverse City, MI  49684

District Forest Manager, Pere Marquette State Forest
Rte 1, 8015 South US131                                 616-775-9727
Cadillac, MI  49601

Trail suitable for skiing & hiking

Location:
 12 miles SW of Traverse City on US31 at near Interlochen
 Trailhead - West 1.5 miles from Interlochen on US31 to Wildwood Rd., then
   north 1 mile to state forest campground

Trail specifications:
   6.3 mi; 3 loop(s); Loop length(s)-2.4, 3.7, 6.3
Typical terrain: Flat to slightly rolling
Skiing ability suggested: Novice
Hiking trail difficulty: Easy
Nordic trail grooming method: Track Set
Suitable for all-terrain bicycle: Yes
Trail use fee: None
Camping: Campground available at trailhead
Drinking water available in snowless months

General Information:
 Maintained by the DNR Forest Management Division

Other contacts:
DNR Forest Management Division Office, Lansing, 517-373-1275
DNR Forest Management Region Office, Roscommon, 517-275-5151

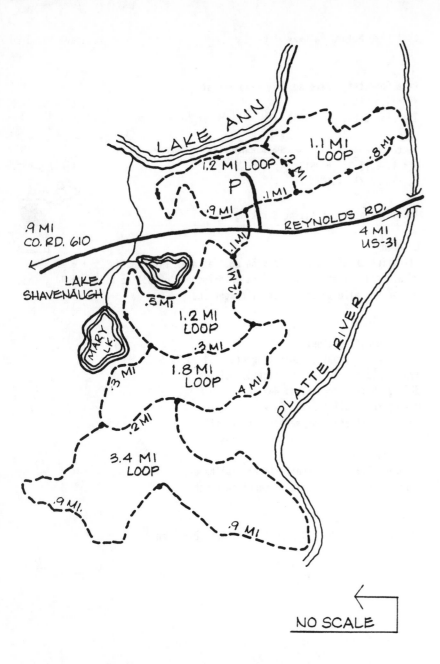

LAKE ANN PATHWAY

NO SCALE

Lake Ann Pathway                                        Revised:  3/05/88

Area Forester, Traverse City Forest Area
404 W 14th St.                                                      616-946-4920
Traverse City, MI  49684

District Forest Manager, Pere Marquette State Forest
Rte. 1, 8015 South US131                                            616-775-9727
Cadillac, MI  49601

Trail suitable for skiing & hiking

Location:
  West of Traverse City between M72 and US31 near Lake Ann
  Trailhead - From Lake Ann west on Almira Rd. to Reynolds Rd., then south
    2.5 miles to Lake Ann State Forest Campground

Trail specifications:
   5.8 mi; 5 loop(s); Loop length(s)-various
Typical terrain: Rolling
Skiing ability suggested: Novice to advanced
Hiking trail difficulty: Easy to moderate
Nordic trail grooming method: Track set
Suitable for all-terrain bicycle: Yes
Trail use fee: None
Camping: At trailhead
Drinking water available

General Information:
  Maintained by the DNR Forest Management Division
  Loops provide interesting skiing for skiers of all skill levels
  The loops west of Reynolds Rd are some of the best designed and groomed
    trails in the DNR system.  Simply a joy to ski!!!

Other contacts:
DNR Forest Management Division Office, Lansing, 517-373-1275
DNR Forest Management Region Office, Roscommon, 517-275-5151

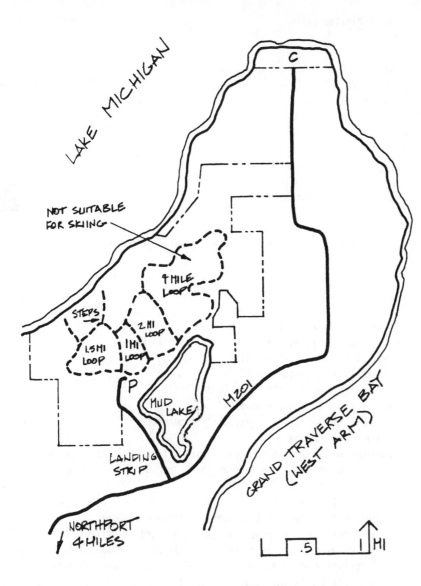

LAKE MICHIGAN

NOT SUITABLE
FOR SKIING

4 MILE
LOOP

STEPS

2 MI
LOOP

1.5 MI
LOOP

1 MI
LOOP

P

MUD
LAKE

M201

GRAND TRAVERSE BAY
(WEST ARM)

LANDING
STRIP

NORTHPORT
4 MILES

.5    1 MI

LEELANAU STATE PARK

Leelanau State Park                           Revised:  8/12/87


Leelanau State Park
Rte 1 Box 49                                  616-386-5422
Northport, Mi  49670


Traverse City State Park
1132 US31 North                               616-947-7193
Traverse City, MI  49684

Trail suitable for skiing & hiking

Location:
 At the north end of the Leelanau Peninsula, 36 miles north of
  Traverse City
 Take Co Rd 629 north out of Northport 3 miles to Densmore Rd (Airport Rd),
  then left to the parking lot


Trail specifications:
  6+ mi; 4 loop(s); Loop length(s)-1.5, 2, 1.5, 4
Typical terrain: Flat to hilly
Skiing ability suggested: Novice to advanced
Hiking trail difficulty: Easy to difficult
Nordic trail grooming method: Track set
Suitable for all-terrain bicycle: Yes
Trail use fee: None, but vehicle entry fee required $2/day, $10/year
Camping: Campground available 4 miles north of trailhead
Drinking water available


General Information:
 Maintained by the DNR Parks Division
 Scenic views of Lake Michigan are provided from an overlook and beach
 Most of the trail system is easy to moderate hiking difficulty except the
  outside loop
 The trail passes through a dune area, hardwoods, pines and along the shore
  of an inland lake to provide plenty of variety
 A pleasant trail system for both hiking and skiing
 The 4 mile loop is not suitable for skiing

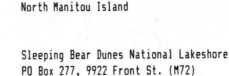

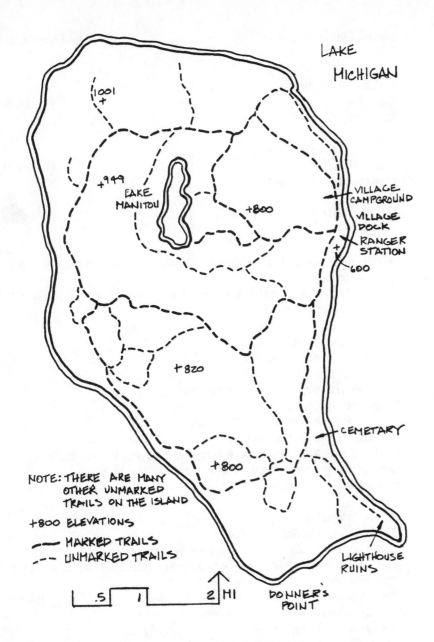

LAKE
MICHIGAN

1001
+

+949
FAKE
MANITOU

VILLAGE
CAMPGROUND

VILLAGE
DOCK

+800

RANGER
STATION

+

600

+820

CEMETARY

+800

NOTE: THERE ARE MANY
OTHER UNMARKED
TRAILS ON THE ISLAND

+800 ELEVATIONS

— · — MARKED TRAILS

— - - UNMARKED TRAILS

LIGHTHOUSE
RUINS

.5      1          2 | HI

DONNER'S
POINT

NORTH MANITOU ISLAND

North Manitou Island                    Revised:  4/07/88

Sleeping Bear Dunes National Lakeshore
PO Box 277, 9922 Front St. (M72)                    616-326-5134
Empire, MI  49630

Trail suitable for hiking only

Location:
 In Lake Michigan, west of Leland, 12 miles offshore

Trail specifications:
   50+ mi; Many⚹ loop(s); Loop length(s)-various
Typical terrain: Flat to hilly
Skiing ability suggested: NA
Hiking trail difficulty: Easy to difficult
Nordic trail grooming method: NA
Suitable for all-terrain bicycle: Not permitted
Trail use fee: None
Camping: One developed campground with wilderness camping permitted ⚹⚹
Drinking water available only at the Ranger Station and campground

General Information:
 Maintained by Sleeping Bear Dunes National Lakeshore
 A wilderness area with very minimal developed facilities. Recommended
   for campers with some backcountry experience. Season 5/30 to 11/15
 ⚹ Since there are a minimum of marked trails and available maps do not
   show all trails and roads, backcountry hiking experience is required
 A very unique island that is worth the effort to reach
 This island is rich in history of the late 1800's to the 1940's
 All campers must register at the Ranger Station on the island
 There is a special deer hunt from 10/15 – 11/15
 Write for brochure and more detailed map needed for hiking
 ⚹⚹Low impact camping methods are required to protect this fragile
   environment. Cooking must be done on portable stoves
 Daily ferry service is available from Leland at 10am  returning to
   Leland by 5pm. Call 616-256-9061 for information and reservations

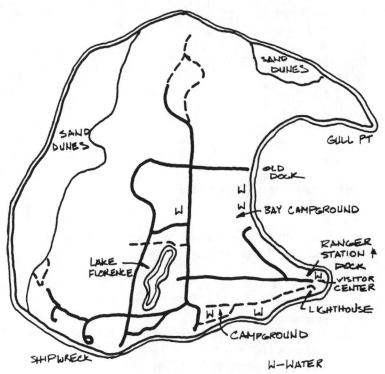

SAND DUNES

SAND DUNES

GULL PT

W OLD DOCK

W BAY CAMPGROUND

W

LAKE FLORENCE

RANGER STATION & DOCK

W VISITOR CENTER

LIGHTHOUSE

W W CAMPGROUND

SHIPWRECK

W—WATER

NOTE: PLEASE RESPECT RIGHTS OF PRIVATE PROPERTY OWNERS

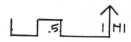

.5    1 MI

# SOUTH MANITOU ISLAND

South Manitou Island                    Revised: 4/07/88

Sleeping Bear Dunes National Lakeshore
PO Box 277, 9922 Front St.(M72)              616-326-5134
Empire, MI  49630

Trail suitable for hiking only

Location:
  In Lake Michigan, west of Leland, 17 miles off shore

Trail specifications:
    11 mi; Many‡ loop(s); Loop length(s)-various
Typical terrain: Flat to hilly
Skiing ability suggested: NA
Hiking trail difficulty: Easy to moderate
Nordic trail grooming method: NA
Suitable for all-terrain bicycle: Not permitted
Trail use fee: None
Camping: Some campgrounds on the island with designated site camping ‡‡
Drinking water available at several locations on the island

General Information:
 Maintained by the Sleeping Bear Dunes National Lakeshore
 ‡ Two track roads are used for hiking trails, as well as many miles of
    foot paths that form a network that reaches every corner of the island
 A very unique island with a very fragile ecosystem that should be
    experienced with great care. Outstanding spring wildflower displays.
 All campers must register at the Ranger Station located at the
    Visitor Center
 ‡‡Most campgrounds are primitive and limited to 6 people. Only a few
    group campgrounds (25 limit) are available on a prior reservation
  basis only by calling 616-352-9611
 Low impact camping methods are required to protect this fragile
    enviornment. Season - Memorial Day through 10/15
 Daily ferry service available from Leland at 10am returning back to
    Leland by 5pm call 616-256-9061 for information and reservations

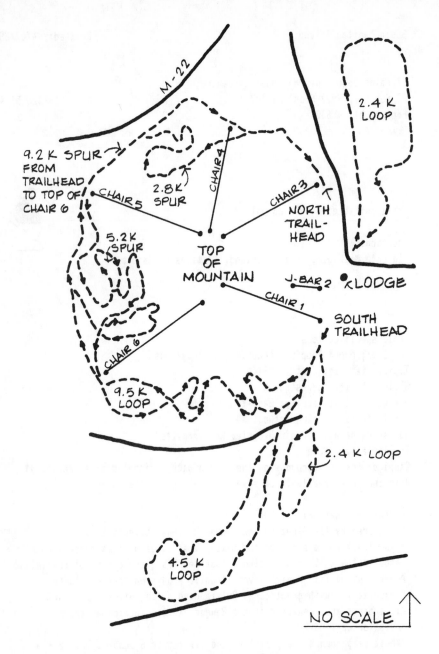

M-22

2.4 K LOOP

9.2 K SPUR FROM TRAILHEAD TO TOP OF CHAIR 6

CHAIR 4

2.8 K SPUR

CHAIR 5

CHAIR 3

NORTH TRAIL-HEAD

5.2 K SPUR

TOP OF MOUNTAIN

J-BAR 2

LODGE

CHAIR 6

CHAIR 1

SOUTH TRAILHEAD

9.5 K LOOP

2.4 K LOOP

4.5 K LOOP

NO SCALE

SUGAR LOAF RESORT

Sugar Loaf Resort                                          Revised: 2/03/88

Sugar Loaf Resort
Route 1                                                    616-228-5461
Cedar, MI  49621                                           800-632-9802

Trail suitable for skiing & hiking

Location:
 From Traverse City, take M72 west for 7 miles, then turn right (north) on
   Co Rd 651 and follow the signs

Trail specifications:
   26 km; 8 loop(s); Loop length(s)-1.2, 2.4, 2.4, 2.8, 4.0, 4.2, 4.5, 4.5
Typical terrain: Flat to very hilly
Skiing ability suggested: Novice to advanced
Hiking trail difficulty: Easy to moderate
Nordic trail grooming method: Double track set daily with skating lane
Suitable for all-terrain bicycle: NA
Trail use fee: $4.00 only for skiing
Camping: None

General Information:
 Privately operated 4 season alpine ski resort with an extensive well
   designed and maintained trail system
 Lodging, ski shop, lessons, restaurants to name only a few features
 Expertly designed trails by John Capper
 Breathtaking views of Lake Michigan
 Torch lit on Saturday nights and special occasions for night skiing

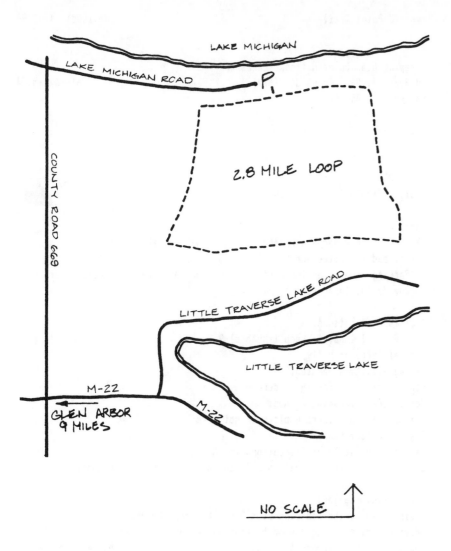

Good Harbor Bay Ski Trail                    Revised: 4/07/88

Sleeping Bear Dunes National Lakeshore
PO Box 277, 9922 Front St. (M72)             616-326-5134
Empire, MI  49630

Trail suitable for skiing only

Location:
  Between Glen Arbor and Leland, north of M22 on Lake Michigan
  Trailhead - On M22 between Little Traverse Lake and Bass Lake, take
    Co Rd 669 to Lake Michigan and turn right and proceed to end of road

Trail specifications:
  2.8 mi; 1 loop(s); Loop length(s)-2.8
Typical terrain: Flat
Skiing ability suggested: Novice
Hiking trail difficulty: Easy
Nordic trail grooming method: None
Suitable for all-terrain bicycle: Not permitted
Trail use fee: None
Camping: Available at 2 locations in the park
Drinking water is not available in the winter at the campgrounds

General Information:
  Maintained by the Sleeping Bear Dunes National Lakeshore
  Trailhead along the shore of Lake Michigan
  Winter accomodations available in Empire at the Lakeshore Inn 326-5145;
    Shady Shores Resort 334-3252; Maple Lane Resort 334-3413; near Maple
    City at the Leelanau Country Inn 228-5060.  See also the Platte Plains
    Trail for other listings in the area.
  This is not a hiking trail!

GOOD HARBOR BAY SKI TRAIL

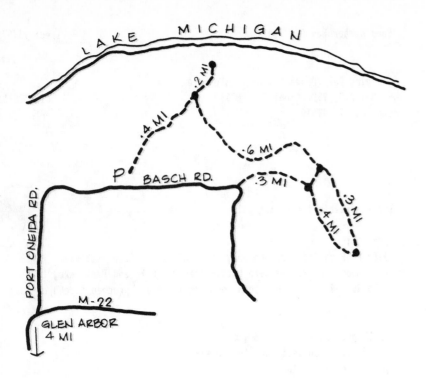

LAKE MICHIGAN

.2 MI

.4 MI

.6 MI

P  BASCH RD.

.3 MI

.4 MI

.3 MI

PORT ONEIDA RD.

M-22

GLEN ARBOR
4 MI

.25      .5 MI

# PYRAMID POINT TRAIL

Pyramid Point Trail                          Revised: 4/07/88

Sleeping Bear Dunes National Lakeshore
PO Box 277, 9922 Front St. (M72)                    616-326-5134
Empire, MI  49630

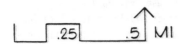

Trail suitable for hiking only

Location:
 Between Glen Arbor and Leland, north of M22 on Lake Michigan
 Trailhead - 5 miles north of Glen Arbor, turn north on Port Oneida Rd.,
   Parking area is on the north side of the road, about .5 mile after Point
   Oneida Rd. turns east.

Trail specifications:
   2.8 mi; 1 loop(s); Loop length(s)-2.8
 Typical terrain: Hilly
 Skiing ability suggested: NA
 Hiking trail difficulty: Moderate
 Nordic trail grooming method: NA
 Suitable for all-terrain bicycle: Not permitted
 Trail use fee: None
 Camping: Available at 2 locations in the park
 Drinking water is not available in the winter at the campgrounds

General Information:
 Maintained by the Sleeping Bear Dunes National Lakeshore
 Wear bright clothing during hunting season 9/15 - 12/15
 Quite varied environments along the trail, including a meadow, beech-maple
   forest, an open sand dune and an outstanding vista of Lake
   Michigan.
 Winter accomodations available in the area. See the Platte Plains Trail
   for listings in the area.

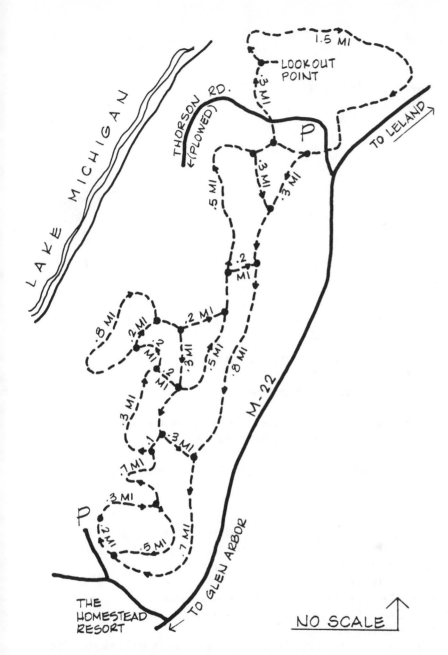

**LAKE MICHIGAN**

THORSON RD. (PLOWED)

1.5 MI

LOOKOUT POINT

.3 MI

P

TO LELAND

.3 MI

.3 MI

.5 MI

.2 MI

.8 MI

.2 MI

.2 MI

.2 MI

.3 MI

.5 MI

.8 MI

.3 MI

.2 MI

.3 MI

.7 MI

.3 MI

M-22

.3 MI

.2 MI

.5 MI

.7 MI

TO GLEN ARBOR

P

THE HOMESTEAD RESORT

HOMESTEAD & BAY VIEW SKI TRAIL

NO SCALE

Bay View Ski Trail                    Revised: 4/07/88

Sleeping Bear Dunes National Lakeshore
PO Box 277, 9922 Front St. (M72)            616-326-5134
Empire, MI  49630

Homestead
Wood Ridge Rd.                              616-334-5000
Glen Arbor, MI  49636

Trail suitable for skiing & hiking

Location:
  Trailhead - About .5 mile west of M22 on Thorson Rd. between Glen Arbor
    and Leland, just north of the Homestead resort.

Trail specifications:
  12 mi; Many loop(s); Loop length(s)-various
Typical terrain: Hilly
Skiing ability suggested: Novice to advanced
Hiking trail difficulty: Moderate
Nordic trail grooming method: Track set Fridays and weekends
Suitable for all-terrain bicycle: Not permitted
Trail use fee: Fri., Sat. & Sun. when groomed $5/day, otherwise none*
Camping: Campground available in park at 2 locations
Drinking water not available

General Information:
  Maintained by the Homestead under permit from the Sleeping Bear Dunes
    National Lakeshore
  * Except holiday weeks when groomed $5/day charge is in effect
  In addition to the Homestead, winter accomodations are available in
    Empire at the Lakeshore Inn 326-5145; Shady Shores Resort 334-3252;
    and Maple Lane Resort 334-3413.  See also the Platte Plains Trail for
    other listings in the area.
  Also known as the Homestead Trail

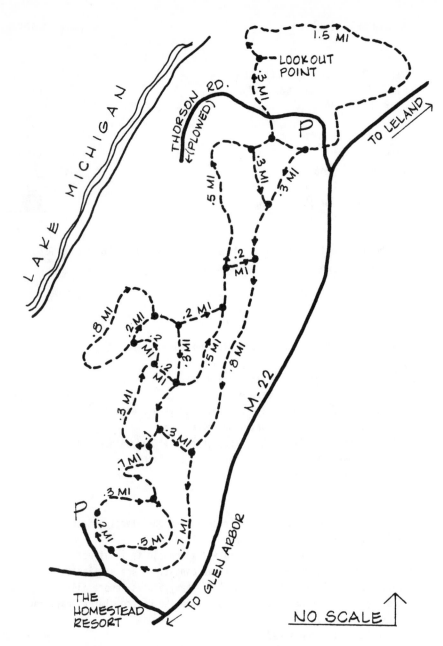

LAKE MICHIGAN

THORSON RD. ←(PLOWED)

1.5 MI

LOOKOUT POINT

.3 MI

P

TO LELAND

.5 MI

.3 MI

.3 MI

.2 MI

.8 MI

.2 MI

.2 MI

.2 MI

.3 MI

.5 MI

.8 MI

.2 MI

.2 MI

M-22

.3 MI

.3 MI

.7 MI

.3 MI

.3 MI

.2 MI

.5 MI

.7 MI

P

TO GLEN ARBOR

THE HOMESTEAD RESORT

TO GLEN ARBOR

NO SCALE

# HOMESTEAD & BAY VIEW SKI TRAIL

204

Homestead                          Revised:  2/02/88

The Homestead  Attn. Pete Edwards
Woodridge Rd.                                    616-334-3041
Glen Arbor, MI  49636                            616-334-5100

Trail suitable for skiing only

Location:
  21 miles NW of Traverse City on M72 to Empire, then 8 miles north on M22
  1 1/2 miles north of Glen Arbor on M22

Trail specifications:
   12 mi; Many loop(s); Loop length(s)-various
Typical terrain: Rolling to hilly
Skiing ability suggested: Novice to advanced
Hiking trail difficulty: NA
Nordic trail grooming method: Track set with some double wide
Suitable for all-terrain bicycle: Not permitted
Trail use fee: Yes
Camping: Campground available in Sleeping Bear Dunes National Lakeshore

General Information:
  The Homestead is a complete 4 seasons resort on Lake Michigan
  Lessons, rentals, snack bar, restaurant, lodging, ice skating, alpine
    skiing, shopping and 10 miles of snowshoe trails
  Very scenic trails overlooking Lake Michigan
  Sleeping Bear Dunes National Lakeshore trails nearby
  PSIA Gold Merit Ski School with telemark lessons available
  Luxurious lodging and fine dining
  A very fine and unique trail booklet is provided which includes flora and
    fauna identification hints, a fine trail map, complete descriptions of
    all trails and identification of unique features from the panoramic
    view of Lookout Pointe
  An excellent and well groomed trail system
  Also known as the Bay View Trail of the Sleeping Bear Dunes National
    Lakeshore

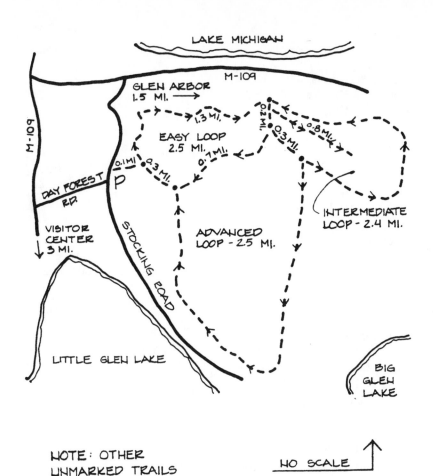

LAKE MICHIGAN

M-109

GLEN ARBOR
1.5 MI. →

M-109

1.3 MI.

0.2 MI.

0.8 MI.

0.3 MI.

EASY LOOP
2.5 MI.

0.1 MI.

0.3 MI.

0.7 MI.

P

DAY FOREST RD.

VISITOR
CENTER
↓ 3 MI.

STOCKING ROAD

ADVANCED
LOOP - 2.5 MI.

INTERMEDIATE
LOOP - 2.4 MI.

LITTLE GLEN LAKE

BIG
GLEN
LAKE

NOTE: OTHER
UNMARKED TRAILS
IN AREA.

NO SCALE

# ALLIGATOR HILL TRAIL

Sleeping Bear Dunes National Lakeshore
PO Box 277, 9922 Front St. (M72)                616-326-5134
Empire, MI  49630

Trail suitable for skiing & hiking

Location:
 Between Glen Haven and Glen Arbor, just south of M109 on Lake Michigan
 Trailhead - 1 mile east of M109 on Day Forest Rd., where Day Forest Rd.
   intersects Stocking Rd. or take Stocking Rd south from M109 just east of
   the DH Day campground entrance.

Trail specifications:
 8.5 mi; 4 loop(s); Loop length(s)-2.5, 5, 5.2, 7.7
Typical terrain: Rolling to hilly
Skiing ability suggested: Novice to advanced
Hiking trail difficulty: Moderate
Nordic trail grooming method: None
Suitable for all-terrain bicycle: Not permitted
Trail use fee: None
Camping: Available at 2 locations in the park
Drinking water available seasonally in campgrounds

General Information:
 Maintained by the Sleeping Bear Dunes National Lakeshore
 Very scenic overlooks of Glen Haven, Lake Michigan and Glen Lake
 Hunting in season: 9/15 to 12/15, please wear bright clothing
 Winter accomodations available in Empire at the Lakeshore Inn 326-5145.
   See also the Platte Plains Trail for other listings in the area.

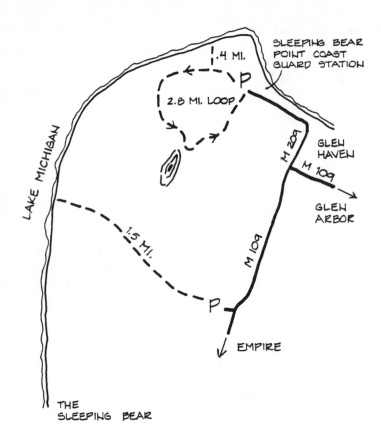

.4 MI.

SLEEPING BEAR
POINT COAST
GUARD STATION

2.8 MI. LOOP

P

LAKE MICHIGAN

M 209

GLEN
HAVEN

M 109

GLEN
ARBOR

1.5 MI.

M 109

P

EMPIRE

THE
SLEEPING BEAR

NO SCALE

# DUNES TRAIL

---

Dunes Trail                                    Revised:  4/07/88

Sleeping Bear Dunes National Lakeshore
PO Box 277, 9922 Front St. (M72)                616-326-5134
Empire, MI  49630

Trail suitable for hiking only

Location:
 South trail - On M109 near the Dune Climb, south of Glen Haven
 North trail - Near Sleeping Bear Dunes Point Coast Guard Station west of
   Glen Haven

Trail specifications:
  4.7 mi *; 2* loop(s); Loop length(s)-3 (round trip), 3.2
Typical terrain: Hilly loose sand
Skiing ability suggested: NA
Hiking trail difficulty: Difficult
Nordic trail grooming method: NA
Suitable for all-terrain bicycle: Not permitted
Trail use fee: None
Camping: Available at 2 locations in the park
Drinking water is not available in the winter at campgrounds

General Information:
 Maintained by the Sleeping Bear Dunes National Lakeshore
 * South trail is a point to point trail of 1.5 miles, 3 miles round trip
    leading to the Lake Michigan shoreline
   North trail is a 2.8 mile loop with a point to point spur of .4 mile
 Groups and families are strongly cautioned to stay togather since
    distances on the dunes are deceiving and its easy to become
    disoriented and lost
 Wear bright clothing during the hunting season 9/15 to 12/15

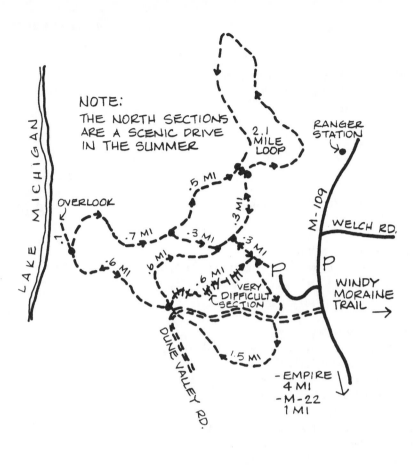

NOTE:
THE NORTH SECTIONS
ARE A SCENIC DRIVE
IN THE SUMMER

2.1 MILE LOOP

RANGER STATION

LAKE MICHIGAN

OVERLOOK

.5 MI

.3 MI

.7 MI

.3 MI

.3 MI

.3 MI

.6 MI

.6 MI

.6 MI

.6 MI

VERY DIFFICULT SECTION

P    P

WELCH RD.

M-109

WINDY MORAINE TRAIL →

DUNE VALLEY RD.

1.5 MI

- EMPIRE 4 MI
- M-22 1 MI

.5          1 MI

SCENIC DRIVE CROSS COUNTRY
SKI TRAIL

Scenic Drive Cross Country Ski Trail          Revised: 4/07/88

Sleeping Bear Dunes National Lakeshore
PO Box 277, 9922 Front St. (M72)                    616-326-5134
Empire, MI  49630

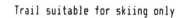

Trail suitable for skiing only

Location:
 SW of Glen Lake on M109
 Trailhead - 3  miles north of Empire on M109 just south of Welch Rd. and
   the park Visitor Center.  A short drive to the trailhead parking is on
   the west side of the road

Trail specifications:
  4.7 mi; Many loop(s); Loop length(s)-various
Typical terrain: Rolling to very steep
Skiing ability suggested: Novice and advanced
Hiking trail difficulty: Moderate to difficult
Nordic trail grooming method: None
Suitable for all-terrain bicycle: Not permitted
Trail use fee: None
Camping: Available at two locations in the park
Drinking water is not available in the winter at the campgrounds

General Information:
 Maintained by the Sleeping Bear Dunes National Lakeshore
 An advanced return trail is very difficult and should only be attempted
   by experienced skiers (see map)
 Spectacular scenic overlook of the shore of Lake Michigan and the dunes
 Across the road from the Windy Moraine Trail
 Parts of this trail are new for 1987
 Previously this trail was known as the Shauger Hill Trail
 Scenic views of Glen Lake, Lake Michigan and the dunes
 Parts of the trail are the Pierce Stocking Scenic Drive used in the
   snowless months. These sections can be skied in both directions
 The downhill sections of the drive are great for telemarking
 Wear bright clothing during hunting season 9/15 - 12/15
 Winter accomodations available in Empire at the Lakeshore Inn 326-5145,
   Shady Shores Resort 334-3252 and Maple Lane Resort 334-3413.

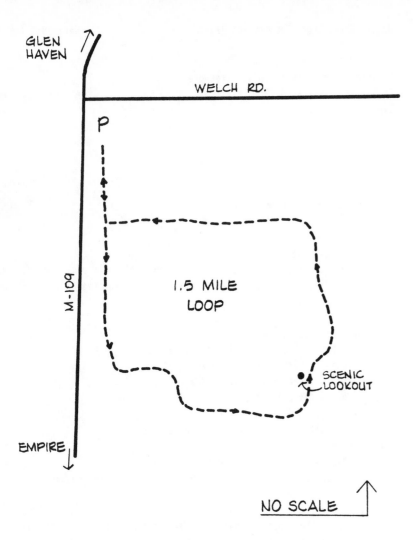

GLEN
HAVEN

WELCH RD.

P

M-109

1.5 MILE
LOOP

SCENIC
LOOKOUT

EMPIRE

NO SCALE

# WINDY MORAINE TRAIL

Sleeping Bear Dunes National Lakeshore
PO Box 277, 9922 Front St. (M72)                    616-326-5134
Empire, MI  49630

Trail suitable for skiing & hiking

Location:
 SW of Glen Lake on M109
  Trailhead -  3 miles north of Empire on M109 and just south of Welch Rd.
  Across from and north of the entrance to the Stocking Scenic Drive.


Trail specifications:
    1.5 mi; 1 loop(s); Loop length(s)-1.5
Typical terrain: Rolling
Skiing ability suggested: Novice
Hiking trail difficulty: Easy
Nordic trail grooming method: None
Suitable for all-terrain bicycle: Not permitted
Trail use fee: None
Camping: Available at two locations in the park
Drinking water not available

General Information:
 Maintained by the Sleeping Bear Dunes National Lakeshore
 Across the road from the Scenic Drive Cross Country Ski Trail
 The trail consists of 1/3 downhill, 1/3 flat and 1/3 uphill
 Wear bright clothing during hunting season 9/15 - 12/15
 Winter accomodations available in Empire at the Lakeshore Inn 326-5145,
   Shady Shores Resort 334-3252 and Maple Lane Resort 334-3413.  See
   also the Platte Plains Trail for other listings in the area.

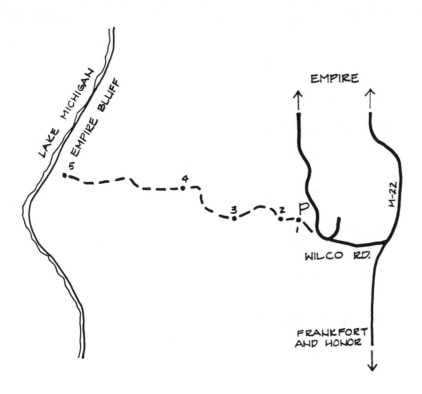

NO SCALE

# EMPIRE BLUFF TRAIL

Sleeping Bear Dunes National Lakeshore
PO Box 277, 9922 Front St. (M72)                616-326-5134
Empire, MI  49630

Trail suitable for skiing & hiking

Location:
 1 mile south of Empire on Wilco Rd. along Lake Michigan

Trail specifications:
   .75 mi; No* loop(s); Loop length(s)-NA
Typical terrain: Hilly
Skiing ability suggested: Intermediate to advanced
Hiking trail difficulty: Moderate
Nordic trail grooming method: None
Suitable for all-terrain bicycle: Not permitted
Trail use fee: None
Camping: Available at two locations in the park
Drinking water not available

General Information:
 Maintained by the Sleeping Bear Dunes National Lakeshore
 Very impressive overlook of Lake Michigan from the end of the trail
 Wear bright clothing during hunting season 9/15 - 12/15
 Winter accomodations available in Empire at the Lakeshore Inn 326-5145;
   Shady Shores Resort 334-3252; and Maple Lane Resort 334-3413.  See also
   the Platte Plains Trail for other listings.
 The trail has some challenging sections. Not recommended for the beginner
 * This is a point to point trail

209

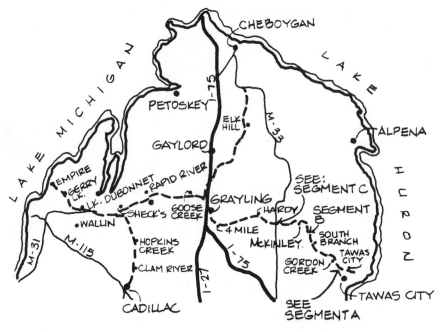

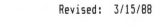

Michigan Trail Riders Association Inc
Chamber of Commerce                                         616-947-5075
Traverse City, MI  49684

DNR Forest Management Division
PO Box 30028                                                517-373-1275
Lansing, MI  48909

Trail suitable for hiking only*

Location:
  Extends from Empire to Tawas with spurs noth to M33 and south from
    Mayfield to Cadillac

Trail specifications:
    302 mi; No** loop(s); Loop length(s)-NA
Typical terrain: Flat to hilly
Skiing ability suggested: NA
Hiking trail difficulty: Easy to difficult
Nordic trail grooming method: NA
Suitable for all-terrain bicycle: No
Trail use fee: None
Camping: Campgounds along trail(see map)
Drinking water at campgrounds

General Information:
  Maintained by the DNR Forest Management and Parks Divisions and the
    Michigan Trail Riders Association
  Connects with sections maintained by the Huron-Manistee National Forest
    in the Tawas to Mio area. See other listings for more detail.
  * Used heavily by horseback riders. Some sections may not be suitable
    for hiking because of extensive loose sand.
  Other trails near or along this trail:
    Midland to Mackinac Pathway, Mason Tract Pathway, Muncie Lakes Pathway
    Wakeley Lake Non-Motorized Area, Corsair Trail, Highbanks Trail
    Ranch Rudolf, Sand Lakes Quiet Area and Loud Creek Pathway
  ** This is a point to point trail across the state from Lake Michigan to
    Lake Huron with spurs north and south
  Other contact:
  DNR Forest Management Region Office, Roscommon, 517-275-5151

NOTE:
SEE SEGMENTS IN MORE
DETAIL ELSEWHERE IN
ATLAS.

• CAMGROUNDS

NO SCALE

SHORE TO SHORE TRAIL

210

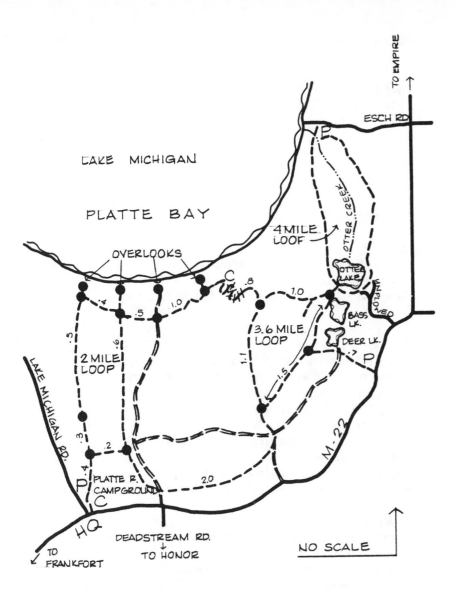

LAKE MICHIGAN

PLATTE BAY

OVERLOOKS

4 MILE LOOF

OTTER CREEK

TO EMPIRE

ESCH RD

OTTER LAKE

C

.8

.4

.5

1.0

1.0

BASS LK.

UNIMPROVED

3.6 MILE LOOP

.6

2 MILE LOOP

1.1

DEER LK.

.7  P

.5

.5

LAKE MICHIGAN RD.

.3

.2

M-22

.4

.2

PLATTE R. CAMPGROUND

2.0

P
C

HQ

DEADSTREAM RD.

TO HONOR

TO FRANKFORT

NO SCALE

PLATTE PLAINS TRAIL

Platte Plains Trail                                    Revised:  4/07/88

Sleeping Bear Dunes National Lakeshore
PO Box 277, 9922 Front St.(M72)                          616-326-5134
Empire, MI  49630

Trail suitable for skiing & hiking

Location:
 North of Platte Lake off M22
 South trailhead - At Platte River Campground
 North trailhead - At the west end of Esch Rd., 1 mile west of M22 and 3.5
    miles south of Empire
 Central trailhead - Just south of Trails End Rd. and M22 intersection
Trail specifications:
  11.7 mi; 3 loop(s); Loop length(s)-various
Typical terrain: Flat to rolling with only one section with hills
Skiing ability suggested: Novice to intermediate
Hiking trail difficulty: Easy to moderate
Nordic trail grooming method: None
Suitable for all-terrain bicycle: Not permitted
Trail use fee: None
Camping: Campground at south trailhead and along trail on Lake Michigan
Drinking water is not available in the winter at the campgrounds

General Information:
 Maintained by the Sleeping Bear Dunes National Lakeshore
 Several overlooks of Lake Michigan
 Extensive trail system of diverse habitat
 Wear bright clothing during hunting season 9/15 - 12/15
 Winter accomodations available in Empire at the Lakeshore Inn 326-5145,
   Shady Shores Resort 334-3252 and Maple Lane Resort 334-3413; Beulah
   at the Bookside Inn 882-7271; in Frankfort at the Frankfort Inn
   352-4303 and Harbor Lights 352-9614; and near Maple City the Leelanau
   Country Inn 228-5060

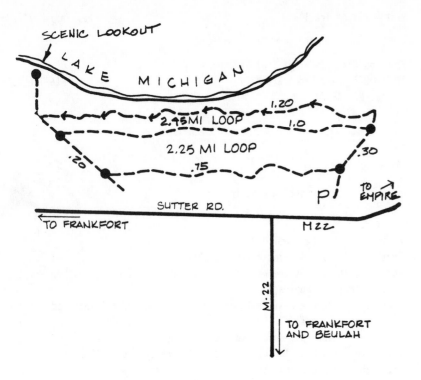

SCENIC LOOKOUT

LAKE MICHIGAN

1.20

2.45 MI LOOP          1.0

2.25 MI LOOP

.30

.20          .75

SUTTER RD.

TO FRANKFORT

M22

TO EMPIRE

P

M-22

TO FRANKFORT
AND BEULAH

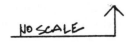

NO SCALE

# OLD INDIAN TRAIL

Sleeping Bear Dunes National Lakeshore
PO Box 277, 9922 Front St. (M72)                    616-326-5134
Empire, MI  49630

Trail suitable for skiing & hiking

Location:
 Between Frankfort and Empire on the north side of Crystal Lake near the
   west end of Long Lake
 Trailhead - At the intersection of M22 and Sutter Rd.

Trail specifications:
   5 mi; 2 loop(s); Loop length(s)-2.3, 4.5
Typical terrain: Flat to rolling with one steep hill
Skiing ability suggested: Novice
Hiking trail difficulty: Easy
Nordic trail grooming method: None
Suitable for all-terrain bicycle: Not permitted
Trail use fee: None
Camping: Available at two locations in the park
Drinking water is not available in the winter at the campgrounds

General Information:
 Maintained by the Sleeping Bear Dunes National Lakeshore
 Scenic view of Lake Michigan along the trail
 Wear bright clothing during hunting season 9/15 - 12/15
 Winter accomodations available in Frankfort at the Harborlights 352-9641,
   Frankfort Inn 352-4303 and Brookside Inn 882-7271.  See also the
   Platte Plains Trail for other listings in the area.

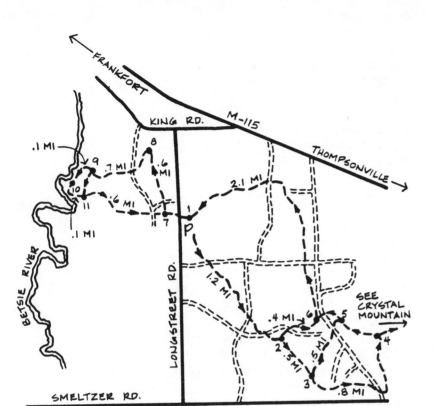

FRANKFORT

KING RD.    M-115

THOMPSONVILLE

.1 MI

8

9   .7 MI    6
            .6 MI

2.1 MI

10

11   .6 MI    1

.1 MI    7    P

BETSIE RIVER

LONGSTREET RD.

.2 MI

.4 MI   6   5

SEE
CRYSTAL
MOUNTAIN

2   .5 MI

.5 MI    4

3

SMELTZER RD.                    .8 MI

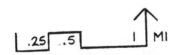

.25   .5    1   MI

# BETSIE RIVER
# PATHWAY

Betsie River Pathway                                          Revised:  3/05/88

Area Forester, Traverse City Forest Area
404 W 14th St.                                               616-964-4920
Traverse City, MI  49684

District Forest Manager, Pere Marquette State Forest
Rte 1, 8015 South US131                                      616-775-9727
Cadillac, MI  49601

Trail suitable for skiing & hiking

Location:
  Between Frankfort and Thompsonville on M115
  Trailhead - West from Thompsonville 5 miles (just beyond Crystal Mt),
    then bear left(south) on King Rd. .5 miles to Longstreet Rd., then left
    again for .75 miles to parking lot on the left

Trail specifications:
   10 mi; 5 loop(s); Loop length(s)-various
Typical terrain: Rolling to hilly
Skiing ability suggested: Novice to intermediate
Hiking trail difficulty: Easy to moderate
Nordic trail grooming method: Track set
Suitable for all-terrain bicycle: Yes
Trail use fee: None
Camping: None
Drinking water not available

General Information:
  Maintained by the DNR Forest Management Division
  Trails west of the parking lot are more difficult than the loops toward
    the east
  Trails connect to Crystal Mountain alpine ski area (trail use fee area)
  The combination of the DNR and Crystal Mountain trails makes for a very
    enjoyable day of skiing
  There is a good ski shop in Beulah if repairs or equipment are needed

Other contacts:
DNR Forest Management Division Office, Lansing, 517-373-1275
DNR Forest Management Region Office, Roscommon, 517-275-5151

213

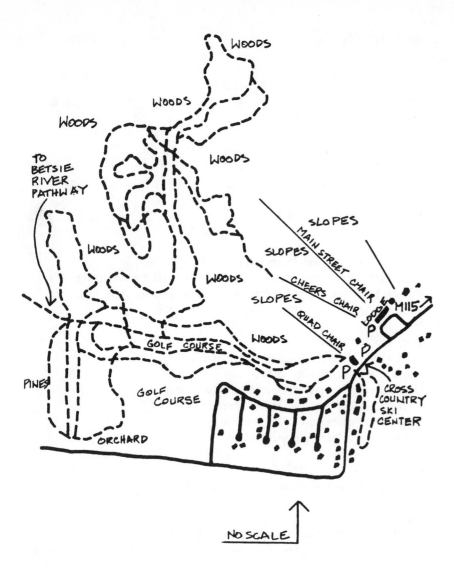

WOODS

WOODS

WOODS

WOODS

TO
BETSIE
RIVER
PATHWAY

WOODS

WOODS

WOODS

PINES

SLOPES

SLOPES

SLOPES

MAIN STREET CHAIR

CHEERS CHAIR

SLOPES

QUAD CHAIR

GOLF COURSE

GOLF
COURSE

ORCHARD

LODGE

M115

P

P

P

CROSS
COUNTRY
SKI
CENTER

NO SCALE

CRYSTAL MOUNTAIN RESORT

Crystal Mountain Resort                    Revised: 4/01/88

Nancy Story, Public Relations Director
Crystal Mountain Resort                    616-378-2911
Thompsonville, MI  49683                   800-321-4637‡

Kirk Davidson, Nordic Director
Crystal Mountain Resort                    616-378-2911
Thompsonville, MI  49683                   800-321-4637‡

Trail suitable for skiing only

Location:
 On M115, 36 miles NW of Cadillac
 28 miles SW of Traverse City via county roads

Trail specifications:
   26 km; 12 loop(s); Loop length(s)-various
Typical terrain: Rolling to very hilly
Skiing ability suggested: Novice to advanced
Hiking trail difficulty: NA
Nordic trail grooming method: Double track set with skating lanes‡‡
Suitable for all-terrain bicycle: NA
Trail use fee: Yes, $4.00/$6.00 with lift ticket privilege
Camping: None

General Information:
 Privately operated 4 season alpine ski area with extensive cross-country
   ski trail system
 Lodging, restaurant, PSIA instruction, rentals, ski shop, entertainment
   and an outdoor pool
 Trails were expertly designed by John Capper
 Trail system connects to the Betsie River Pathway to the west
 Very scenic views from the trail
 6 km lighted trail
 ‡ In Michigan only
 ‡‡ Power tiller grooming on 12 km
 12 km of skating trail
 Quality skating ski and classic ski rentals available
 Trail access can be gained from the Cheers Chairlift
 The cross country ski center is at the golf course clubhouse

214

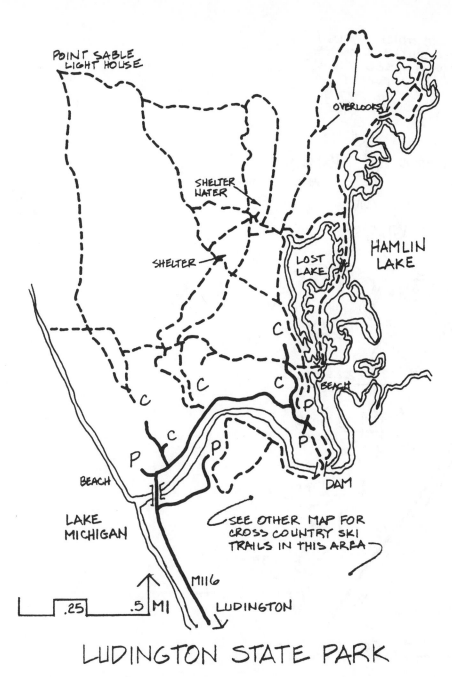

POINT SABLE LIGHT HOUSE

OVERLOOKS

SHELTER WATER

SHELTER

HAMLIN LAKE

LOST LAKE

C

C

C

BEACH

C

C

C

P

P

P

P

P

P

BEACH

LAKE MICHIGAN

DAM

SEE OTHER MAP FOR CROSS COUNTRY SKI TRAILS IN THIS AREA

M116

LUDINGTON

.25     .5 MI

LUDINGTON STATE PARK

Ludington State Park                    Revised:  3/28/88

Ludington State Park
Box 709                                              616-843-8671
Ludington, MI  49431

DNR Parks Division Office

                                                         517-373-1270

Trail suitable for skiing & hiking

Location:
 North of Ludington at the end of M116

Trail specifications:
    25 mi; 17 loop(s); Loop length(s)-various
Typical terrain: Rolling to hilly
Skiing ability suggested: Novice to advanced
Hiking trail difficulty: Easy to difficult
Nordic trail grooming method: Track set as needed
Suitable for all-terrain bicycle: Yes
Trail use fee: None, but vehicle entry fee required $2/day, $10/year
Camping: Campgrounds in the park
Drinking water available in the park

General Information:
 Maintained by the DNR Parks Division
 Extensive trail system
 Some hiking trails are not suitable for skiing and some ski trails are not
    available for hiking
 In the summer the park is a favorite destination for many campers
 Some trails are not well marked. Be sure to take both hiking and ski trail
    maps with you in the winter
 Shelters and toilets are available along the trail system
 1,699 acres have been designated as a Wildnerness Natural Area.  This
    area includes the park land from Big Sable Lighthouse to north the the
    boundary (which is the south boundary of the Nordhouse Dunes, managed
    by the Forest Service).  No motorized vehicles allowed in this area
    of the park.

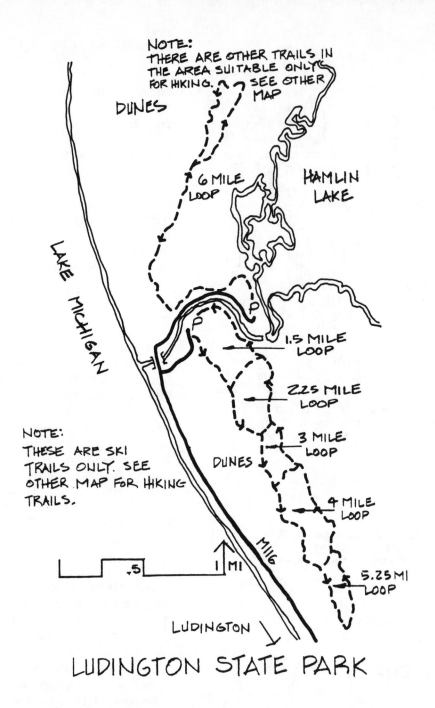

NOTE:
THERE ARE OTHER TRAILS IN THE AREA SUITABLE ONLY FOR HIKING. SEE OTHER MAP

DUNES

6 MILE LOOP

HAMLIN LAKE

LAKE MICHIGAN

NOTE:
THESE ARE SKI TRAILS ONLY. SEE OTHER MAP FOR HIKING TRAILS.

1.5 MILE LOOP

2.25 MILE LOOP

3 MILE LOOP

DUNES

4 MILE LOOP

.5    1 MI

M116

5.25 MI LOOP

LUDINGTON

LUDINGTON STATE PARK

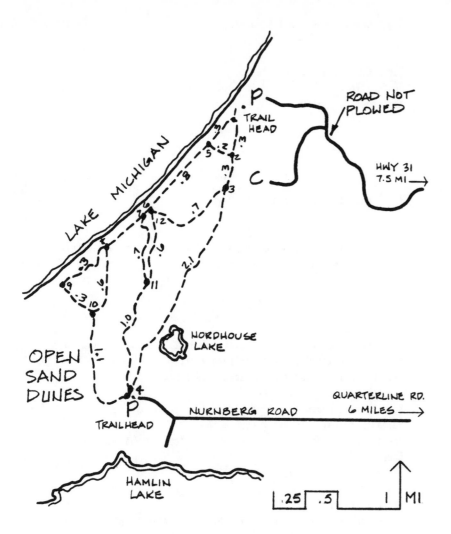

OPEN
SAND
DUNES

LAKE MICHIGAN

ROAD NOT
PLOWED

P
TRAIL
HEAD

C

HWY 31
7.5 MI →

NORDHOUSE
LAKE

P
TRAILHEAD

NURNBERG ROAD

QUARTERLINE RD.
6 MILES →

HAMLIN
LAKE

.25   .5         1  MI

# NORDHOUSE DUNES TRAILS

Manistee Ranger District, Huron-Manistee National Forest
1658 Manistee Highway                                    616-723-2211
Manistee, MI  49660

Forest Supervisor, Huron-Manistee National Forest
421 S. Mitchell St.                                      616-775-2421
Cadillac, MI  49601

Trail suitable for hiking & skiing

Location:
 Between Ludington and Manistee on Lake Michigan
 South trailhead - At west end of Nurnberg Rd., 6 miles west of
    Quarterline Rd.
 North trailhead - Lake Michigan Recreation Area which is at the west end
    of FH 5629, 7.5 miles from US31 (9 miles south of Manistee)
Trail specifications:
    10 mi; 8+ loop(s); Loop length(s)-.6 to 2.2
Typical terrain: Flat to hilly
Skiing ability suggested: Intermediate to advanced
Hiking trail difficulty: Moderate
Nordic trail grooming method: None
Suitable for all-terrain bicycle: No
Trail use fee: None
Camping: Campground available at Lake Michigan Recreation Area
Drinking water available at campground and picnic area

General Information:
 Maintained by Manistee Ranger District, Huron-Manistee National Forest
 Recommended only for advanced skiers with winter survival skills
 Trails not designed for skiing but are skiable
 Some trails in dune area along Lake Michigan shore
 Lake Michigan Recreation Area is located at the north trailhead off
   FR 5629, 7.5 miles west of US31. Campground contains 98 paved parking
   spurs with direct access to Lake Michigan. Fee charged for camping.
 FR 5629 is not plowed.  Access must be gained via Nurnberg Rd.
 Trails are located within the Nordhouse Dunes Wilderness
 1200 acres of wooded sand dunes
 700 acres of open sand
 4 miles of beach on Lake Michigan

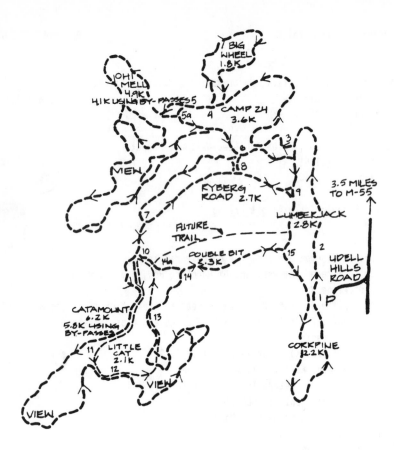

BIG M
CROSS COUNTRY SKI AREA

Big M Cross Country Ski Area                    Revised:  2/03/88


Big M Cross Country Ski Area
PO Box 196                                      616-723-2575
Manistee, MI  49660                             616-723-6062

Trail suitable for skiing only

Location:
  About 18 miles east of Manistee and 7 miles west of Wellston on M55, then
    south 3.5 miles on Udell Hills Rd.


Trail specifications:
   30 km; 6 loop(s); Loop length(s)-1.8, 2.5, 3.2, 3.6, 4.0, 5.2
Typical terrain: Rolling to extremely hilly
Skiing ability suggested: Novice to advanced
Hiking trail difficulty: NA
Nordic trail grooming method: Track set
Suitable for all-terrain bicycle: NA
Trail use fee: None, but donations accepted.  Annual membership $10
Camping: None
Drinking water not available


General Information:
  Developed and maintained by the Manistee Cross Country Ski Council in
    cooperation with the Huron-Manistee National Forest
  Trails in the Huron-Manistee National Forest
  Expertly designed trails by John Capper
  On the site of the former Big M alpine ski area
  A very scenic trail system
  Food and lodging in Wellston
  Rentals available in Manistee at Sports World 723-5908 or
    Northwind Sports 723-2255
  Call Tom Moerdyk at 848-4431 for snow conditions
  Write for free brochure

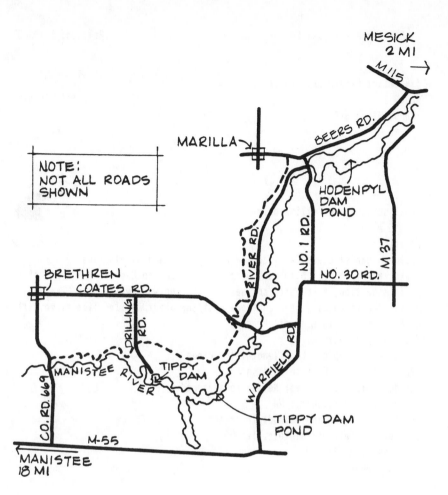

MESICK 2 MI

MARILLA

BEERS RD.

HODENPYL DAM POND

NO. 1 RD.

NO. 30 RD.

M 37

M 115

RIVER RD.

NOTE: NOT ALL ROADS SHOWN

BRETHREN

COATES RD.

DRILLING RD.

WARFIELD RD.

MANISTEE RIVER

TIPPY DAM

TIPPY DAM POND

CO. RD. 669

M-55

MANISTEE 18 MI

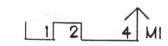

1 2 4 MI

# NORTH COUNTRY TRAIL- MANISTEE

North Country Trail - Manistee          Revised: 12/12/87

Manistee Ranger District, Huron-Manistee National Forest
1658 Manistee Highway                    616-723-2211
Manistee, MI  49660

Forest Supervisor, Huron-Manistee National Forest
421 S. Mitchell St.                      616-775-2421
Cadillac, MI  49601

Trail suitable for hiking & skiing

Location:
 From Marilla go north .5 mile to Beers Rd., then east 2 miles to trailhead
 From Brethren go east on Coats Hwy 7 miles to trail
 From Brethren go east on Coats Hwy 2.5 miles, then south 1.75 miles on
  Drilling Rd. to trail
 From Brethren go south 2.5 miles to the bridge and trailhead
Trail specifications:
  20.2 mi; No loop(s); Loop length(s)-NA
Typical terrain: Rolling to hilly
Skiing ability suggested: Advanced
Hiking trail difficulty: Moderate
Nordic trail grooming method: None
Suitable for all-terrain bicycle: Not permitted
Trail use fee: None
Camping: Camping is permitted 200' from trail
Drinking water is not available along the trail

General Information:
 Maintained by Manistee Ranger District, Huron-Manistee National Forest
 Recommended only for skiers with good winter survival skills
 The trail follows a ridge that parallels the Manistee River
 Excellent views of the Hodenpyl Pond and the Manistee River Valley
 Trail is marked with blue diamond blazes
 For further information about the North Country Trail contact the
  North Country Trail Association, PO Box 311, White Cloud, Mi 49349 or
  USDI, Mid West Region, 1709 Jackson St, Omaha, Nebraska 68102

Timberlane Nordic Ski Center, Inc                    Revised: 11/03/87


Timberlane Nordic Ski Center, Inc
Route 1                                              616-266-5780
Irons, MI  49644


Trail suitable for skiing only

Location:
 Between Manistee and Cadillac, SW of Wellston and NW of Irons
 Take Harvey Rd. (10 Mile Rd.) west out of Irons to Bass Lake Rd. at "T"
   intersection, then north and west continuing west while Bass Lake Rd.
   turns north again, then continue west for about 1 mile, Timberlane will
   be on the north side of the road
Trail specifications:
   25 km; 4 loop(s); Loop length(s)-various
Typical terrain: Flat to rolling
Skiing ability suggested: Novice to advanced
Hiking trail difficulty: NA
Nordic trail grooming method: Track set
Suitable for all-terrain bicycle: NA
Trail use fee: $3.50
Camping: None


General Information:
 Privately operated touring center
 Lodging, snack bar, lessons, warming area, sauna and rentals
 Lodging types include a bunkhouse, lodge and 3 cabins
 A very pleasant area that should not be missed
 Most trails are wooded. Very little open field skiing
 Write or call for information

# No Trail Map

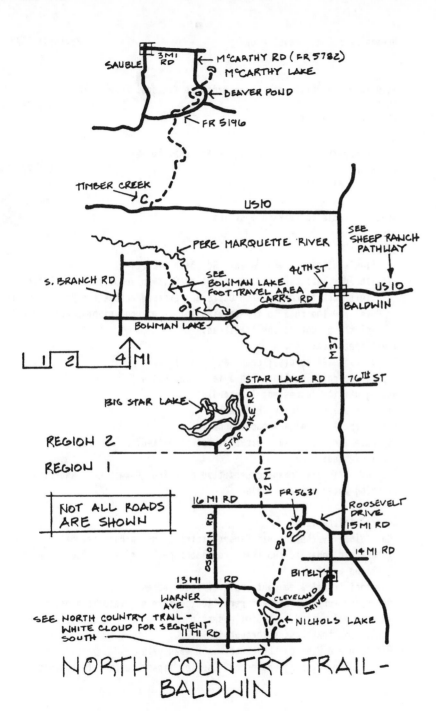

SAUBLE — 3 MI RD

McCARTHY RD (FR 5782)
McCARTHY LAKE
BEAVER POND
FR 5196
TIMBER CREEK — C
US 10
PERE MARQUETTE RIVER
SEE SHEEP RANCH PATHWAY
46TH ST
S. BRANCH RD
SEE BOWMAN LAKE FOOT TRAVEL AREA
CARRS RD
US 10
BALDWIN
BOWMAN LAKE
1 2 4 MI
BIG STAR LAKE
STAR LAKE RD
76TH ST
M37
REGION 2
REGION 1
NOT ALL ROADS ARE SHOWN
2 MI
FR 5631
16 MI RD
ROOSEVELT DRIVE
15 MI RD
OSBORN RD
C
B
14 MI RD
13 MI RD
BITELY
WARNER AVE
CLEVELAND DRIVE
SEE NORTH COUNTRY TRAIL - WHITE CLOUD FOR SEGMENT SOUTH
C
NICHOLS LAKE
11 MI RD

NORTH COUNTRY TRAIL - BALDWIN

North Country Trail - Baldwin                Revised: 12/02/87

Baldwin Ranger District, Huron-Manistee National Forest
PO Box Drawer D                                      616-745-4631
Baldwin, MI  49304

Forest Supervisor, Huron-Manistee National Forest
421 S. Mitchell St.                                  616-775-2421
Cadillac, MI  49601

Trail suitable for hiking & skiing

Location:
 Trailhead - From Baldwin take M37 south 3 miles to 76th St, then west
   2.5 miles to the trailhead on the south side of the road
 Trailhead - From Bitely take Cleveland Drive west 3.5 miles to Nichols
   Lake R.A. Trail crosses the road west of the entrance to the R.A.
 Trailhead - Bowman Lake Foot Travel Area ‖
Trail specifications:
   19+mi‖‖; No loop(s); Loop length(s)-NA
Typical terrain: Flat to hilly
Skiing ability suggested: Advanced
Hiking trail difficulty: Difficult
Nordic trail grooming method: None
Suitable for all-terrain bicycle: Not permitted
Trail use fee: None
Camping: Campgound at Nichols Lake Recreation Area ‖‖‖
Drinking water available only at Nichols Lake

General Information:
 Maintained by the Baldwin Ranger District, Huron-Manistee NF
 Not designed for skiing. For experienced skiers only
 ‖ Not contiguous with the main 12 mile segment
 ‖‖ This segment of the NCT is not completed.  Three sections of this
  segment are shown on the map.
 See the NCT - White Cloud, for the adjacent segment to the south
 One of the shorter sections of the trail connects with the Bowman
  Lake Foot Travel Area
 ‖‖‖ Camping is also permitted 200' from the trail
 For more information about the North Country Trail, contact the
  North Country Trail Association, PO Box 311, White Cloud, MI 49349
  or the USDI, Mid West Region, 1709 Jackson St, Omaha, NE 68102

FR 5596

PERE MARQUETTE RIVER

FR 5168

BOWMAN
LAKE

56th ST.

EVERGREEN RD.

BALDWIN
6 MI

|___|‾‾|___|     ↑
      .5      1 | MI

# BOWMAN LAKE
FOOT TRAVEL AREA

Baldwin Ranger District, Huron-Manistee National Forest
PO Box Drawer D                                             616-745-4631
Baldwin, MI  49304

Forest Supervisor, Huron-Manistee National Forest
421 S. Mitchell St.                                        616-775-2421
Cadillac, MI  49601

Trail suitable for hiking & skiing

Location:
 6 miles west of Baldwin on Carr Rd (56th Street)
 Trailhead - Take Carrs Rd. west out of Baldwin about 2.5 miles, then take
   a left fork to continue on Carrs Rd, proceed across the Pere Marquette
   River and the road to the parking lot is on your right about 1.5 miles
   past the bridge to the trailhead.
Trail specifications:
   3.7 mi*; 1** loop(s); Loop length(s)-1.2**
Typical terrain: Rolling with a few steep hills
Skiing ability suggested: Intermediate
Hiking trail difficulty: Moderate
Nordic trail grooming method: None
Suitable for all-terrain bicycle: Not permitted
Trail use fee: None
Camping: Primitive camping permitted away from Bowman Lake shoreline
Drinking water not available


General Information:
 Maintained by the Baldwin Ranger District, Huron-Manistee National Forest
 * Many old unmarked two track roads and paths are available for wilderness
   skiing and hiking
 The foot travel area contains over 1,000 acres
 Motorized vehicles are not permitted in this non-motorized area
 ** Does not include a 2.5 mile section of the North Country Trail -
   Baldwin, that passes through the area.
 Pan fish and Bass can be caught in Bowman Lake
 Carry out everything you bring. Use low impact camping techinques.

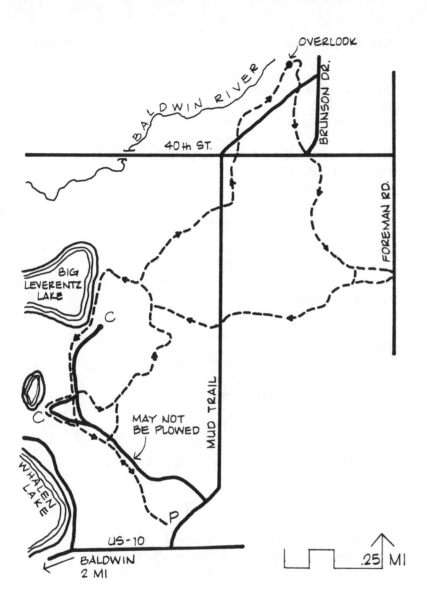

**Sheep Ranch Pathway**

Revised: 3/06/88

Area Forester, Baldwin Forest Area
Rte 2, Box 2810
Baldwin, MI  49304

616-745-4651

District Forest Manager, Pere Marquette State Forest
Rte 1, 8015 South US131
Cadillac, MI  49601

616-775-9727

Trail suitable for skiing & hiking

Location:
 2 miles east of Baldwin on US10, then north on Mud Trail, parking lot
   immediately on the left (west)

Trail specifications:
  4.5 mi; 2 loop(s); Loop length(s)-1,2,3
Typical terrain: Flat to slightly rolling
Skiing ability suggested: Novice
Hiking trail difficulty: Easy
Nordic trail grooming method: None
Suitable for all-terrain bicycle: Yes
Trail use fee: None
Camping: Campgrounds along trail but with limited facilities in winter
Drinking water available

General Information:
 Maintained by the DNR Forest Management Division
 Swamps, low hills, Baldwin River, two lakes and small creeks will be found
   along this trail
 Snowmobilers may be present in the area, sorry.
 Pit toilet at parking lot

**SHEEP RANCH PATHWAY**

Other contacts:
DNR Forest Management Division Office, Lansing, 517-373-1275
DNR Forest Management Region Office, Roscommon, 517-275-5151

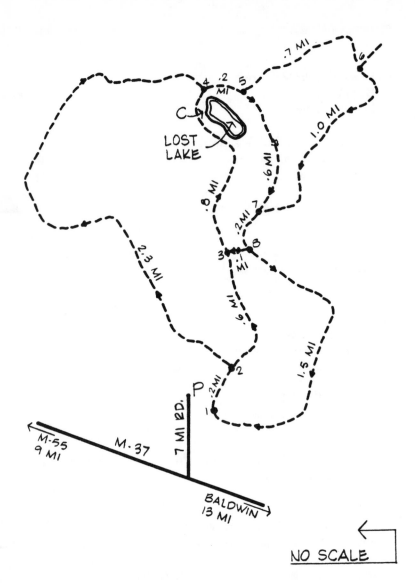

**PINE VALLEYS PATHWAY**

Pine Valleys Pathway                    Revised:  3/05/88

Area Forester, Baldwin Forest Area
Rte 2, Box 2810                         616-745-4651
Baldwin, MI  49304

District Forest Manager, Pere Marquette State Forest
Rte 1, 8015 South US131                 616-775-9727
Cadillac, MI  49601

Trail suitable for skiing & hiking

Location:
 Between Baldwin and M55 on M37
 17 miles north of Baldwin and 9 miles south of M55, then east on 7 Mile Rd
   .2 mile to parking lot


Trail specifications:
   8.2 mi; 4 loop(s); Loop length(s)-various
Typical terrain: Flat to slightly rolling
Skiing ability suggested: Novice
Hiking trail difficulty: Easy
Nordic trail grooming method: None
Suitable for all-terrain bicycle: Yes
Trail use fee: None
Camping: None
Drinking water not available

General Information:
 Maintained by the DNR Forest Management Division
 The southern loops are more interesting than the northern loop that passes
   through a recent clear cut area

Other contacts:
DNR Forest Management Division Office, Lansing, 517-373-1275
DNR Forest Management Region Office, Roscommon, 517-275-5151

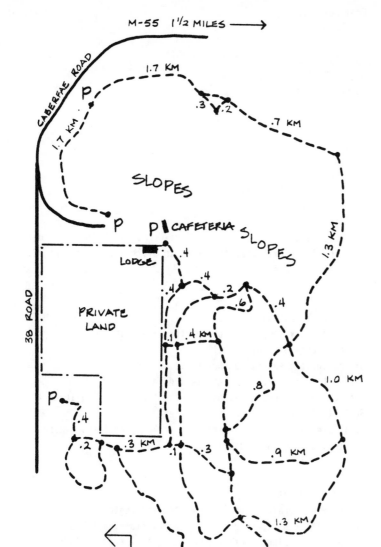

Cadillac Ranger District, Huron-Manistee National Forest
1800 West M55                                              616-775-8539
Cadillac, MI  49601

Forest Supervisor, Huron-Manistee National Forest
421 S. Mitchell St.                                        616-774-2421
Cadillac,

Trail suitable for skiing & hiking

Location:
 From M55/115 junction take M55 west 13 miles to Caberfae Rd., then north
   2 miles to trailheads
 Trailhead - west end of the downhill area parking lot
 Trailhead - take Caberfae Rd north .5 mile to 38 Rd., then west about
   1 mile to parking lot on the south
Trail specifications:
   11.5 mi; Many loop(s); Loop length(s)-various
Typical terrain: Slightly rolling to hilly with some wet land
Skiing ability suggested: Novice to intermediate
Hiking trail difficulty: Easy
Nordic trail grooming method: None‡
Suitable for all-terrain bicycle: Yes
Trail use fee: None
Camping: Backcountry camping permitted along trail
Drinking water available nearby


General Information:
 Maintained by Cadillac Ranger District, Huron-Manistee National Forest
 Ski shop, first aid, rentals and lodging at the adjacent Caberfae Ski
   Area.
 Interesting trails that are well worth the time to ski.  Not all sections
   of the trails are well designed, but the scenery and terrain make for a
   rewarding experience
‡ Since this trail is popular, the trail is usually skied in well.

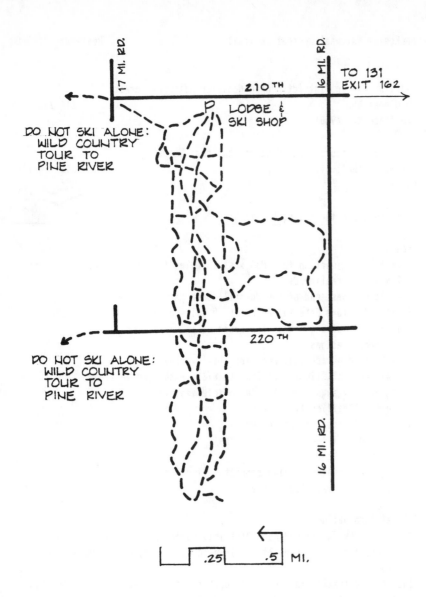

17 MI. RD.

210TH

16 MI. RD.

TO 131
EXIT 162

P LODGE &
SKI SHOP

DO NOT SKI ALONE:
WILD COUNTRY
TOUR TO
PINE RIVER

220TH

DO NOT SKI ALONE:
WILD COUNTRY
TOUR TO
PINE RIVER

16 MI. RD.

.25    .5  MI.

COOL SKI AREA

Cool Ski Area                                    Revised:  3/28/88

Cool Ski Area
5557 N 210th Ave                                 616-768-4624
Le Roy, MI  49655

Trail suitable for skiing & hiking

Location:
 16 miles south of Cadillac and 8 miles north of Reed City on US131
 Exit US131 at exit 162, then west to 210th St., then north 2.5 miles
   to the ski area

Trail specifications:
   50 km; Many loop(s); Loop length(s)-various
Typical terrain: Flat to hilly
Skiing ability suggested: Novice to advanced
Hiking trail difficulty: Easy to moderate
Nordic trail grooming method: Track set with skating lanes ‡
Suitable for all-terrain bicycle: Yes
Trail use fee: $5/day on weekends, weekday are less. Season passes available
Camping: Camping area available

General Information:
 Privately operated, family owned touring center
 One of the best touring centers in the state, with something for everyone.·
   One of the older touring centers, established in 1976
 Lodging of all kinds from ski-in cabins to a bunk house
 Ski shop, rentals, restaurant, warming house, lessons, moonlight & guided
   tours, snowshoe rental, ice skating pond and clinics
 Site of several races in early January
 Trails are a delight to ski with ammenities of benches, fire pits and a
   portion of the trail is lighted.
 Trails pass through a variety of terrain and vegatation
 ‡ Some trails are double tracked and all are well groomed
 Owned and operated by Mike and Norma Cool who are dedicated to make your
   time at their ski area as enjoyable as possible
 Write or call for brochure and reservations

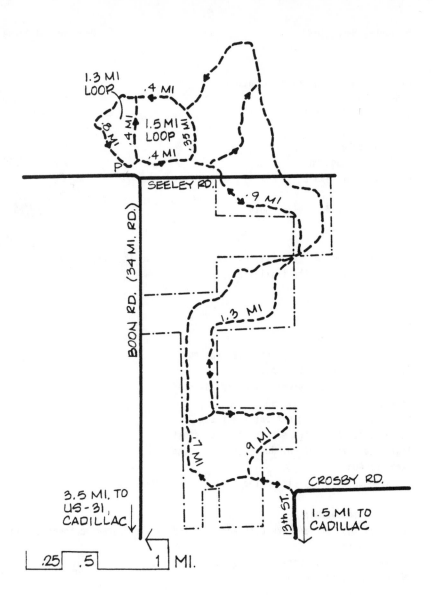

1.3 MI LOOP

.4 MI

.4 MI

.4 MI

1.5 MI LOOP

.35 MI

.4 MI

SEELEY RD.

.9 MI

BOON RD. (34 MI. RD.)

1.3 MI

.9 MI

.7 MI

3.5 MI. TO US-31, CADILLAC

CROSBY RD.

13th ST.

1.5 MI TO CADILLAC

.25  .5  1 MI.

## CADILLAC PATHWAY

Cadillac Pathway                          Revised: 3/05/88

Area Forester, Kalkaska Forest Area
Government Center, 605 North Birch          616-258-9471
Kalkaska, MI  49464

District Forest Manager, Pere Marquette State Forest
Rte 1, 8015 South US131                     616-775-9727
Cadillac, MI  49601

Trail suitable for skiing & hiking

Location:
 Trailhead - North from Cadillac on US131, then right on 13th St. for 1.5
   miles to the point where the road turns south(at playground)
 Trailhead - North from Cadillac on US131, then right on 34 Mile Rd.
   (Boon Rd.) 3.5 miles to Seeley Rd (the road turns north) and the parking
   lot will be found just past the turn on the right
Trail specifications:
   11.3 mi; 9 loop(s); Loop length(s)-various
Typical terrain: Flat to rolling with some hills
Skiing ability suggested: Novice to intermediate
Hiking trail difficulty: Easy
Nordic trail grooming method: Track set usually
Suitable for all-terrain bicycle: Yes
Trail use fee: None
Camping: Campgrounds in the Cadillac area
Drinking water not available

General Information:
 Maintained by the DNR Forest Management Division
 The west loops are more challenging for the more advanced skier
 The east loops off Boon Rd are over more level terrain
 Parking for access to the trailhead on 13th St is in the Wexford-
   Missaukee Intermediate School District building
 A rather good DNR pathway for skiing
 Near MIssaukee Mountain (north of Lake City)

Other contacts:
DNR Forest Management Division Office, Lansing, 517-373-1275
DNR Forest Management Region Office, Roscommon, 517-275-5151

227

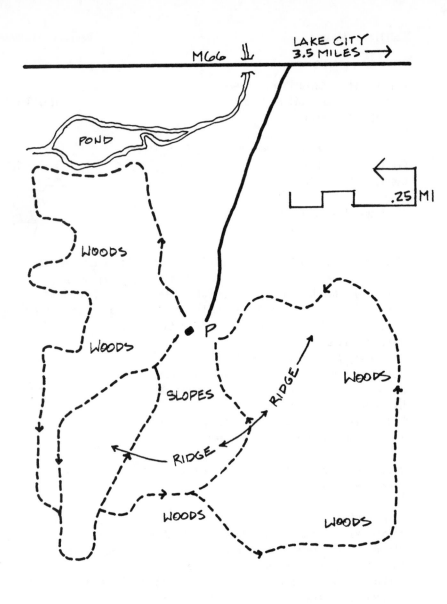

## MISSAUKEE MOUNTAIN

Missaukee Mountain Ski Association
N Morey Rd                                      616-839-7575
Lake City, MI  49651                            616-839-4561

Teri VanderLaan
4439 W. Jennings Rd                             616-839-2548
Lake City, MI  49651

Trail suitable for skiing only

Location:
 3.5 miles north of Lake City on M66 (Morey Rd) to the entrance road
   leading west to the trailhead

Trail specifications:
 5 mi; 3 loop(s); Loop length(s)-various
Typical terrain: Flat to hilly
Skiing ability suggested: Novice to advanced
Hiking trail difficulty: NA
Nordic trail grooming method: Track set
Suitable for all-terrain bicycle: Not permitted
Trail use fee: None, but donations are accepted
Camping: None
Drinking water available in the lodge

General Information:
 Owned by the City of Lake City and operated by the Missaukee Mountain Ski
   Association
 Lodge, snack bar, rentals and lessons available
 Near the Cadillac Pathway

The top phone number is only answered on winter weekends
The second phone number is the Lake City clerks office

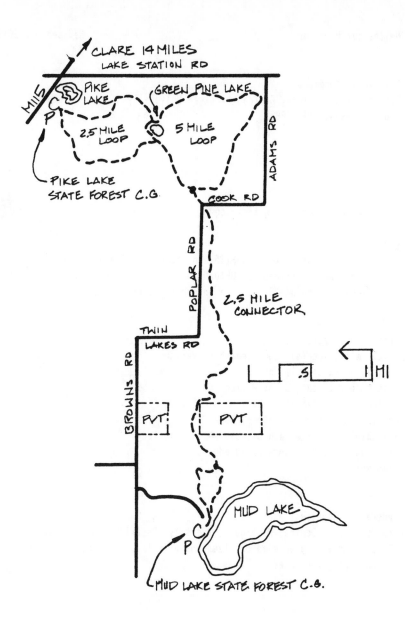

Green Pine Lake Pathway                           Revised: 4/01/88

Area Forester, Au Sable State Forest
801 N. Silver Leaf, PO Box 337                    517-426-9205
Gladwin, MI  48624

District Forest Manager, Au Sable State Forest
191 South Mt. Tom Rd.                             517-826-3211
Mio, MI  48647

Trail suitable for skiing & hiking

Location:
 14 miles NW of Clare on M115 at the Pike Lake State Forest Campground

Trail specifications:
 8.5 mi; 3 loop(s); Loop length(s)-2.5, 5, 1, 2.5(connector)
Typical terrain: Flat to slightly rolling
Skiing ability suggested: Novice
Hiking trail difficulty: Easy
Nordic trail grooming method: None
Suitable for all-terrain bicycle: Yes
Trail use fee: None
Camping: Campground available at trailhead
Drinking water available at campgrounds

General Information:
 Maintained by the DNR Forest Management Division

GREEN PINE LAKE PATHWAY

Other contacts:
DNR Forest Management Division Office, Lansing, 517-373-1275
DNR Forest Management Region Office, Roscommon, 517-275-5151

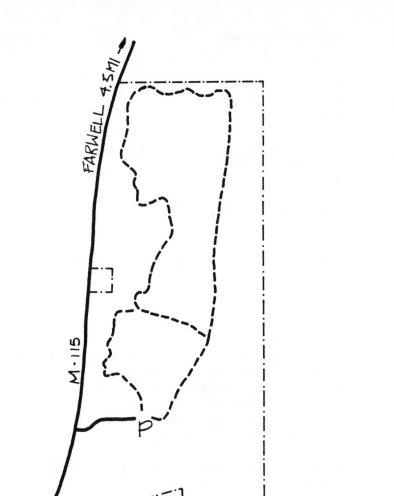

FARWELL 4.5 MI

M-115

P

.25 MI.

# NEITHERCUT WOODLAND

Neithercut Woodland
Department of Biology, Central Michigan University          517-774-3412
Mount Pleasant, MI  48859

Trail suitable for hiking & skiing

Location:
 4.5 miles west of Farwell on M115, on the south side of the road
 Property starts just west of US10/M115 intersection (the west end of the
    divided section of US10).  The entrance is about 1 mile farther west.

Trail specifications:
   2.5 mi; 3 loop(s); Loop length(s)-various
Typical terrain: Rolling
Skiing ability suggested: Novice
Hiking trail difficulty: Easy
Nordic trail grooming method: None
Suitable for all-terrain bicycle: Not permitted
Trail use fee: Donations accepted
Camping: None

General Information:
 Maintained by Central Michigan University, Department of Biology
 This is primarily an outdoor classroom with trails for hiking and skiing
    containing 250 acres

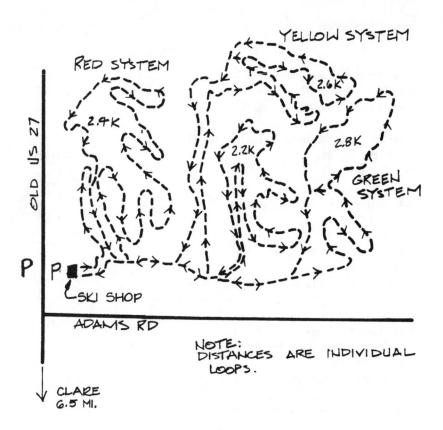

RED SYSTEM

YELLOW SYSTEM

2.4K

2.6K

2.2K

2.8K

GREEN SYSTEM

OLD US 27

P    P ■
    └ SKI SHOP

ADAMS RD

NOTE:
DISTANCES ARE INDIVIDUAL
LOOPS.

↓ CLARE
  6.5 MI.

NO SCALE ↑

# CHALET CROSS COUNTRY

Chalet Cross Country                                    Revised:  3/20/88

Chalet Cross Country Inc
5931 S. Clare Ave                                       517-386-9697
Clare, MI  48617

Downtown Drugs
523 McEwan                                              517-386-9905
Clare, MI  48617

Trail suitable for skiing only

Location:
 6.5 miles north of Clare on old US27
 From the north US10/27 Clare exit, take Clare Ave (Old 27) north 5.5 miles
   to the top of the hill.  Parking on both sides of Old 27


Trail specifications:
  10 km; 6‡ loop(s); Loop length(s)-1 to 2.8
Typical terrain: Flat to hilly
Skiing ability suggested: Novice to advanced
Hiking trail difficulty: NA
Nordic trail grooming method: Track set with skating trails ‡‡
Suitable for all-terrain bicycle: NA
Trail use fee: Yes
Camping: None


General Information:
 Privately operated touring center
 Warming area, lessons, rentals and ski shop
 Open from 10am to 7pm
 ‡ 4 trail systems
 ‡‡ Green and Blue Systems are tracked; Red and Yellow Systems are
   packed for skating

231

NOTE: SOME ROADS SHOWN
MAY NOT BE PLOWED.

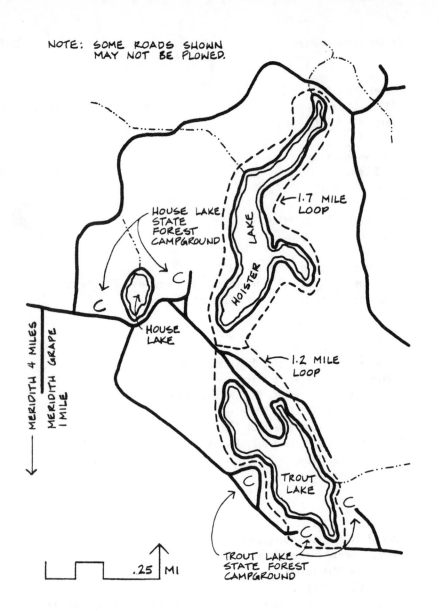

HOUSE LAKE
STATE
FOREST
CAMPGROUND

HOISTER LAKE

1.7 MILE
LOOP

HOUSE
LAKE

1.2 MILE
LOOP

MERIDITH 4 MILES

MERIDITH GRADE 1 MILE

TROUT
LAKE

TROUT LAKE
STATE FOREST
CAMPGROUND

.25 MI

# TROUT LAKE PATHWAY

Trout Lake Pathway

Revised: 3/13/88

Area Forester, Roscommon Forest Area
Box 158
Houghton Lake Heights, MI  48630

517-422-5522

District Forest Manager, Au Sable State Forest
191 S. Mt. Tom Rd.
Mio, MI  48647

517-826-3211

Trail suitable for skiing & hiking

Location:
 In the NW corner of Gladwin County
 2 miles east of Meridith
 1 mile north of M18 off the Meridith Grade

Trail specifications:
    2.7 mi; 2 loop(s); Loop length(s)-1.2, 1.7
Typical terrain:
Skiing ability suggested: Novice
Hiking trail difficulty: Easy
Nordic trail grooming method: None
Suitable for all-terrain bicycle: Yes
Trail use fee: None
Camping: Available along the trail
Drinking water is available

General Information:
 Maintained by the DNR Forest Management Division

Other contacts:
 DNR Forest Management Division Office, Lansing, 517-373-1275
 DNR Forest Management Region Office, Roscommon, 517-275-5151

# Region 3

# Region 3

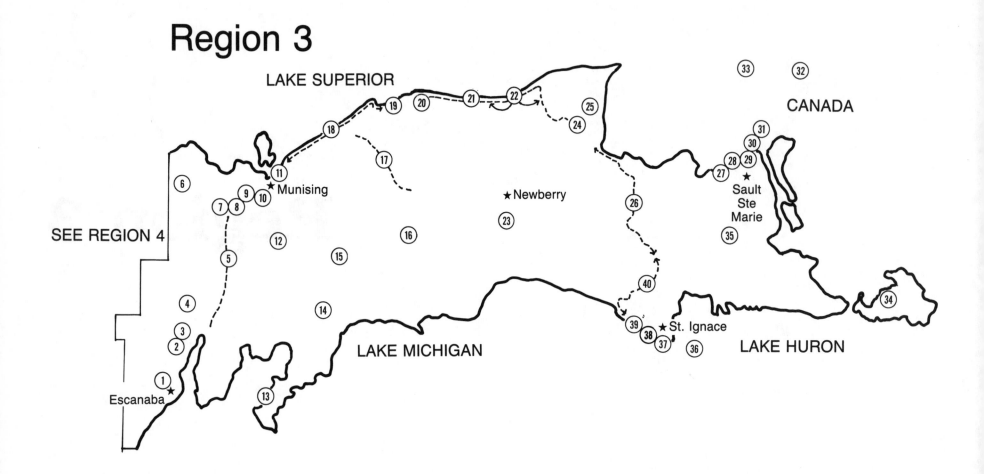

LAKE SUPERIOR

CANADA

SEE REGION 4

★ Newberry

★ Munising

★ Sault Ste Marie

LAKE MICHIGAN

★ St. Ignace

LAKE HURON

Escanaba

# Region 3 Contents

# Trail Notes

OVERLOOK

6.3 MILES

7.7 MILES

4.5 MILES

30TH STREET

STOP SIGN

STOP SIGN

US2/41

ST FRANCIS HOSPITAL

ESCANABA 2 MILES

NO SCALE

# ESCANABA
# CROSS COUNTRY SKI PATHWAY

Department of Recreation, City of Escanaba
121 S. 11th St.                                  906-786-4141
Escanaba, MI  49829

Trail suitable for skiing only

Location:
 On N. 30th St. (dead end street) in Escanaba, .5 mile north of US2/41 on
   the west side of town, just before St. Francis Hospital located on
   US2/41

Trail specifications:
   17.3 km; 3 loop(s); Loop length(s)-7.2, 10.1, 17.3
Typical terrain: Flat to rolling
Skiing ability suggested: Novice to advanced
Hiking trail difficulty: NA
Nordic trail grooming method: Track set daily or as needed
Suitable for all-terrain bicycle: Not permitted
Trail use fee: $1/day at trailhead or $5/season
Camping: None in area
Drinking water not available

General Information:
 Maintained by the City of Escanaba
 Within the city limits but in a very heavily forested area
 Within 15 miles of 4 other trails; Days River Pathway, Rapid River Cross-
   Country Ski Trail, Cedar River Pathway and Gladstone Cross Country Ski
   Trail.  See these other listings

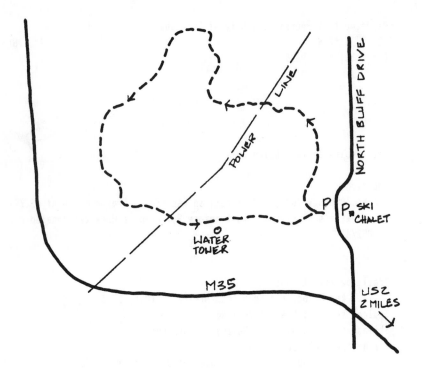

**GLADSTONE**
**CROSS COUNTRY SKI TRAIL**

Gladstone Sports Park
Box 32                                          906-428-2311
Gladstone, MI  49837

Trail suitable for skiing & hiking

Location:
 From Gladstone follow US2/41, then north on M35 2 miles, then west 1/4
   mile on North Bluff Drive

Trail specifications:
   3 mi; 1 loop(s); Loop length(s)-3
Typical terrain: Flat to slightly rolling
Skiing ability suggested: Novice
Hiking trail difficulty: Easy
Nordic trail grooming method: Double track set
Suitable for all-terrain bicycle: Yes
Trail use fee: None
Camping: Campground available within 3 miles of the park
Drinking water available

General Information:
 Municipally operated recreation area by City of Gladstone
 Warming area and snack bar available
 Sledding, tubing and downhill ski hills available

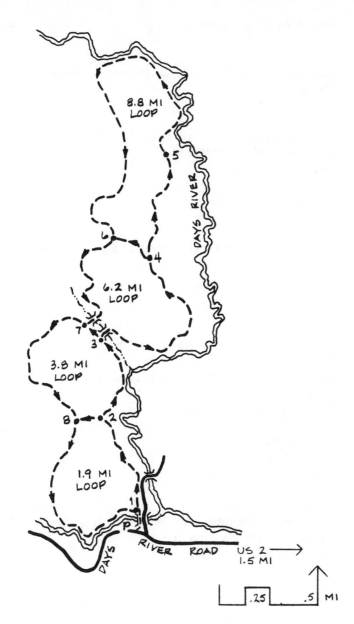

Days River Pathway                               Revised: 3/06/88


Asst Area Manager, Escanaba Forest Area
6833 US2/41 & M35                                906-786-2351
Gladstone, MI  49835


District Forest Manager, Escanaba River State Forest
6833 US2/41 & M35                                906-786-2351
Gladstone, MI  49835


Trail suitable for skiing & hiking

Location:
 3 miles north of Gladstone on US2/41, then west 2 miles on Days River Rd.


Trail specifications:
   9 mi; 3 loop(s); Loop length(s)-1.9, 3.8, 6.2, 8.8
Typical terrain: Rolling with some steep hills
Skiing ability suggested: Novice to advanced
Hiking trail difficulty: Easy to moderate
Nordic trail grooming method: Track set
Suitable for all-terrain bicycle: Yes
Trail use fee: Donations accepted for trail grooming
Camping: None
Drinking water is not available

General Information:
 Maintained by the DNR Forest Management Division
 Overlooks the Days River at several locations
 Deer usually seen along trail


# DAYS RIVER PATHWAY

Other contacts:
DNR Forest Management Division Office, Lansing, 517-373-1275
DNR Forest Management Region Office, Marquette, 906-228-6561

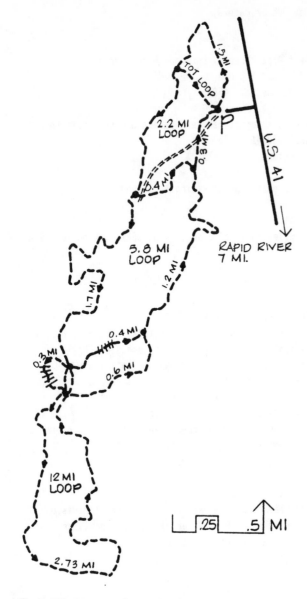

**2.2 MI LOOP**

TOT LOOP

.2 MI

0.3 MI

0.4 MI

**5.8 MI LOOP**

RAPID RIVER 7 MI.

1.7 MI

1.2 MI

0.4 MI

0.3 MI

0.6 MI

U.S. 41

**12 MI LOOP**

2.73 MI

.25 .5 MI

# RAPID RIVER
# CROSS COUNTRY SKI TRAIL

Rapid River Cross Country Ski Trail                    Revised: 11/29/87

Rapid River Ranger District, Hiawatha National Forest
8181 US 2                                             906-474-6442
Rapid River, MI  49878

Forest Supervisor, Hiawatha National Forest
PO Box 316, 2727 N. Lincoln Rd.                       906-786-4062
Escanaba, MI  49829

Trail suitable for skiing only

Location:
 North of Escanaba and 7 miles north of Rapid River on US41

Trail specifications:
   9 mi; 4 loop(s); Loop length(s)-1.8 to 9
Typical terrain: Flat to very hilly
Skiing ability suggested: Novice to advanced
Hiking trail difficulty: NA
Nordic trail grooming method: Track set
Suitable for all-terrain bicycle: Not permitted
Trail use fee: None
Camping: None
Drinking water is not available

General Information:
 Maintained by the Rapid River Ranger District, Hiawatha National Forest
 Designed for cross country skiing
 Well marked and maintained

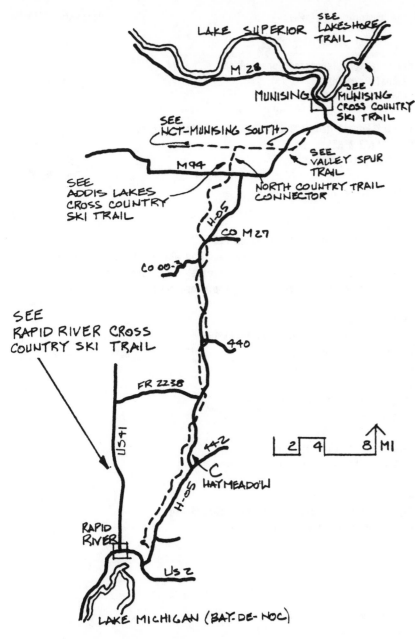

BAY DE NOC-GRAND ISLAND TRAIL

Bay De Noc - Grand Island Trail                    Revised: 11/29/87


Munising Ranger District, Hiawatha National Forest
601 Cedar St., PO Box 160                          906-387-2512
Munising, MI  49862

Rapid River Ranger District, Hiawatha National Forest
8181 Hwy 2                                         906-474-6442
Rapid River, MI  49878

Trail suitable for hiking only

Location:
  South trailhead - 2 miles east of Rapid River on US2, turn north on Co Rd
    509, then north 1.5 miles to parking lot on west side of road
  Central trailhead - same as above but travel north on 509 for 16 miles.
    Parking lot on east side of the road
  North trailhead - 10 miles SW of Munising on M94 at Ackerman Lake
Trail specifications:
  40 mi; No* loop(s); Loop length(s)-NA
Typical terrain: Rolling
Skiing ability suggested: NA
Hiking trail difficulty: Moderate to difficult
Nordic trail grooming method: NA
Suitable for all-terrain bicycle: Not permitted
Trail use fee: None
Camping: At the Haymeadow Campground and primitive camping is permitted
Drinking water available at campgound and trailheads


General Information:
  Maintained by the Munising and Rapid River Ranger Districts of
    the Hiawatha National Forest
  Also used for horseback riding
  Haymeadow Creek Campground has a .5 mile hiking trail to a waterfalls
  Haymeadow Creek is an excellent trout stream
  Near the Rapid River Cross Country Ski Trail. See other listing
  North Country Trail - Munising South is 3 miles north of north trailhead
    via the North Country connector trail
  * This is a point to point trail
  Write for more information

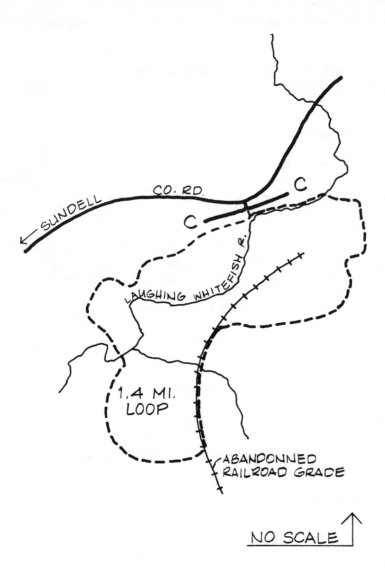

SUNDELL ← CO. RD.

LAUGHING WHITEFISH R.

C   C   C

1.4 MI. LOOP

ABANDONNED RAILROAD GRADE

NO SCALE

TYOGA HISTORICAL PATHWAY

Area Forester, Ishpeming Forest Area
632 Teal Lake Rd                                906-485-1031
Ishpeming, MI  49849

District Forest Manager, Escanaba River State Forest
6833 US41/2 & M35                              906-786-2351
Gladstone, MI  49837

Trail suitable for hiking only

Location:
 Between Marquette and Munising on M28
 Trailhead - North from M28 toward Laughing Whitefish Falls State Forest
   Campground.  Pass the Laughing Whitefish Falls State Scenic Site and
   continue north several miles to the campground.

Trail specifications:
   1.4 mi; 1 loop(s); Loop length(s)-1.4
Typical terrain: Hilly
Skiing ability suggested: NA
Hiking trail difficulty: Moderate
Nordic trail grooming method: NA
Suitable for all-terrain bicycle: No
Trail use fee: None
Camping: Campground at trailhead
Drinking water available at campground

General Information:
 Maintained by the DNR Forest Management Division
 Developed as a interperative trail

Other contacts:
DNR Forest Management Region Office, Marquette, 906-228-6561
DNR Forest Management Division Office, Lansing. 517-373-1275

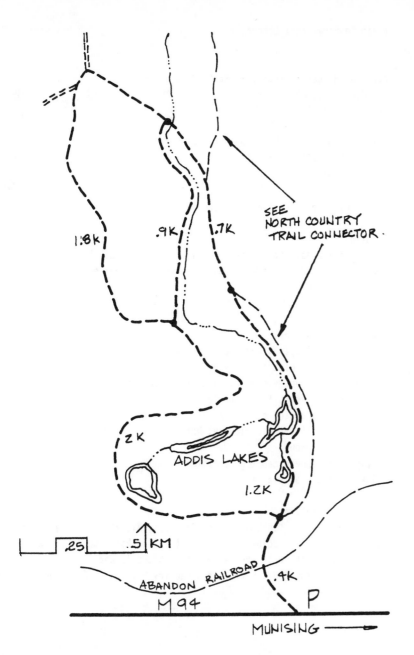

1.8k

.9K  .7K

SEE
NORTH COUNTRY
TRAIL CONNECTOR.

2 K

ADDIS LAKES

1.2K

.25  .5 KM

ABANDON RAILROAD

.4K

M 94

P

MUNISING →

ADDIS LAKES CROSS COUNTRY SKI TRAIL

Addis Lakes Cross Country Ski Trail                    Revised: 3/28/88

Munising Ranger District, Hiawatha National Forest
601 Cedar St., PO Box 160                              906-387-2512
Munising, MI  49862

Forest Supervisor, Hiawatha National Forest
PO Box 316, 2727 N. Lincoln Rd.                        906-786-4062
Escanaba, MI  49826

Trail suitable for skiing only

Location:
 South trailhead - On M94, 10 miles west of Munising
 North trailhead - North Country Trail - Munising South


Trail specifications:
   7 km; 2 loop(s); Loop length(s)-various
 Typical terrain: Flat to rolling
 Skiing ability suggested: Intermediate
 Hiking trail difficulty: NA
 Nordic trail grooming method: None
 Suitable for all-terrain bicycle: Not permitted
 Trail use fee: None
 Camping: Wilderness camping permitted
 Drinking water not available

General Information:
 Maintained by the Munising Ranger District, Hiawatha National Forest
 Adjacent to the North Country Trail Connector. See other listing
 Not available for hiking since the trail passes through marshes

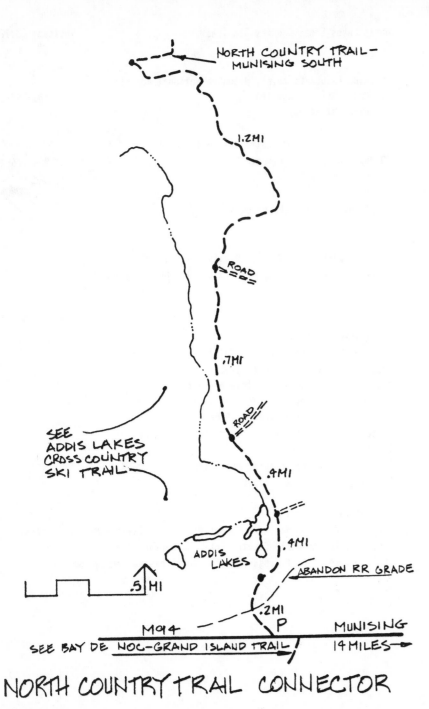

NORTH COUNTRY TRAIL CONNECTOR

North Country Trail Connector                          Revised: 2/20/88

Munising Ranger District, Hiawatha National Forest
601 Cedar St., PO Box 160                              906-387-2512
Munising, MI  49862

Forest Supervisior, Hiawatha National Forest
PO Box 316, 2727 N. Lincoln Rd.                        906-786-4062
Escanaba, MI  49829

Trail suitable for hiking & skiing

Location:
 North trailhead - North Country Trail - Munising South
 South trailhead - On M94, 10 miles southwest of Munising

Trail specifications:
   2.9 mi; No loop(s); Loop length(s)-NA
Typical terrain: Flat to rolling
Skiing ability suggested: Intermediate to advanced
Hiking trail difficulty: Moderate
Nordic trail grooming method: None
Suitable for all-terrain bicycle: Not permitted
Trail use fee: None
Camping: Wilderness camping permitted
Drinking water not available

General Information:
 Maintained by the Munising Ranger District, Hiawatha National Forest
 This is a point to point trail connecting the North Country Trail -
   Munising South, with the Bay De Noc - Grand Island Trail
 Adjacent to the Addis Lakes Cross Country Ski Trail. See other listing

244

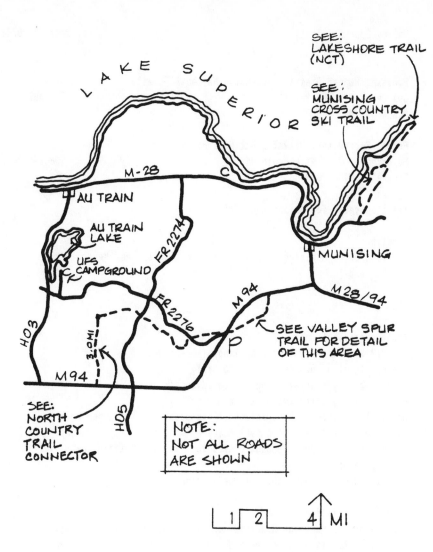

SEE:
LAKESHORE TRAIL
(NCT)

SEE:
MUNISING
CROSS COUNTRY
SKI TRAIL

LAKE SUPERIOR

M-28

AU TRAIN

AU TRAIN
LAKE

UFS
CAMPGROUND

FR 2274

MUNISING

FR 2276

M 94

M 28/94

SEE VALLEY SPUR
TRAIL FOR DETAIL
OF THIS AREA

HO3

3.0 MI

M 94

HO5

SEE:
NORTH
COUNTRY
TRAIL
CONNECTOR

NOTE:
NOT ALL ROADS
ARE SHOWN

1 2 4 MI

# NORTH COUNTRY TRAIL-
# MUNISING SOUTH

North Country Trail - Munising South            Revised: 3/28/88

Munising Ranger District, Hiawatha National Forest
601 Cedar St., PO Box 160                        906-387-2512
Munising, MI  49862

Forest Supervisior, Hiawatha National Forest
PO Box 316, 2727 N. Lincoln Rd.
Escanaba, MI  49829                              906-786-4062

Trail suitable for hiking & skiing

Location:
  Trailhead - SW of Munising 1.5 miles west of M28 on M94, on south side of
    the road
  Trailhead - On M94 between HO5 and HO3 at Ackerman Lake. See North Country
    Trail Connector for more information

Trail specifications:
  9 mi; No* loop(s); Loop length(s)-NA
Typical terrain: Rolling to hilly
Skiing ability suggested: Advanced
Hiking trail difficulty: Moderate to difficult
Nordic trail grooming method: None
Suitable for all-terrain bicycle: Not permitted
Trail use fee: None
Camping: Trailside camping is permitted
Drinking water available at Valley Spur trailhead

General Information:
 Maintained by the Munising Ranger District, Hiawatha National Forest
 Short part of the Valley Spur Ski Trail (2 miles)
 West end of this section, ends about 3 miles east of HO3 road
 Recommended only for skiers with good winter survival skills
 For further information about the North Country Trail contact the
  North Country Trail Association, PO Box 311, White Cloud, MI 49349 or
  USDI, Mid West Region, 1709 Jackson St., Omaha, Nebraska 68102
 This trail was not designed for skiing. Use caution if attempting to ski
  trail
 * Like the entire North Country Trail, is is a point to point trail
 Write the Munising Ranger District for more information

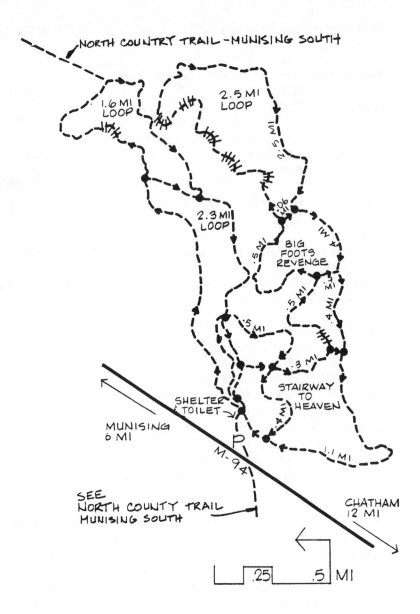

NORTH COUNTRY TRAIL - MUNISING SOUTH

1.6 MI LOOP

2.5 MI LOOP

2.3 MI LOOP

.06 MI

BIG FOOTS REVENGE

.5 MI

.5 MI

.4 MI

.3 MI

STAIRWAY TO HEAVEN

.4 MI

SHELTER TOILET

P

M-94

MUNISING 6 MI

SEE NORTH COUNTY TRAIL MUNISING SOUTH

CHATHAM 12 MI

1.1 MI

.25  .5 MI

## VALLEY SPUR SKI TRAIL

Valley Spur Ski Trail

Revised: 2/20/88

Munising Ranger District, Hiawatha National Forest
601 Cedar St., PO Box 160
Munising, MI 49862

906-387-2512

Forest Supervisor, Hiawatha National Forest
PO Box 316, 2727 N. Lincoln Rd.
Escanaba, MI 49829

906-786-4062

Trail suitable for skiing and hiking

Location:
  6 miles SW of Munising on M94, to the parking lot on the south side of
    the road

Trail specifications:
  19.2 km; Many loop(s); Loop length(s)-various
Typical terrain: Gently rolling to hilly
Skiing ability suggested: Novice to advanced
Hiking trail difficulty: Moderate
Nordic trail grooming method: Track set usually 3 times per week
Suitable for all-terrain bicycle: Yes
Trail use fee: $2/day, season passes for family and individuals available
Camping: None
Drinking water is available at the warming hut

General Information:
  Maintained by Munising Ranger District, Hiawatha National Forest
  A warming hut is open on weekends, with food service and ski rentals
  Outdoor toilet is available at the trailhead
  Forest cover includes hardwoods with conifer-ringed valleys
  Part of the North Country Trail - Munising South
  An excellent trail system for all levels of skill.  A trail not to be
    passed by.
  Near the Munising Cross Country Ski Trail, another great trail to ski.

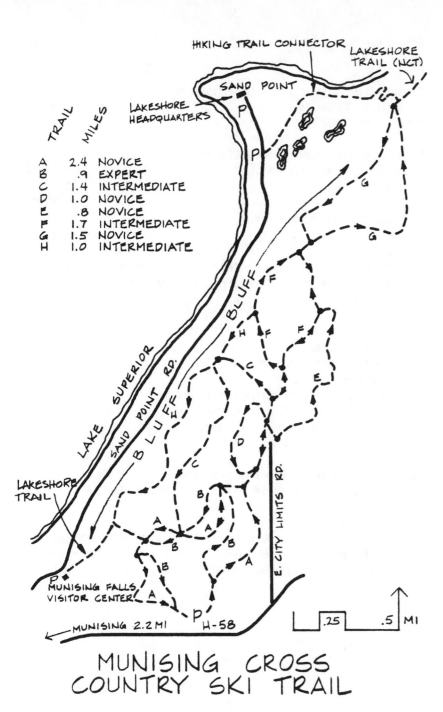

| TRAIL | MILES | |
|---|---|---|
| A | 2.4 | NOVICE |
| B | .9 | EXPERT |
| C | 1.4 | INTERMEDIATE |
| D | 1.0 | NOVICE |
| E | .8 | NOVICE |
| F | 1.7 | INTERMEDIATE |
| G | 1.5 | NOVICE |
| H | 1.0 | INTERMEDIATE |

HIKING TRAIL CONNECTOR

LAKESHORE TRAIL (NCT)

SAND POINT

LAKESHORE HEADQUARTERS

P
P
P

G
G

BLUFF

F
F
F
H
F
F

LAKE SUPERIOR

SAND POINT RD.

BLUFF

C
H
C
E
D
C

B
A
A
B
A
B
B
A
B
A

E. CITY LIMITS RD.

LAKESHORE TRAIL

P
MUNISING FALLS
VISITOR CENTER
A
P
MUNISING 2.2 MI    H-58

.25    .5 MI

# MUNISING CROSS COUNTRY SKI TRAIL

Munising Cross Country Ski Trail                Revised: 2/20/88

Pictured Rocks National Lakeshore
PO Box 40                                        906-387-3700
Munising, MI  49862                              906-387-2607

Trail suitable for skiing only

Location:
 NE of Munising on H58
 Trailhead - Take H58 east from the blinking traffic light on M28 in
   Munising about 2.2 miles to the parking lot on the north side of the
   road. The left fork is Sand Point Rd. to the the Lakeshore Headquarters.

Trail specifications:
 12 mi; Many loop(s); Loop length(s)-various
Typical terrain: Rolling to hilly
Skiing ability suggested: Novice to advanced
Hiking trail difficulty: NA
Nordic trail grooming method: Track set twice a week
Suitable for all-terrain bicycle: Not permitted
Trail use fee: None
Camping: Campgrounds not open in the winter‡
Drinking water is not available

General Information:
 Maintained by the Pictured Rocks National Lakeshore
 ‡ Camping is permitted 200' off the trail
 Mostly hilly terrain with frozen waterfalls and canyons and some
   beautiful scenic vistas across Munising Bay to Grand Island
 All trails are well marked and with maps at each intersection
 Degree of difficulty signs are at the start of each loop
 A well designed and well groomed trail that should not be missed
 A connector trail starts near the Lakeshore Headquarters and ends at the
   north end of the trail system(not suitable for skiing)
 The section of the trail along the cliff is part of the Lakeshore Trail
   (see separate entry for more detail) which is also part of the North
   Country Trail
 Pets are not permitted on the trail
 Near the Valley Spur Trail, another great ski trail

247

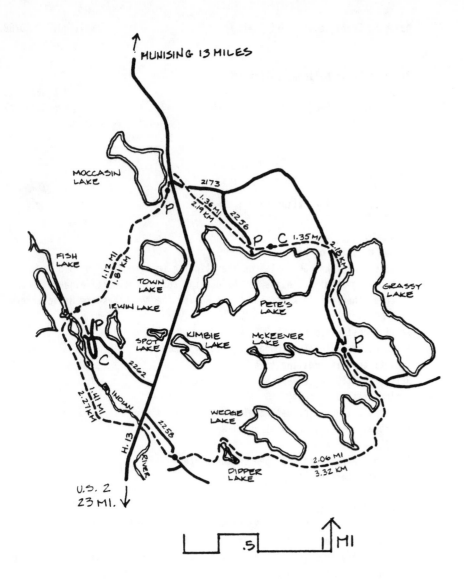

MUNISING 13 MILES

MOCCASIN LAKE

2173
1.36 MI
2.19 KM
2256

FISH LAKE

1.12 MI
1.81 KM

TOWN LAKE

IRWIN LAKE

SPOT LAKE

KIMBIE LAKE

P C 1.35 MI
2.18 KM

PETE'S LAKE

McKEEVER LAKE

GRASSY LAKE

P

2262

1.41 MI
2.27 KM

INDIAN

H.13

RIVER

2258

WEDGE LAKE

DIPPER LAKE

2.06 MI
3.32 KM

U.S. 2
23 MI.

.5          1 MI

BRUNO'S RUN

Munising Ranger District, Hiawatha National Forest
601 Cedar St, PO Box 160                    906-387-2512
Munising, MI  49862

Forest Supervisor, Hiawatha National Forest
PO Box 316, 2727 N. Lincoln Rd.             906-786-4062
Escanaba, MI  49829

Trail suitable for skiing & hiking

Location:
  Take M28 south from Munising 4 miles to Wetmore, then south 11 miles
    on H13 (FH13) to the Moccasin Lake Picnic Area where the trailhead
    is located

Trail specifications:
  11.7 km; 1 loop(s); Loop length(s)-11.7
Typical terrain: Rolling
Skiing ability suggested: Intermediate to advanced
Hiking trail difficulty: Easy to moderate
Nordic trail grooming method: Not groomed
Suitable for all-terrain bicycle: Yes
Trail use fee: None
Camping: Pete's Lake and Widwaters campgrounds are along the trail
Drinking water at Moccasin Lake, Pete's Lake and Wadewaters CG's

General Information:
  Maintained by the Munising Ranger District, Hiawatha National Forest
  Trail is for more experienced skiers
  Scenic views and rolling terrain makes for a very interesting trail

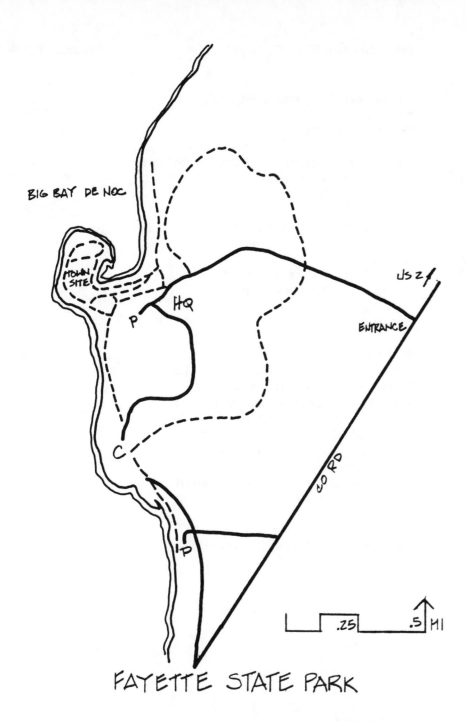

**FAYETTE STATE PARK**

BIG BAY DE NOC

MTOWN SITE

P    HQ

ENTRANCE

C

CO RD

US 2

P

.25    .5 MI

Fayette State Park                    Revised: 3/28/88

Fayette State Park
13700 13.25 Lane                      906-644-2603
Garden, MI  49835

DNR Parks Division Office

                                      517-373-1270

Trail suitable for skiing & hiking

Location:
 SW of Manistique via US2 and M183
 On the west shore of the Garden Peninsula near the south end

Trail specifications:
  5 mi; Several loop(s); Loop length(s)-various
Typical terrain: Flat to hilly
Skiing ability suggested: Novice to intermediate
Hiking trail difficulty: Easy
Nordic trail grooming method: Track set
Suitable for all-terrain bicycle: Yes
Trail use fee: None, but vehicle entry fee required $2/day, $10/year
Camping: Campground is open all year
Drinking water is available

General Information:
 Maintained by the DNR Parks Division
 Scenic overlook along trail
 A unique restored village of the 1800's, settled to house the iron
   smelting workers who worked there
 The Blessing of the Fleet event is held on the last Saturday in June
 Heritage Days are held on on the first weekend of August
 Modern visitor center, 15 restored buildings, dock, swimming beach and
   picnic area

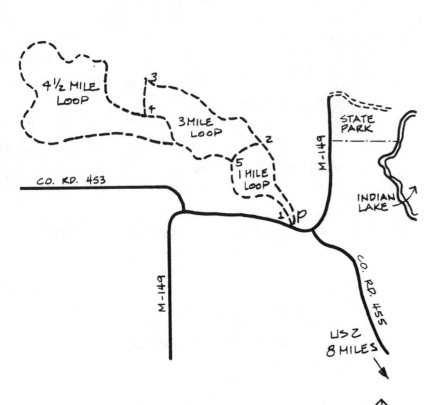

INDIAN LAKE PATHWAY

Area Forester, Shingleton Forest Area
M28                                          906-452-6236
Shingleton, MI  49884                        906-341-6917

District Forest Manager, Lake Superior State Forest
PO Box 445, 309 W. McMillan                  906-239-5131
Newberry, MI  49868

Trail suitable for skiing & hiking

Location:
 9 miles NW of Thompson on M149 and
 1 mile west of Palms Brook State Park

Trail specifications:
   4 mi; 3 loop(s); Loop length(s)-1, 2, 3.5
Typical terrain: Gently rolling to hilly
Skiing ability suggested: Novice to advanced
Hiking trail difficulty: Moderate
Nordic trail grooming method: Track set
Suitable for all-terrain bicycle: Yes
Trail use fee: None
Camping: None at trail but available nearby*
Drinking water not available

General Information:
 Maintained by the DNR Forest Management Division

Other contacts:
 DNR Forest Management Division Office, Lansing, 517-373-1275
 DNR Forest Management Region Office, Marquette, 906-228-6561

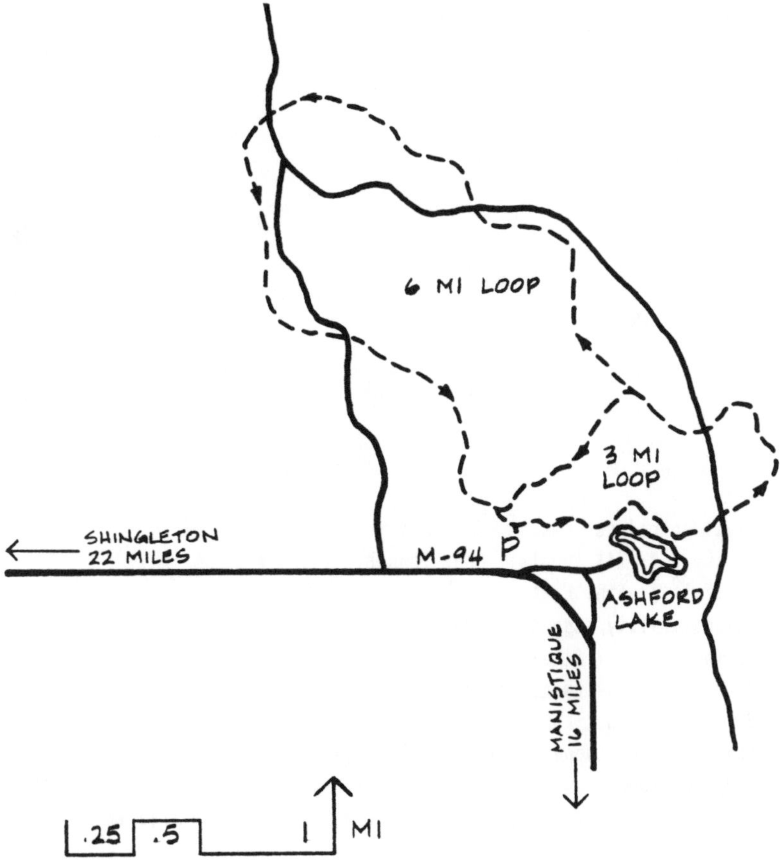

Area Forester, Shingleton Forest Area
M28                                                         906-341-6917
Shingleton, MI  49884

District Forest Manager, Lake Superior State Forest
PO Box 445, 309 W. McMillan St.                            906-239-5131
Newberry, MI  49868

Trail suitable for skiing & hiking

Location:
 16 miles north of Manistique on M94
 22 miles south of Shingleton on M94

Trail specifications:
  7 mi; 2 loop(s); Loop length(s)-3, 6
Typical terrain: Flat to gently rolling
Skiing ability suggested: Novice to intermediate
Hiking trail difficulty: Easy
Nordic trail grooming method: Track set
Suitable for all-terrain bicycle: Yes
Trail use fee: None
Camping: None
Drinking water not availble

General Information:
 Maintained by the DNR Forest Management Division

**6 MI LOOP**

**3 MI LOOP**

SHINGLETON
22 MILES

M-94  P

ASHFORD
LAKE

MANISTIQUE
16 MILES

.25  .5     1  MI

# ASHFORD LAKE PATHWAY

Other contacts:
DNR Forest Management Division Office, Lansing, 517-373-1275
DNR Forest Management Region Office, Marquette, 906-228-6561

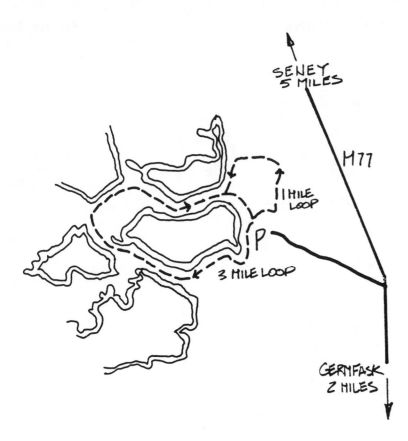

Seney National Wildlife Refuge                    Revised: 7/13/87


Seney National Wildlife Refuge
HCR2, Box 1                                        906-586-9851
Seney, MI  49883                                   906-586-9801

Trail suitable for skiing & hiking

Location:
 2 miles north of Germfask and 5 miles south of Seney (M28) on M77


Trail specifications:
    10+ mi*; 2** loop(s); Loop length(s)-1, 3**
Typical terrain: Flat
Skiing ability suggested: Novice
Hiking trail difficulty: Easy
Nordic trail grooming method: None
Suitable for all-terrain bicycle: Yes
Trail use fee: None in winter, $2.00/car from 5/15 to 9/30
Camping: None
Drinking water available at the Visitors Center from 5/15 to 9/30

General Information:
 Maintained by the Fish and Wildlife Service
 * Mostly gravel roads
 ** Ski trails listed only.
 Warming shelter available
 Prohibited for use by ORV's and snowmobiles
 Over 95,000 acres containing over 250 species of birds

SENEY
5 MILES

M77

1 MILE LOOP

P

3 MILE LOOP

GERMFASK
2 MILES

NO SCALE

SENEY
NATIONAL WILDLIFE REFUGE

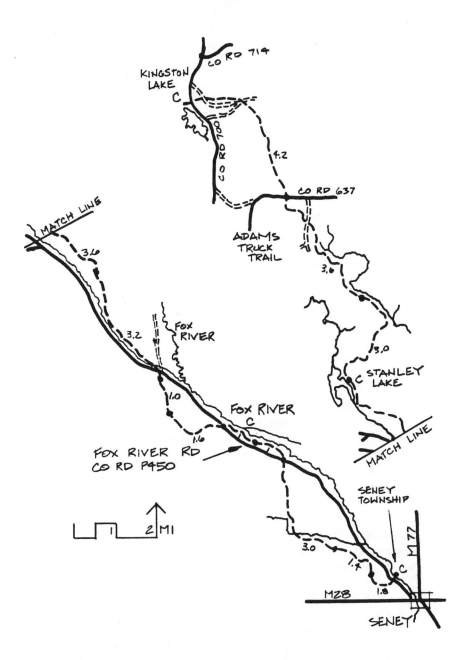

KINGSTON LAKE C

CO RD 714

CO RD 700

4.2

CO RD 637

ADAMS TRUCK TRAIL

3.6

MATCH LINE

3.6

3.2

FOX RIVER

STANLEY LAKE C

3.0

FOX RIVER C

1.0

MATCH LINE

1.6

FOX RIVER RD CO RD P450

SENEY TOWNSHIP

3.0

1.4

M 77

M28

1.8

C

SENEY

1    2 MI

## FOX RIVER PATHWAY

Fox River Pathway                                    Revised: 3/06/88

Area Forester, Shingleton Forest Area
M28                                                  906-452-6236
Shingleton, MI  49884

District Forest Manager, Lake Superior State Forest
PO Box 445, 309 W. McMillan                          906-239-5131
Newberry, MI  49868

Trail suitable for hiking only

Location:
 North trailhead - Kingston Lake Campground on Co Rd 714 (H58 or Kingston
   Lake Rd.)
 South trailhead - .5 mile north of Seney on Co Rd 450 (Fox River Rd.) at
   Seney Township Campground

Trail specifications:
  27.5 mi; No* loop(s); Loop length(s)-NA
Typical terrain: Flat to hilly
Skiing ability suggested: NA
Hiking trail difficulty: Moderate to difficult
Nordic trail grooming method: NA
Suitable for all-terrain bicycle: Yes
Trail use fee: None
Camping: Four campgrounds available along the trail
Drinking water available at campgrounds

General Information:
 Maintained by the DNR Forest Management Division
 Not frequently used trail but does pass through some very beautiful and
   isolated land
 Since the trail is rather isolated, prepare well for the trip because
   emergency assistance will not be available very easily
 21 marked locations along the trail provide interesting information about
   the history of the area
 * This is a point to point trail

Other contacts:
DNR Forest Management Division Office, Lansing, 517-373-1275
DNR Forest Management Region Office, Marquette, 906-228-6561

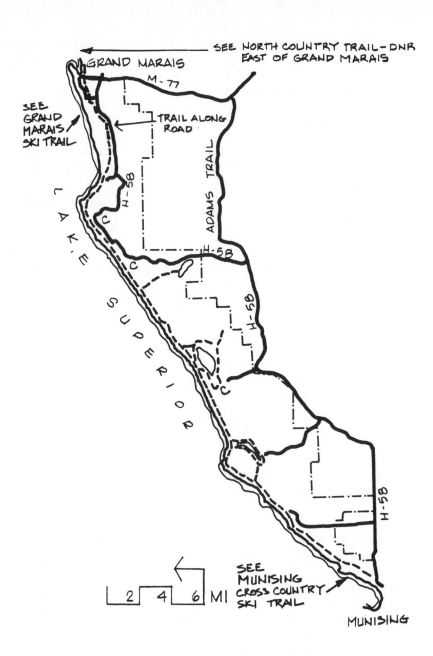

SEE NORTH COUNTRY TRAIL-DNR
EAST OF GRAND MARAIS

GRAND MARAIS
M-77

SEE GRAND MARAIS SKI TRAIL

TRAIL ALONG ROAD

ADAMS TRAIL

H-58

H-58

H-58

LAKE SUPERIOR

SEE MUNISING CROSS COUNTRY SKI TRAIL

MUNISING

2  4  6 MI

## LAKESHORE TRAIL

Lakeshore Trail                                    Revised:  2/20/88

Pictured Rocks National Lakeshore
PO Box 40                                          906-387-3700
Munising, MI  49862                                906-387-2607

Trail suitable for hiking only

Location:
 From Munising to Sable Falls west of Grand Marais
 West trailhead - Munising Falls, northeast of Munising
 East trailhead - About 5 miles west of Grand Marais on H58
 Other trailheads are all accessible from H58

Trail specifications:
 43 mi; No loop(s); Loop length(s)-NA
Typical terrain: Flat to hilly
Skiing ability suggested: NA
Hiking trail difficulty: Easy to moderate
Nordic trail grooming method: NA
Suitable for all-terrain bicycle: Not permitted
Trail use fee: None
Camping: 13 backcountry campgounds are along the trail
Limited drinking water is available along the trail *

General Information:
 Maintained by the Pictured Rocks National Lakeshore
 A segment of the North Country Trail
 Permits are required for the backcountry campsite. 30% of the sites are
   reservable
 * Only the following locations have drinking water-Munising Falls, Park
   Headquarters, Miner's Castle, Miner's Beach, Little Beaver Campground
   Twelvemile Beach Campground, Hurricane River Campground and Grand Sable
   Visitor Center. Most campgrounds have access to untreated Lake Superior
   water that must be boiled or treated with a filter. Some campgrounds
   have no water available
 Parties of 9 to 20 people must use group backcountry campsites only and
   must make reservations
 Open fires are prohibited at Chapel and Mosquito Campgrounds
 Pets are not allowed in the backcountry

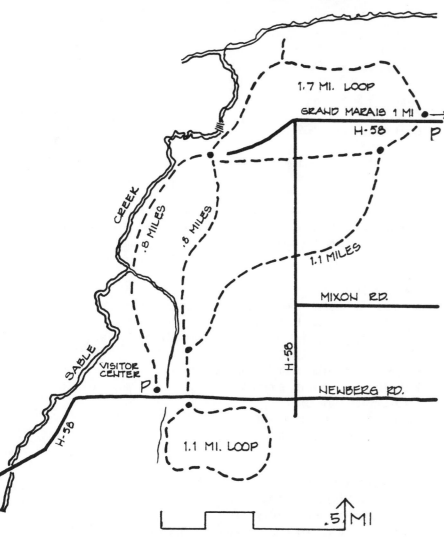

LAKE SUPERIOR

1.7 MI. LOOP

GRAND MARAIS 1 MI.

H-58

P

CREEK

SABLE

.8 MILES

.8 MILES

1.1 MILES

MIXON RD.

H-58

VISITOR CENTER

P

NEWBERG RD.

H-58

1.1 MI. LOOP

.5 MI

# GRAND MARAIS
# SKI / SNOWSHOE TRAILS

Grand Marais Cross Country Ski & Snowshoe Trail        Revised: 2/20/88

Pictured Rocks National Lakeshore
PO Box 40                                               906-387-3700
Munising, MI  49862                                     906-387-2607

Pictured Rock National Lakeshore
PO Box 395                                              906-494-2669
Grand Marais, MI  49839

Trail suitable for skiing only

Location:
  1 mile west of Grand Marais on H58 (just inside the park boundary) or
  1 mile west of M77 on Newberg Rd.

Trail specifications:
   5.1 mi; Several loop(s); Loop length(s)-various
Typical terrain: Flat to rolling with some steep hills
Skiing ability suggested: Novice to intermediate
Hiking trail difficulty: Easy
Nordic trail grooming method: Track set
Suitable for all-terrain bicycle: Not permitted
Trail use fee: None
Camping: Campgrounds closed in the winter ✸
Drinking water available at campgrounds

General Information:
 Maintained by the Pictured Rocks National Lakeshore
 ✸ Backcountry camping is permitted 200' off the trail
 View of Sable Falls and Lake Superior from the trail
 The Grand Marais district office is located on Coast Guard Point in
    Grand Marais
 A map is in place at each trail intersection
 Pets are not permitted on the ski trails

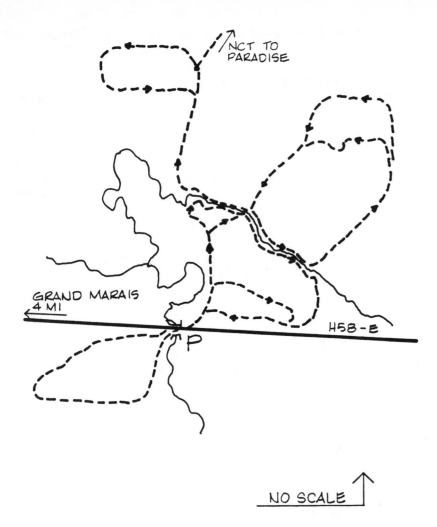

NCT TO
PARADISE

GRAND MARAIS
4 MI

H58-E

P

NO SCALE

SCHOOL FOREST SKI TRAIL

School Forest Ski Trail                    Revised: 1/13/88


Grand Marais Chamber of Commerce
PO Box 139                                    906-494-2766
Grand Marais, MI  49839


Kathleen R Baker
PO Box 118                                    906-494-2766
Grand Marais, MI  49839


Trail suitable for skiing & hiking

Location:
 4 miles east of Grand Marais on H58 just past the creek
 Parking lot on right side of road. Short walk from parking lot to the
   trailhead (look for sign on left).


Trail specifications:
   15+ mi; 6 loop(s); Loop length(s)-various
Typical terrain: Flat to rolling
Skiing ability suggested: Novice to intermediate
Hiking trail difficulty: Easy to moderate
Nordic trail grooming method: Track set weekly
Suitable for all-terrain bicycle: Yes
Trail use fee: None
Camping: Camping not permitted
Drinking water not available


General Information:
 Maintained by the community of Grand Marais
 Food and lodging in Grand Marais
 Connects to the North Country Trail
 Site of the Polar Bear Cross Country Ski Race the first week of February
 Well marked trail with beautiful north country scenery

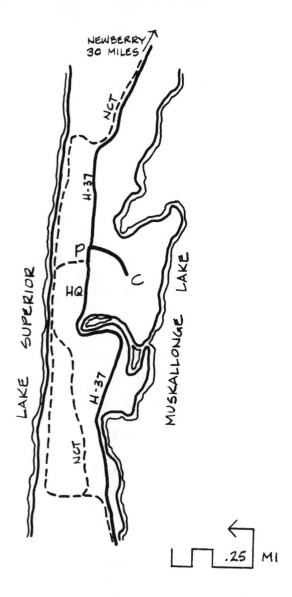

NEWBERRY
30 MILES

NCT

H-37

LAKE SUPERIOR

P

HQ

C

MUSKALLONGE LAKE

H-37

NCT

.25 MI

MUSKALLONGE LAKE
STATE PARK

Muskallonge Lake State Park                    Revised:  3/28/88


Muskallonge Lake State Park
Rte 1, PO Box 245                              906-658-3338
Newberry, MI  49868


DNR Parks Division Office

517-373-1270


Trail suitable for hiking only

Location:
 30 miles north of Newberry on Co Rd 407 (H37)
 18 miles east of Grand Marais on Co Rd 407


Trail specifications:
   1.5 mi; 1 loop(s); Loop length(s)-1.5
Typical terrain: Rolling to hilly
Skiing ability suggested: NA
Hiking trail difficulty: Easy
Nordic trail grooming method: NA
Suitable for all-terrain bicycle: Yes
Trail use fee: None, but vehicle entry fee required $2/day, $10/year
Camping: Campground in the park
Drinking water avaiable

General Information:
 Maintained by the DNR Parks Division
 Part of the North Country Pathway
 Site of a logging town of the 1800's
 Good agate hunting along Lake Superior near trail
 Wildlife and many birds frequently seen in area


257

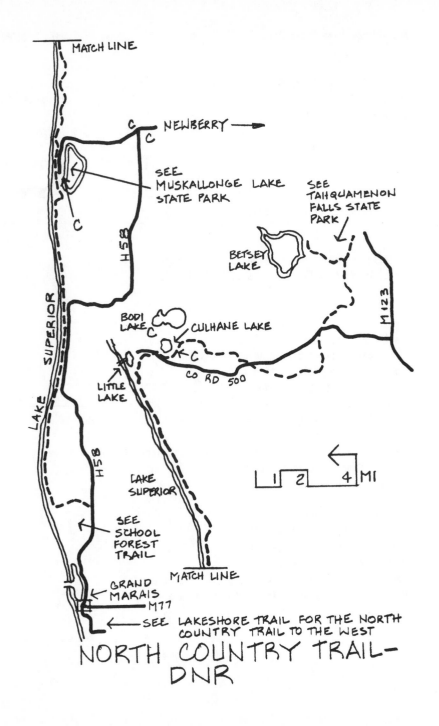

DNR Forest Management Region 1 Office
1990 US41 South                                906-228-6561
Marquette, MI  49855

Tahquamenon Falls State Park
Rte 48, Box 225                                906-492-3415
Paradise, MI  49768                            517-373-1270

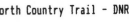

Trail suitable for hiking only

Location:
 From Tahquamenon Falls State Park to Pictured Rocks National Lakeshore
 Trailheads - Grand Marais, Tahquamenon Falls SP, Muskallonge Lake SP
   Lake Superior State Forest Campground and Two Hearted River State Forest
   Campground

Trail specifications:
   50+ mi; No* loop(s); Loop length(s)-NA
Typical terrain: Flat to very hilly
Skiing ability suggested: Not recommended
Hiking trail difficulty: Moderate to difficult
Nordic trail grooming method: None
Suitable for all-terrain bicycle: Not permitted
Trail use fee: None
Camping: Numerous campgrounds along the trail
Drinking water available at campgrounds

General Information:
 Maintained by the DNR
 Excellent wilderness hiking trail
 Recommended for skiing only to those with excellent winter survival skills
   The trail was not designed for skiing.
 * Like the entire North Country Trail system, this is a point to point
   trail.

Other contact:
 DNR Forest Management Divison Office, Lansing, 517-373-1275
 For more information about the North Country Trail contact the
   North Country Trail Association, PO Box 311, White Cloud, MI
   49349 or the USDI, Midwest Region, 1709 Jackson St., Omaha, NE
   68102-2571

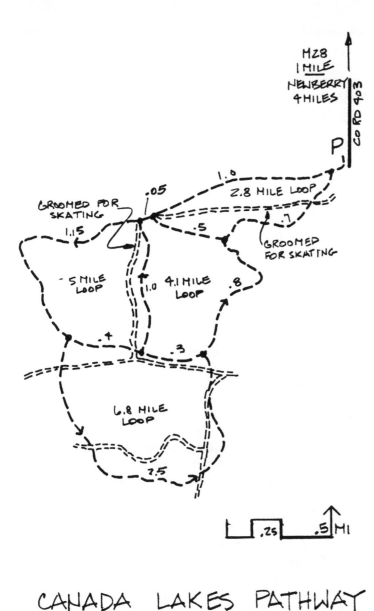

Canada Lakes Pathway                                  Revised:  3/06/88

M28
1 MILE
NEWBERRY
4 MILES

CO RD 403

P

1.0

.05

2.8 MILE LOOP

GROOMED FOR
SKATING

1.15

.5

.7

GROOMED
FOR SKATING

- 5 MILE
LOOP

1.0

4.1 MILE
LOOP

.8

.4

.3

6.8 MILE
LOOP

2.5

.25        .5 MI

# CANADA LAKES PATHWAY

Area Forester, Newberry Forest Area
PO Box 428, South M123                           906-293-3293
Newberry, MI  49868

District Forest Manager, Lake Superior State Forest
PO Box 445, 309 West McMillan St.                 906-293-5131
Newberry, MI  49868

Trail suitable for hiking & skiing

Location:
  5.5 miles SE of Newberry
  Trailhead - East 1 mile from the Jct of M123 and M28 to Co Rd 403, then
     south 1.5 miles to parking lot


Trail specifications:
    7.7 mi‡; 4‡ loop(s); Loop length(s)-2.8, 4.1, 5, 6.8
Typical terrain: Gently rolling
Skiing ability suggested: Novice to intermediate
Hiking trail difficulty: Easy
Nordic trail grooming method: Track set twice weekly or as needed
Suitable for all-terrain bicycle: Yes
Trail use fee: Donation accepted at trailhead for grooming trails
Camping: Available in area ‡‡
Drinking water not available

General Information:
  Maintained by the DNR Forest Management Division
  ‡ Does not include all trails groomed for skating
  Well groomed and very enjoyable skiing trail
  ‡‡ Campgrounds
     North Country Campground, 4 miles north of Newberry on M123
     State Forest Campground, 2 miles west of Newberry off Co Rd 405
     KOA Campground south of Newberry
  Food and lodging in Newberry
  Logging museum in Newberry


Other contacts:
DNR Forest Management Division Office, Lansing, 517-373-1275
DNR Forest Management Region Office, Marquette, 906-228-6561

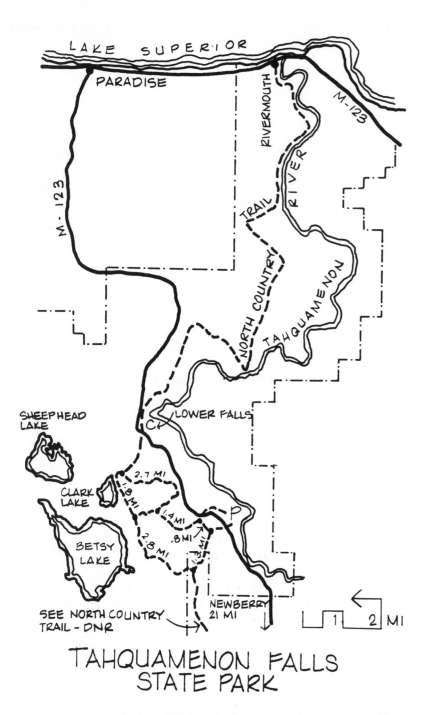

SHEEPHEAD
LAKE

CLARK
LAKE

BETSY
LAKE

2.7 MI
.8 MI
1.4 MI
2.8 MI
.8 MI
.3 MI

LOWER FALLS

C.

P

SEE NORTH COUNTRY
TRAIL - DNR

NEWBERRY
21 MI

1    2 MI

# TAHQUAMENON FALLS
# STATE PARK

Tahquamenon Falls State Park                    Revised: 3/28/88

Tahquamenon Falls State Park
Rte 48, Box 225                                 906-492-3415
Paradise, MI  49768

DNR Parks Division Office

517-373-1270

Trail suitable for skiing & hiking

Location:
 12 miles west of Paradise on M123

Trail specifications:
   25 mi*; 3+** loop(s); Loop length(s)-various
Typical terrain: Flat to rolling
Skiing ability suggested: Novice to intermediate
Hiking trail difficulty: Easy to moderate
Nordic trail grooming method: Track set weekly
Suitable for all-terrain bicycle: Yes
Trail use fee: None, but vehicle entry fee required $2/day, $10/year
Camping: Avaialble in the park in snowless months only
Drinking water is available in the park during snowless months only

General Information:
 Maintained by the DNR Parks Division
 Hiking and skiing trails many not be identical
 Food and lodging available in Paradise and Newberry
 * Also point to point trails in the system included in the 25 miles
 Some of the trails are part of the North Country Trail
 Paradise Pathway is nearby
 ** Skiing trails are 4 miles long with one loop.  Wilderness skiing is
    also available on hiking trails but deep snow will make that quite
    difficult

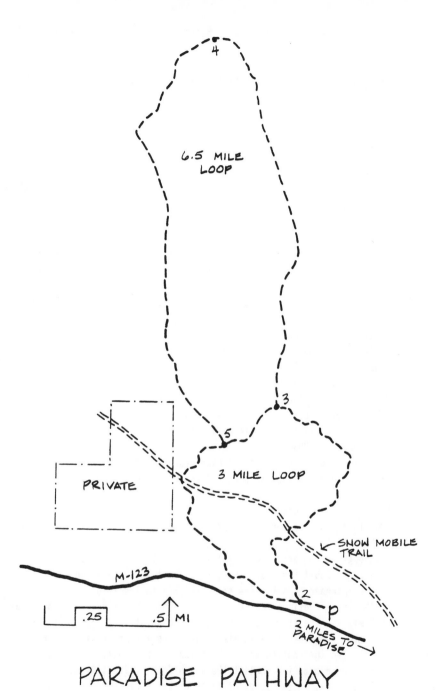

Area Forester, Newberry Forest Area
PO Box 428, South M123                              906-293-3293
Newberry, MI  49868

District Forest Manager, Lake Superior State Forest
PO Box 445, 309 West McMillan                      906-293-5131
Newberry, MI  49868

Trail suitable for skiing & hiking

Location:
 1 mile west of Paradise on M123

Trail specifications:
   6.7 mi; 2 loop(s); Loop length(s)-3, 6.5
Typical terrain: Rolling
Skiing ability suggested: Novice to intermediate
Hiking trail difficulty: Easy
Nordic trail grooming method: Track set once per week or as needed
Suitable for all-terrain bicycle: Yes
Trail use fee: None
Camping: Campground at Tahquamenon Falls SP (limited facilities in winter) ‡
Drinking water not available

General Information:
 Maintained by the DNR Forest Management Division
 Food and lodging available in Paradise throughout the year
 ‡ Andrus Lake and Shelldrake State Forest Campgrounds available in summer
 Shipwreck Museum at Whitefish Point (closed in winter)
 Rentals available in Paradise
 Tahquamenon Falls State Park trails are nearby

Other contacts:
DNR Forest Management Division Office, Lansing, 517-373-1275
DNR Forest Management Region Office, Marquette, 906-228-6561

261

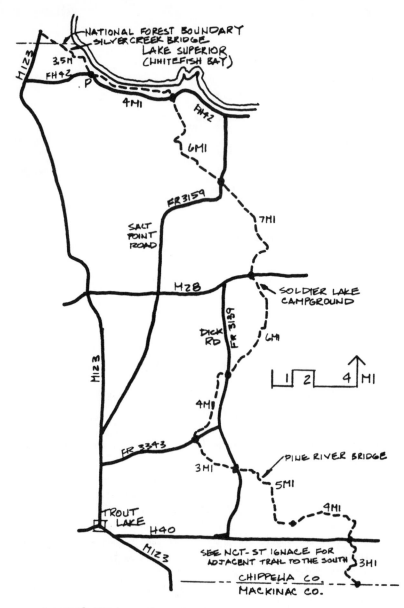

## NORTH COUNTRY TRAIL- SAULT STE MARIE

North Country Trail - Sault Ste. Marie          Revised: 4/01/88

Sault Ste. Marie Ranger District, Hiawatha National Forest
4000 I75 Business Loop                          906-635-5311
Sault Ste Marie, MI  49783

Forest Supervisor, Hiawatha National Forest
PO Box 316, 2727 N. Lincoln Rd.                 906-786-4062
Escanaba, MI  49829

Trail suitable for hiking only

Location:
 Near East Lake at the Chippewa Co Line to Tahquamenon Falls State Park
 South trailhead - Lookout on East Lake Dr. on Chippewa Co Line just south
   of H40
 North trailhead - On FR 42(east of M123) .5 mile west of Lake Superior.
   Parking is available ‼
Trail specifications:
   42 mi; No loop(s); Loop length(s)-NA
Typical terrain: Flat to rolling
Skiing ability suggested: NA
Hiking trail difficulty: Moderate to difficult
Nordic trail grooming method: NA
Suitable for all-terrain bicycle: Not permitted
Trail use fee: None
Camping: Campground at Soldier Lake near M28 ‼‼
Drinking water is available at Soldier Lake Campground


General Information:
 Maintained by the Sault Ste. Marie Ranger District, Hiawatha National
   Forest
 Connects to the North Country Trail - St. Ignace, on the south
 Write the Sault Ste. Marie Ranger District for a detailed map
 It is intended to make this trail skiable in the future
 ‼ The trail continues north of the National Forest boundary for about
   2 miles.  The trail can then be picked up at the River Unit Campground
   of the Tahquamenon Falls State Park. See the State Park for more
   detailed information on that section of the trail.
 For more information contact the North Country Trail Association,
   PO Box 311, White Cloud, MI 49349 or the USDI, Midwest Region,
   1709 Jackson St., Omaha, NE 68102-2571
 ‼‼ As with all of the North Country Trail, wilderness camping is
   permitted 200' from the trail

262

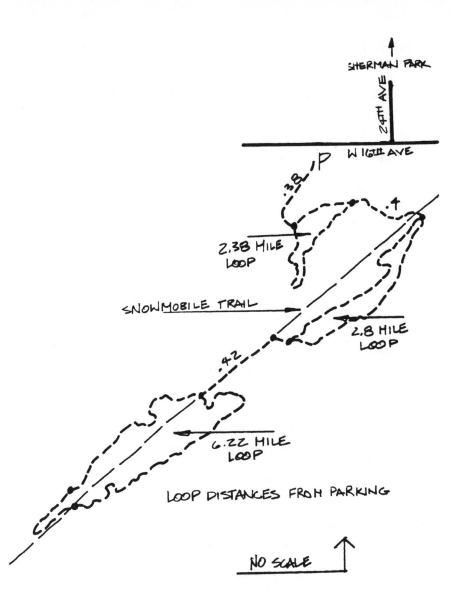

SHERMAN PARK

24TH AVE

W 16TH AVE

P

.38

2.38 MILE
LOOP

SNOWMOBILE TRAIL

2.8 MILE
LOOP

.42

6.22 MILE
LOOP

LOOP DISTANCES FROM PARKING

NO SCALE

ALGONQUIN
CROSS COUNTRY SKI TRAIL

Algonquin Cross Country Ski Trail                Revised:  3/23/88

Area Forester, Sault Ste. Marie Forest Area
2001 Ashmun St.                                     906-635-5281
Sault Ste. Marie, MI  49783

DNR District Office
PO Box 445                                          906-293-5131
Newberry, MI  49868

Trail suitable for skiing & hiking

Location:
 2 miles west of I75, SW of Sault Ste. Marie, Michigan
 Take 3 Mile Rd. exit off of I75, then west on 3 Mile Rd to 20th St. W,
   then north on 20th St. W to 16th Ave. W, then west on 16th Ave W to the
   trail that is on south side of the road

Trail specifications:
   15 km; 3 loop(s); Loop length(s)-2.1, 3.2, 15
Typical terrain: Flat to rolling
Skiing ability suggested: Novice
Hiking trail difficulty: Easy
Nordic trail grooming method: Track set twice weekly or more if needed
Suitable for all-terrain bicycle: Yes
Trail use fee: None, but donations are accepted to groom the trail
Camping: Campgrounds avaialble locally
Drinking water not available at trailhead

General Information:
 Maintained by the DNR Forest Management Division
 Although near Sault Ste. Marie, the trail is very secluded in a mixed
   hardwood and evergreen forest
 A snowmobile trail passes through trail system but there has been no
   know conflict
 A very popular trail with the local skiers
 Food and lodging in Sault Ste Marie

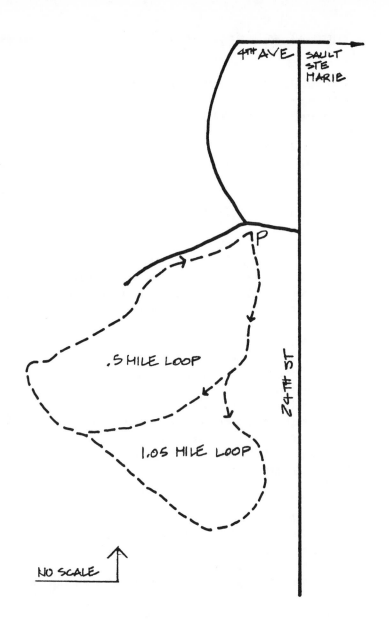

4TH AVE

SAULT STE MARIE

P

.5 MILE LOOP

1.05 MILE LOOP

24TH ST

NO SCALE

SHERMAN PARK

City Parks and Recreation Department, City of Sault Ste. Marie
325 Court St                                    906-632-6853
Sault Ste Marie, MI   49783

Sault Area Chamber of Commerce
2581 I75 Bus. Loop                              906-632-3301
Sault Ste Marie, MI   49783                     800-MISAULT

Trail suitable for skiing & hiking

Location:
  West of Sault Ste. Marie at 4th St. and 24th Ave, across the street from
     the water pumping station on the shore of Lake Superior
  Exit I75 at Easterday west(the name changes to 4th and then Oak), turn
     right on 4th Ave W., park entrance is at the end of 4th Ave W.

Trail specifications:
  1.7 km; 2 loop(s); Loop length(s)-.8, 1.1
Typical terrain: Flat
Skiing ability suggested: Novice
Hiking trail difficulty: Easy
Nordic trail grooming method: Track set occiasionally ‡
Suitable for all-terrain bicycle: Not permitted
Trail use fee: None
Camping: Available in the area
Drinking water not available in winter

General Information:
  Maintained by the city Parks and Recreation Department
  ‡ Call ahead for grooming schedule
  Just north of Algonquin Cross Country Ski Trail
  Food and lodging available nearby

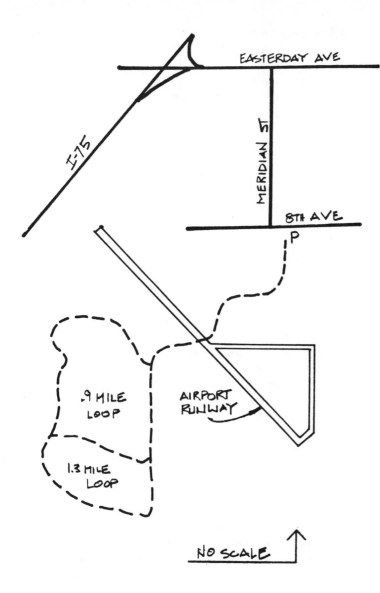

EASTERDAY AVE

I-75

MERIDIAN ST

8TH AVE

P

AIRPORT RUNWAY

.9 MILE LOOP

1.3 MILE LOOP

NO SCALE

SAULT NORDIC SKI TRAIL

Sault Nordic Ski Trail                    Revised: 2/09/88

City Parks & Recreation Department, City of Sault Ste. Marie
325 Court St.                              906-635-5341
Sault Ste Marie, MI  49783

Sault Area Chamber of Commerce
2581 I75 Bus. Loop                        906-632-3301
Sault Ste Marie, MI  49783                800-MISAULT

Trail suitable for skiing only

Location:
 1 mile west of the I75 Business Loop at 8th Ave and Meridian St. in
 Sault Ste. Marie
 Exit I75 at Easterday, then east to Meridian, then south on Meridian to
 8th Ave, then east 100' on 8th Ave to parking lot on south side of the
 road. Trailhead at sign
Trail specifications:
  2.5 km; 2 loop(s); Loop length(s)-1.7, 2.2
Typical terrain: Flat
Skiing ability suggested: Intermediate
Hiking trail difficulty: NA
Nordic trail grooming method: Track set occasionally ‡
Suitable for all-terrain bicycle: Not permitted
Trail use fee: None
Camping: None, but available in Sault Ste. Marie
Drinking water not available at the trailhead

General Information:
 Maintained by the city Parks and Recreation Department.
 ‡ Call ahead for trail gooming schedule
 Food and lodging nearby
 Access to the wooded trail sections is across an open level area that is
   used by snowmobiles

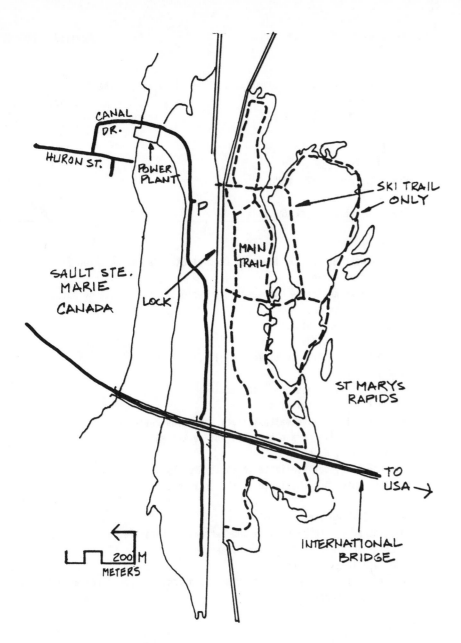

CANAL DR.

HURON ST.

POWER PLANT

P

SAULT STE. MARIE CANADA

LOCK

MAIN TRAIL

SKI TRAIL ONLY

ST MARYS RAPIDS

TO USA →

INTERNATIONAL BRIDGE

200 M
METERS

SAULT STE. MARIE CANAL

Sault Ste. Marie Canal                    Revised: 4/20/88


Sault Ste. Marie Canal
PO Box Sault Ship Canal, Canal Drive      705-942-6262
Sault Ste. Marie, Canada  P6B 1P0


Trail suitable for hiking & skiing

Location:
 Along the Canadian Soo Locks under the International Bridge
 Turn right past customs and right again on Huron Street to Canal Drive,
  then left on Canal Drive past the power generating station to the locks
  parking lot.

Trail specifications:
  5 km ‡; 1 loop(s); Loop length(s)-3
 Typical terrain: Flat
 Skiing ability suggested: Novice
 Hiking trail difficulty: Easy
 Nordic trail grooming method: Track set
 Suitable for all-terrain bicycle: No
 Trail use fee: None
 Camping: None
 Drinking water avaialble

General Information:
 Maintained by the Parks Canada
 ‡ Approximate distance only. Ski trail is longer since it encorporates
   additional distance over the frozen Whitefish Island and adjacent water.
 Interpretive trail with displays describing the natural and cultural
   features of the area.
 Since a major wall failure in the lock on July 22, 1987, the locks have
   been closed to navigation.

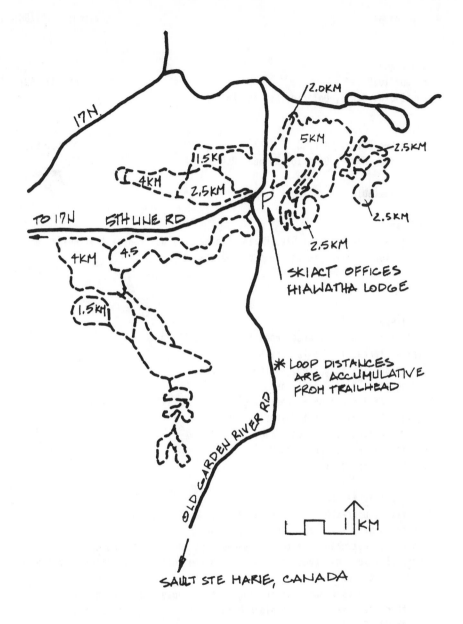

STAR SYSTEM/KINSHEN SKI TRAILS

Skiact c/o Don Scott
99 Foster Drive, PO Box 580                    705-759-3898
Sault Ste Marie, Ontario, Canada  P6A 5N1      705-942-0383

HATS
99 Foster Drive, Level 3                        800-461-6020
Sault Ste Marie, Ontario, Canada  P6B 5X6


Trail suitable for skiing & hiking

Location:
 10 miles north of International Bridge, then take Hwy 17N to 5th Line,
   then right 2 miles to Hiawatha Lodge


Trail specifications:
   50 km; 10 loop(s); Loop length(s)-2, 4, 5, 5, 5, 7.5, 18, 2.5, 2.5, 5
Typical terrain: Flat to very hilly
Skiing ability suggested: Novice to advanced
Hiking trail difficulty: Easy to moderate
Nordic trail grooming method: Track set with a double track daily
Suitable for all-terrain bicycle: Yes
Trail use fee: $8/day, $15/weekend, $22.50/season/adult (Canadian) ‡
Camping: None
Drinking water is available

General Information:
 Maintained by Skiact
 Warming hut and scenic resting decks along trail system
 Warming area, restaurant, snack bar, sauna, target range, biathlon
   range, rentals and a 150' vertical alpine slope
 Established over 30 years ago as a cross country ski area by Finnish
   residents of the Soo, this area is one of the finest trail systems in
   the Great Lakes area.
 2 km lighted trail with 2 tracks and a skating lane, 7 nights a week
 ‡ $50/season/family, $10/season/student, $50/uni-pass/season, seniors 65
   and older and children 12 and under ski free (Canadian funds)
 Ski shops in Soo Canada: Duke of Windsor, 655 Queen St. E., 942-1550;
   Collegiate Sports, 33 Queen St. E., 942-0510; Old Ski House,
   282 Wellington St. W.; The Ski Specialist, 121 Elgin at King St.
 Planned future improvements of $1,000,000 over the next 3 years

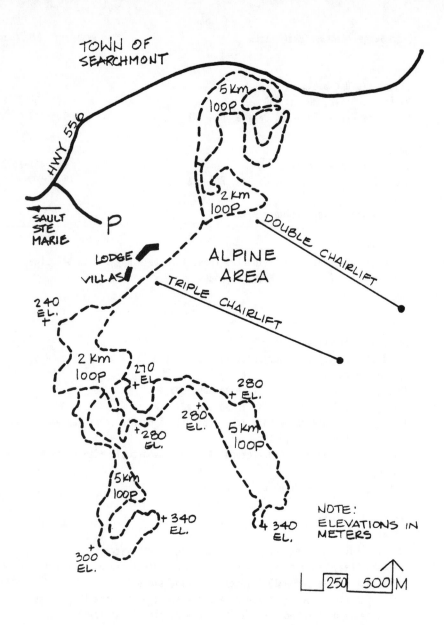

TOWN OF SEARCHMONT

HWY 556

SAULT STE MARIE

P

LODGE

VILLAS

5 km loop

2 km loop

ALPINE AREA

DOUBLE CHAIRLIFT

TRIPLE CHAIRLIFT

240 EL. +

2 km loop

270 EL. +

280 EL. +

280 EL. +

+ 280 EL.

5 km loop

5 km loop

+ 340 EL.

+ 340 EL.

+ 300 EL.

NOTE: ELEVATIONS IN METERS

250  500 M

SEARCHMONT

Searchmont                                    Revised: 4/02/88

Searchmont
PO Box 1029                                   705-759-4881
Sault Ste. Marie, Ontario, Canada  P6A 5N5

HATS
99 Foster Drive, Level 3                      800-461-6020
Sault Ste. Marie, Ontario, Canada  P6A 5X6

Trail suitable for skiing & hiking

Location:
 8 miles north of Sault Ste. Marie, Canada on 17N, then east at Heyden on
   556 for 17 miles to the town of Searchmont

Trail specifications:
   15 km; 5 loop(s); Loop length(s)-2, 2, 5, 5, 5, 8
Typical terrain: Flat to very hilly
Skiing ability suggested: Novice to advanced
Hiking trail difficulty: Easy
Nordic trail grooming method: Single track set 14' wide with a skating lane
Suitable for all-terrain bicycle: Yes
Trail use fee: $8/day (Canadian)
Camping: None available nearby
Drinking water available

General Information:
 Privately operated alpine ski area
 Cross country ski trails new for 1987/88
 Lodging, restaurant, rentals, lessons, ski shop and day nursery
 Very fine well designed trail system in the wooded area adjacent to the
   alpine slopes
 Trails are wide enough for skating with a single track on the right
 Further trail expansion is planned to double the total trail distance for
   the 88/89 ski season
 The novice trail is separate from the intermediate/advanced trails
 Over 120 meter elevation change in the intermediate/advanced trails
 Near Stokely Creek and Star System/Kinsman ski trails

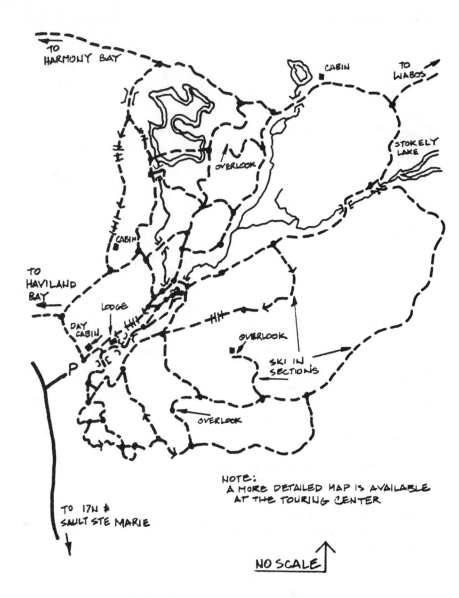

NOTE:
A MORE DETAILED MAP IS AVAILABLE
AT THE TOURING CENTER

NO SCALE

STOKELY CREEK
SKI TOURING CENTER

Stokely Creek Ski Touring Center                     Revised:  2/01/88

Stokely Creek Ski Touring Center
Karalash Corners                                     705-649-3421
Goulais River, Ontario, Canada  P0S 1E0

HATS
99 Foster Drive, Level 3                             800-461-6020
Sault Ste. Marie, Ontario, Cananda  P6A 5X6

Trail suitable for skiing and hiking

Location:
 21 miles north of Sault Ste Marie Canada on 17N.  Follow the signs east
   off Rte 17N just past the Buttermilk alpine ski area

Trail specifications:
   100 km‡; Many loop(s); Loop length(s)-various
Typical terrain: Flat to severly hilly and beyond!
Skiing ability suggested: Novice to advanced
Hiking trail difficulty: Moderate to difficult
Nordic trail grooming method: Double track set‡
Suitable for all-terrain bicycle: Excellent ATB area
Trail use fee: Yes
Camping: None
Drinking water available at the day skiers cabin and lodge

General Information:
 Privately operated ski touring center
 One of the premier ski touring centers in the midwest. Named one of the
   24 best touring centers in North America by Cross Country Skier magazine
 Site of the annual Wabos Loppet, held in March each year
 Good skiing is usually available through the end of March
 The terrain and scenery is simply spectactular.  One trail loop is 17 km
   with another trail going past a summer hang glider launching platform.
   Two trails have over 600 feet of vertical change.
 Warming area and lodging is available
 Winter lodging reservations should be made by Thanksgiving
 ‡ Approximate distance. Does not include ski-in trails
 Four new trails recently added, which go to Harmony Beach and Haviland
  Bay on Lake Superior, Taylor Creek Canyon Trail and the Hakon Lien Trail
  that goes to the top of King Mountain!!!

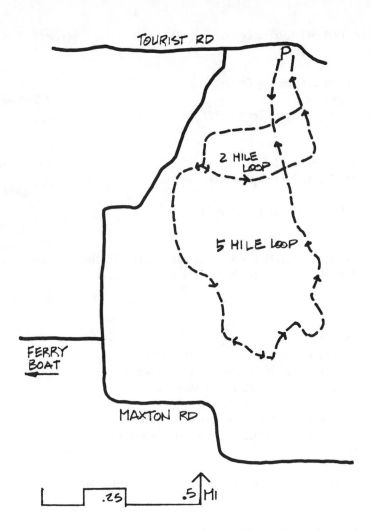

TOURIST RD

P

2 MILE LOOP

5 MILE LOOP

FERRY BOAT

MAXTON RD

.25 .5 MI

## DRUMMOND ISLAND SKI TRAIL

Drummond Island Ski Trail                                    Revised:  2/05/88


Domino's Lodge
PO Box 26                                                    906-493-5234
Drummond Island, MI   49726


Eastern UP Regional Planning & Development Commission
524 Ashmun St.                                               906-635-1581
Sault Ste Marie, MI   49783

Trail suitable for skiing only

Location:
 Take ferry from Detour to Drummond Island
 Trailhead on Tourist Rd., parking lot at Domino's Lodge


Trail specifications:
   7 mi; 2 loop(s); Loop length(s)-2, 5
Typical terrain: Rolling to hilly
Skiing ability suggested: Novice to intermediate
Hiking trail difficulty: NA
Nordic trail grooming method: None
Suitable for all-terrain bicycle: Not permitted
Trail use fee: None
Camping: None
Drinking water available at Domino's Lodge

General Information:
 Maintained by Domino's Lodge
 Wildlife fed along the forested trail
 Food and lodging available on island
 Ferry schedule includes 13 trips per day from 6:40am to 11:30pm

I75
5 MILES

TONE RD
1 MILE

WILSON RD

P

2 MILE
LOOP

6.3 MILE
LOOP

NO SCALE

PINE BOWL PATHWAY

Pine Bowl Pathway                                Revised:  3/23/88

Area Forester, Sault Ste. Marie Forest Area
Box 798, 2001 Ashmun St.                                906-635-5281
Sault Ste. Marie, MI  49783

District Forest Manager, Lake Superior State Forest
PO Box 445, South M123                                  906-293-5131
Newberry, MI  49868

Trail suitable for skiing & hiking

Location:
 16 miles south of Sault Ste. Marie on I75 at the Kinross exit 378
 Trailhead - Exit I75 east on Tone Rd. 4 miles to Wilson Rd., then south
  .75 mile to parking lot


Trail specifications:
   5.7 mi; 2 loop(s); Loop length(s)-2, 5.7
Typical terrain: Flat to rolling
Skiing ability suggested: Novice
Hiking trail difficulty: Easy
Nordic trail grooming method: Track set weekly or more if needed
Suitable for all-terrain bicycle: Yes
Trail use fee: Donations accepted at trailhead
Camping: None
Drinking water not available


General Information:
 Maintained by the DNR Forest Management Division
 Wooded trails
 Food and lodging available in Kinross
 Popular trail with local skiers


Other contacts:
DNR Forest Management Division Office, Lansing, 517-373-1275
DNR Forest Management Region Office, Marquette, 906-228-6561

271

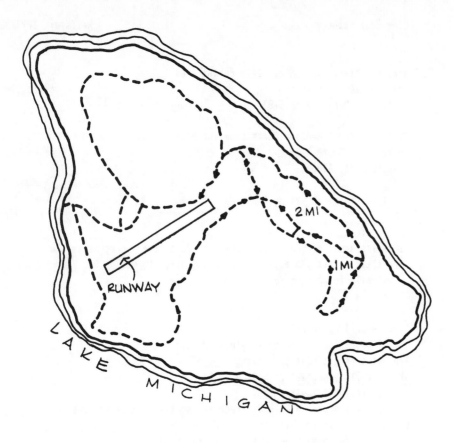

NO SCALE ↑

## MACKINAC ISLAND

Mackinac Island                                    Revised: 2/05/88


Eastern UP Tourist Association
100 Marley St.                                      906-643-7343
St Ignace, MI  49781


Director
Mackinac Island Chamber of Commerce                906-643-8918
Mackinac Island, MI  49757                          906-436-5473


Trail suitable for hiking & skiing

Location:
 Located in the Straits of Mackniac
 Take ferry in summer airplane in winter (contact Eastern UP Tourist
    Association for schedules)


Trail specifications:
    25+ mi*; Many loop(s); Loop length(s)-various
Typical terrain: Rolling
Skiing ability suggested: Novice to advanced
Hiking trail difficulty: Easy to moderate
Nordic trail grooming method: Track set occasionally
Suitable for all-terrain bicycle: Yes
Trail use fee: None
Camping: None
Drinking water available

General Information:
 Maintained by the Mackinac Island State Park Commission
 * Skiing trails are 3 miles, with loops of 1 & 2 miles
 Food and lodging available in summer and food only in winter
 Bicycle rentals available on the island

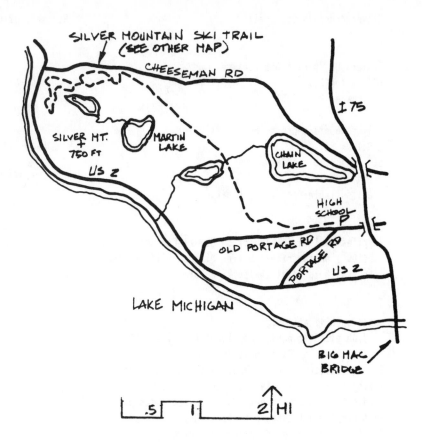

SILVER MOUNTAIN SKI TRAIL
(SEE OTHER MAP)

CHEESEMAN RD

SILVER MT.
+
750 FT

MARTIN
LAKE

CHAIN
LAKE

I 75

US 2

HIGH
SCHOOL
P

OLD PORTAGE RD

PORTAGE RD

US 2

LAKE MICHIGAN

BIG MAC
BRIDGE

.5  1  2 HI

## ST. IGNACE TOWN TRAIL

St. Ignace Town Trail                    Revised:  2/05/88

Eastern UP Tourist Association
100 Marley St.                           906-643-7343
St. Ignace, MI  49781

Silver Mountain Cross Country Ski Club
3 Balsam St.                             906-643-7082
St Ignace, MI  49781

Trail suitable for skiing only

Location:
 Trailhead - La Salle High School, Old Portage Rd., St. Ignace
 Trailhead - Silver Mt. Ski Area, Cheeseman Rd., 7 miles west of St. Ignace
   on US2

Trail specifications:
   6 mi*; No** loop(s); Loop length(s)-NA
Typical terrain: Flat to slightly rolling
Skiing ability suggested: Novice
Hiking trail difficulty: NA
Nordic trail grooming method: Packed as needed
Suitable for all-terrain bicycle: NA
Trail use fee: Donations accepted
Camping: None available
Drinking water not available along the trail

General Information:
 Maintained by the St. Ignace and the Silver Mt Cross Country Ski Club
 * Connects Silver Mt. Cross-Country Ski Area with St. Ignace by means of
   a point to point trail.
 ** This is a point to point trail

273

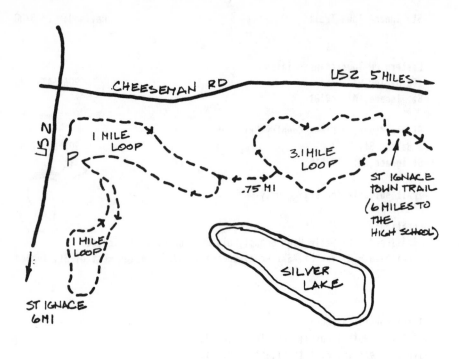

CHEESEMAN RD

US2 5 MILES →

US 2

P

1 MILE LOOP

3.1 MILE LOOP

.75 MI

ST IGNACE TOWN TRAIL
(6 MILES TO THE HIGH SCHOOL)

1 MILE LOOP

ST IGNACE 6 MI

SILVER LAKE

NO SCALE

# SILVER MOUNTAIN SKI TRAIL

Silver Mountain Ski Trail                    Revised: 2/09/88

Eastern UP Tourist Association
100 Marley St.
St Ignace, MI  49781                         906-643-7343

Silver Mountain Cross Country Ski Club
3 Balsam St.                                 906-643-7082
St. Ignace, MI  49781

Trail suitable for skiing & hiking

Location:
  4 miles west of St. Ignace on US2 at Cheeseman Rd., right to first drive
    (200') on the right (Silver Mt. downhill ski area entrance).
  The trailhead is at the parking lot.


Trail specifications:
   3.35 mi; 3 loop(s); Loop length(s)-1, 1, 3.1
Typical terrain: Flat to hilly
Skiing ability suggested: Novice to intermediate
Hiking trail difficulty: Easy to moderate
Nordic trail grooming method: Track set occasionally✸
Suitable for all-terrain bicycle: Not permitted
Trail use fee: None, donations accepted
Camping: None
Drinking water available at warming hut in winter


General Information:
  Maintained by the Silver Mt. Cross-Country Ski Club
  The west end of the St Ignace Town Trail
  ✸ Call ahead to check on trail grooming schedule
  Use the Silver Mountain alpine ski area parking lot

SAND DUNES
CROSS COUNTRY SKI TRAIL

.6MI
.2M
.9MI
BREVOORT
8 MILES
1.5 MI
.25   .5 MI
BREVOORT LAKE RD
H57
.4MI
.7MI
.4MI   .4MI
.7MI
I-75
11 MILES

LAKE MICHIGAN

Sand Dunes Cross Country Ski Trail                Revised: 3/20/88

St. Ignace Ranger District, Hiawatha National Forest
1498 West US2                                      906-643-7900
St Ignace, MI  49781

Eastern UP Tourist Association
100 Marley                                         906-643-7343
St Ignace, MI  49781

Trail suitable for skiing & hiking

Location:
  11 miles west of I75 (St. Ignace) on US2, then north on Brevoort Lake Rd.
  (H57) .5 miles to parking lot

Trail specifications:
  15.6 km; 7 loop(s); Loop length(s)-2.4, 4.7, 7.6, 8.5, 10, 11.8, 12.3
Typical terrain: Rolling to hilly
Skiing ability suggested: Novice to advanced
Hiking trail difficulty: Easy to moderate
Nordic trail grooming method: Track set as needed
Suitable for all-terrain bicycle: Not permitted
Trail use fee: Donations accepted to cover grooming costs
Camping: Seasonal camping available at the NF campground 7 miles west
Drinking water not available

General Information:
  Built by the St. Ignace Ranger District, Hiawatha National Forest,
    Silver Mountain Cross Country Ski Club and 12 other local groups
  Groomed by the Silver Mountain Cross-Country Ski Club
  Excellent ski trail with varied forest cover and well designed loops
    with scenic overlooks of Lake Michigan. The entire trail was
    contoured to provide for a delightful skiing experience
  By passes for difficult sections are provided on the intermediate loops
  The open area at the trailhead was the site of the Round Lake Civilian
    Conservation Corps Camp that started in 1935
  Site of the annual Dunes Day Loppet held the first Saturday in March
  Food and lodging in St. Ignace

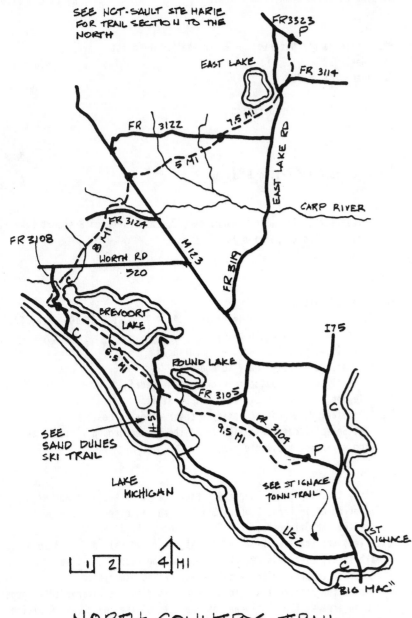

SEE NOT-SAULT STE MARIE FOR TRAIL SECTION TO THE NORTH

FR3323
P

EAST LAKE

FR 3114

FR 3122

7.5 MI

EAST LAKE RD

5 MI

CARP RIVER

FR 3124

FR3108

8 MI

WORTH RD

520

M123

FR3119

BREVOORT LAKE

6.5 MI

ROUND LAKE

I75

FR 3105

SEE SAND DUNES SKI TRAIL

H57

9.5 MI

FR 3104

C

P

LAKE MICHIGAN

SEE ST IGNACE TOWN TRAIL

US2

ST IGNACE

C

1  2    4 MI

C

"BIG MAC"

# NORTH COUNTRY TRAIL ST. IGNACE

North Country Trail - St. Ignace        Revised: 4/02/88

St. Ignace Ranger District, Hiawatha National Forest
1498 West US2                                        906-643-7900
St. Ignace, MI  49781


Forest Supervisor, Hiawatha National Forest
PO Box 316, 2727 N. Lincoln Rd.                      906-786-4062
Escanaba, MI  49829

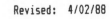

Trail suitable for hiking only

Location:
 North and east of St Ignace
 South trailhead - 1.5 miles west of I75 on Castle Rock Rd.
 North trailhead - Just east of East Lake Rd. (NE of East Lake) on FR 3323
 Lake Michigan trailhead - 11 miles west of St Ignace on US2, then 1.8
   miles north on Co Rd H57 (Brevoort Lake Rd.)
Trail specifications:
 35 mi; No** loop(s); Loop length(s)-NA
Typical terrain: Rolling
Skiing ability suggested: NA
Hiking trail difficulty: Moderate
Nordic trail grooming method: NA
Suitable for all-terrain bicycle: Not permitted
Trail use fee: None
Camping: Campgounds along trail *
Drinking water available at the developed campground


General Information:
 Maintained by the St. Ignace Ranger District, Hiawatha National Forest
 Part of the North Country Trail
 The trail is fully marked but not all sections are brought up to trail
   standards.
 * Developed campground is located at Brevoort Lake Campground with
   70 sites, toilets and drinking water.
   Primitive campgrounds are located on the south side of the trail
   near the Pt. Aux Chenes River, on the south side of Lake Brevoort and
   20 feet from the trail, 1/4 mile east of FR3119. Also wilderness
   camping is permitted 200' from the trail
 ** Like the entire North Country Trail, this is a point to point trail
 For more information contact the North Country Trail Association,
   PO Box 311, White Cloud, MI 49349 or the USDI, Midwest Region, 1709
   Jackson St, Omaha, NE 68102-2571

# Region 4

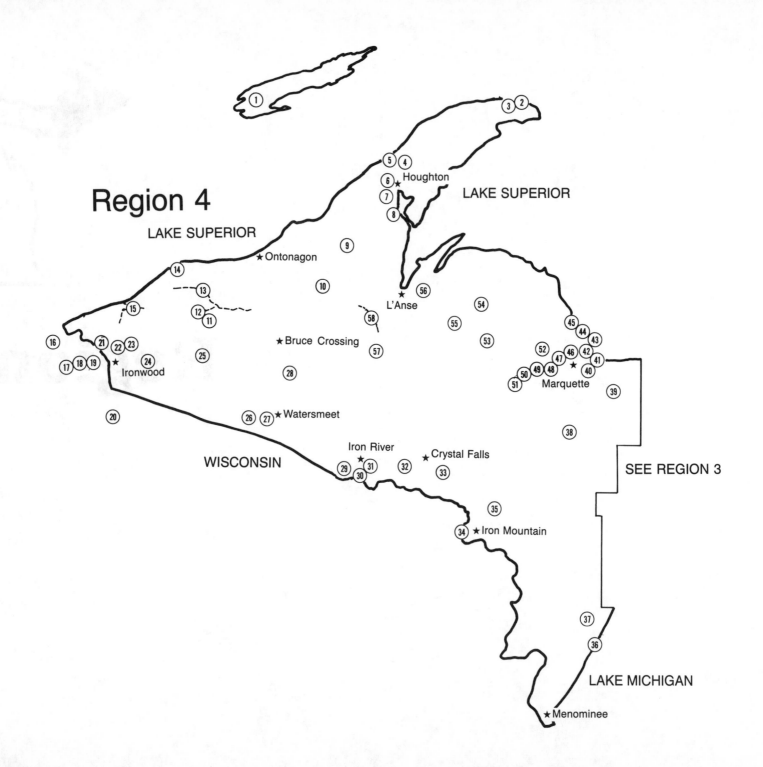

Region 4

LAKE SUPERIOR

LAKE SUPERIOR

★Ontonagon

Houghton

★L'Anse

★Bruce Crossing

Ironwood ★

★Watersmeet

WISCONSIN

Iron River ★

★Crystal Falls

Marquette

SEE REGION 3

★Iron Mountain

LAKE MICHIGAN

★Menominee

# Region 4 Contents

# Trail Notes

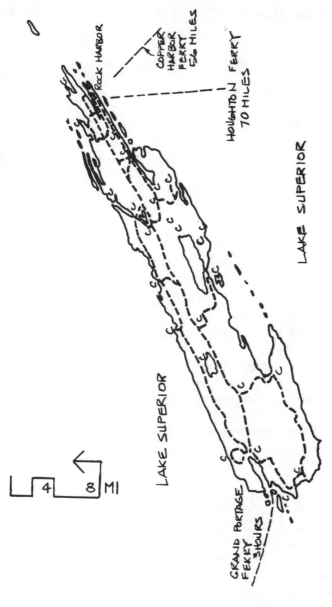

ISLE ROYALE NATIONAL PARK

Isle Royale National Park                              Revised: 3/20/88


Isle Royale National Park
87 N. Ripley St                                     906-482-0984
Houghton, MI  49931

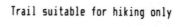

Trail suitable for hiking only

Location:
 70 miles north of Houghton in Lake Superior
  Ferry services from Houghton, Copper Harbor and Grand Portage
  Sea plane service from Houghton


Trail specifications:
   165 mi; Many loop(s); Loop length(s)-various
Typical terrain: Flat to very steep
Skiing ability suggested: NA
Hiking trail difficulty: Easy to extremely difficult
Nordic trail grooming method: NA
Suitable for all-terrain bicycle: Not permitted
Trail use fee: $2/person entry fee
Camping: Available throughout the park
Drinking water available at campgrounds and ranger stations

General Information:
 Maintained by the National Park Service
 The most rugged and remote area in Michigan
 The extreme beauty of this island is a delight to the senses
 Be completely prepared before attempting to do any extensive hiking on
   the island.  Write to the Park for information on hiking/camping/
   boating recommendations before planning your trip.
 Complete lodge facilities are available at Rock Harbor for those not
   interested in extensive hiking but reservations must be made months in
   advance to assure accomodation.
 Likewise, reservations on the two ferry boats should be made a month in
   advance of departure to assure space on board
 Write for information brochures and catalog pf publications available
 Park season Apr 16th - Oct 31st. Full services are available June-August
 NOT OPEN IN THE WINTER

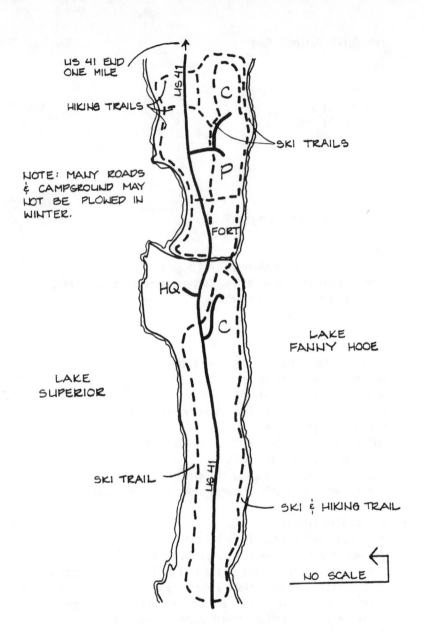

US 41 END
ONE MILE

HIKING TRAILS

US 41

C

SKI TRAILS

NOTE: MANY ROADS
& CAMPGROUND MAY
NOT BE PLOWED IN
WINTER.

P

FORT

HQ

C

LAKE
FANNY HOOE

LAKE
SUPERIOR

SKI TRAIL

US 41

SKI & HIKING TRAIL

NO SCALE

# FORT WILKINS STATE PARK

Fort Wilkins State Park                    Revised:  3/28/88

Fort Wilkins State Park
US41 East                                  906-289-4215
Copper Harbor, MI  49918

DNR Parks Division Office

                                           517-373-1270

Trail suitable for skiing & hiking

Location:
 Just east of Copper Harbor on US41

Trail specifications:
   4.2 mi; 4 loop(s); Loop length(s)-various
Typical terrain: Flat
Skiing ability suggested: Novice
Hiking trail difficulty: Easy
Nordic trail grooming method: Track set twice weekly
Suitable for all-terrain bicycle: Yes
Trail use fee: None, but vehicle entry fee required $2/day, $10/year
Camping: In park
Drinking water available

General Information:
 Maintained by the DNR Parks Division
 Rentals available at the Lake Fanny Hooe Resort at the west end of Lake
    Fanny Hooe 906-289-4451
 Hiking and ski trails may not all be identical trails
 Snowmobiles are not permitted in the park
 Copper Harbor Pathway is nearby.  See other listing.

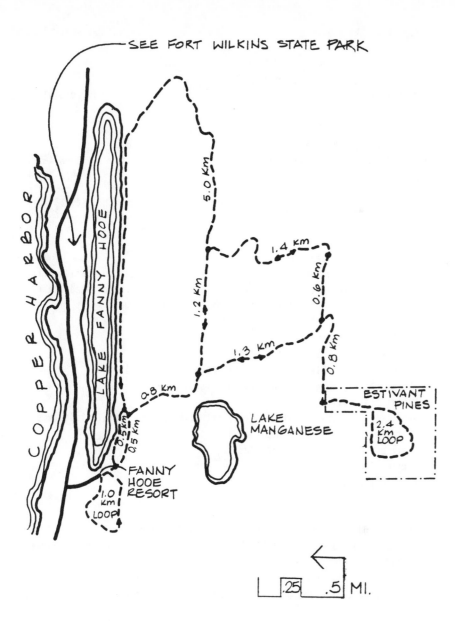

SEE FORT WILKINS STATE PARK

COPPER HARBOR

LAKE FANNY HOOE

5.0 KM

1.4 KM

1.2 KM

0.6 km

1.3 KM

0.8 KM

0.8 KM

0.5 km
0.5 km

FANNY HOOE RESORT

1.0 KM LOOP

LAKE MANGANESE

ESTIVANT PINES

2.4 KM LOOP

.25  .5 MI.

COPPER HARBOR PATHWAY

Copper Harbor Pathway                    Revised: 4/18/88

Area Forester, Baraga Forest Area
Box 440                                        906-353-6651
Baraga, MI  49908

Park Manager
Fort Wilkins State Park                        906-289-4215
Copper Harbor, MI  49918

Trail suitable for skiing & hiking

Location:
 Trailhead - West end of Lake Fanny Hooe near Lake Fanny Hooe Resort

Trail specifications:
   18.7 km; 5 loop(s); Loop length(s)-1, 8, 10.1, 14.1, 3.4
Typical terrain: Rolling to hilly
Skiing ability suggested: Intermediate to advanced
Hiking trail difficulty: Moderate
Nordic trail grooming method: Track set
Suitable for all-terrain bicycle: Yes
Trail use fee: None
Camping: Available at Fort Wilkins SP and Lake Fanny Hooe Resort
Available at Fort Wilkins SP and Lake Fanny Hooe Resort

General Information:
 Maintained by the DNR Forest Management and Parks Divisions
 Rentals and lodging available from Fanny Hooe Resort at the west end of
   Lake Fanny Hooe 906-289-4451
 Groomed by Fort Wilkins State Park
 Estivant Pines loop is owned by the Michigan Nature Association.  It is
   not groomed for skiing.  The trail was developed only for hiking.
 Other contacts:
 DNR Forest Management Region Office, Marquette, 906-228-6561
 DNR Forest Management Division Office, Lansing, 517-373-1275
 Clyde Wescoat, Brockway Inn, Copper Harbor, MI 49918 906-289-4588
 Keweenaw Tourism Council, 1197 Calumet Ave., Calumet, MI 49913
   906-482-2388
 Keweenaw Peninsula Chamber Of Commerce, 326 Sheldon Ave.,
   Houghton, MI 49931     906-482-5240 or 337-4579

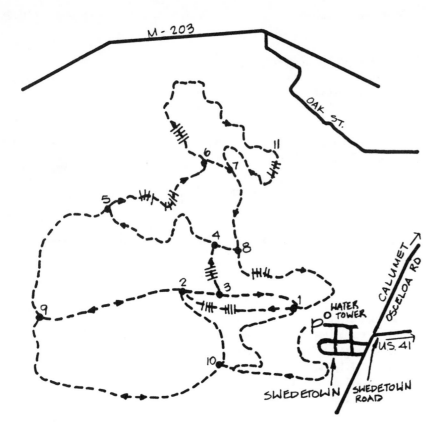

M-203

OAK ST.

| NAME | TRAIL | LENGTH |
|------|-------|--------|
| GREEN | 1-3-2-9-10-2-3-1 | 5.0 Km. |
| BLUE | 1-10-1 | 2.0 Km. |
| RED | 1-2-3-4-8-1 | 2.5 Km |
| RED | 1-2-3-4-5-6-7-8-1 | 5.0 Km |
| RED | 1-2-3-4-5-6-11-7-8-1 | 7.5 Km |

NO SCALE

SWEDETOWN SKI TRAIL

284

Swedetown Ski Trail                          Revised: 3/23/88

Copper Island Cross Country Ski Club
PO Box 214                                    906-337-4520
Calumet, MI  49913

Keweenaw Tourism Council
PO Box 336, 1197 Calumet Ave                  906-482-2388
Calumet, MI  49913                            906-337-4579

Trail suitable for skiing and hiking

Location:
  1 mile SW of Calumet on Osceloa Rd
  Trailhead - Take Swedetown Rd west from US41 (just before tourist office,
    sign at intersection), then left on Osceloa Rd, then an immediate right
    into Swedetown and west to trailhead past water tower

Trail specifications:
  12 km; Several loop(s); Loop length(s)-various
  Typical terrain: Flat to gently rolling with some hills
  Skiing ability suggested: Novice to intermediate
  Hiking trail difficulty: Easy
  Nordic trail grooming method: Track set with skating lane, 4 times/week
  Suitable for all-terrain bicycle: Yes
  Trail use fee: Donations accepted
  Camping: None
  No drinking water available

General Information:
  Maintained by Copper Island Cross-Country Ski Club
  Rentals and ski shop at the Cross-Country Sports, 507 Oak St., Calumet,
    337-4520.
  Site of the Season Opener Ski Race (first race of the season for the
    the midwest) and the Great Bear Chase Race (last event of the season
    for the midwest).
  Normal ski season begins in November and goes through March
  Skiing available on the Keweenaw Peninsula through April.  The Annual
    "Picnic in the Snow" event is held on the 2nd or 3rd Sunday in April.
    This event has been held for the last 16 years.
  Accomodations and food available in Calumet
  Other contact:
  Keweenaw Peninsula Chamber of Commerce, 326 Shelden Ave.,
    Houghton, MI 49931  906-482-5240 or 337-4579

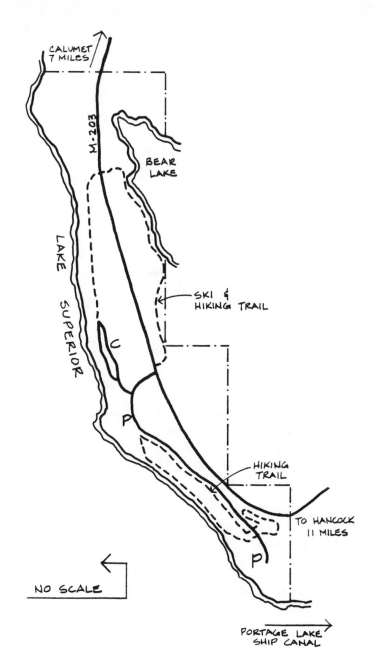

CALUMET
7 MILES

M-203

BEAR
LAKE

LAKE SUPERIOR

SKI &
HIKING TRAIL

U

P

HIKING
TRAIL

TO HANCOCK
11 MILES

NO SCALE

P

PORTAGE LAKE
SHIP CANAL

McLAIN STATE PARK

McLain State Park                              Revised:  3/28/88

McLain State Park
M 203                                          906-482-0278
Hancock, MI  49930

DNR Parks Division Office
                                               517-373-1270

Trail suitable for skiing & hiking

Location:
 7 miles west of Calument on M-203 and
 11 miles west of Hancock on M-203


Trail specifications:
  3 mi; 1 loop(s); Loop length(s)-3
Typical terrain: Flat to rolling
Skiing ability suggested: Novice
Hiking trail difficulty: Easy
Nordic trail grooming method: Packed as needed
Suitable for all-terrain bicycle: Yes
Trail use fee: None, but vehicle entry fee required $2/day, $10/year
Camping: Campground on site
Drinking water

General Information:
 Maintained by the DNR Parks Division
 Trail along Lake Superior and Bear Lake
 3 mile fitness trail

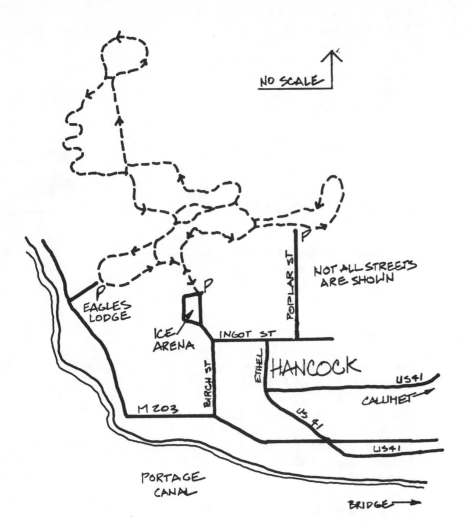

NO SCALE

NOT ALL STREETS
ARE SHOWN

EAGLES
LODGE

ICE
ARENA

INGOT ST

POPLAR ST

HANCOCK

ETHEL

BIRCH ST

US41
CALUMET

US 41

M 203

US41

PORTAGE
CANAL

BRIDGE →

MAASTO HIIHTO SKI TRAIL

Maasto Hiihto Ski Trail                    Revised:  2/22/88

Houghton-Hancock Ski Club c/o City of Hancock
City Hall                                             906-483-1770
Hancock, MI  49930

Kewennaw Tourism Council
PO Box 336, 1197 Calumet Ave                          906-482-2388
Calumet, MI  49913                                   906-337-4579

Trail suitable for skiing only

Location:
 Northwest edge of Hancock
 Trailhead - Behind the Houghton County Arena at Birch and Ingot Streets
 Trailhead - North end of Popular St
 Trailhead - Off M203 behind the Eagles Club, NW of town

Trail specifications:
   15 km; Many loop(s); Loop length(s)-1.5 to 6.5
Typical terrain: Hilly
Skiing ability suggested: Intermediate to Advanced
Hiking trail difficulty: NA
Nordic trail grooming method: Track set occasionally
Suitable for all-terrain bicycle: NA
Trail use fee: Donations accepted
Camping: Campground not available nearby
Drinking water not available

General Information:
 Maintained by the Houghton-Hancock Ski Club and the City of Hancock
 Maintained when funds are available - call ahead
 A simply fantastic nordic ski trail
 The trail map is the best that was available at publishing time.  Check
   with local ski shops or the tourist office before skiing for any changes
   in the course and directions to it

Other contact:
Keweenaw Peninsula Chamber of Commerce, 326 Shelden Ave.,
   Houghton, MI 49931    906-482-5240 or 337-4579

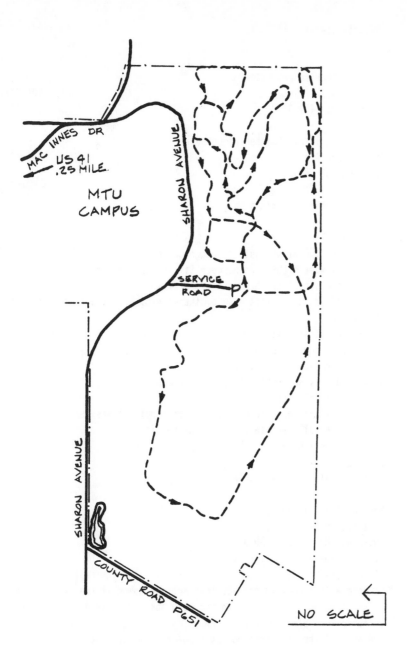

MAC INNES DR

US 41
.25 MILE.

MTU
CAMPUS

SHARON AVENUE

SERVICE
ROAD

P

SHARON AVENUE

COUNTY ROAD P651

NO SCALE

## MTU TRAIL

MTU Trail                                    Revised: 2/24/88

Keweenaw Tourism Center
PO Box 336, 1197 Calumet Ave               906-337-4579
Calumet, MI  49913                         906-338-7982

Keweenaw Peninsula Chamber of Commerce
326 Shelden Ave                            906-482-5240
Houghton, MI  49931

Trail suitable for skiing only

Location:
 On the MTU campus between Sharon Ave and Manninen Rd
 Entrance to trail on Sharon Ave

Trail specifications:
    8 km; Several loop(s); Loop length(s)-various#
Typical terrain: Flat to very hilly
Skiing ability suggested: Novice to advanced
Hiking trail difficulty: Easy
Nordic trail grooming method: Track Set about 4 times/week
Suitable for all-terrain bicycle: Yes
Trail use fee: None
Camping: Camping available in area
Drinking water not available

General Information:
 Trails maintained on a regular basis by Michigan Technological University
 # Outside loop is 6.2 km
 Cut offs from the main loop will bypass the most difficult trail
    sections which would reduce the required ability from advanced to an
    intermediate novice
 A beautiful wooded trail system on the edge of the MTU campus.

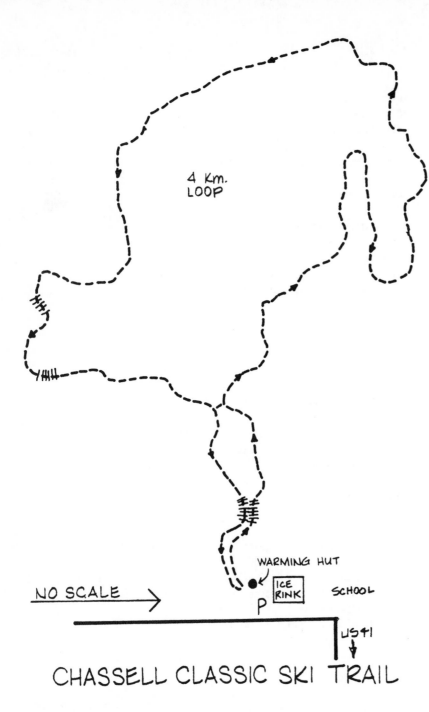

4 Km.
LOOP

NO SCALE →

WARMING HUT

ICE RINK

P

SCHOOL

US41

CHASSELL CLASSIC SKI TRAIL

Chassell Classic Ski Trail                    Revised: 2/24/88

Keweenaw Tourism Council
PO Box 336                                    906-337-4579
Calumet, MI  49913                            800-338-7982

Keweenaw Peninsula Chamber Of Commerce
362 Sheldon Ave                               906-482-5240
Houghton, MI  49931

Trail suitable for Skiing only

Location:
 In Chassell, 7 miles south of Houghton on US41
 One block west of US41 on Hancock St. in Chassell next to the ice rink
   near the school at the north end of town
 Trail starts on the left side of the warming building that is next to the
   ice rink
Trail specifications:
 4 km; 1 loop(s); Loop length(s)-4
Typical terrain: Slightly rolling
Skiing ability suggested: Novice to intermediate
Hiking trail difficulty: NA
Nordic trail grooming method: Track set about 3 times per week ⚹
Suitable for all-terrain bicycle: Not permitted
Trail use fee: None
Camping: None
Drinking water not available

General Information:
 Maintained by Chassell
 Warming shelter available
 ⚹ Trail not designed for skating
 A well designed trail that is a delight to ski. The rolling terrain is
   used effectively to provide long rolling downhill runs with a minimum
   of climbing.  The mostly wooded with some open field skiing provides
   for a very pleasant experience.
 Because of the open sections it's not recommended when its windy

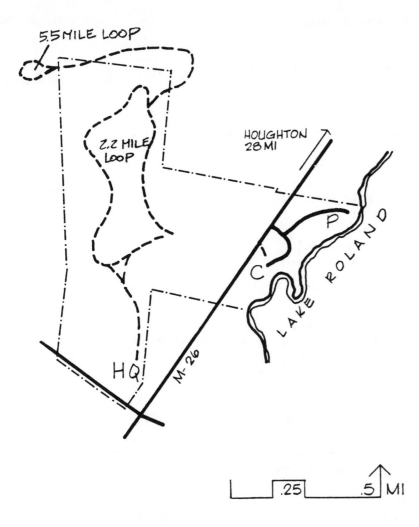

5.5 MILE LOOP

2.2 MILE LOOP

HOUGHTON 28 MI

C I P

LAKE ROLAND

HQ

M-26

|___|___|.25|___|___|.5|MI

# TWIN LAKES STATE PARK

Twin Lakes State Park                          Revised: 3/28/88

Twin Lakes State Park
Rte 3, Box 234                                 906-288-3321
Toivola, MI  49965

DNR Parks Division Office

                                               517-373-1270

Trail suitable for skiing & hiking

Location:
 28 miles south of Houghton on M-26

Trail specifications:
    5 mi; 2 loop(s); Loop length(s)-2.5, 5
 Typical terrain: Flat to rolling
 Skiing ability suggested: Novice
 Hiking trail difficulty: Easy
 Nordic trail grooming method: Track set once/week minimum
 Suitable for all-terrain bicycle: Yes
 Trail use fee: None, but vehicle entry fee required $2/day, $10/year
 Camping: Campground available in park, year-round‡
 Drinking water available‡‡

General Information:
 Maintained by the DNR Parks Division
 ‡ Limited facilities in winter. Call ahead to make arrangements
 ‡‡ Available at headquarters in the winter
 Two overlooks along the trail, which can permit a view of Lake Superior on
     a clear day
 Restaurant and lounge across M26 from park headquarters

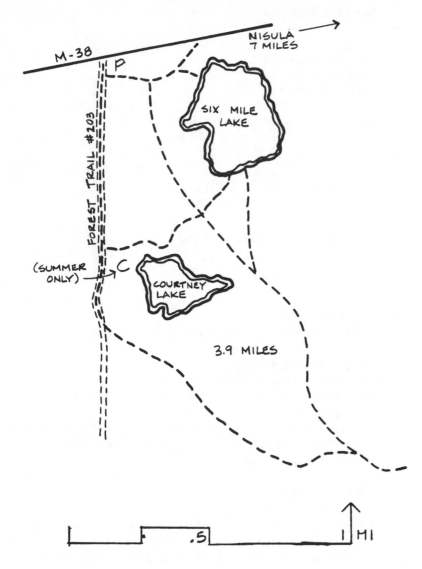

NISULA
7 MILES

M-38

P

FOREST TRAIL #203

SIX MILE LAKE

(SUMMER ONLY) → C

COURTNEY LAKE

3.9 MILES

.5        1 MI

# OLD GRADE SKI TRAIL

Old Grade Ski Trail                                    Revised:  3/20/88

Ontonagon Ranger District, Ottawa National Forest
PO Box 217                                             906-884-2411
Ontonagon, MI  49953

Forest Supervisor, Ottawa National Forest
East US2                                               906-932-1330
Ironwood, MI  49938                                    800-562-1201

Trail suitable for skiing & hiking

Location:
 West of Baraga on M38
 7 miles west of Nisula at Courtney Lake Recreation Area on FH203

Trail specifications:
   3.9 mi; Several loop(s); Loop length(s)-various
 Typical terrain: Gently rolling
 Skiing ability suggested: Novice
 Hiking trail difficulty: Easy
 Nordic trail grooming method: None
 Suitable for all-terrain bicycle: Yes
 Trail use fee: None
 Camping: Campgound at trailhead open in snowless months
 Drinking water available when the campground is open

General Information:
 Maintained by the Ontonagon Ranger District, Ottawa National Forest
 Courtney Lake has a very nice swimming area
 Many other unmarked trails in the area for wilderness skiing
 Trail is not well marked
 FR 203 is plowed to some privately owned cabins near campground

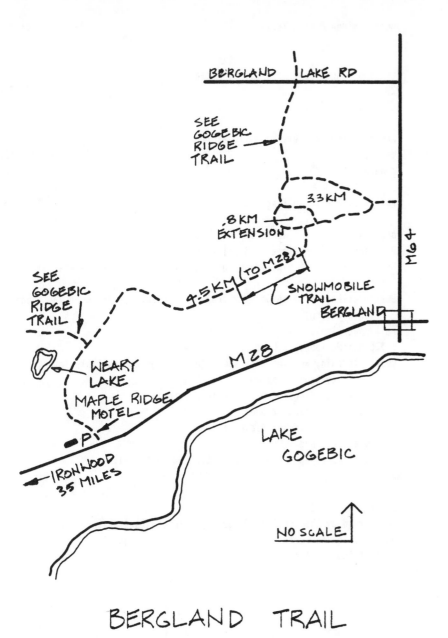

BERGLAND TRAIL

Bergland Ranger District, Ottawa National Forest
PO Box 126, M28                                       906-575-3441
Bergland, MI 49910

Forest Supervisor, Ottawa National Forest
East US2                                              906-932-1330
Ironwood, MI 49938                                    800-562-1201

Trail suitable for skiing only

Location:
 Trailhead - .4 mile north of the Bergland on M64.  Park on the road.
 Trailhead - Maple Ridge Motel, 2.5 miles west of Bergland on M28.,

Trail specifications:
  8.7 km; 3‡ loop(s); Loop length(s)-3.3, 4.1, 12.3 ‡
Typical terrain: Rolling to hilly
Skiing ability suggested: Novice to intermediate
Hiking trail difficulty: NA
Nordic trail grooming method: Track set by Chamber of Commerce
Suitable for all-terrain bicycle: NA
Trail use fee: None
Camping: Campground available at Lake Gogebic State Park
Drinking water available in Bergland

General Information:
 Maintained by the Bergland Ranger District, Ottawa National Forest
 A well marked but not frequently used ski trail
 Food and lodging available in Bergland
 ‡ Also a point to point trail section
 Part of the Eagle Ridge section is a snowmobile trail
 Part of the Gogebic Ridge Hiking Trail.  See other listing
 Via the Gogebic Ridge Hiking Trail, the North Country Trail - Bergland
   can be reached

291

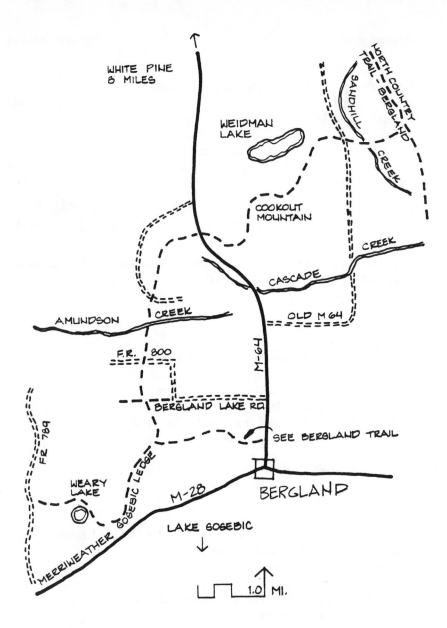

## GOGEBIC RIDGE HIKING TRAIL

Gogebic Ridge Hiking Trail                    Revised:  4/02/88

Bergland Ranger District, Ottawa National Forest
M28                                           906-575-3441
Bergland, MI  49910

Forest Supervisor, Ottawa National Forest
East US2                                      906-932-1330
Ironwood, MI  49938                           800-562-1201

Trail suitable for hiking only

Location:
 Bergland Trail trailhead - 3 miles north of Bergland on M64
 West trailhead - 1.5 miles north of M28 on FR 789, 3 miles west of
   Bergland
 East trailhead - North Country Trail - Bergland Segment near the Sandhill
   Creek crossing
Trail specifications:
 5.5 mi; No loop(s); Loop length(s)-NA
Typical terrain: Rolling with some steep grades not suitable for skiing
Skiing ability suggested: NA
Hiking trail difficulty: Moderate to difficult
Nordic trail grooming method: NA
Suitable for all-terrain bicycle: Yes
Trail use fee: None
Camping: Wildnerness camping permitted 200' off trail
None

General Information:
 Maintained by the Bergland Ranger District, Ottawa National Forest
 Connects to the North Country Trail - Bergland Segment
 Part of the Bergland Trail

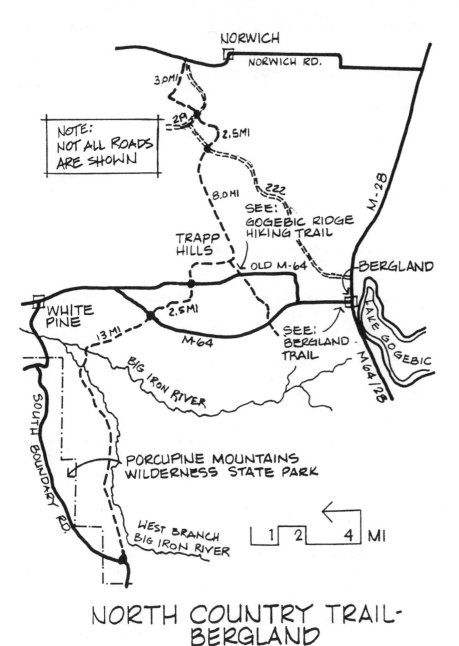

# NORTH COUNTRY TRAIL-
# BERGLAND

NOTE:
NOT ALL ROADS
ARE SHOWN

North Country Trail - Bergland                    Revised: 4/01/88

Bergland Ranger District, Ottawa National Forest
PO Box 126, M28                                   906-575-3441
Bergland, MI  49910

Forest Supervisor, Ottawa National Forest
East US2                                          906-932-1330
Ironwood, MI  49938                               800-562-1201

Trail suitable for hiking only

Location:
 West trailhead-S. Boundary Rd adjacent to Procupine Mountains State Park
 East trailhead-NE of Bergland, 10 miles north of M28 on Norwich Rd, at the
   intersection of FH 219
 Trailhead-7 miles north of Bergland on M64
 Other trailheads available
Trail specifications:
  29 mi; No loop(s); Loop length(s)-NA
Typical terrain: Very hilly
Skiing ability suggested: Advanced
Hiking trail difficulty: Difficult
Nordic trail grooming method: None
Suitable for all-terrain bicycle: Not permitted
Trail use fee: None
Camping: There are no developed campsites✻
Boil all water at least 5 minutes or use filter

General Information:
 Maintained by the Bergland Ranger District, Ottawa National Forest
 This is a point to point trail
 Connected to the east end of the Gogebic Ridge Trail
 Recommended only for skiers with winter survival skills
 Most streams do not have bridges
 Formally the Trap Falls section of the North Country Trail
 A more detailed trail map is available from the Bergland Ranger District
   office
 ✻ Wilderness camping is permitted 200' from the trail


For more information about the North Country Trail, contact the
 North Country Trail Association, PO Box 311, White Cloud, MI 49349 or
 USDI, Midwest Region, 1709 Jackson St., Omaha, NE 68102-2571

293

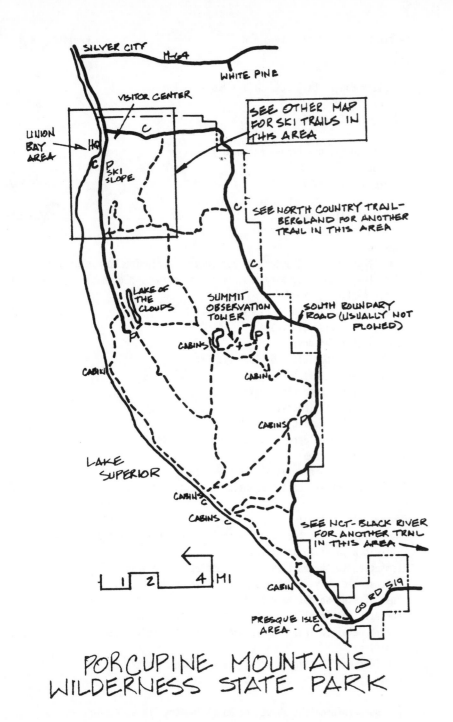

SILVER CITY
M-64
WHITE PINE

VISITOR CENTER

SEE OTHER MAP
FOR SKI TRAILS IN
THIS AREA

UNION
BAY
AREA

HQ
C
P SKI
SLOPE

SEE NORTH COUNTRY TRAIL-
BERGLAND FOR ANOTHER
TRAIL IN THIS AREA

LAKE OF
THE CLOUDS

SUMMIT
OBSERVATION
TOWER

SOUTH BOUNDARY
ROAD (USUALLY NOT
PLOWED)

CABINS

CABIN

CABIN

CABINS

LAKE
SUPERIOR

CABINS
C

CABINS C

SEE NCT-BLACK RIVER
FOR ANOTHER TRAIL
IN THIS AREA

1  2    4 MI

CABIN

CO RD 519

PRESQUE ISLE
AREA
C

# PORCUPINE MOUNTAINS WILDERNESS STATE PARK

Porcupine Mountains Wilderness State Park                Revised:  3/23/88

Porcupine Mountains Wildnerness State Park
599 M107                                                906-885-5275
Ontonagon, MI  49953

DNR Parks Division Office

517-373-1270

Trail suitable for skiing & hiking

Location:
17 miles west of Ontonagon on the shore of Lake Superior


 Note: there are two trail maps. One for skiing and another map at a larger
       scale for all hiking trails.
Trail specifications:
   85+ mi*; Many loop(s); Loop length(s)-various
Typical terrain: Rolling to very hilly
Skiing ability suggested: Novice to intermediate
Hiking trail difficulty: Easy to difficult
Nordic trail grooming method: Track set regularly
Suitable for all-terrain bicycle: Yes
Trail use fee: None, but vehicle entry fee required $2/day, $10/year
Camping: Available in park, facilities may be limited during the winter
Drinking water available throughout park (limited locations in winter)

General Information:
 Maintained by the DNR Parks Division
 A unique state park at the shore of Lake Superior
 Rentals, warming area, snack bar and alpine skiing available.
 * Only about 25 mi of the trails were designed for skiing.  Most of these
   ski trails are not used for hiking trails in the summer.
 Extensive wilderness hiking trail system has been developed throughout
   the park complete with shelters and cabins available for rent.
 One ski trail leads to the top of the alpine slope for a very
   spectacular panoramic view of Lake Superior.
 Back country cabins are available on a reservation basis for rent
   throughout the year.
 Lodging and restaurants are available in Ontonagon and Silver City
 For additional information contact the Ontonagon Co. Tourist Association,
   PO Box 266, Ontonagon, MI 49953  906-884-4735

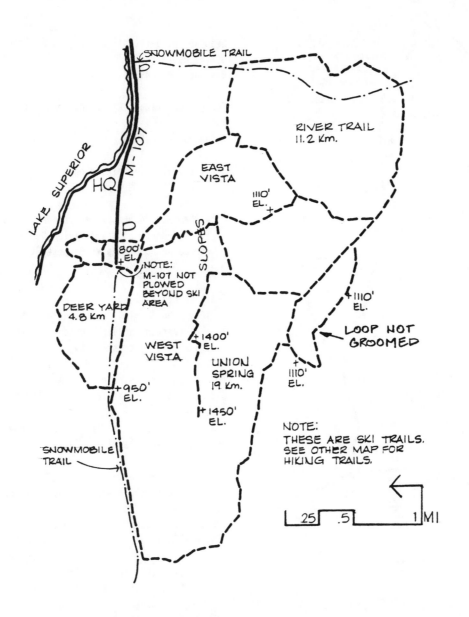

SNOWMOBILE TRAIL

P

RIVER TRAIL
11.2 Km.

LAKE SUPERIOR

HQ

M-107

EAST
VISTA

1110'
EL. +

P

800'
EL. +

SLOPES

NOTE:
M-107 NOT
PLOWED
BEYOND SKI
AREA

1110'
EL. +

DEER YARD
4.8 Km.

LOOP NOT
GROOMED

WEST
VISTA

+ 1400'
EL.

UNION
SPRING
19 Km.

+
1110'
EL.

+ 950'
EL.

+ 1450'
EL.

NOTE:
THESE ARE SKI TRAILS.
SEE OTHER MAP FOR
HIKING TRAILS.

SNOWMOBILE
TRAIL

.25   .5                    1 MI

# PORCUPINE MOUNTAINS
# WILDERNESS STATE PARK

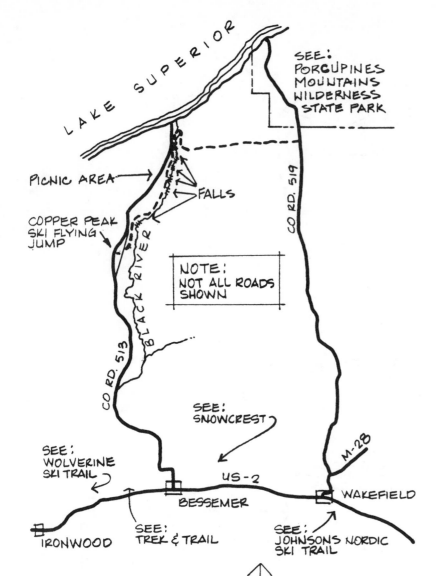

Bessemer Ranger District, Ottawa National Forest
500 N. Moore St.                                          906-667-0261
Bessemer, MI  49911

Forest Supervisor, Ottawa National Forest
East US 2                                                906-932-1330
Ironwood, MI  49938                                      800-562-1201

Trail suitable for hiking only

Location:

 Trailhead-Co Rd 513, 11 miles north of Bessemer near Copper Peak
 Trailhead-North of Wakefield on Co Rd 519, .5 mile south of the
   Porcupine Mountains Wilderness State Park boundary


Trail specifications:
   10 mi; No loop(s); Loop length(s)-NA
Typical terrain: Rolling to very hilly
Skiing ability suggested: NA
Hiking trail difficulty: Difficult
Nordic trail grooming method: NA
Suitable for all-terrain bicycle: Not permitted
Trail use fee: None
Camping: Campgound at Black River Harbor on Lake Superior ⚹
Drinking water is available at the Black River Harbor campground ⚹⚹

General Information:
 Maintained by the Bessemer Ranger District, Ottawa National Forest
 This is a point to point trail
 Most streams do not have bridges at this time
 Several falls are along the trail on the Black River.
 ⚹ Also as with all of the North Country Trail, wilderness camping is
   permitted 200' from the trail
 ⚹⚹ Drinking water is also available at the Potawatomi and Gorge Falls
    Picnic Area
 Copper Peak is the largest ski jump in the United States
 For more information about the North Country Trail contact the
   North Country Trail Association, PO Box 311, White Cloud, MI 49349 or
   USDI, Midwest Region, 1709 Jackson St., Omaha, NE 68102-2571
 A more detailed map is available from the Bessemer Ranger District
   office

# NORTH COUNTRY TRAIL- BLACK RIVER

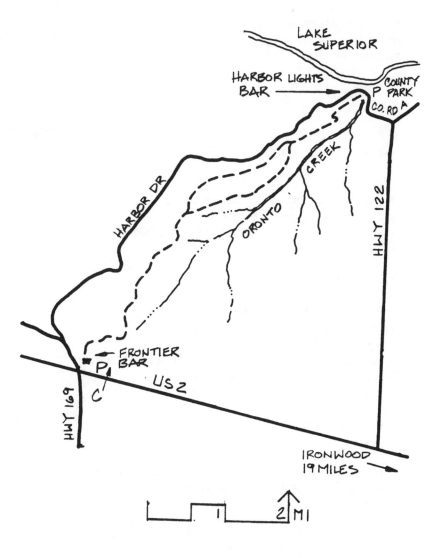

CEDAR TRAIL

Iron County Extension Service
Court House                                     715-561-2695
Hurley, WI  54534

Frontier Bar c/O John Innes
HCR Box 481                                     715-893-2461
Saxon, WI  54559

Trail suitable for skiing only

Location:
  18 miles west of Ironwood on US2 at the intersection of US2 and Hwy 169
  South trailhead - Frontier Bar on US2 at Hwy 169
  North trailhead - Harbor Lights Bar on Co Rd A


Trail specifications:
  12 km; No** loop(s); Loop length(s)-NA
Typical terrain: Flat to hilly
Skiing ability suggested: Intermediate
Hiking trail difficulty: NA
Nordic trail grooming method: Track set 3 times/week
Suitable for all-terrain bicycle: NA
Trail use fee: Donations accepted for trail maintenance only
Camping: Campgrounds at either end of trail *
Drinking water available at both trailheads

General Information:
 Maintained by volunteers and Wisconsin Conservation Corps
 Grooming done by the Harbor Lights and Frontier Bars(volunteer)
 The trail is a 600 foot decent to Lake Superior
 Light meals available at bothe trailhead taverns
 Picturesque ravines and mature forest along trail
 * County park, campground and harbor at north trailhead
   Private campground with showers and trailer hook-ups available at the
    south trailhead
 ** This is a point to point trail
This and other Iron County trails were developed through the close
  cooperation of concerned local citizen groups and the Iron County
  Forestry Department.  Donations by users are an essential part of
  the fund raising program to maintain these trails.

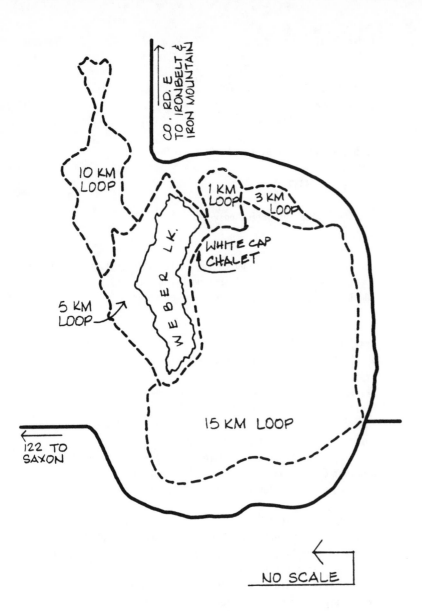

10 KM LOOP

CO. RD. E TO IRONBELT & IRON MOUNTAIN

1 KM LOOP

3 KM LOOP

WHITE CAP CHALET

WEBER LK.

5 KM LOOP

15 KM LOOP

122 TO SAXON

NO SCALE

WHITECAP MOUNTAINS NORDIC

Whitecap Mountains Nordic                    Revised: 2/22/88

Whitecap Mountains Nordic
PO Box D                                      715-561-2227
Montreal, WI  54550

Trail suitable for skiing only

Location:
 West of Ironwood on Hwy 77, turn north past Iron Belt Wisconsin on Co Hwy
  E, then follow signs to the ski area
 Area is about 20 minutes west of Ironwood Wisconsin


Trail specifications:
  30 km; 7 loop(s); Loop length(s)-2, 3, 5, 6, 8, 12, 15
Typical terrain: Rolling to hilly
Skiing ability suggested: Novice to advanced
Hiking trail difficulty: NA
Nordic trail grooming method: Single track set with skating
Suitable for all-terrain bicycle: Yes‡
Trail use fee: $5/day
Camping: None
Drinking water available


General Information:
 Privately operated alpine ski area with extensive nordic ski trails
 Food, lodging, lessons, ski shop, entertainment and alpine skiing
   available
 Trails designed by former US Olympic Team coach Sven Wiik
 3 km lighted trail available all night, 7 nights a week.
 Site of the Run For The Rings Race
 Beautiful trails in undeveloped land around Weber Lake and through the
   Whitecap Mountains
 West end of the 16 km Uller Trail from Montreal, WI (see other listing)
 ‡ All terrain bike race held in August
 Trail ticket allows use of rope tows
 Races are held on Monday nights and are video taped
 An extensive, well designed and well groomed trail system
 Write Steve Ketterhagen, Nordic Director for additional information

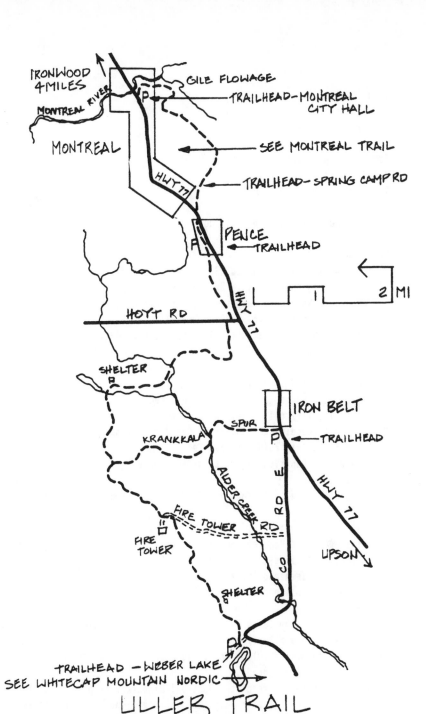

ULLER TRAIL

Uller Trail                                    Revised: 4/14/88

Iron County Extension Service
Court House                                    715-561-2695
Hurley, WI 54534

Penokee Rangers Inc c/o Mike Fauerbach
HRC Box 360                                    715-682-9151
Sason, WI 54559                                evenings

Trail suitable for skiing & hiking

Location:
 East trailhead - Montreal Public Trail at the Montreal City Hall
 Middle trailhead - On Hwy 77 at Pence
 Middle trailhead - On Hwy 77 at west end of Iron Belt (Krankkala Spur)
 West trailhead - Weber Lake next to Whitecap Mountains Nordic on Co Hwy E

Trail specifications:
 16 km%; No loop(s); Loop length(s)-none
Typical terrain: Flat to hilly
Skiing ability suggested: Intermediate to advanced
Hiking trail difficulty: Moderate to difficult
Nordic trail grooming method: Track set as needed
Suitable for all-terrain bicycle: NA
Trail use fee: Donation requested at trailheads
Camping: None
Drinking water available in communities along the trail

General Information:
 Maintained by the Penokee Rangers Inc (a local non-profit cross-country
   ski club)
 A surprisingly well established ski trail with little interferance from
   snowmobiles, even though there are few signs to prohibit snowmobile use
   of the trail.
 Since this trail is funded solely by the donations of its users, it is
   essential that you make a donation to fund the grooming
 The Montreal Trail located at the east end of the Uller is also maintained
   by the Penokee Rangers Inc.
 This trail traverses the top of the scenic Penokee Mountains from
   Montreal to Weber Lake and nearby Whitecap Mountains Nordic
 Rustic cabin and shelter along the trail
 Because of the remote nature of much of the trail, it is recommended
   for more experienced skiers.  Don't ski alone on this trail.

299

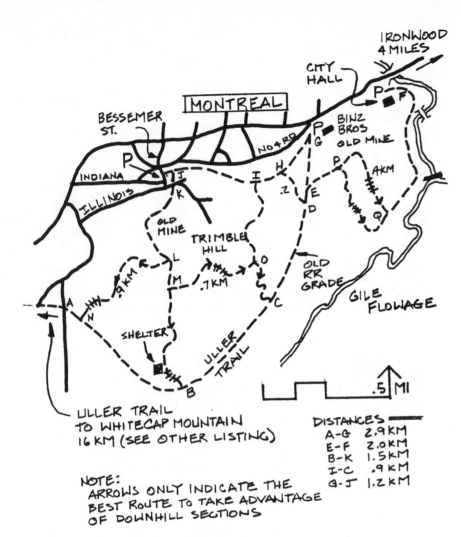

IRONWOOD
4 MILES

CITY
HALL

MONTREAL

P

BINZ
BROS
OLD MINE

BESSEMER
ST.

No 4 RD

P
G

H

P

4KM

INDIANA

J

I

.2

E

Q

ILLINOIS

K

D

OLD
MINE

TRIMBLE
HILL

O

OLD
RR
GRADE

.9KM

R

L

GILE
FLOWAGE

M

.7KM

C

A

N

SHELTER

ULLER
TRAIL

B

.5 MI

ULLER TRAIL
TO WHITECAP MOUNTAIN
16 KM (SEE OTHER LISTING)

DISTANCES
A-G   2.9KM
E-F   2.0KM
B-K   1.5KM
I-C    .9KM
G-J   1.2KM

NOTE:
ARROWS ONLY INDICATE THE
BEST ROUTE TO TAKE ADVANTAGE
OF DOWNHILL SECTIONS

MONTREAL PUBLIC TRAIL

Montreal Public Trail                                    Revised:  4/14/88

Iron County Extension Service
Court House                                              715-561-2695
Hurley, WI  54534


Penokee Rangers Inc.
301 Birch St.                                            715-561-5623
Pence, WI  54553

Trail suitable for skiing & hiking


Location:
 4 miles west of Ironwood via US2 and Wisconsin Hwy 77
 Trailhead - In Montreal take Bessemer south to trailheads(2) at the
   corners of No 4 Rd & Bessemer and Illinois & Bessemer.
 Trailhead - Montreal City Hall on Hwy 77
 Trailhead - West end of Montreal on Spring Camp Rd
Trail specifications:
   15.5km; Many loop(s); Loop length(s)-various
Typical terrain: Rolling to hilly
Skiing ability suggested: Novice to intermediate
Hiking trail difficulty: Easy to moderate
Nordic trail grooming method: Track set 3 to 4 times per week
Suitable for all-terrain bicycle: Yes
Trail use fee: Donation requested at trailhead
Camping: None
Drinking water available Monday - Friday at the Montreal City Hall


General Information:
 Maintained by the Penokee Rangers (a local non-profit ski club)
 A delightful trail system in the hills above Montreal.
 Shelter cabin is along the trail
 Trail is well designed with several long downhill runs and beautiful
   scenery.
 The east end of the 16 km Uller Trail (see other listing) to Weber Lake
   Whitecap Mountain Nordic (see other listing)
 Portion of the trail (Uller Trail) is double track on the old Montreal
   Iron Mine railroad grade.
 Many historic remanents of the Montreal Mine (the deepest iron mine in
   the world, almost 1 mile deep) are visible along the trail including
   tailing piles, many old structures and the railroad grade cut
   through bedrock.
 Also contact Randall Meyer, PO Box 102, Montreal, WI, 54550 715-561-4658

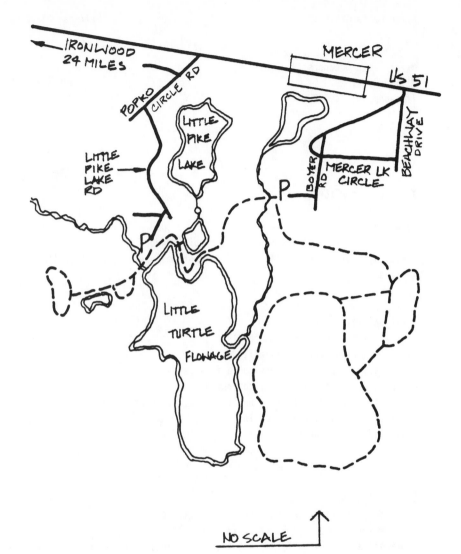

MECCA SKI TRAIL

Mecca Ski Trail                                    Revised: 3/24/88

Iron County Extenision Service
Court House                                        715-561-2695
Hurley, WI  54534

Mecca Ski Club c/o John Olson
DNR Ranger Station                                 715-476-2646
Mercer, WI  54547

Trail suitable for Skiing only

Location:
 23 miles south of Ironwood on US51 at Mercer Wisconsin.
 Traihead - About 1 mile west of Mercer, take Popko Circle Rd. south to
    Little Pike Lake Rd., turn left(south) to trailhead
 Trailhead - South of Mercer DNR Ranger Station. Park in Ranger Station
    south lot
Trail specifications:
 17 km; Several loop(s); Loop length(s)-various
Typical terrain: Rolling glacial esker
Skiing ability suggested: Novice to intermediate
Hiking trail difficulty: NA
Nordic trail grooming method: Track set weekly
Suitable for all-terrain bicycle: NA
Trail use fee: Donations accepted
Camping: None
Drinking water available in Mercer

General Information:
 Maintained by the Mecca Ski Club
 Well designed and interesting ski trail
 Shelter along trail at a scenic wetland vista

This and other Iron County trails were developed through the close
 cooperation of various local citizen groups and the Iron County
 Wisconsin Forestry Department.  Donations by trail users are an
 essential part of the fund raising program to maintain these trails.

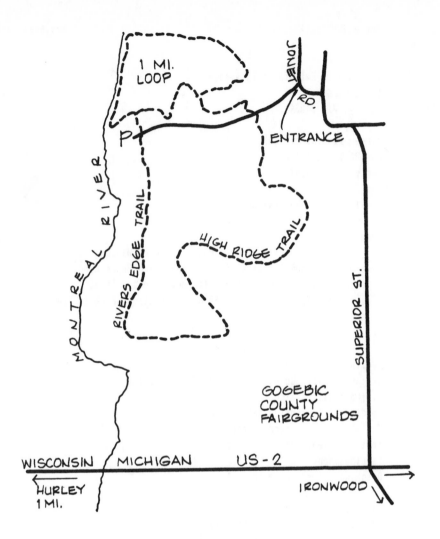

1 MI. LOOP

MONTREAL RIVER

P

ENTRANCE

JUNET RD.

RIVERS EDGE TRAIL

HIGH RIDGE TRAIL

SUPERIOR ST.

GOGEBIC COUNTY FAIRGROUNDS

WISCONSIN / MICHIGAN   US-2

HURLEY 1 MI.

IRONWOOD

NO SCALE

## RIVER FALLS TRAIL

River Falls Trail                                    Revised:  3/03/88

River Falls Outdoors
N10675 Junet Rd.                                     906-932-5638
Ironwood, MI  49938

Trail suitable for Skiing only

Location:
 Along the Montreal River 4 miles north of Ironwood
 Take Superior St. north to Junet Rd., west on Junet to the Lodge (follow
  signs)

Trail specifications:
   3 mi; 2 loop(s); Loop length(s)-1, 2
 Typical terrain: Rolling to hilly
 Skiing ability suggested: Novice to intermediate
 Hiking trail difficulty: Easy to moderate
 Nordic trail grooming method: Double track set several times each week
 Suitable for all-terrain bicycle: Yes
 Trail use fee: $2.00/day *
 Camping: Yes
 Drinking water available at lodge

General Information:
 Privately operated touring center and outfitter
 * Free when staying at River Falls Outdoors
 Cottages and lodge with complete facilities including sauna and fireplace
 Overlooking the Montreal River and falls
 Outfitting services available for mountain bike trips, hiking trips in
  the Porcupine Mountains and canoe trips in the Sylvania Area area
  rivers

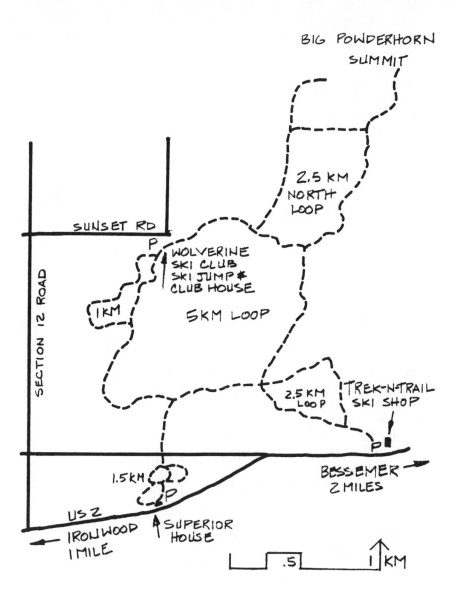

BIG POWDERHORN SUMMIT

2.5 KM NORTH LOOP

SUNSET RD

WOLVERINE SKI CLUB SKI JUMP & CLUB HOUSE

1 KM

5 KM LOOP

SECTION 12 ROAD

2.5 KM LOOP

TREK-N-TRAIL SKI SHOP

1.5 KM

BESSEMER 2 MILES

US 2

IRONWOOD 1 MILE

SUPERIOR HOUSE

.5     1 KM

WOLVERINE SKI TRAIL

Wolverine Ski Trail                                    Revised:  4/14/88

Wolverine Nordic Ski Corporation
PO Box 303                                             906-667-0034
Ramsay, MI  49959                                      906-663-6919

Trek & Trail
East US 2                                              906-663-4791
Bessemer, MI  49911

Trail suitable for skiing only

Location:
 Wolverine Hill trailhead - East of Ironwood on US2 1 mile, then north
  on Section 12 Rd 1.25 miles, then east .5 mile on Sunset Rd to the ski
  jumping complex.
 Trailheads also at Big Powderhorn, Trek & Trail ski shop and The
  Superior House restaurant on US2
Trail specifications:
  14 km; 5 loop(s); Loop length(s)-various
Typical terrain: Rolling to hilly with some flat sections
Skiing ability suggested: Novice to intermediate
Hiking trail difficulty: NA
Nordic trail grooming method: Track set usually Monday and Friday
Suitable for all-terrain bicycle: No
Trail use fee: Donation of $2/day is requested to groom trails
Camping: None


General Information:
 Maintained by the Wolverine Ski Club
 A trail connects to the top Big Powderhorn alpine ski hill
 A trail connects with the Trek and Trail ski shop on US2, 663-4791
 A trail connects with the Superior House restaurant on US2, 932-1804
 The trail offers a variety of scenery, maple hardwood forests, old
  homesteads, scenic overlooks, streams, a beaver dam, "ice falls", and ski
  jumps.
 Very popular trail, but large enough so you don't get the feeling
  of being crowded.
 Well designed ski trail for the novice and intermediate skier
 Near many other trails including Johnson's in Wakefield, Snowcrest and
  several Wisconsin trails just across the state line.
 Write for accomodation and other information: Gogebic Area Convention
  & Visitor Bureau, East US2, Ironwood, MI 906-932-4850

303

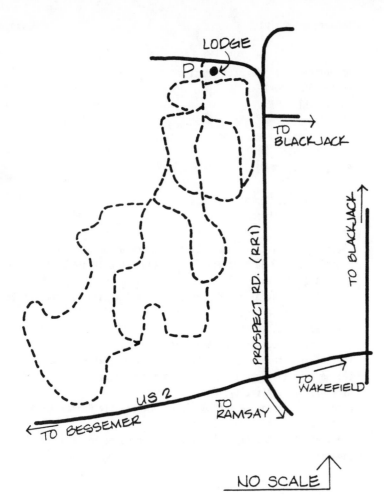

SNOWCREST

Snowcrest                                    Revised:  2/22/88


Snowcrest Corporation
Rte 1, Box 18                                906-663-6916
Bessemer, MI  49911                          906-667-0587


906-667-0405

Trail suitable for skiing only

Location:
 Between Wakefield and Bessemer, turn north at Country Corner Store
  (Prospect Rd), turn left again about 1.25 miles (follow signs). The lodge
  is on the left.


Trail specifications:
   32 km; 6 loop(s); Loop length(s)-1, 2, 3, 6, 7, 10
 Typical terrain: Rolling to hilly in wooded and open field trails
 Skiing ability suggested: Novice to advanced
 Hiking trail difficulty: NA
 Nordic trail grooming method: Track set
 Suitable for all-terrain bicycle: NA
 Trail use fee: $4/day
 Camping: None
 Drinking water available in the lodge


General Information:
 Privately operated lodge with ski trails
 Lodging and warming area available
 Many other cross-country trails are nearby

WAKEFIELD
US 2

BEDELL ST.

OLD US 2

MC VICHIE

SCENIC
OVERLOOK

4.0 KM

3.2 KM

CREEK

P

4.0 KM

2.4 KM

1.6 KM

1.6 KM

4.5 KM

3.2 KM

SCENIC
OVERLOOK

NO SCALE

# JOHNSON'S NORDIC SKI TRAILS

Johnson's Nordic Trails
Box 160, Old US2                                          906-224-4711
Wakefield, MI  49968

Bessemer Ranger District - Ottawa National Forest
500 N. Moore St.                                          906-667-0261
Bessemer, MI  49911

Trail suitable for skiing only

Location:
 On the south side of Old US2, 2 miles east of Wakefield
 Turn right off US2 on Bedell St., then 2 blocks turn left and proceed
    1 mile on old US2 to the trailhead

Trail specifications:
   25 km; 8 loop(s); Loop length(s)-1.6, 1.6, 3.2, 2.4, 4.5, 4.5, 4.0
Typical terrain: Flat to rolling
Skiing ability suggested: Novice to advanced
Hiking trail difficulty: NA
Nordic trail grooming method: Track set with skating lane‡
Suitable for all-terrain bicycle: NA
Trail use fee: $4/day adults, $2/day children
Camping: Campground not available
Drinking water available

General Information:
 Privately operated cross country ski area in the Ottawa National Forest
 Warming area, rentals and ski shop available
 Perfectly groomed and track set trails with outstanding scenery.
 Site of the annual Early Season Classic 10km Race, held in mid-December.
 ‡ 5 of the 8 loops are 10 to 12 feet wide for skating
 The warming cabin built in 1906 was once the home for a Finnish family of
    8 people.
 Skiing is usually available from Thanksgiving into April
 Lodging available locally: Ravenhurst 229-5249
                           Regal Motel 229-5122
                           Granto's Motel 224-8099
                           Medford House 224-5151
Write or call Gogebic Area Convention & Visitor Bureau(Big Snow Country)
   for more information, East US2, Ironwood, MI 49938  906-932-4850

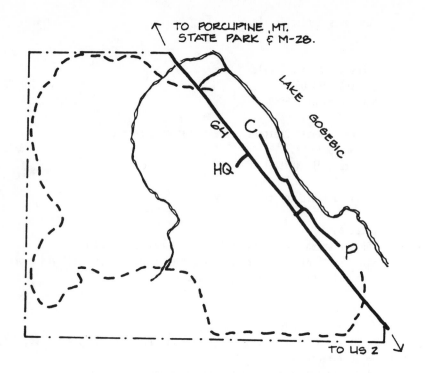

↑ TO PORCUPINE, MT.
STATE PARK & M-28.

LAKE GOGEBIC

64

C

HQ

P

TO US 2 →

NO SCALE ↑

# LAKE GOGEBIC STATE PARK

Lake Gogebic State Park                    Revised: 8/02/87

Lake Gogebic State Park
HC 1, Box 139                              906-842-3341
Marenisco, MI  49947

Trail suitable for skiing & hiking

Location:
 13 miles NE of Marenisco on the west shore of Lake Gogebic on M64
 14 miles south of Bergland on M64

Trail specifications:
   2 mi; 1 loop(s); Loop length(s)-2
Typical terrain: Hilly
Skiing ability suggested: Intermediate
Hiking trail difficulty: Moderate
Nordic trail grooming method: Packed
Suitable for all-terrain bicycle: Yes
Trail use fee: None, but vehicle entry fee required $2/day, $10/year
Camping: Campground in park.  Limited facilities in the winter

General Information:
 Maintained by the DNR Parks Division
 Trail is a self-guided nature trail
 All types of forest cover is present along trail

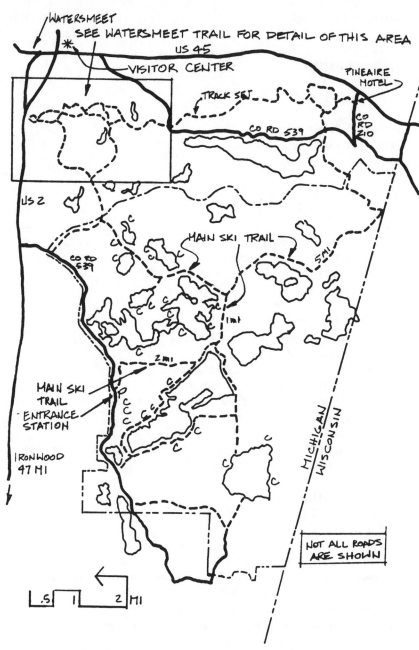

WATERSMEET

SEE WATERSMEET TRAIL FOR DETAIL OF THIS AREA

US 45

VISITOR CENTER

PINEAIRE MOTEL

TRACK SET

CO RD 539

CO RD 210

US 2

MAIN SKI TRAIL

CO RD 539

5 MI

1 MI

2 MI

MAIN SKI TRAIL ENTRANCE STATION

IRONWOOD 47 MI

MICHIGAN
WISCONSIN

NOT ALL ROADS ARE SHOWN

.5  1  2 MI

# SYLVANIA RECREATION AREA

Sylvania Recreation Area                         Revised:  3/24/88

Sylvania Recreation Area
Watersmeet Ranger District, Ottawa National Forest        906-358-4551
Watersmeet, MI  49969

Forest Supervisor, Ottawa National Forest
East US2                                                  906-932-1300
Escanaba, MI  49938                                       800-562-1201

Trail suitable for skiing & hiking

Location:
  4 miles west of Watersmeet to Hwy 535, then south 4 miles(watch for signs)
  Skiing trailhead - Plowed parking lot at entrance station
  Hiking trailhead - West of main campground
  Visitor Center - US2/US45 intersection, just east of the park entrance

Trail specifications:
   30 mi ✻; 1 ✻✻ loop(s); Loop length(s)-7
Typical terrain: Flat to rolling
Skiing ability suggested: Intermediate to advanced
Hiking trail difficulty: Easy to difficult
Nordic trail grooming method: None
Suitable for all-terrain bicycle: Not permitted
Trail use fee: None
Camping: Available in recreation area. Limited facilites in winter
Drinking water available. Limited in winter

General Information:
  Maintained by the Watersmeet Ranger District, Ottawa National Forest
  11.3 mile established ski trail.  Excellent back country skiing
  Trail connects with the Watersmeet Trail at two locations (skiing only)
  Ski shop and lodging in Watersmeet and Land O' Lakes, Wisconsin
  Many lakes in the area provide for excellent canoeing
  ✻ Ski trails are less total length
  Recently this area has been established as a designated Wilderness
  Large area of virgin Northern Hardwoods an Hemlock with some Pine
  Excellent area for winter camping
  Winter wildlife include deer, coyote, fisher, martin, squirrels birds.
   etc.
  ✻✻ Most of the trail system is a point to point type
  Great area for canoeing. Many lakes and portages provided.

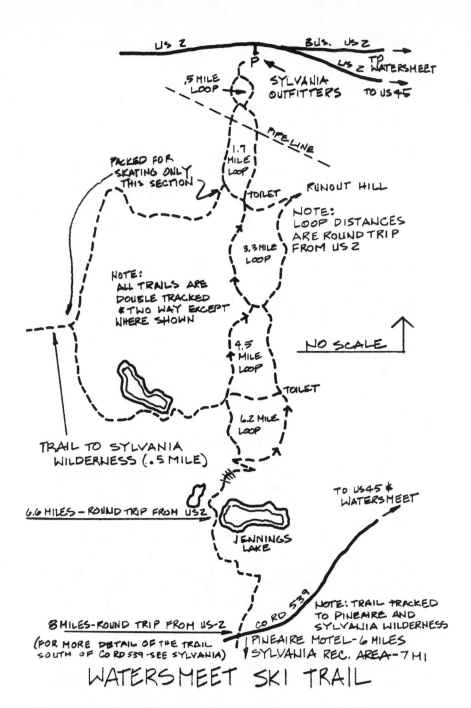

US 2

BUS. US2

P

US 2 TO WATERSMEET

.5 MILE LOOP

SYLVANIA OUTFITTERS

TO US 45

PIPELINE

1.7 MILE LOOP

PACKED FOR SKATING ONLY THIS SECTION

TOILET

RUNOUT HILL

NOTE: LOOP DISTANCES ARE ROUND TRIP FROM US 2

3.3 MILE LOOP

NOTE: ALL TRAILS ARE DOUBLE TRACKED & TWO WAY EXCEPT WHERE SHOWN

4.5 MILE LOOP

NO SCALE

TOILET

6.2 MILE LOOP

TRAIL TO SYLVANIA WILDERNESS (.5 MILE)

6.6 MILES - ROUND TRIP FROM US 2

JENNINGS LAKE

TO US 45 & WATERSMEET

8 MILES - ROUND TRIP FROM US 2

(FOR MORE DETAIL OF THE TRAIL SOUTH OF CO RD 539 - SEE SYLVANIA)

CO RD 539

NOTE: TRAIL TRACKED TO PINEAIRE AND SYLVANIA WILDERNESS

PINEAIRE MOTEL - 6 MILES
SYLVANIA REC. AREA - 7 MI

WATERSMEET SKI TRAIL

Watersmeet Ski Trail                    Revised: 4/02/88

Sylvania Outfitters
West US2                                 906-358-4766
Watersmeet, MI  49969

Watersmeet Ranger District
Ottawa National Forest                   906-358-4551
Watersmeet, MI  49969

Trail suitable for skiing only

Location:
 North trailhead - 1 mile west of Watersmeet at Sylvania Outfitters
 South trailhead - 1 mile north of Land O' Lakes, Wisconsin on US45, then
    turn west on Co Rd 210, parking on north side near Pineaire Motel

Trail specifications:
   21.5 mi; 7* loop(s); Loop length(s)-.5, 1, 1.7, 3.3, 4.5, 6.2, 8.2
Typical terrain: Flat to hilly
Skiing ability suggested: Novice to advanced
Hiking trail difficulty: Easy to difficult
Nordic trail grooming method: Track set daily as needed **
Suitable for all-terrain bicycle: Yes
Trail use fee: Donations accepted
Camping: Campground available nearby and wilderness camping permitted
Drinking water available at Sylvania Outfitters

General Information:
 Maintained by Sylavnia Outfitters and Pineaire Motel in cooperation with
    the Ottawa National Forest
 Ski shop, warming area, rentals, lessons available at Sylavnia Outfitters
 Two trails connect to the Sylvania Wilderness trail system
 Accomodations and food available at the Pineaire Motel   906-544-3800
 Accomodations and food available in Watersmeet, contact the Chamber of
    Commerce or Sylvania Outfitters for information.
 * Additional non-loop track set trails are not listed
 ** Trail from Jennings Lake to the Pineaire Motel is track set weekly
 A well designed and well groomed trail system with long downhill runs.
 Generally the southbound travel is uphill with northbound travel being
    downhill.  However, because of the trail layout, the uphill climbs are
    not difficult and are interrupted with downhill sections.  Danger Hill
    is 160 feet in elveation above the ski shop.

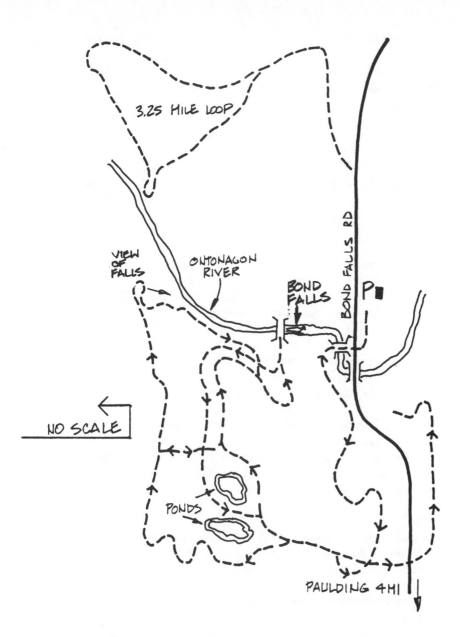

3.25 MILE LOOP

VIEW OF FALLS

ONTONAGON RIVER

BOND FALLS RD

BOND FALLS

P

NO SCALE

PONDS

PAULDING 4 MI

BOND FALLS SKI TRAIL

Bond Falls Ski Trail                                    Revised:  1/11/88


Bond Falls Outpost
PO Box 37                                              906-827-3708
Bruce Crossing, MI  49912


Trail suitable for skiing only

Location:
  Between Watersmeet and Bruce Crossing on US45, then east from Paulding
    4 miles on Bond Falls Rd


Trail specifications:
   10 km; Several loop(s); Loop length(s)-various
Typical terrain: Flat to rolling
Skiing ability suggested: Novice to intermediate
Hiking trail difficulty: NA
Nordic trail grooming method: Track set as needed
Suitable for all-terrain bicycle: NA
Trail use fee: $2.00/day
Camping: Avaialble nearby
Drinking water available at the Outpost

General Information:
 Maintained by local ski shop
 Food, ski shop, warming area and rentals are available at the Bond Falls
   Outpost
 The very scenic Bond Falls is along trail


309

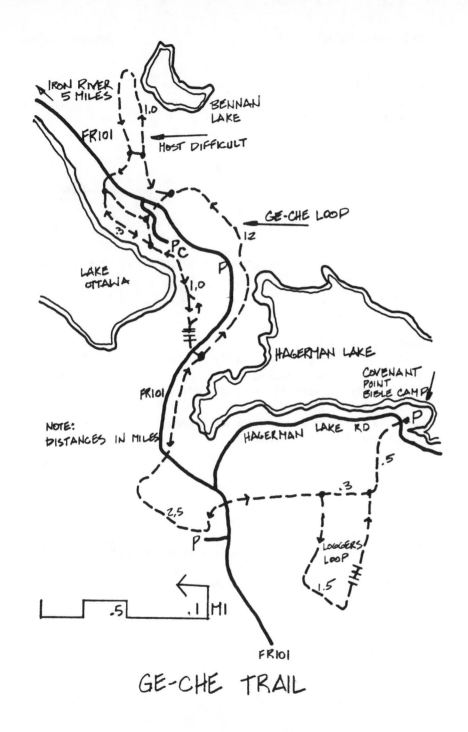

GE-CHE TRAIL

Ge-Che Trail                                    Revised:  4/17/88


Iron River Ranger District, Ottawa National Forest
801 Adams St.                                   906-265-5139
Iron River, MI  49935


Covenant Point Bible Camp
Hagerman Lake                                   906-265-2117
Iron River, MI  49935

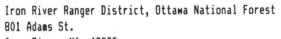

Trail suitable for hiking & skiing


Location:
  West trailhead - 8 miles SW of Iron River on US2/M73, then north on
    Hagerman Lake Rd. to Covenant Point Bible Camp
  East trailhead - 3 miles SW of Iron River on US2 M73 to FR 101, then right
    to Lake Ottawa National Forest campground


Trail specifications:
  9 mi; 4 loop(s); Loop length(s)-1.5, 2.2, 2.5, 2.8
Typical terrain: Flat to rolling
Skiing ability suggested: Novice to intermediate
Hiking trail difficulty: Easy to moderate
Nordic trail grooming method: Track set by the Convenant Point Bible Camp‡
Suitable for all-terrain bicycle: Yes
Trail use fee: Donations accepted to pay for grooming at trailheads
Camping: Summer camping available at the National Forest campground
Drinking water available at the bible camp and NF campground (summer)


General Information:
  Maintained by the Covenant Point Bible Camp in cooperation with the
    Ottawa National Forest, Iron River Ranger District.
  Rentals and group accomodations available from the Covenant Point Bible
    Camp.
  ‡ Groomed occasionally but not the entire system all of the time.  Call
    them if more information is desired.


Other contact:
Forest Supervisior, Ottawa National Forest, Ironwood, 800-562-2101

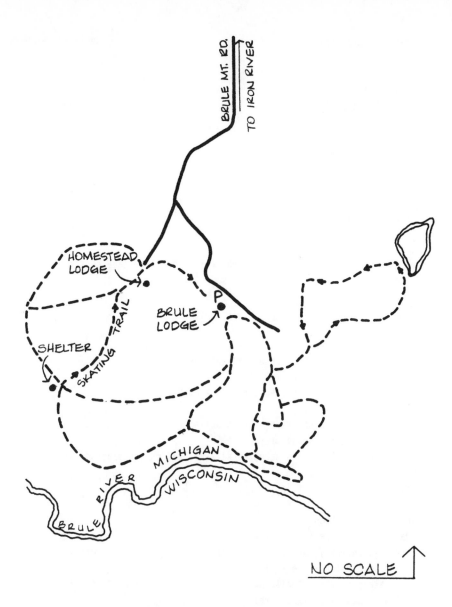

# SKI BRULE/ SKI HOMESTEAD

NO SCALE

Ski Brule/Ski Homestead, Att. Bruce Clark
397 Brule Mountain Rd.                                    906-265-4957
Iron River, MI  49935                                    800-338-7174

906-265-4821

Trail suitable for skiing only

Location:
 6 miles SW of Iron River between M189 and M73.
 Follow signs from both M189 and M73 to the ski area
 Trailhead is at the Ski Brule Lodge

Trail specifications:
  23 km; 5 loop(s); Loop length(s)-various
Typical terrain: Flat to hilly
Skiing ability suggested: Novice to advance
Hiking trail difficulty: Easy to moderate
Nordic trail grooming method: Single track set with skating lane
Suitable for all-terrain bicycle: Yes
Trail use fee: $5/day
Camping: None

General Information:
 Privately operated alpine ski area
 Instruction, lodging, restaurant, ski shop and snack bar are available
 A very nice trail system for all levels of skill
 Shelters along trails
 Site of the Brule River Run ski race held in January
 Horse back riding, ATB riding and white water rafting trips available
   in summer months
 Pig roast every Thursday and Saturday nights at the Homestead

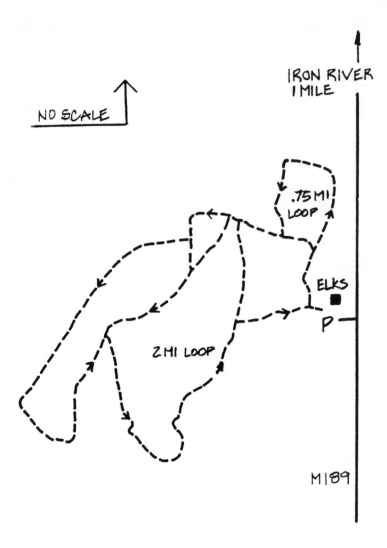

NO SCALE

IRON RIVER
1 MILE

.75 MI
LOOP

ELKS

P

2 MI LOOP

M189

IRON LAND SKI TRAIL

Iron Land Ski Trail                                     Revised:  4/18/88

Iron County Chamber of Commerce
1 East Genesee St.                                      906-265-3822
Iron River, MI  49935

Nordic Skiers United
362 East Siding Rd.                                     906-265-2953
Iron River, MI  49935

Trail suitable for skiing only

Location:
 1 mile south of Iron River on M189 behind the Elks Lodge on the west side
   of the road

Trail specifications:
   5 km; 4 loop(s); Loop length(s)-various
Typical terrain: Rolling to hilly
Skiing ability suggested: Novice to intermediate
Hiking trail difficulty: NA
Nordic trail grooming method: Track set on occasion
Suitable for all-terrain bicycle: NA
Trail use fee: Donations accepted at trailhead or grooming and maintenance
Camping: None
Drinking water not available

General Information:
 Maintained by the Nordic Skiers United
 Trail is entirely on private property.  Respect private property rights
   and do not leave the trail.
 Some steep climbs but all downhill sections have straight out runs so
   that almost any skill level can handle the trail.
 The Elks Club is not open to the public.

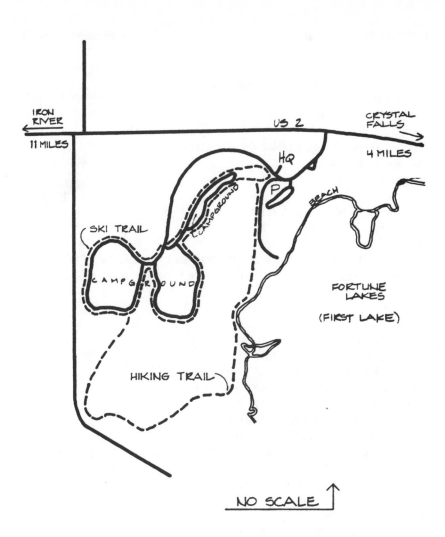

IRON
RIVER
11 MILES

US 2

CRYSTAL
FALLS

4 MILES

HQ

P

BEACH

SKI TRAIL

CAMPGROUND

CAMPGROUND

FORTUNE
LAKES

(FIRST LAKE)

HIKING TRAIL

NO SCALE

# BEWABIC STATE PARK

Bewabic State Park                        Revised:  8/14/87

Bewabic State Park
1933 US2 West                             906-875-3324
Crystal Falls, MI  49920

DNR Parks Division Office

                                          517-373-1270

Trail suitable for hiking & skiing

Location:
 4 miles west of Crystal Falls on US2

Trail specifications:
   2 mi; 1 loop(s); Loop length(s)-2
Typical terrain: Rolling to hilly
Skiing ability suggested: Novice
Hiking trail difficulty: Easy
Nordic trail grooming method: Packed
Suitable for all-terrain bicycle: No
Trail use fee: None, but vehicle entry fee required $2/day, $10/year
Camping: Campground available in park from May 15th to October 15th


General Information:
 Maintained by the DNR Parks Division
 Some ski trail sections use unplowed campground roads
 Hiking trail is a separate system

LOOP 1
3.4 MILES

TO M-69
1 MILE

GLIDDEN LAKE

P,C

LOOP 2
4.5 MILES

LOOP 3
3.9 MILES

.25    .5 MI

# LAKE MARY PLAINS PATHWAY

Lake Mary Plains Pathway                    Revised:  3/05/88

Area Forester, Crystal Falls Forest Area
PO Box 300                                  906-875-6622
Crystal Falls, MI  49920

District Forest Manager, Copper Country State Forest
US41 North, Box 440                         906-353-6651
Baraga, MI  49908

Trail suitable for skiing & hiking

Location:
 4 miles west of Crystal Falls on M69, then south on Lake Mary Plains Rd.
  1 mile to trailhead at Glidden Lake State Forest Campground

Trail specifications:
   10 mi; 3 loop(s); Loop length(s)-3.4, 6.2, 9.5
Typical terrain: Flat to rolling with some steep hills
Skiing ability suggested: Novice & expert trails ‡
Hiking trail difficulty: Moderate
Nordic trail grooming method: Track set
Suitable for all-terrain bicycle: Yes
Trail use fee: Donations accepted at the trailhead for trail grooming
Camping: Campground at trailhead
Drinking water available at trailhead

General Information:
 Maintained by the DNR Forest Management Division
 Deer commonly seen along trail
 Forest fire occoured in an area that the trail passes through
 ‡ Because of the hills, none of the trails area rated intermediate
 One of the better DNR trails that I've skied

Other contacts:
DNR Forest Management Division Office, Lansing, 517-373-1275
DNR Forest Management Region Office, Marquette, 906-228-6561

314

Pine Mountain Lodge                                    Revised: 11/21/87


Pine Mountain Lodge
N3332 Pine Mountain Rd.                                906-774-2747
Iron Mountain, MI  49801

Trail suitable for skiing only

Location:
 2 miles north of Iron Mountain


Trail specifications:
    10 km; 2 loop(s); Loop length(s)-5, 5
Typical terrain: Rolling to hilly
Skiing ability suggested: Novice to intermediate
Hiking trail difficulty: NA
Nordic trail grooming method: Track set
Suitable for all-terrain bicycle: NA
Trail use fee: None
Camping: Available nearby


General Information:
 Privately operated full facility alpine ski area with lodging,restaurant,
    tennis courts, indoor pool, golf course and convention facilities.
 90 meter ski jump in view of the trails.

# No Trail Map

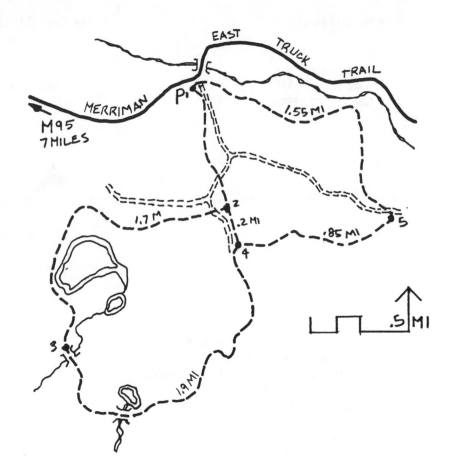

MERRIMAN EAST PATHWAY

Merriman East Pathway                                    Revised: 3/06/88

Area Forester, Norway Forest Area
PO Box 126                                               906-563-9247
Norway, MI  49870

District Forest Manager, Copper Country State Forest
US41 North, Box 440                                      906-353-6651
Baraga, MI  49908

Trail suitable for skiing & hiking

Location:
 North of Iron Mountain about 6 miles to the Merriman Truck Trail, then
   east about 7 miles to trailhead located just before the
   Mitchell Creek bridge


Trail specifications:
    9.5 mi; 2 loop(s); Loop length(s)-5.6, 9.4
Typical terrain: Rolling
Skiing ability suggested: Intermediate
Hiking trail difficulty: Moderate
Nordic trail grooming method: None
Suitable for all-terrain bicycle: Yes
Trail use fee: None
Camping: Developed campground not available nearby
Drinking water not available

General Information:
 Maintained by the DNR Forest Management Division
 Skiers should have some winter survival skills since this trail is
   somewhat isolated and is not groomed in the winter

Other contacts:
DNR Forest Management Division Office, Lansing, 517-373-1275
DNR Forest Management Region Office, Marquette, 906-228-6561

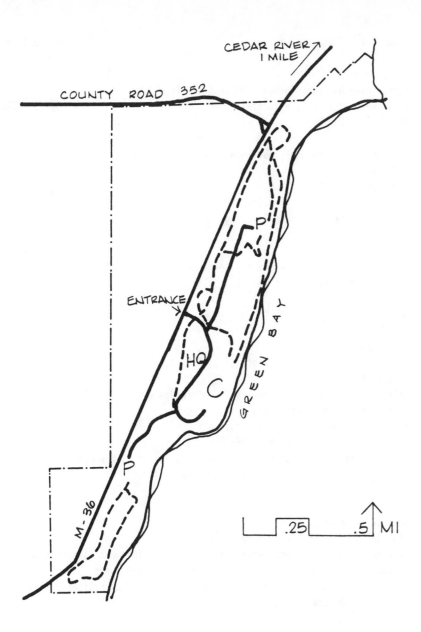

CEDAR RIVER
1 MILE

COUNTY ROAD 352

ENTRANCE

P

HQ

C

GREEN BAY

M-36

P

⌐‾⌐‾ .25 ⌐‾ .5 ⌐ MI

WELLS STATE PARK

Wells State Park                                    Revised: 12/03/87

Wells State Park
M35                                                906-863-9747
Cedar River, MI  49813

DNR Parks Division Office

                                                   517-373-1270

Trail suitable for skiing & hiking

Location:
 South of Escanaba and 1 mile south of Cedar River on Lake Michigan
   on M35

Trail specifications:
   7 mi; 4 loop(s); Loop length(s)-1.1, 1.3, 1.6, 3
Typical terrain: Flat to gently rolling
Skiing ability suggested: Novice to intermediate
Hiking trail difficulty: Easy to moderate
Nordic trail grooming method: Track set once a week or after 4" snowfall
Suitable for all-terrain bicycle: Yes
Trail use fee: None, but vehicle entry fee required $2/day, $10/year
Camping: Campground in park. Open all year
Drinking water available in park

General Information:
 Maintained by the DNR Parks Division
 Hiking and ski trails may not be identical
 6 very rustic cabins are available for rent that house up to 16 people
 Snowmobiling permitted in park except on ski trails
 Many cross country ski trail nearby to the north of Wells State Park
 Ski rentals available in Escanaba and Menominee
 Virgin forest throughout park
 3 miles of Lake Michigan shoreline
 Established in 1925 by the children of John Wells, a local lumberman, who
   donated the land.
 Many of the buildings were constuction by the CCC in the 1930's & 1940's

317

# CEDAR RIVER PATHWAY

US 2
14 MI

US 41
11 MI

CEDAR RIVER

RIVER ROAD

4

7 MILE LOOP

6

5 MILE LOOP

3    5

7

3.5 MILE LOOP

2

8

C    1

2 MILE LOOP

9

P

M-35
6 MI

.25 MI

Cedar River Pathway                                    Revised:  3/06/88

Forest Fire Officer, Escanaba River State Forest
Department of Natural Resources                        906-753-6317
Stephenson, MI  49987

District Forest Manager, Escanaba River State Forest
6833 US41/2 & M35                                      906-786-2351
Gladstone, MI  49837

Trail suitable for skiing & hiking

Location:
  1.5 miles north of Cedar River (town) on M35. Then north on Co Rd 551
    (River Rd) for 6 miles to the trailhead

Trail specifications:
  8 mi; 4 loop(s); Loop length(s)-2, 3.5, 5, 7
Typical terrain: Gently rolling
Skiing ability suggested: Novice to intermediate
Hiking trail difficulty: Easy
Nordic trail grooming method: Track set
Suitable for all-terrain bicycle: Yes
Trail use fee: None, but donations accepted for trail grooming
Camping: Campground along trail (ski-in only) ✻
Drinking water available at campground

General Information:
 Managed by the DNR Forest Management Division
 Trails touch on the Cedar River at several locations and pass through a
   variety of forest cover including pine, birch and aspen.
 ✻ Campgrounds also available at Wells State Park on Lake Michigan near
   the town of Cedar River.

Other contacts:
DNR Forest Management Division Office, Lansing, 517-373-1275
DNR Forest Management Region Office, Marquette, 906-228-6561

318

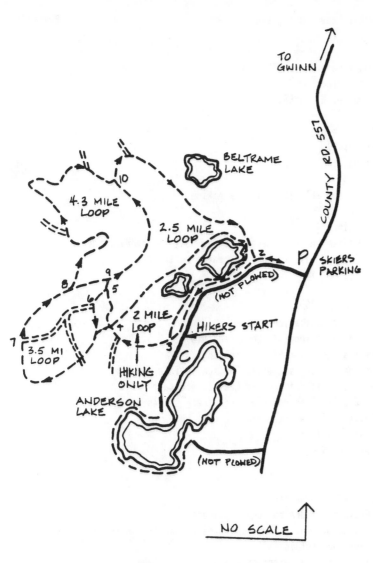

TO
GWINN

COUNTY RD. 557

BELTRAME
LAKE

4.3 MILE
LOOP

2.5 MILE
LOOP

10

9

8

5

6

7

3.5 MI
LOOP

2 MILE
LOOP

(NOT PLOWED)

P SKIERS
PARKING

HIKERS START

HIKING
ONLY

ANDERSON
LAKE

C

(NOT PLOWED)

NO SCALE

ANDERSON LAKE
PATHWAY

Anderson Lake Pathway                    Revised:  3/06/88

Area Forester, Gwinn Forest Area
PO Box 800                                           906-346-9201
Gwinn, MI  49841

District Forest Manager, Escanaba River State Forest
PO Box 445, US2/41 & M35                              906-786-2351
Gladstone, MI  49837

Trail suitable for skiing & hiking

Location:
 7 miles SW of Gwinn on Co Rd 557 at the Anderson Lake Campground

Trail specifications:
    6+ mi‡; 4‡ loop(s); Loop length(s)-2, 2.5, 3.5, 4.3‡
Typical terrain: Rolling to hilly
Skiing ability suggested: Novice to intermediate
Hiking trail difficulty: Easy
Nordic trail grooming method: None
Suitable for all-terrain bicycle: Yes
Trail use fee: None
Camping: Campground at site
Drinking water available seasonally

General Information:
 Maintained by the DNR Forest Management Division
 Designed as an interpretive trail with points of interest marked
 ‡ Ski trails don't include the 2 mile loop around the two lakes and do
    require skiing on the access road to the campground.

Other contacts:
DNR Forest Management Division Office, Lansing, 517-373-1275
DNR Forest Management Region Office, Marquette, 906-228-6561

319

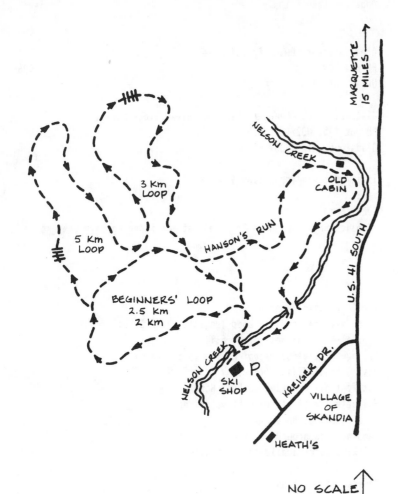

Maple Lane Touring Center                          Revised: 3/23/88

Maple Lane Touring Center
124 Kreiger Dr.                                    906-942-7662
Skandia, MI  49885

Ron Stenfors
PO Box 83                                          906-942-7230
Skandia, MI  49885

Trail suitable for skiing & hiking

Location:
  15 miles south of Marquette via US41 to Skandia, then right on Kreiger Dr.
    for .2 mile to touring center on the right


Trail specifications:
   14 km; 4 loop(s); Loop length(s)-2, 2.5, 3, 5
Typical terrain: Flat to rolling
Skiing ability suggested: Novice to intermediate
Hiking trail difficulty: Easy to moderate
Nordic trail grooming method: Track set as needed
Suitable for all-terrain bicycle: NA
Trail use fee: Yes
Camping: None


General Information:
 Privately operated nordic ski area
 Ski shop, rentals, warming area and snack bar is available
 Snowshoe rentals
 Ski repair, maintenance and waxing available
 A small but well designed and groomed trail system that is a lot of fun
 Mostly forested trails
 New 3km skating loop for 1988/89 season
 Within 10 minutes of fine food and lodging
 Ski school on weekends
 Ski videos available
 Ski season is from December through March

MAPLE LANE
TOURING CENTER

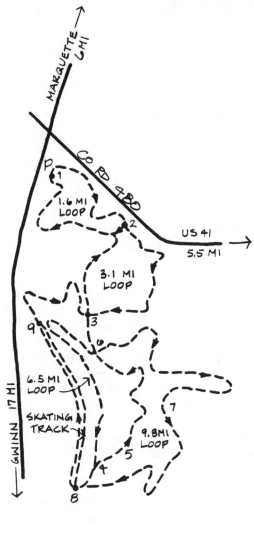

BLUEBERRY RIDGE
PATHWAY

NO SCALE

Area Forester, Ishpeming Forest Area
Box 632, Teal Lake Road                     906-485-1031
Ishpeming, MI  49849

DNR Marquette Repair Facility
110 Ford Rd.                                906-249-1497
Marquette, MI  49849

Trail suitable for skiing & hiking

Location:
 6 miles south of Marquette on Co Rd 553 at Co Rd 480

Trail specifications:
    12 mi; 5 loop(s); Loop length(s)-1.6, 3.1, 3.1, 2.9, 1.25
Typical terrain: Flat to hilly
Skiing ability suggested: Novice to advanced
Hiking trail difficulty: Easy to moderate
Nordic trail grooming method: Track set with skating lanes ⚹
Suitable for all-terrain bicycle: Yes
Trail use fee: Donations accepted at the trailhead
Camping: Campgrounds available nearby in Marquette area
Drinking water not available

General Information:
 Maintained by the DNR Forest Management Division
 A completely new trail in 1987. Relocated from the west side of Co Rd 553.
 Food available near trail
 Very popular Marquette area ski trail
 ⚹ A skating loop (1.25 km) is not included in distance shown. Loops 4 and
   5 on occasion may be groomed for skating only.
 Use by NMU as a nordic training site.
 Loops 1 & 2 are generally flat to rolling with loops 4 & 5 being hilly.
 This trail is groomed and track set frequently.

Other contacts:
DNR Forest Management Division Office, Lansing, 517-373-1275
DNR Forest Management District Office, Gladstone, 906-786-2351
DNR Forest Management Region Office, Marquette, 906-228-6561

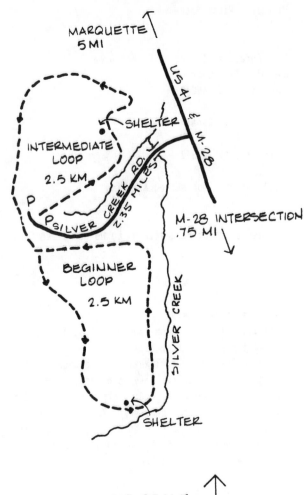

MARQUETTE
5 MI

SHELTER

US 41 & M-28

INTERMEDIATE
LOOP
2.5 KM

SILVER CREEK RD.

2.35 MILES

P
P
SILVER CREEK RD.

M-28 INTERSECTION
.75 MI

BEGINNER
LOOP
2.5 KM

SILVER CREEK

SHELTER

NO SCALE

SILVER CREEK TRAIL-
MARQUETTE

Silver Creek Trail - Marquette          Revised:  2/22/88


Marquette County Natural Resources Commission
Court House                                              906-228-1535
Marquette, MI  49855


Marquette Chamber of Commerce
510 S. Front Street                                      906-226-6591
Marquette, MI  49855                                     800-544-4321


Trail suitable for skiing & hiking

Location:
 South of Marquette, 2.3 miles west off US41 at the end of Silver Creek Rd;
   .5 mile north of the M28/US41 intersection


Trail specifications:
   5 km; 2 loop(s); Loop length(s)-2.5, 2.5
Typical terrain: Rolling
Skiing ability suggested: Novice & intermediate
Hiking trail difficulty: Easy to moderate
Nordic trail grooming method: None
Suitable for all-terrain bicycle: Yes
Trail use fee: None
Camping: Contact Chamber of Commerce
Drinking water not available at trail


General Information:
 Maintained by the Marquette County Natural Resources Commission
 Warming shelter available on both loops
 Trail follows along branches of the Silver Creek

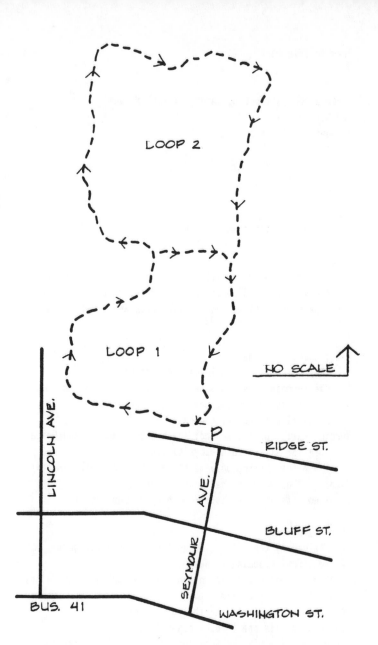

LOOP 2

LOOP 1

NO SCALE

P

RIDGE ST.

BLUFF ST.

WASHINGTON ST.

LINCOLN AVE.

SEYMOUR AVE.

BUS. 41

FIT STRIP SKI TRAIL

Fit Strip Ski Trail                                          Revised:  3/24/88

Parks and Recreation Department, City of Marquette
300 Baraga Ave                                              906-228-8200
Marquette, MI  49855                                        ext 213

Trail suitable for skiing & hiking

Location:
  Take Washington St. .5 mile west of the downtown area to Seymour St, then
     proceed north to Ridge St., then west on Ridge St. to the parking lot.
     The trailhead is directly north of the parking lot.

Trail specifications:
   1.8 km; 2 loop(s); Loop length(s)-1, 1.7
Typical terrain: Flat to somewhat hilly
Skiing ability suggested: Novice to intermediate
Hiking trail difficulty: Easy
Nordic trail grooming method: Track set Monday and Friday‡
Suitable for all-terrain bicycle: Not permitted
Trail use fee: Skiing only $5/child, $8/adult, $15/ family‡‡
Camping: Available in the Marquette area

General Information:
  Maintained by the Parks Department, City of Marquette
  1.7 km lighted loop to 11pm
  Trails for traditional and skating styles
  ‡ Additional grooming as needed
  ‡‡ Per season, double for non-city residents (includes Presque Isle Trail)
  Moderately forested area

323

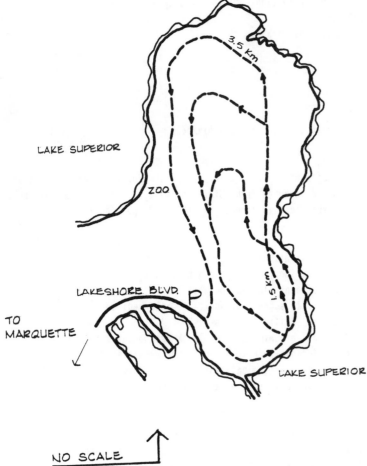

LAKE SUPERIOR

ZOO

3.5 Km

1.5 km

LAKESHORE BLVD.

P

TO MARQUETTE

LAKE SUPERIOR

NO SCALE

# PRESQUE ISLE PARK

Presque Isle Park                    Revised:  3/24/88

Parks & Recreation Department, City of Marquette
300 Baraga Ave
Marquette, MI  49855

906-228-8200
ext 213

800-544-4321

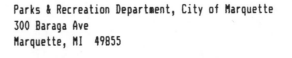

Trail suitable for skiing & hiking

Location:
 2 miles north of Marquette along lakeshore at Presque Isle Park
 Take Lakeshore Blvd north to Peter White Dr(2 miles)
 Trailhead-Adjacent to Peter White Drive and plowed parking lots


Trail specifications:
  5 km; 3 loop(s); Loop length(s)-various
Typical terrain: Flat to somewhat hilly
Skiing ability suggested: Novice to intermediate
Hiking trail difficulty: Moderate
Nordic trail grooming method: Track set on Monday and Friday⚹
Suitable for all-terrain bicycle: Yes
Trail use fee: Skiing only $5/child, $8/adult, $15/family⚹⚹
Camping: Available in the Marquette area
Drinking water is available from May through October


General Information:
 Maintained by the City of Marquette, Parks Department
 ⚹ Additional grooming as needed
 Both wide (vehicle drive in summer) and narrow (foot paths) trails are
   available to the skier
 A small city zoo is along the return trail
 Interior trails are through dense forests
 Beautiful view of Lake Superior and winter ice formations
 Also a snow shoe trail avaialble which is not listed
 Traditional and skating style trails
 ⚹⚹ Per season, double for non-ciy residents(Fit Strip Ski Trail included)
 Because of the warming effect of Lake Superior, this trail looses its
   snow cover earlier than the inland trails in the Marquette and
   Ishpeming area.

324

Marquette County Road Commission
N. 2nd St.                                         906-486-8462
Ishpeming, MI  49849

Trail suitable for hiking only

Location:
 North from Marquette along Lake Superior on Co Rd 550 about 5 miles

## No Trail Map

Trail specifications:
   .5 mi; 1 loop(s); Loop length(s)-,5
Typical terrain: Hilly, with many stairs
Skiing ability suggested: NA
Hiking trail difficulty: Moderate
Nordic trail grooming method: NA
Suitable for all-terrain bicycle: No
Trail use fee: None
Camping: None
Water not available

General Information:
 Maintained by the Marquette County Road Commission
 Near Harlow Lake Pathway
 Very scenic changing panoramic views of the Lake Superior shoreline

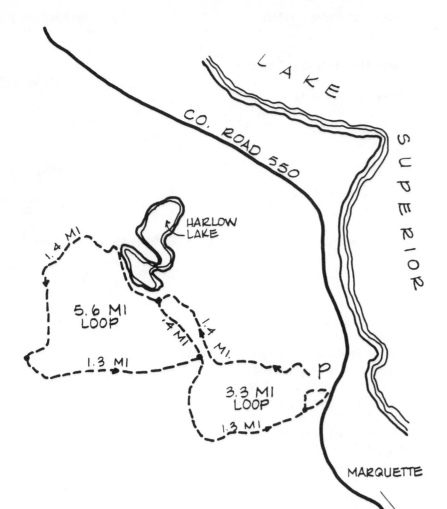

Harlow Lake Pathway                          Revised:  3/06/88

Area Forester, Ishpeming Forest Area
Box 632, Teal Lake Rd.                                  906-485-1031
Ishpeming, MI  49849

DNR Marquette Repair Facility
110 Ford Rd.                                            906-249-1497
Marquette, MI  49849

Trail suitable for skiing & hiking

Location:
 5 miles north of Marquette on Co Rd 550
 Trail is on the west side of the road

Trail specifications:
   6 mi; 2 loop(s); Loop length(s)-3.3, 5.6
 Typical terrain: Rolling to hilly
 Skiing ability suggested: Intermediate
 Hiking trail difficulty: Moderate
 Nordic trail grooming method: Track set weekly or as needed ‡
 Suitable for all-terrain bicycle: Yes
 Trail use fee: Donations accepted at trailhead
 Camping: None
 Drinking water not available along trail

General Information:
 Maintained by the DNR Forest Management Divison
 ‡ Trail is not wide enough to permit skating

HARLOW LAKE PATHWAY

Other contacts:
 DNR Forest Management Division Office, Lansing, 517-373-1275
 DNR Forest Management District Office, Gladstone, 906-786-2351
 DNR Forest Management Region Office, Marquette, 906-228-6561

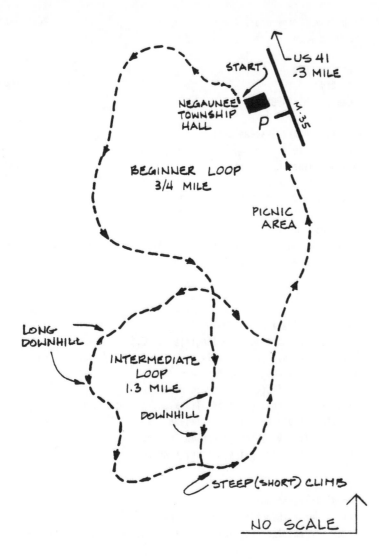

LONG DOWNHILL

INTERMEDIATE LOOP 1.3 MILE

DOWNHILL

STEEP (SHORT) CLIMB

NO SCALE

START

US 41 .3 MILE

NEGAUNEE TOWNSHIP HALL

P

M35

BEGINNER LOOP 3/4 MILE

PICNIC AREA

# NEGAUNEE TOWNSHIP TOURING TRAIL

Negaunee Township Touring Trail                    Revised: 10/12/87

Negaunee Township Hall
RR, M35                                            906-475-4216
Negaunee, MI  49866

Superior Shores Systems Inc
Rte 3, Box 1024                                    906-486-6706
National Mine, MI  49865

Trail suitable for skiing only

Location:
  Trailhead - NW corner of the Negaunee Township Offices located .4 mile
    south of US41 on M35 (intersection is just east of airport)
    (Trailhead is not well signed - look behind the main county office
    building)

Trail specifications:
  3 km; 2 loop(s); Loop length(s)-1.2, 2
Typical terrain: Mostly flat with some rolling sections
Skiing ability suggested: Novice to intermediate
Hiking trail difficulty: Easy
Nordic trail grooming method: Track set on occasion
Suitable for all-terrain bicycle: Yes
Trail use fee: None, but donations are accepted
Camping:


General Information:
  Maintained by the Superior Shores Skiers, Inc., Rte 3, Box 1024,
    National Mine, MI 49865
  Small but well maintained trail with several long downhill sections
  Directions on the map are suggested skiing directions by the author to
    take advange of the downhill sections and to avoid a very difficult and
    dangerous downhill section. They are not the directions that are posted
    at the trail.

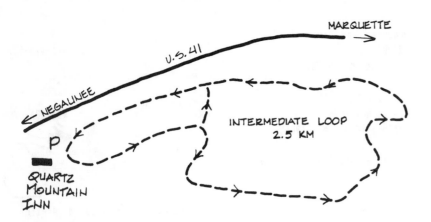

MARQUETTE

U.S. 41

NEGAUNEE

P

QUARTZ
MOUNTAIN
INN

INTERMEDIATE LOOP
2.5 KM

NO SCALE

CARP RIVER FORGE TRAIL

Iron Town USA
City Bldg                                                    906-475-9814
Negaunee, MI  49866

Superior Shores Systems Inc.
Rte 3, Box 1024                                              906-486-6706
National Mine, MI  49865

Trail suitable for skiing & hiking

Location:
  Between Negaunee and Marquette on US41 at the Quartz Mountain Inn, west of
    the Marquette Co. Airport on US41

Trail specifications:
   2.8 km; 2 loop(s); Loop length(s)-1, 2.5
Typical terrain: Flat to hilly
Skiing ability suggested: Novice
Hiking trail difficulty: Easy to moderate
Nordic trail grooming method: Track set occasionally
Suitable for all-terrain bicycle: No
Trail use fee: Donations accepted to groom the trail
Camping: Available in the Marquette area

General Information:
 Maintained by Superior Shores Systems Inc.
 Snack bar and lodging available at the Quartz Mountain Inn, 906-475-7165

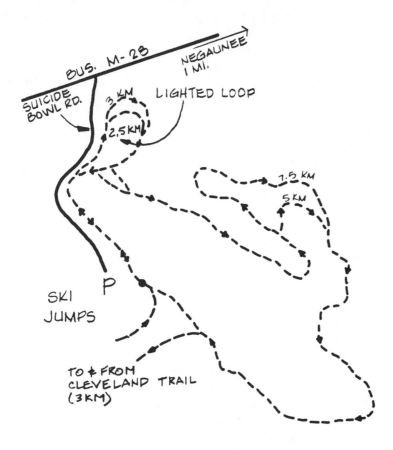

SKI
JUMPS

TO & FROM
CLEVELAND TRAIL
(3KM)

NO SCALE

SUICIDE BOWL

Suicide Bowl                                    Revised:  3/20/88

Ishpeming Ski Club c/o Mike Tonkin
612 N. 3rd St.                                      906-486-8786
Ishpeming, MI  49849                               800-544-4321

Ishpeming Ski Club c/o Knut Strom
191 Bluff St.                                      906-485-1747
Ishpeming, MI  49849

Trail suitable for skiing only

Location:
 Between Ishpeming and Nagaunee on Business M28

Trail specifications:
   12 km‡; 4 loop(s); Loop length(s)-2.5, 3, 5, 7.5
Typical terrain: Rolling to extremely hilly
Skiing ability suggested: Intemediate to expert
Hiking trail difficulty: Moderate
Nordic trail grooming method: Track set with skating lane ‡‡
Suitable for all-terrain bicycle: Not permitted
Trail use fee: $2.00/day, available at ski shops and the C. of C. ‡‡‡
Camping: Available in the area
Drinking water not available

General Information:
 Maintained by the Ishpeming Ski Club, founded in 1887
 Site of many events for both skiing and jumping
 Connected to Cleveland Trail with two separate one way 3 km trails
 One of the finest ski trail systems in the state
 Originally designed by Norman Juhola of Ishpeming
 ‡ Connected to the Cleveland Ski Trail to make a 23 km loop
 ‡‡ Groomed weekly as needed
 ‡‡‡ Season memberships available at $15.00
 Site of 5 ski jumps (10, 20, 30, 50 & 70 meters)
 2.5 km lighted trail

329

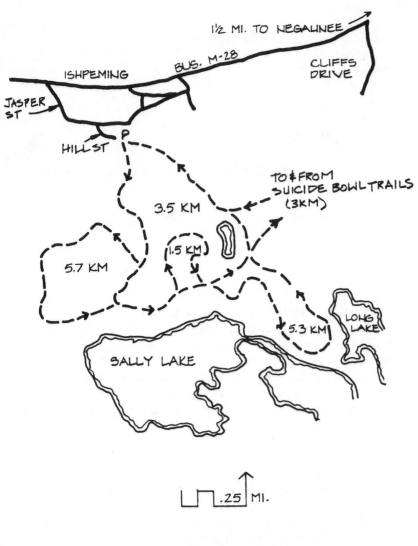

1½ MI. TO NEGAUNEE

ISHPEMING    BUS. M-28    CLIFFS DRIVE

JASPER ST

HILL ST

P

3.5 KM

TO & FROM SUICIDE BOWL TRAILS (3KM)

5.7 KM

1.5 KM

5.3 KM

LONG LAKE

SALLY LAKE

.25 MI.

# CLEVELAND
# CROSS COUNTRY SKI TRAIL

Cleveland Cross Country Ski Trail                    Revised: 3/20/88

Ishpeming Ski Club c/o Mike Tonkin
612 N. 3rd St.                                       906-486-8786
Ishpeming, MI  49849                                906-486-9957

Ishpeming Ski Club c/o Knut Strom
191 Bluff St.                                       906-485-1747
Ishpeming, MI  49849

Trail suitable for skiing and hiking

Location:
 On the south side of Ishpeming via Jasper St south off Bus M28, then right
   on Hill St. to the parking lot.  Trailhead is not signed

Trail specifications:
   10 km *; 5 loop(s); Loop length(s)-3.5 to 8
Typical terrain: Rolling to very hilly
Skiing ability suggested: Intermediate to expert
Hiking trail difficulty: Moderate
Nordic trail grooming method: Double track set **   SKATING NOT PERMITTED
Suitable for all-terrain bicycle: Not permitted
Trail use fee: $2.00/day, available at ski shops and Chamber of Commerce***
Camping: None
Drinking water not available

General Information:
 Maintained by the Ishpeming Ski Club on Cleveland Cliffs Co. property
 Absolutely one of the finest ski trail systems in the state
 Connected to the Suicide Bowl system with two separate 3 km trails
 Originally developed by Norman Juhola of Ishpeming
 * Connected to the Suicide Bowl Trails to make a 23 km loop
 ** Groomed weekly as needed
 *** Season memberships available at $15.00

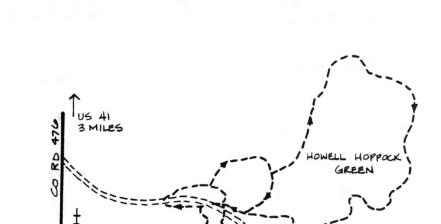

Superior Shores Systems Inc
Rte 3, Box 1024                           906-486-6706
National Mine, MI  49865                  800-544-4321

Ishpeming Chamber of Commerce
661 Palms Ave                             906-486-4841
Ishpeming, MI  49849

Trail suitable for skiing only

Location:
 At National Mine on Co. Rd. 476 3 miles south of US41
 From westbound US41 in Ishpeming, proceed 1 mile west to yellow blinker,
  turn south on Lakeshore Dr.,, then proceed .4 mile to Washington St,
  turn right(west) and proceed 2.7 miles to National Mine (unmarked)
 Trailhead is 200 feet west on road to Tilden Mine (just south of A-frame)
Trail specifications:
  20 km; 6 loop(s); Loop length(s)-.5 to 10
Typical terrain: Rolling to very hilly
Skiing ability suggested: Novice to advanced
Hiking trail difficulty: NA
Nordic trail grooming method: Groomed for skating‡
Suitable for all-terrain bicycle: NA
Trail use fee: Donations accepted to maintain the trail
Camping: None in the area
Water available at the A-Frame office

General Information:
 Built and maintained by the Delta Trail Systems & Superior Shore Skiers
 The A-frame is the warming house with showers and toilets
 Biathlon range planned for 88-89
 Start of the Red Earth Loppet
 Very significant elevation changes on trail system
 Few signs to trailhead or on trail.  Ask for directions at A-frame.
 Some sections of the trail may be restricted for competition use only
   during training sessions
 ‡ Trails would be track set on request

331

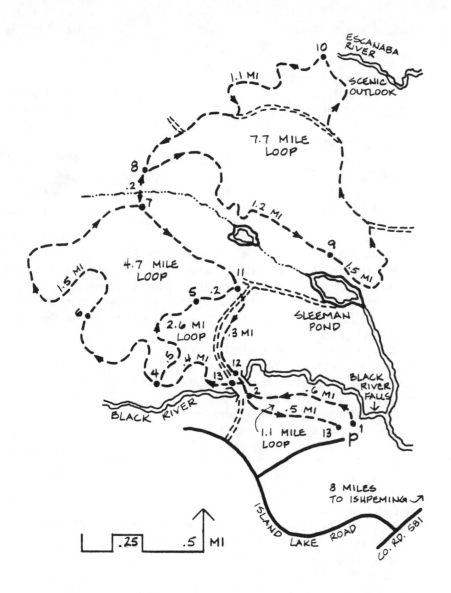

BLACK RIVER PATHWAY

Black River Pathway                                    Revised: 3/05/88

Area Forester, Ishpeming Forest Area
Box 632, Teal Lake Rd.                                 906-485-4193
Ishpeming, MI  49849

DNR Marquette Repair Facility
110 Ford Rd.                                           906-249-1497
Marquette, MI  49849

Trail suitable for skiing & hiking

Location:
  SW of Ishpeming on Co Rd 581, then right on Island Lake Rd. 1/2 mile, then
    right again to trailhead

Trail specifications:
  9.2 mi; 4 loop(s); Loop length(s)-1.1, 2.6, 4.7, 7.7
Typical terrain: Flat to hilly
Skiing ability suggested: Novice to advanced
Hiking trail difficulty: Easy to moderate
Nordic trail grooming method: None
Suitable for all-terrain bicycle: Yes
Trail use fee: None
Camping: Campgrounds are available at trailhead and in Marquette area
Drinking water not available

General Information:
  Maintained by the DNR Forest Management Division
  Black River Falls and a scenic overlook of the Escanaba River are along
    the trail
  Temporarily rerouted due to forest fire and logging operations

Other contacts:
DNR Forest Management Division Office, Lansing, 517-373-1275
DNR Forest Management District Office, Gladstone, 906-786-2351
DNR Forest Management Region Office, Marquette, 906-228-6561

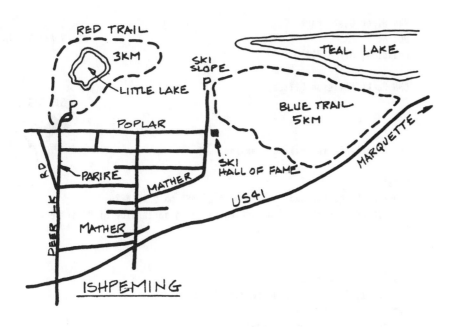

AL QUAAL RECREATION AREA

Al Quaal Recreation Area
City of Ishpeming, 100 Division St.              906-486-6181
Ishpeming, MI  49849                            906-486-8301

Trail suitable for skiing only

Location:
 Red Trail-From M41(stop light) in Ishpeming, turn north on Deer Lake Rd.,
  continue straight onto Prairie to park entrance. Trailhead is just
  inside entrance on left side before park sign.
 Blue Trail-Same as above, but right at park entrance on Poplar St. to the
  end of the street, then left (north) to downhill ski area rope tow.
Trail specifications:
  8 km; 2 loop(s); Loop length(s)-3, 5
Typical terrain: Flat to somewhat hilly
Skiing ability suggested: Novice to intermediate
Hiking trail difficulty: NA
Nordic trail grooming method: Track set twice weekly *
Suitable for all-terrain bicycle: Not permitted
Trail use fee: $2/day or season pass is available
Camping: None


General Information:
 Maintained by the City of Ishpeming
 Warming hut, restrooms and a small alpine slope are part of the area
 Site of the annual Ski Hall of Fame Race held in February
 Sledding area and toboggan run that is 1500' long
 Near the Ski Hall of Fame
 * Trail not suitable for skating
 When I skied the trails, it appeared to me that the posted distances were
  reversed.  I believe the Red Trail is about 3km and the Blue Trail is
  about 5 km.  That is the way I have shown them on the map.
 The trails were both very well designed and scenic along the shores of
  Little Lake and Teal Lake.

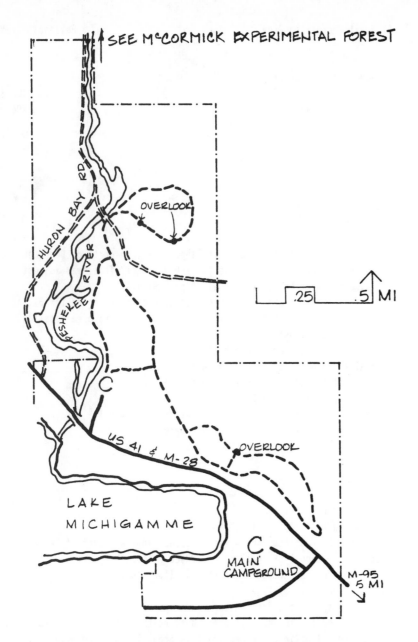

SEE McCORMICK EXPERIMENTAL FOREST

OVERLOOK

HURON BAY RD.

PESHEKEE RIVER

.25    .5 MI

C

US 41 & M-28

OVERLOOK

LAKE
MICHIGAMME

C

MAIN
CAMPGROUND

M-95
5 MI

# VAN RIPER STATE PARK

Van Riper State Park                                    Revised:  4/01/88

Van Riper State Park
Box 66                                                  906-339-4461
Champion, MI  49814

DNR Parks Division Office

                                                        517-373-1270

Trail suitable for hiking & skiing

Location:
  West of Marquette and 5 miles west of M95 on US41/M28
  Trailhead is west of main park entrance on north side of US41/M28 at the
    rustic campground

Trail specifications:
   4.5 mi; 4 loop(s); Loop length(s)-various
Typical terrain: Hilly
Skiing ability suggested: Advanced
Hiking trail difficulty: Moderate to difficult
Nordic trail grooming method: None
Suitable for all-terrain bicycle: No
Trail use fee: None, but vehicle entry fee required $2/day, $10/year
Camping: Campground available at trailhead and on Lake Michigamme
Water is available at both campgrounds

General Information:
  Maintained by the DNR Parks Divison
  Overlooks along the trail

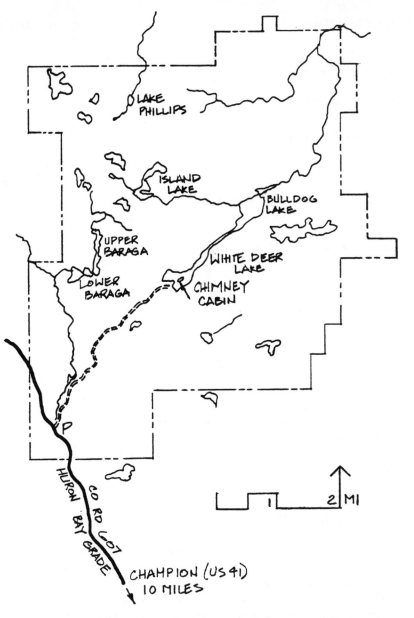

## McCORMICK EXPERIMENTAL FOREST

(map labels) LAKE PHILLIPS · ISLAND LAKE · BULLDOG LAKE · UPPER BARAGA · WHITE DEER LAKE · LOWER BARAGA · CHIMNEY CABIN · P · HURON BAY GRADE · CO RD 607 · CHAMPION (US 41) 10 MILES · 1 2 MI

McCormick Experimental Forest                    Revised: 3/23/88

Kenton Ranger District, Ottawa National Forest
M28                                               906-852-3500
Kenton, MI  49943

Forest Supervisor, Ottawa National Forest
East US2                                          906-932-1330
Ironwood, MI  49938                               800-562-1201

Trail suitable for skiing & hiking

Location:
 12 miles north of US41 from Champion on Co Rd 607 (Huron Bay Grade)

Trail specifications:
   8 mi; 2 loop(s); Loop length(s)-3.5, 7
Typical terrain: Rolling to very hilly with rock outcrops
Skiing ability suggested: Advanced
Hiking trail difficulty: Moderate to difficult
Nordic trail grooming method: None
Suitable for all-terrain bicycle: Not permitted
Trail use fee: None
Camping: No developed campground, but wilderness camping is permitted
No drinking water available

General Information:
 Maintained by the Kenton Ranger District, Ottawa National Forest
 Formerly owned by Cyrus McCormick, son of the inventor of the reaper
   harvesting machine
 Very rugged, isolated and scenic area
 Nearest developed campground is at Van Riper State Park on US41
 Recommended only for skiers with winter survival skills since the area is
   very isolated
 Total forest acreage is over 17,600 acres
 Write for more information

335

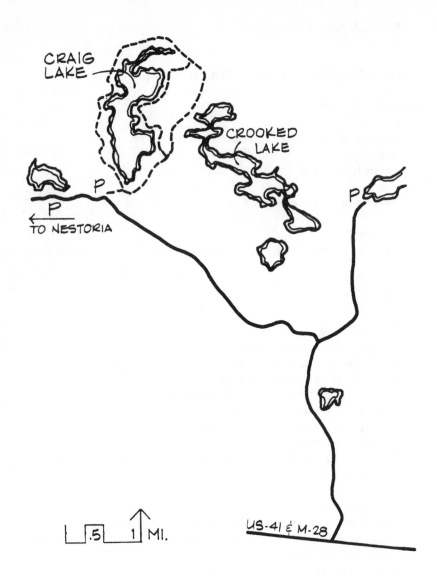

CRAIG LAKE

CROOKED LAKE

P

P
← TO NESTORIA

US-41 & M-28

.5   1 MI.

# CRAIG LAKE STATE PARK

Craig Lake State Park                                    Revised: 11/21/87

Van Riper State Park
PO Box 66                                                906-339-4461
Champion, MI  49814

DNR Parks Division Office

                                                         517-373-1270

Trail suitable for hiking & skiing

Location:
 West of Marquette and 2 miles west of Michigamme on US41 at Craig Lake Rd.

Trail specifications:
   17+ mi; Many loop(s); Loop length(s)-various
Typical terrain: Rolling to hilly with rock outcrops
Skiing ability suggested: Advanced
Hiking trail difficulty: Difficult
Nordic trail grooming method: None - Wilderness area
Suitable for all-terrain bicycle: Not permitted
Trail use fee: None
Camping: No developed campgrounds within the park (see below)
Drinking water not available in park

General Information:
 Maintained by the DNR Parks Division
 This is a wilderness state park with no facilities
 Two-track roads and foot paths, developed by the former private owners,
   are throughout the property may be use but no trail system has been
   developed since the DNR became the owner.
 Suitable for skiing by those with winter survival skills only
 Camping: Wildnerness camping permitted 100 off existing trails
          Developed campgrounds available at Van Riper State Park and
            Michigamme Shores (privately operated campground located at the
            west end of Lake Michigamme on US41)
 Craig Lake State Park is managed by Van Riper State Park

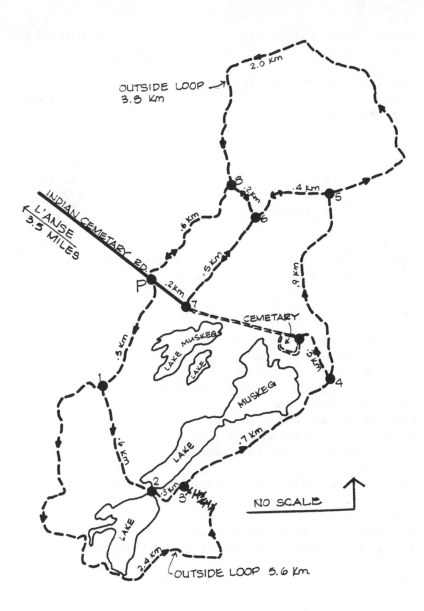

OUTSIDE LOOP
3.8 Km

2.0 Km

INDIAN CEMETERY RD.

L'ANSE
3.5 MILES

.2 Km

.4 Km

.6 Km

.5 Km

.9 Km

P

.2 Km

7

CEMETARY

LAKE MUSKEG

LAKE

.5 Km

.5 Km

4

1

MUSKEG

.6 Km

LAKE

.7 Km

2

.3 Km

3

NO SCALE

LAKE

2.4 Km

OUTSIDE LOOP 5.6 Km

PINERY LAKES TRAIL

Pinery Lakes Trail                                    Revised:  2/24/88

Baraga County Tourist Association
PO Box 556                                           906-524-7444
Baraga, MI  49908

Baragaland Cross Country Ski Club
c/o Indian Country Sales                             906-524-6518
L'Anse, MI  49946

Trail suitable for skiing only

Location:
 From downtown L'Anse take Main St. north 1.6 miles to Indian Cemetery Rd.,
    then right 2.5 miles to the trailhead.  Park along the road.

Trail specifications:
    15 km; 4 loop(s); Loop length(s)-various
Typical terrain: Rolling to hilly
Skiing ability suggested: Novice to advanced
Hiking trail difficulty: NA
Nordic trail grooming method: Track set with skating lane
Suitable for all-terrain bicycle: NA
Trail use fee: Donations accepted at trailhead
Camping: Available nearby

General Information:
 Maintained by the Baragaland Cross-Country Ski Club
 Site of the Baragaland Cross-Country Ski Race held the 2nd Sunday in
    February
 Indian Country Sales is the local ski shop in L'Anse
 Indian cemetary dating back to the 1840's is along the trail
 Also contact: Baragaland Cross-Country Ski Club
                Rte 1, Box 122A
                L'Anse, MI 49946
 Well designed and maintained trail system

337

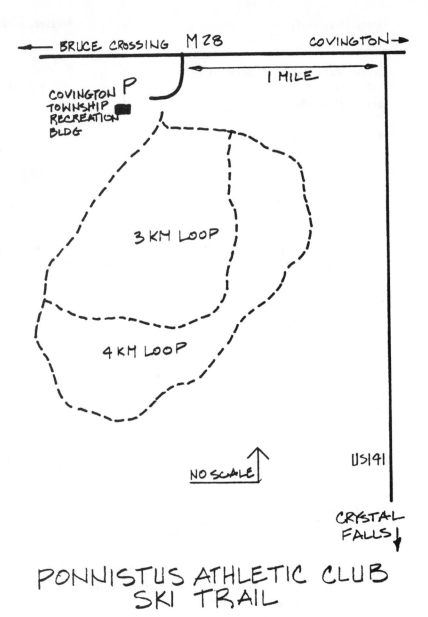

BRUCE CROSSING ← M 28 COVINGTON →

1 MILE

COVINGTON P
TOWNSHIP
RECREATION
BLDG

3 KM LOOP

4 KM LOOP

NO SCALE

US 141

CRYSTAL
FALLS ↓

# PONNISTUS ATHLETIC CLUB SKI TRAIL

Ponnistus Athletic Club Ski Trail          Revised: 3/24/88

Baraga County Tourist Association
PO Box 556                                  906-524-7444
Baraga, MI  49908

Glenn Maki
Rte 1, Box 15                               906-524-6429*
Covington, MI  49919                        906-335-2270**

Trail suitable for skiing only

Location:
  16 miles south of L'Anse on M28 to Covington, then continuing east from
   Covington on M28 1 mile to the Covington Recreation Building

Trail specifications:
   7 km; 2 loop(s); Loop length(s)-3, 4
Typical terrain:
Skiing ability suggested: Novice to intermediate
Hiking trail difficulty: NA
Nordic trail grooming method: Track set
Suitable for all-terrain bicycle: No
Trail use fee: None, but donations accepted
Camping: None
Drinking water available in the recreation bldg, when its open

General Information:
  Maintained by the Ponnistus Athletic Club
  Warming shelter in the recreation building, when its open
  * days
  ** evenings

338

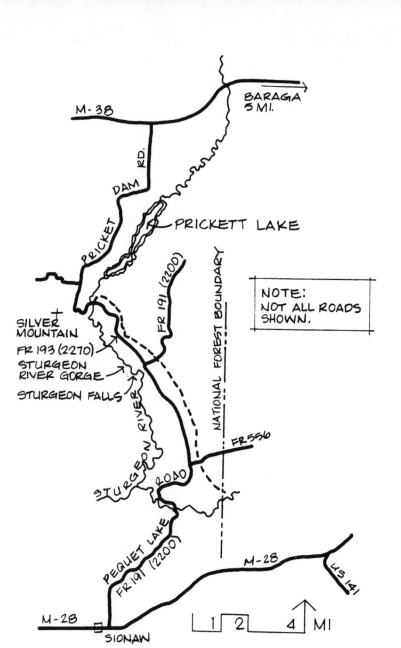

## NORTH COUNTRY TRAIL - STURGEON RIVER

North Country Trail - Sturgeon River                    Revised:  4/02/88

Kenton Ranger District, Ottawa National Forest
M28                                                     906-852-3501
Kenton, MI  49943

Forest Supervisor, Ottawa National Forest
East US2                                                906-932-1330
Ironwood, MI  49938                                     800-562-1201

Trail suitable for hiking & skiing

Location:
 Trail parallels the Sturgeon River Gorge east of FR191 (new FR2200) & 193
  (new FR2270) from Sturgeon River bridge on FR193 (new FR2270) to the
  east boundary of the National Forest.
 Trailhead - Take FR191 (new FR2200) north from M28 just east of Sidnaw
  for about 9 miles to the trail access point (east side of FR2200).
Trail specifications:
  10 mi; No loop(s); Loop length(s)-NA
Typical terrain: Very hilly
Skiing ability suggested: Advanced
Hiking trail difficulty: Difficult
Nordic trail grooming method: None
Suitable for all-terrain bicycle: Not permitted
Trail use fee: None
Camping: There are no developed campsites &
Drinking water not available along trail

General Information:
 Maintained by the Kenton Ranger District, Ottawa National Forest
 This is a point to point trail
 Only skiers with good winter survival skills should attempt this trail
 Most streams do not have bridges
 Terrain and remoteness in the nearby Sturgeon River Gorge are
  exceptional, even for the Upper Peninsula. District Ranger comment
 A more detailed map is available from the Kenton Ranger District office
 Like all of the North Country Trail, wilderness camping is permitted 200'
  from the trail
 For more information about the North Country Trail contact the
  North Country Trail Association, PO Box 311, White Cloud, MI 49349 or
  USDI, Midwest Region, 1709 Jackson St., Omaha, NE 68102-2571

339

# Trail Notes

# Hiking Primer

When I used to take groups of YMCA boys to Isle Royale National Park, I always told them that the goal of any hiking trip should be to get the maximum enjoyment out of the experience with the minimum of effort and discomfort. When looking back on that statement and the context that I said it in, I still believe that to be true today. The entire trip should be planned with that single goal in mind, regardless of the destination or the length of the trip. The key word in the last sentence is "plan". There is no such thing as too much planning. In today's high pressure lifestyle, the opportunity to get away from it all becomes a precious commodity that should not be wasted. Lack of proper planning can ruin the best of intentions.

This chapter is not intended to be a complete discussion on the subject but rather a starting point to begin the development of your hiking trip. You should visit your local library or camping equipment store for other books on the subject and more detail on specific subjects of interest that I do not provide you with. Two books that I recommend are *Walking Softly in the Wilderness* by John Hart and *The New Complete Walker* by Colin Fletcher. Also *Backpacker* magazine is an excellent source of information on current developments in camping equipment.

The comments that follow are intended for spring through fall hiking trips. For information on winter camping, consult your library or camping store.

## Equipment

Generally, the beginning hiker usually is over equipped with not only too much gear but it is over designed for the intended purpose. Not only will that cost more but it makes a pack heavier than it should be. As my general rule, if you have to think twice about an item you are considering, usually you won't need it.

The four most important pieces of equipment that will either make or break a trip are the pack, tent, sleeping bag and boots.

Take care in your selections and ask your hiking friends for their thoughts on the subject.

*Sleeping Bag*: For the Michigan climate, a sleeping bag that has a range to 20 degrees is very adequate. To reduce bulk and weight, a down bag is best but it will soak up water if allowed to get wet. A bag with man-made insulation will not absorb water, but is bulkier than down insulation, however they cost much less. Should you be camping in the U.P. in the early spring or late fall, a warmer bag or adding a liner may be necessary. The style of the bag is a personal decision, depending on how much room you prefer. For colder weather camping, a built in flap at the shoulders or drawstring is a nice feature to look for when selecting your bag.

Some would consider a sleeping pad an essential part of the sleeping bag. Because of its bulk, it usually is left behind to save weight and space. For longer hikes, I would strongly urge its inclusion. Nothing is worse than not getting a good nights sleep or waking up sore, with 20 miles ahead of you.

Along with the sleeping bag you should include a stuff bag to pack it in. This is easier than rolling it up and actually better for goose down bags than rolling them up the same way every time.

*Boots*: Since most of Michigan's terrain is not too demanding the heavy lug boot commonly used in the mountains are not really necessary in Michigan. On the contrary, because of the sand and light soils that are often found on Michigan trails, the lug sole can cause unnecessary erosion damage to the trail.

More importantly, boots should be water proof because of the frequent rains that occur throughout the state as well as the wet lands that are often crossed. Properly applied Snow Seal is the best product that I have found to water proof boots. Remember, the construction of the boot is a major factor on how well the boot can keep out the water. Check with your camping store to select the best boot for your needs.

Before going on your hiking trip make sure that the boots are well broken in. Wearing your boots during your conditioning period is an excellent way to get you and your gear ready for the trip.

Part of your foot wear should be an extra pair of lightweight shoes to wear when in camp. Also if your boots get wet, you will have something else to wear while they are drying. The sneakers will give your feet a rest as well.

*Pack*: High technology has made a major impact in the design of packs. Generally you have two design choices, the older external frame or the relatively new internal frame design. Both have their advantages. Summer hiking is best with an external frame, since this design usually allows for more air circulation between the pack and your back. However, some say that the internal frame is more comfortable. The internal pack is better for winter ski touring, since arm movement will be less restricted and the pack is usually more compact. The choice is yours.

Size is another consideration. The larger pack allows you to place everything inside including your sleeping pad and bag. Smaller packs require that these items be strapped on the outside. With everything on the inside, you get the added protection from the rain, and equipment usually stays cleaner when not exposed.

The most important consideration is to have the pack properly sized to your body. Unlike knit ski hats, one size does not fit all. To be sure that you are getting the properly sized pack, visit several stores and have them size the pack for you. This way you will have a better chance at getting one that fits properly.

*Tent*: The Michigan climate demands the use of a tent. Frequent rains and numerous types of insects makes it essential that you use a tent if you intend to sleep well. One that is fitted with a rainfly is better than the less expensive coated type since the rain fly design permits plenty of mosquito netted openings for the cloudless nights. If you can find one with "no-see-um" netting, so much the better. It's not necessary to purchase the most expensive tent on the market, since they are designed to withstand severe wind and weather conditions usually not found in Michigan.

*Stove*: With stoves now being a requirement in some areas of Michigan you should consider including one on your equipment list. Once I got used to mine, I found it more convenient than an open fire. My meal cooked sooner and water boiled faster and with much less of a mess to pots and pans. In times of high fire risk you may be required to use one, or go without a hot meal. In addition, its easier to minimize your impact on the land when you don't have to collect wood and build a fire ring. Further, you will not have to carry a hatchet or saw. Most of the stoves on the market will serve you well. Of course, the Seva and Optimus brands have been around for along time, proving their value with years of excellent trouble free service. I suggest you ask your camping friends for their recommendations.

In addition to these major items above the following suggested checklist of equipment should be considered:

water bottle
fuel bottle
nestle pots with covers
pot holder or insulated glove
cup, spoon and knife (fork is not needed)
cooking spoon
multi tool pocket knife (Swiss Army knife type)
biodegradable dish soap and pot scrubber
dish towel
flashlight or other light source
20' nonelastic rope
first aid kit
water filter and iodine tablets
first aid kit
whistle
blister protection (mole skin, etc)
stick type insect repellent
leather gloves (keeps hands clean when doing dirty jobs)
compass
watch
toilet paper
maps
personal items (comb, soap, toothbrush, toothpaste, etc)
towel and wash cloth
food
mosquito net hat
repair kit (thread, needle, duct tape, etc)
2 plastic garbage bags

Additional equipment that you might consider, depending on the type of hike you are taking may include:

| | |
|---|---|
| camera | pedometer |
| guides | thermometer |
| binoculars | paper and pencil |

## Clothing

Like in the winter, the layer system should be followed. This system provides the maximum of warmth for the minimum of weight. Further, it allows you to maintain a comfortable body temperature in a wide range of weather.

Jackets: A windshell is essential when the weather is cool. This item does not add much weight but provides the necessary protection in windy/cool conditions. Rain gear which includes a jacket with hood, could be used instead of the windshell. The jacket should be made of a Gore-tex type fabric to reduce the amount of perspiration that occurs when wearing rain gear. Since I don't care for the condensing perspiration, I take along a wide brimmed hat and just get wet in light rains (when it really starts coming down hard, I stop and cover up with a poncho until it abates). Usually by the time camp is reached, I'm dry anyway.

For northern regions of the state and during the spring and fall, a down vest would be a nice addition to keep warm in the morning, evening and on cool days.

Shirts: The best is a long sleeved button shirt with a collar. The weight will depend on the time of year. During the warm days the sleeves can be rolled up. When down and buttoned they protect your arms from insects without adding an additional layer when its not needed.

Pants: Shorts are great, if you understand that insects just love you to wear them. Plan on wearing long, loose fitting cotton pants for general use. Jeans are very durable but they also chafe the skin. The long pants also protect your skin from thorny bushes and nettles.

Socks: These are especially important items. Wearing 2 pair will help prevent blisters. The smooth fabric socks should be against your skin and wool against the boot. Take two extra pair along to change into often. Wash the extra pair and hang them on your pack to dry in warm weather or around your waist next to your skin when its too cool or on rainy days. Your body warmth will act as a drier. Remember, dirty socks cause blisters much faster than clean ones. Polypropylene socks are just as good to use in the summer as they are in the winter and for the exact same reason. They can be worn as inner socks to wick away the moisture.

Undergarments: I recommend cotton fabrics or again polypropylene to wick off moisture and reduce the chance for hypothermia. Even if the temperature is above 32 degrees, hypothermia remains a danger that must constantly be protected against.

## First Aid, Health and Safety

An ounce of prevention . . . need I say more. Adding to what has been previously said about hypothermia, clean socks and so on, insects and allergies can be the most troublesome. If you have a medical problem, prepare well and do what ever you can in advance of the trip to preclude a problem from occurring.

Insects are another issue. By wearing long sleeves and long pants and sealing up spaces where insects can reach the skin, much of the problem will be reduced. In addition by forgoing the wearing of scented products you will reduce the possibility of attracting insects. Of course, insect repellant is a must. The stick form I find quite good since it can be applied around the face without fear of getting it in the eyes. It also weighs less for the amount of usable produce and it can't spill. When the insects become really aggressive a netting hat may be your only alternative.

The best way to keep from getting injured is not to take chances or get overly tired. If unanticipated problems or difficult terrain require more energy than you have take several breaks daily and reduce the length of your planned hike for the day and/or the entire trip.

Check your feet often. Do it at rest periods, lunch and in the evening. If redness is observed, place some moleskin over the area so that a blister will not occur. You must keep your feet in good condition if you expect to enjoy your outing.

If an accident occurs, a well equipped first aid kit is essential. It doesn't need to be large though. I suggest you contact the

American Red Cross to get suggestions on what it should contain before purchasing one. Also remember that just because you don't use it, it may not be in usable condition when you need it. Items may deteriorate over time. Check it before each trip and make replacements when necessary. Be sure you know how to use it before you take your trip. A class in first aid and CPR would be well worth the time. Don't forget that the most essential first aid item is water. Keep your water bottle full when ever you can.

*Water*: Purification of water is absolutely necessary throughout Michigan. All kinds of contaminants have made drinking water directly out of streams or lakes dangerous. Using a 3 micron filter (on Isle Royale a .4 micron filter is required to eliminate intestinal bacteria) or boiling the water for at least 2 minutes should do the job. Since experts don't agree, you may want to combine both methods for the best protection. Halazone and chlorine methods are no longer recommended as safe and should not be used. Use of iodine is effective for some types of bacteria. If at all possible, take along extra water. Water weighs about 9 lbs per gallon, but it's usually better than all the extra weight of fuel needed for boiling, not to mention the time required and the taste it has after the disinfecting process.

*Food*: Food selection is the most subjective and my discussion will be very limited for that reason. However, a few general suggestions are in order for the novice hiker.

Try out everything you intend to take before the trip. Its better to have a disaster in the kitchen than on the trail. Food is critical on a hiking trip and 20 miles out is no place to experiment.

Take more than you think you will need, if it isn't possible to purchase additional supplies along the trail. You will eat much more on a hike than you ever did before.

Keep it simple. Prepared cold or hot cereals as the basis for breakfast is best. To that you can add finger foods and hot chocolate. Leave the hot cakes, eggs, bacon, etc., home, even in the freeze dried form. It takes too much time to prepare and clean up. For lunch, finger food again. It takes too much time to get a fire going and your stove will usually be deep in your pack. Gorp, cheese, hard crackers, peanut butter, pop tarts, raisins, fresh fruit, dried fruit, etc are good choices to start

with. For dinner dive into the freeze dried selections that are available at your camping store. Also your grocery store has many very suitable dishes including macaroni and cheese and numerous instant foods that can be combined with freeze dried food for a inexpensive and filling meal.

Be sure to take along a little extra finger food in case it becomes impractical to cook an evening meal because of insects or rain.

## Getting Yourself and Your Equipment into Condition

I cannot emphasize this point enough. Practice hikes around your neighborhood or local park may look funny when carrying all of your gear and wearing your boots but it will not only get you in shape but also break in your gear. Expect some soreness. If you don't develop any, you have not taken long enough hikes. It's better to hurt some at home than for the pain to ruin your trip later. Being out of shape can ruin a trip.

From your conditioning program you should be better qualified to choose a hike that is appropriate for your condition. It might be a good idea to take a practice overnight hike to a nearby campground to try out your equipment. This is the easiest way to check out your gear . . . and yourself. If changes or modifications need to be made in your gear to better fit your needs, making those changes at home is much easier and more effective than on the trail.

With thoughtful planning, asking questions of knowledgeable hikers and salespeople, and using good quality equipment that is appropriate for your individual needs, your first hiking trip should be a pleasant experience that you will long remember.

# History of Nordic Skiing

*by Danforth Holley*

Like you, I love skiing, especially Cross Country. I also love our beautiful State of Michigan, which boasts such a vast number of wilderness areas with terrain uniquely suited to Cross Country Skiing that it is fast becoming one of the nation's leading areas for this great ancient sport.

Would you be startled to know that Cross Country Skiing is at least 4,000 years old? On the Island of Rødøy in Northern Norway is a stone-age rock carving depicting a man on skis. This 4,000 year old figure is surrounded by animal figures (not pictured here) which suggests he is a hunter who owes his fame more to his ability to ski than to bag a hearty meal.

Ancient skis have been unearthed in Finland, Sweden and Norway. Ancient Norwegian ski finds include the Øvrebø ski which is about 2,500 years old. The number and quality of workmanship of these various skis is an astounding and fascinating history of man's resourcefulness in an inhospitable environment.

Our first written reference to skis and skiers is found in early Viking sagas from 900 to 1100 A.D., replete with male and female ski gods, hunting, friendly competition, and warfare on skis.

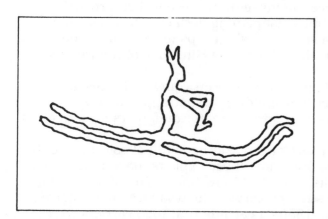

*Stone Age Rock Carving Depicting a Man on Skis. From the Isle of Rødøy in Norway.*

The earliest skis were made of large animal bones which were smoothed on the joint ends to produce a flat surface that allowed for a swift, gliding motion. These were strapped to the feet with skin or thongs. The world's oldest known skis, made of bone, are displayed at the Djugarden Museum in Stockholm and are at least 4,000 years old.

The first historical account of skis used in warfare was during the Battle of Oslo in 1200 A.D. when King Sverre of Sweden sent scouts on skis to spy on the Norwegian enemy camp. Feeling as fiesty as they were fleet on foot, the Swedes continued to use skis in the Wars of 1521, 1576, 1590 and 1610 A.D.

The long tradition of skis in warfare has given birth to great competitive events throughout the world. Here in Michigan the annual North American Vasa Race, of which I am proud to be one of the founders, is patterned after the world's longest ski race (85 kilometers) held each March in Dalecarlia, Sweden, which attracts some of the world's best Cross Country racers. The race honors the Swedish patriot, Gustavus Vasa, who in 1521 skied from Salen to Moran, Sweden, to lead his countrymen against King Christian II of Denmark. The North American Vasa in recognition of Gustavus Vasa and "loppet" meaning long distance, is a 25 kilometer (16 miles) and a 50 kilometer (32 miles) race, held in Traverse City.

Another race you should know about is the American Birkebeiner Race held each year near Cable, Wisconsin. Initiated in 1973, this 55 kilometer Cross Country back-buster is also patterned after a similar race, this time in Norway, that commemorates a Viking saga about the rescue of a Norwegian child Prince in 1206. "Birkebeiner" means birch legs, referring to the leggings worn by the king's warriors.

The actual sport of skiing, as opposed to its purely practical application in hunting and warfare, began in the Telemark District of Norway in the 1850s when the Norwegian, Sondre Nordheim invented the toe-piece and heel-strap binding which gave proper control of skis for the first time. Impromptu races

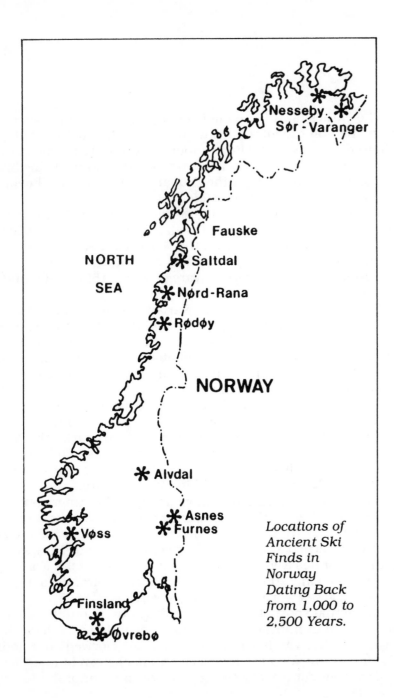

Locations of Ancient Ski Finds in Norway Dating Back from 1,000 to 2,500 Years.

and jumping contests were held and in the 1850s an annual get-together of ski enthusiasts was held with accompanying one- and two-day festivals. Skiing became fashionable in the 1860s when the Royal Family organized an annual ski-jumping tournament at Holmenkollen, near Oslo, appointed a committee to draft rules, and donated a trophy. This contest soon became the greatest national sports event in Norway and Cross Country and other forms of skiing were added. Today, one can visit the famous Holmenkollen Jump and Museum.

In the U.S.A., ski teams were sent to the Olympics in the 1930s. In the 1940s and 50s most of the Cross Country Skiing was still done by racers. However, in the 60s, snowbelt families began to get interested in Cross Country Skiing. Early in the decade, there was only one annual open Cross Country Race with less than 100 racers, but by the early 70s, the sport had really caught on.

Here in the U.S.A., two developers have been to modern skiing what Sondre Nordheim was to ancient skiing—Howard Head having pioneered the wood and metal ski and I am credited with the first fiberglass ski, the first L-shaped edge, plastic snow, and Holley Speed Spray, which are all in the Ski Hall of Fame in Ishpeming, Michigan. Ishpeming, which is located in the Upper Peninsula, may sound like an unlikely place for the Hall of Fame, but it is especially appropriate because at the time skiing was becoming a sport, Swedes and Norwegians were coming to Michigan at the onset of the lumber boom. Not only does the museum represent their ardent interest in skiing, but at Ishpeming is the famous "Suicide Hill," one of the most famous ski jumps in the world, and in nearby Ironwood is the "Ski Flying Hill," one of the world's largest jumps.

Cross Country Skiing has also been going on in this area since the Nordic settlers' children first strapped on their home-made skis as their fathers and grandfathers used to do in the Old World.

The history of Cross Country Skiing is full of colorful events and characters and one man whose exploits made him a legend in his own time was John A. "Snow-Shoe" Thompson. A native of the Telemark District of Norway, he was lured to California by gold fever in the 1850s. Learning that mail carriers were hard pressed to make it over the mountains in winter, he set up a route and carried mail on skis across the Sierras. His skill and daring on his hand-carved skis were unmatched, whether in schussing hills at mile-a-minute clips, leaping obstacles 30, 40 and 50 yards, or slaloming down slopes with serpentine grace. He is considered by many to be the Father of American Skiing and has been memorialized since 1946 by an annual Cross Country Ski Race. It is interesting to note he used skis that were 8'9½" long and one long pole to veer his course from one side to another. One pole was a tradition that he brought from Norway.

During World War II the famous American 10th Mounties Division is credited by General Mark Clark as having been a leading factor in winning the war in Italy with their bold Alpine maneuvers for which a special dual purpose binding was utilized for combined Alpine and Cross Country Skiing.

But enough of books and history. It is time to enter the wintery wonders of Michigan, and you will not find yourself alone. The woods are "silent, dark and deep," but also becoming, peopled by those eager to commune with nature without the snarling and fuming intrusion of snowmobiles. Cross Country Skiing equipment is reasonably inexpensive and trail expenses minimal. Skiing with a good rucksack on your back, loaded with good wine, bread and cheese, isn't too dear. For those who love the wildlife, photographing beautiful landscapes, deer, elk, rabbits, birds and whomever else you might run across in the wild woods; for those who look for a close-knit family sport which doctors claim is one of the best of all around exercises; for those who seek clean air and serenity—there is no better sport.

The most revolutionary change to cross country skiing since the change to two ski poles instead of the single long pole used by "Snow Shoe Thompson" occurred in the early 1980's when Bill Kock adopted the ice skating movement to cross-country skiing. It immediately changed the face of racing because skating produced much faster speeds than could ever be made by the classic diagonal stride method. This technique gave birth to a completely new line of cross country ski equipment. Even though there has been considerable emphasis on this new skating technique, the general cross-country skiing public remains loyal to the diagonal stride as the preferred technique. (See the skating section in the chapter on technique for more information)

But enough of history. It is my fervent wish that you take advantage of the years of work and preparation that have gone into the making of this Atlas by going out and exploring the unparalleled beauty of Michigan's ski trails.

# Snowfall and Cross-Country Skiing Opportunities

Two independent weather factors impact cross country skiing snow conditions in Michigan. These factors are (1) precipitation and the "lake effect" and (2) temperature and its fluctuations during the winter. That is why the amount of snow available for skiing varies so greatly from one area of the state to another.

In Michigan, winter precipitation is greatly magnified by the role that the great lakes play, commonly referred to as the "lake effect". This "lake effect" greatly enhances the quality of snowfall as well as determining its location. "Lake effect" refers to the effect that lakes, specifically for Michigan they are Lakes Michigan and Superior, have on significantly increasing the amount of snowfall on land along southeast shorelines of these two bodies of water, especially if the shoreline orientation is SW-NE. This orientation is important since the prevailing winter storms come over Michigan from the NW. As the storms pass over the relatively warm water of the Great Lakes in early winter, they pick up moisture and continue inland where it deposits this moisture on the relatively cold land in the form of snow. There are several locations in Michigan where this "lake effect" is quite obvious. In order of greatest to least impact they are:

1. The Lake Superior shoreline from Wisconsin to Copper Harbor. The western end of this area is called Big Snow Country.
2. The area centered around Gaylord, extending from Burt Lake on the north to Kalkaska and Crawford Counties on the south.
3. The Leelanau Peninsula and extending south to a line from Mesick west to Lake Michigan.
4. The Huron Mountains in north-central Upper Peninsula.
5. Along the Lake Superior shoreline from Munising to Grand Marais.
6. The remaining north half of the Upper Peninsula not mentioned previously.
7. Along the Lake Michigan shore from Muskegon to Van Buren county.

The impact of this "lake effect" is shown graphically in Figure 1.

*Average Annual Snowfall in Inches*

*FIGURE 1*

348

However, even with significant snowfall, if the temperature is not cold enough any amount of snow will melt. In areas where the snowfall is minimal, fluctuations in temperature above freezing can significantly reduce or eliminate the snow cover. Refer to Figure 2 to see where the most consistently cold areas of the state are located.

When combining both snowfall and temperature, Figure 3 illustrates where and for how long snow cover of 6″ or more can be found throughout the state. The major fatality of this combination is southwest Michigan. Although this area gets as much snow as at the Big Mac Bridge the number of days of snow cover of 6″ or more is no greater than Tawas. What this means is that when the frequent storms dump the snow in the southwest corner of the State its time to go skiing right then and not wait for the weekend. At the minimum, change your weekend plans and go skiing, since the skiing conditions the following weekend could be significantly different.

This discussion further reinforces the fact that "going up north" will not guarantee snow for skiing, especially in marginal snow seasons. That is why I have included phone number(s) with all the trails to allow you to call ahead to check on snow conditions. I recommend that you use them to insure a pleasurable ski tour. In addition, the Northern Michigan Nordic Ski Council has established a toll free number to call for information on current snow conditions in the area served by the Council. That number is 800-521-0675 or you can call 517-786-2211.

As a guideline you can expect snow for skiing in Region 1 from early January to mid February, in Region 2 from mid December to late February, in Region 3 from late November to late March and in Region 4 from mid November to early April. This schedule may require you to travel to the most favorable section of the region to find that snow, but it should be possible to find sufficient snow for skiing.

*Mean Number of Days Per Year*
*When the Maximum Temperature Does Not Exceed 32°F*

*FIGURE 2*

349

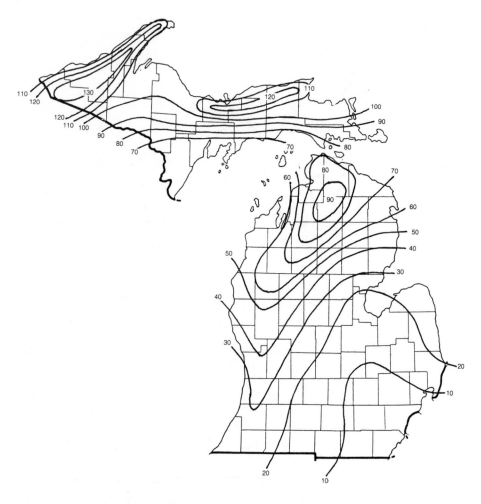

*Average Number of Days Per Season
When the Accumulated Snow Depth is 6" Or More*

FIGURE 3

# Ski Tour Planning Guide

## A Word of Caution

Planning a ski tour, whether it is only a few hours long or will involve the entire day, requires serious planning. Outdoor recreation in the winter can be extremely rewarding, but proper precautions should be taken because of hazardous weather conditions that you may encounter.

The effect of wind during the winter is very critical since it accentuates the low temperatures on the human body. Commonly called the Wind Chill Factor, the temperature is usually well below the actual air temperature reading. When combined with moisture on your body, this problem is greatly compounded. Since wet clothing draws off body heat, it is extremely important to stay as dry as possible and adequately protected from the wind with proper clothing. If care is not taken, you could become affected by hypothermia, frostbite or both. Either condition is dangerous but can be avoided if care is taken.

Frostbite is the freezing of skin and/or appendages as the result of inadequate protection from cold temperatures. Hands, feet, face and ears are especially vulnerable to this condition. The first danger signal is a tingling or numb sensation. If treated early, usually by improving blood circulation, warming the effected area and adding dry clothing (being sure to remove wet clothing first) should correct the problem. In the case of the face, your companions should check each other often for any signs of visible frostbite, in the form of white or gray patches of skin. If for some reason frostbite does occur, warm the affected area gradually and protect it from any additional exposure while continuing to improve blood circulation. Under no circumstances should you massage, rub, apply high heat or break blisters, for this will only aggravate the condition. Your most important concerns should be to prevent additional frostbite and keep the effected area as clean as possible. In the case of fingers and toes, keep them separated with sterile gauze.

Hypothermia is another condition that you should also guard against. This condition is harder to recognize and often affects its victims without their knowledge. Only constant vigilance on the part of all your companions will keep this problem from affecting your group.

Hypothermia is caused by the drastic lowering of the body core temperature resulting from exposure to cool or cold temperature, wind, moisture and coupled with fatigue. It's not necessary to have extremely low temperatures for this condition to occur. It can happen very rapidly and may in extreme cases result in death if not treated promptly. Symptoms include uncontrolled shivering, heavy speech, fumbling, extreme fatigue, stiff joints, irrationality, bluish lips, dilated pupils and breathing difficulties. In mild cases, treatment involves replacing wet clothing with dry, then rewarming the entire body by wrapping the victim in blankets, clothing or placing them in a sleeping bag to allow their own remaining body heat to rewarm themselves. If possible, give the victim warm liquids and food to warm them internally. In more severe cases, it may be necessary to provide additional heat by sharing the body heat of another through direct skin to skin contact. Of course, the victim should be taken to a medical facility when possible. If you guard against the possibility of contracting hypothermia by staying dry, warm and do not become overly tired, this problem should not occur.

Both hypothermia and frostbite can be prevented through the proper selection and use of clothing. The following section should be helpful in that regard.

## Clothing Suggestions

Thoughtful choice and proper use of clothing is the single most important consideration that will make your tour an enjoyable experience. Clothing selection is a very individual matter since the conditions under which it is worn are unique to you alone. The speed you ski, your technique, the length of the tour, your perspiration rate, weather conditions and your tolerance of cold temperatures will all affect the type of clothing you should wear. An outfit that is perfect for someone else may be very uncomfortable for you. For those reasons, the only

## Wind Speed Cooling Power of Wind
### Expressed as "Equivalent Chill Temperature"

| mph | Local Temperature (°F) | | | | | | | | | | | |
|---|---|---|---|---|---|---|---|---|---|---|---|---|
| calm | 40 | 30 | 20 | 10 | 5 | 0 | -10 | -20 | -30 | -40 | -50 | -60 |
| | Equivalent Chill Temperature | | | | | | | | | | | |
| 5 | 35 | 25 | 15 | 5 | 0 | -5 | -15 | -25 | -35 | -45 | -55 | -70 |
| 10 | 30 | 15 | 5 | -10 | -15 | -20 | -35 | -45 | -60 | -70 | -80 | -95 |
| 15 | 25 | 10 | -5 | -20 | -25 | -30 | -45 | -60 | -70 | -85 | -100 | -110 |
| 20 | 20 | 5 | -10 | -25 | -30 | -35 | -50 | -65 | -80 | -95 | -110 | -120 |
| 25 | 15 | 0 | -15 | -30 | -35 | -45 | -60 | -75 | -90 | -105 | -120 | -135 |
| 30 | 10 | 0 | -20 | -30 | -40 | -50 | -65 | -80 | -95 | -110 | -125 | -140 |
| 35 | 10 | -5 | -20 | -35 | -40 | -50 | -65 | -80 | -100 | -115 | -130 | -145 |
| 40 | 10 | -5 | -20 | -35 | -45 | -55 | -70 | -85 | -100 | -115 | -130 | -150 |
| Danger | | | Higher Danger (flesh may freeze in 1 min.) | | | Great Danger (flesh may freeze in 30 seconds) | | | | | | |

accurate way to determine what is correct for you, especially in different weather conditions is by experimentation. The following suggestions you may find useful as a starting point to determine what is correct for you.

More than anything else, the clothing you choose should accomplish three objectives. It should keep you WARM, regardless of the temperature or how much it changes; DRY, regardless of the amount of moisture your body produces or falls on you in the form of snow or sleet; and your clothing should allow for the MAXIMUM AMOUNT OF BODY MOVEMENT WITHOUT DISCOMFORT.

The easiest way to keep warm is to wear several layers of lightweight clothing rather than a single heavy garment. Not only does this permit you to adjust the amount of clothing to the activity level or change in weather conditions but the layers of clothing develop air space between them which add to the insulating value of the clothing without adding weight. If you rely on one heavy garment, you will likely be either too warm or too cold most of the time, not to mention the bulkiness of such clothing.

Even with the proper number of layers, some perspiration will develop. It is therefore essential that it be evaporated as rapidly as possible in order to stay dry. To accomplish this, I have found polypropylene fabric to be quite effective. When dry, it creates a thin layer of warm air, and when wet it promotes evaporation. Another source of moisture that should be prevented from collecting is caused by external sources, either from falling snow or sleet or by snow being picked up on clothing as a result of falls or normal skiing. If the snow is dry it should be removed, being careful not to push it into the fabric. The exception is on knee socks if worn, where small amounts of dry snow should be left untouched since this adds insulating quality. Obviously in moist snow or sleet conditions, a water repellant outer garment is the order of the day.

The third requirement of cross country ski clothing is that it should provide completely unrestricted movement of all parts of the body. Snug or tight fitting clothing will soon chafe skin and may restrict blood circulation, not to mention the general uncomfortable feeling. For maximum comfort, any garment that may bind in the shoulders, waist, knees or thighs should be avoided. This is why much of the new cross country clothing is made of stretch fabric.

Since the head radiates about 40% of body heat, it is the single most important part of your anatomy in controlling the overall body temperature. With proper use of head gear, total perspiration can be kept to a minimum, making the job of staying dry much easier. Depending on the weather conditions you may choose anything from not wearing any head protection in very warm weather, to a full knit ski mask or balaclava for maximum protection from wind and snow. In between these two extremes, a headband and light knit ski cap are very useful for most situations. When planning a day tour, it might be a good idea to put a knit ski mask or balaclava in your pack in case the weather turns windy or cold.

Hand protection is another very individual matter. Control of poles vs. warmth will be the major decision you will have to make. In most situations, gloves should be suitable for most everyone. But in cold weather you might consider a polypropylene glove liner or for even colder conditions mittens may be required. For all day tours, taking a pair of mittens in your pack might be wise, since weather conditions could change for the worst. Effectiveness of gloves are directly related to fit. Tight fitting gloves restrict blood and can defeat the benefits of good quality gloves if they are improperly sized. Snug but not tight should be the rule for gloves.

Like gloves, socks should also be made of polypropylene since wicking of moisture is critical to maintain warmth in the feet as well. The number of socks are a personal decision, however I have found that using only one pair of mid weight polypropylene socks in properly sized boots keep my feet warm even in the coldest weather. Other options include silk socks next to your skin, with a pair of wool socks over them. If the weather gets extremely cold, try putting a pair of old socks over your boots. You may be surprised at how well it works.

Assuming you have sufficient layers of clothing to keep warm, don't forget to include a wind shell in your pack. Wind chill can be devastating if you're not properly protected. Don't be caught without that protection.

Remember, getting too warm is just as bad as too cold. Don't over dress. Plan on being a little cool when starting out on a tour. The physical activity will warm you. If you must wear a jacket, plan on taking a pack to put it in when you warm up. Overheating will drain your energy. Be award that extra perspiration will cool you quickly when you stop skiing. Plan on covering up with a jacket before you get cold.

## Equipment and Food Checklist

The amount of gear you need to take with you will depend on the length, location and trail or area you intend to ski. Nevertheless, it's very important that you take along a few items to make your tour safe and enjoyable.

Since it is very uncomfortable to carry things in your pocket, a "fanny pack" is convenient for most short tours. Not only is it just the right size, but unlike a day pack nothing is covering your back to restrict evaporation. Of course, for the day long tour, a larger day pack that allows complete freedom of movement for your arms is essential. Both types of packs come in many different shapes and sizes to suit your specific needs.

The following are items you might consider taking with you depending on the length of your tour:

## Equipment and Food Checklist

1. If you have wood skis, I highly recommend taking a spare ski tip. I have seen people having to walk miles in deep snow for the lack of this $8 item.
2. Trail map.
3. Wax/cork/scraper—Usually one wax for warm temperatures (above 32) and another wax for cold temperatures (below 32) should be enough.
4. Waterproof matches if you intend to be out all day.
5. Knife—For meals and emergencies.
6. Protection for your lips.
7. Sunglasses with a strap to keep them from coming off in a fall.
8. Extra mittens or gloves.
9. Food—This is very subjective but I have found that raisins, bananas, hot water, apples, oranges, dried fruit and cookies work well as trail lunches.
10. Whistle—to signal for help when lost.
11. Small first aid kit.

## Ski Tour Checklist

When planning a ski tour the following list should help you make the tour a safe trip.

1. Check skis and poles for breaks and loose screws.
2. Choose companions carefully. Their skill and strength will determine the length of your tour. Never ski faster than the slowest skier in your group.
3. Check your map and decide on the route or area you intend to ski.
4. Be sure you have all necessary equipment and food.
5. Choose clothing for anticipated weather conditions. At least one member of the group should take additional clothing for unexpected problems that might occur.
6. Leave your trip schedule with a responsible person and contact them on your return.

## One Last Comment

This section is only intended as a brief summary of the topics covered and not as a conclusive reference. For detailed information on subjects such as winter camping, orienteering, skiing technique, regional trail guides and racing, I suggest that you contact your local ski shop or bookstore for publications relating to your interest area. I would recommend that you subscribe to the *Great Lakes Skier*, a seasonal newspaper of skiing (both downhill and cross-country) for the Great Lakes region. It is an excellent and timely publication of events and tours in the Great Lakes area (mostly Michigan). It can be purchased at many ski shops and ski areas or by mail. Their address is 7990 West Grand River Ave, Suite C, Brighton, MI 48116. 313-227-4200.

# Waxing for Recreational X-C Skiers

*by Danforth Holley*

*Alumnus Certified Professional Cross Country Ski Instructor (Nordic)*

Proper waxing is one of the key elements for the maximum enjoyment of the sport. Contrary to public opinion, the skills needed to properly wax skis is very overrated. The method for waxing is simple and with some practice only takes a few minutes before each tour and not the long time that is often thought.

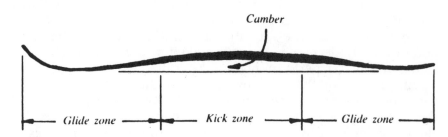

## Definitions to Understand for Proper Waxing

*Camber*—The curve of the ski. This allows for more uniform body weight distribution throughout the length of the ski in order to permit the ski to glide across the snow farther.

*Glide Zone*—Actually there are two zones. The front ¹/₃ of the ski and the rear ¹/₃ of the ski.

*Glide Wax*—Special waxes, some color coded, some not, applied to the Glide Zones of the ski for the sole purpose of creating maximum glide across the snow.

*Kick Zone*— Approximately the center ¹/₃ of the ski extending forward from a point directly under the rear of the heel plate.

*Kick Wax*—Special color coded hard and soft waxes corresponding to the various temperature and snow conditions applied to the kick zone of the ski.

*Klister*—A special soft kick wax used when snow is wet or ski tracks are icy.

## Characteristics of Snow

The only aspect that makes waxing appear difficult is trying to wax skis when there is almost unlimited combinations of snow and temperature conditions. This problem can be simplified if you are award of what snow is actually made. Though snow often appears soft and velvety, it is actually made of tiny crystals of frozen water. The hardness and sharpness of these crystals determines the snow characteristics and; therefore, the proper wax to be used. The colder the temperature, the sharper the crystals and the warmer the temperature, the duller the crystals. The variety of waxes available are designed to match the characteristics of snow so that the crystals will only penetrate a given depth of the wax. This limited penetration of the wax permits you to push against the snow and be released by it at almost the same time. Therefore, harder wax is generally for colder temperatures (sharp crystals) and softer wax is for warmer temperatures (dull crystals). The exception to this occurs when there is ice on the ski track, in which case a klister (soft wax) is required.

## Ski Preparation

Now we begin . . . If the skis are brand new, they should be given some pre-wax preparation. Starting with clean, dry skis, the first step is to prepare the running surface or base. Sand the base with very fine sandpaper (#120 to #400) to get the base as smooth as possible and to remove any hairs that remain from the manufacturing process, should you have that type of ski. Then, thoroughly flush with water several times and completely dry the ski with a lint free towel. This step is not absolutely necessary but will make for more effortless skiing and better performance on the trail.

Since most skis that are now sold are of fiberglass construction with synthetic bases, this chapter will deal with these skis, however, the same method can be used with the older wooden skis by applying a pine tar to the wooden bases for moisture proofing and adhering purposes and then putting kick wax over the entire length of the ski and vary its thickness, with more wax on the center of the ski than at either end.

## Waxing Waxless Skis

Another most important updating is that most fiberglass skis with synthetic soles are so-called waxless skis but never the less, there is a new concept and great trend toward waxing or technically it could be termed lubricating or a combination of both of these so-called waxless skis. This can be accomplished by use of specially formulated lubricants over the entire ski which greatly enhances the glide and also protects the pattern or kick area from excessive wear and icing. The glide area can also be waxed with a universal wax (preferably hot waxed) and the pattern area (fish scales, diamonds, steps, etc.) can be lubricated with one of several products available for this specific purpose.

## General Waxing Information on Waxable Skis

The first step is to wax the glide zones of the ski. For best results, the glider wax will work the best and remain longest on the skis when it is melted and penetrates into the pores of the base. The type of wax needed is not critical for the beginner, since the wrong selection will only result in a very minimal reduction in glide length, a problem you should not find annoying. Many manufacturers provide a wide range and also "universal" glide zone waxes which are very suitable for recreational skiers, and should be chosen initially. In fact, there is one universal glider wax that can also be used in the kick area by applying thicker layers.

To apply the glide wax, position the ski horizontally on a work bench, between two saw horses or anywhere so that the ski will not see-saw on the ski binding. With the use of an old clothes iron (don't plan to use it for clothes again), press the chosen wax against the iron so that the resulting liquid wax drips off the point of the iron onto the ski base to form a long thin ribbon. Once the wax starts melting, you must work fast or it will end up in a big puddle on the ski. Be sure not to allow the wax to smoke since this will change the character of the wax. Next heat the wax into the base by rubbing the iron on the base. This action will not only spread the wax, but also melt a portion of the wax zone. The wax has been sufficiently heated when the top of the ski (the side of the ski away from the snow) near the tip and tail feels warm to the touch. Then place the ski outside to cool completely. Once cooled, repeat the process several times to get maximum penetration of the wax into the pores of the base. If at any time the iron appears to drag on the ski when ironing in the wax, additional wax should be added to that portion of the ski. Caution: If when ironing, the base turns white, STOP IRONING IMMEDIATELY. The base has gotten too hot. It should cool before proceeding. Next, scrape off the ridged glider wax to produce a smooth uniform surface. The best tool for this is a plastic scraper, available at most ski shops. Unlike metal, plastic will not gouge the ski base. Be sure to also remove all the wax out of the groove. Keeping the groove to its full depth is very important because it helps you to control the skis.

Up to this point, all the work can be done most anytime, even well in advance of the ski tour, however, the remaining steps can only be completed when the conditions of the snow that is to be skied on are known.

The following step involves applying the correct kick wax on the remaining center ⅓ of the ski. The proper application of this wax is very important since it allows you not to slip backward when you put weight on your ski to kick backwards.

To select the correct wax to apply, you must first know the type of snow that you are going to ski. If you are at the ski area this can easily be done by grasping a handful of snow and then opening your hand. If the snow remains powdery, then a hard kick wax is needed. On the other hand, if it turns into a ball of wet snow, or ice is in the tracks of the ski trail, then a soft wax is required. Remember to always crayon the wax on evenly in short, rapid strokes covering the entire ski bottom. What you then do depends on the snow temperature. If it is very cold, say less than 20°F., rub the wax out to a gloss with a waxing cork. Nearer freezing, smooth the wax surface slightly with a cork but leave it a bit rough.

## For the Intermediate Skier

Many wax manufacturers have developed "two wax" systems designed especially for beginners that eliminate the rainbow of colored waxes that are on the market. One wax is for above 32°F. and one is for below 32°F. I would highly suggest starting out with one of these systems. They all work reasonably well except in some icy conditions, where klister is still required. After some experience is gained in waxing with these waxes you may want to graduate to the multi-colored wax system.

To apply the wax, choose the correct wax as mentioned above or by using a reliable weather report the night before the tour. By knowing what condition the snow is at that time, you can put on the first layer in your home. Though not absolutely necessary but to make the kick wax more durable, a thin layer of green (for cold weather) and blue (for warmer weather) can be ironed into the base as a first or binder layer. If the two wax system is used, select the proper one of the two and proceed accordingly. To iron on the wax, first crayon a uniform layer of the chosen wax onto the kick zone. Then with an iron, smooth out the wax the same way as done for the glider wax application. After the ski has cooled, scrape off excess wax to produce a uniform layer. If the conditions you anticipate will require additional wax, use a cork instead of a scraper to smooth out the wax. If you don't know what the conditions will be, just leave the wax on and wait until the next day. It is

much faster to scrape off wax than to add it. Not only will this method eliminate, for the most part, the need to purchase special binder wax (not worth the money for the beginning skier) but you will reduce the time normally needed to wax once you arrive at the skiing site.

## For the Serious Tourer

If you have not melted in any kick wax, wait until you are at the trail head to choose the correct wax to apply. Refer to a wax chart and do not hesitate to ask a few people who have skied the trail. With that information, you should have a good idea with which wax to start. If there is a choice between two colors, choose the colder of the two, since it is much easier to add a warmer (softer) wax over a colder (harder) wax than the reverse. Ever try to spread peanut butter over jelly? That is what it is like. Once the wax is evenly crayoned over the entire kick zone, buff the wax out with a cork to make a smooth uniform layer. Add another layer or two and then try out the skis on the snow. Be sure to ski at least 300 feet, so the wax will have an opportunity to set up properly on the skis. If slipping still occurs when attempting to kick backward, the next question is should I add more wax of the same color or go on to the next warmer (softer) wax? Adding more thin layers of the same wax is much safer than using the next softer wax, since that may result in suing a wax that is too soft which will cause ice to form on the skis. The ice will cause poor kick and glide. However, later in the day if the temperature increases, a softer wax may be needed. But don't confuse lack of kick after skiing a while with warmer weather conditions. It may be a result of loss of kick wax which is causing the slipping. When waxing the kick zone, remember it does not extend beyond the heel of the boot. In most cases kick wax added back of that point will only reduce glide and have little effect on improving kick.

If the conditions are very warm (above 40°F.) or the ski track is icy, klister will most likely be needed. In wet conditions where red hard wax is not quite enough, yellow klister in the tin can be used with good success. However, if the track is icy, usually only tube klister will be effective. Spray on klisters are not recommended.

To apply klister try to do it in a warm room. That will make the job much easier. If the tube of klister you have selected from that wax chart is cold, warm the tube with a propane torch. With a clean ski free of wax, apply a thin ribbon of klister along each side of the groove for about two-thirds the length of the normal kick zone starting with the heel end. Klister does not require as much contact with the ice to be equally effective as hard wax does on powder snow. While still warm, and using your finger or the stick provided with the klister, evenly smooth it out, covering the width of the ski. This will take some practice to do it well. If the klister becomes hard before you finish, warm up the klister with the torch using quick long swings so that the flame will not damage the base. Once the klister is spread, let the ski cool *completely* outdoors before skiing on them. It is a good idea to take along a small tube of waterless hand soap (available at most ski shops) to clean your hands. After skiing, remove all of the klister with a scraper and wax remover before packing up, since warm klister tends to get on everything.

For waxable skis, that is about it, with one important exception. It is always necessary to remove all waxes including sticky klister and by far, the best method is to use the very best wax remover sold in bulk cans with a dauber and in spray cans. It will save much time and produces a clean ski. Remember, for best results of waxing it is absolutely necessary to apply the new wax on thoroughly cleaned bottoms.

This chapter is, I believe, the first material written on waxing that categorizes for the x-c skier in a crystal clear way the methods for the beginner, intermediate and serious recreational skier.

Also, it is a first writing in a general way and not mentioning any brand names. You do not have to stick to any one brand as mentioned in most ski books. In all honesty, there are a number of good waxes or lubricants available to the skiing public.

Most Important, Good Tour.

# Skiing Technique Fundamentals

*by Danforth Holley*

*Alumnus Certified Professional Ski Instructor of America (Nordic)*

This chapter is not intended to provide you with complete and comprehensive instruction. Rather, it is intended in this book to give the beginner an idea of the basic movements in the sport of cross country skiing. Many of the movements illustrated on the following pages appear quite easy to execute. However, if you have never had a pair of skis attached to your feet before, you will notice from the first moment, a degree of clumsiness that can only be eliminated by practice and instruction. Instruction is critically important to achieve maximum enjoyment from the sport. This chapter is not intended to be a substitute for instruction, but rather an aid to it. These following pages cannot and should not replace the personal instructor who will be able to recognize a flaw and correct the problem, an aspect that no amount of reading and practice can replace.

Good technique is not difficult or complex, but rather the natural and effortless way to propel yourself on skis. The basic movement, the diagonal stride is directly related to normal walking, but is refined and adapted for use with skis. Good technique does not require the beginner to ski fast or for long distances. That will come with the experience and desire to do so, if you choose. It does, however, result in the same efficiency that the racers have when they ski. The key word here is efficiency. Regardless if you are 15 or 50, a citizen racer to be or just a Sunday afternoon tourer, good technique will allow you to get the maximum enjoyment out of the sport while expending the least amount of energy. This is especially important if you are not, athletically oriented. Without good technique, regardless of how strong you may be, you will struggle, plod along and most likely become frustrated. But this need not happen if you learn the basic cross country technique.

As a beginner, the easiest place to learn to ski is at a nordic ski area which has a prepared ski track that is mechanically made. This might seem at first totally contradictory to the whole idea of cross country skiing, which is supposed to promote the idea of making your own trail wherever you choose, but like a lot of things, that will come later. Good tracks will not only reduce your apprehension, but will also speed your progress and mastery of the technique. If a prepared track is not available, get some of your skiing friends to make a track a few hundred yards long for you. Practice on it before tackling the trail.

But first things first. . . . Before you get on the snow, you must first learn how to get in your ski equipment. Usually the skis are put on first, since hands must be free to secure the ski boot to the binding. The only difficulty with putting on skis is to make sure that the correct ski goes on the proper foot. This might seem trite, but I have seen many beginners 2 miles from the parking lot, having great difficulty skiing, not realizing that the skis are reversed!!! For 75mm bindings there is a small symbol of a foot or words stamped on the binding to help you determine which ski is for what foot. An easier way to make this determination is by the shape of the binding. These bindings are not symmetrical. The binding will protrude further out one side of the ski than the other. The side that occurs on will be the ski for that foot.

On the newer SNS, NNN and similar bindings, should you have a pair, the bindings *are* symmetrical so the skis can be interchanged, though that is not recommended. I suggest placing a small piece of tape on the right ski, to make proper identification easy.

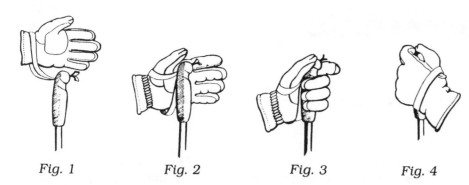

*Fig. 1*     *Fig. 2*     *Fig. 3*     *Fig. 4*

Properly grasping the poles is also very important, for safety as well as for enjoyment. First, place you hand through the strap when the strap is *above* the pole as shown in figure 1. The most common error is to do this with the strap hanging down. Then lower your hand as shown in figure 2 so that the strap is in your palm. Next grip the pole as shown in figures 3 and 4. The index finger should fit snugly just below the top of the pole. If this does not occur, adjust the strap accordingly. Unlike downhill poles that have straps, the cross country ski pole strap is intended to take most of the force of poling without the need for a tight grip of your hand. This eliminates considerable strain and allows blood to flow freely through your fingers to keep them warm. In addition, with this configuration, if the pole basket gets snagged on a branch, the strap and pole will have the tendency to slide off your hand rather than bind to it. A very important safety feature.

## Diagonal Stride

The diagonal stride, the basic technique of cross country skiing is somewhat similar to walking in that opposite arm and leg move together. To learn the stride, begin walking on skis in a ski track on level ground. Do not use poles at first since this will only hinder natural arm movement. Like walking, do not shuffle your feet in the track. When bringing the rear foot forward, lift the foot completely so that body weight is completely transferred to the opposite foot. As the rear foot moves forward and passes the other one, it should begin to

glide as the foot that was passed begins to push to propel you forward. After this begins to feel comfortable, poles can be added to increase glide. They are not intended to be balancing devices, for this will only push your body from side to side with little effect on forward glide. They should be placed in the snow only a few inches outside the edge of the track for maximum effect.

In figure 1, the skier has just planted the left pole. The left ski has just completed the kick and the weighted right ski is about to complete the forward glide. Notice the fingers on the right hand are not gripping the pole. The proper pole strap position discussed earlier, will allow the fingers to relax in order to promote good blood circulation to reduce cold fingers and frostbite. As the hand moves forward, the pole will naturally move back into the hand ready to be gripped loosely as shown in figure 2. In figure 2, the left leg and right arm are swinging forward in unison, while the left pole is pushing. In figure 3, as the left foot passes the right, the right ski begins to kick. The right arm continues to swing forward.

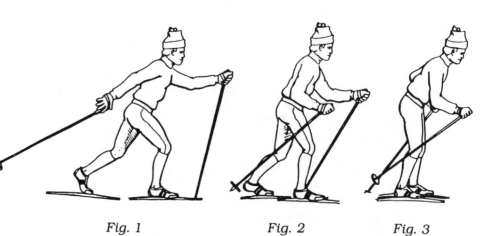

*Fig. 1*          *Fig. 2*          *Fig. 3*

In figure 4, the right ski continues to the end of the kick while the left pole finishes the push. The left ski is still gliding forward. Figure 5 is opposite figure 1 with the left ski nearing the end of its glide and the right pole is relaxed and open. A tight grip will greatly reduce arm swing tiring you quickly. The

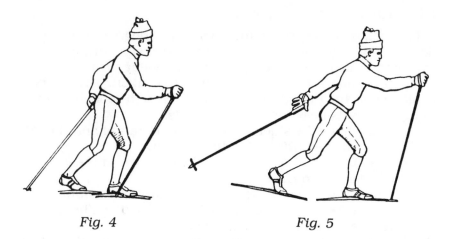

Fig. 4                    Fig. 5

## Double Pole Stride (see below)

The double pole stride is a modification of the diagonal stride where both poles are used in unison to increase glide. The leg movements are identical; however, when one leg kicks, both arms swing forward in a natural opposing movement as illustrated in figures 1 and 3. As the kicking leg comes forward, both poles are planted firmly into the snow (figure 4). As both feet come side by side, the poles are pushed backward, with both feet gliding, as shown in figure 5.

Without the leg movement, another technique is available to you, which is the double pole. With legs side by side, just swing both arms in unison, planting both poles together and pushing off together. Using this technique on any downhill grade, no matter how gradual, will dramatically increase glide much more than by using the diagonal stride.

pole, instead of trailing out behind you will end almost straight up in the air, reducing glide distance and balance.

The objective of the diagonal stride is to develop maximum glide. But, don't try to force natural movements of your body. First keep the stride short to maintain balance and maximum body weight shift to the kicking leg. Do not try to imitate others. As your balance improves, the glide will become longer.

Fig. 1          Fig. 2          Fig. 3          Fig. 4          Fig. 5          Fig. 6

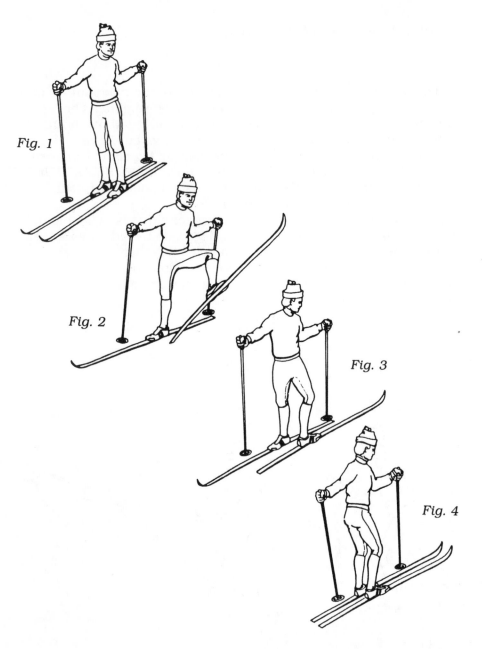

Fig. 1

Fig. 2

Fig. 3

Fig. 4

## Kick Turn

The kick turn is very useful when a 180-degree turn is desired in a very confined location where a star turn can't be executed. This turn is also quicker than a star turn.

Figure 1 shows the skier intending to turn left. The left pole is planted at the tail of the skis, while the right pole is to the right of the skis near the tips of the skis.

Figure 2 shows the skier with the left ski raised and the tail in the snow at the *midpoint* of the right ski.

In figure 3, the left ski has been placed down in the opposite direction, parallel to the right ski.

And finally, in figure 4 the right ski is brought around behind the left ski to be positioned parallel to the left ski. The new opposite direction has been achieved.

Pole position may vary somewhat; however, you will quickly realize that a pole in a slightly incorrect position will make it impossible to execute this turn.

## Star Turn

For the beginner, the least difficult way to change direction when not moving is by executing the star turn. Starting with parallel skis, lift the ski in the direction you wish to turn (lift is shown here). Angle that ski slightly, while making sure not to let the ski tails overlap each other. The skier then lifts the right ski and repositions it parallel to the left one. Repeat the process until the desired direction is reached.

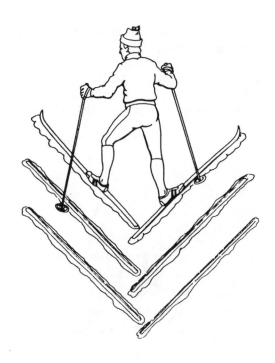

## Climbing with a Diagonal Stride

When climbing gradual hills it is important for you to maintain glide and momentum for as long as possible; hopefully until you reach the top. By using a shortened version of the diagonal stride, maintain upper body position directly over the forward leg to maximize weight on the kicking leg. To increase this weight as the slope becomes steeper, separate your skis a few inches if possible to force total body weight shift to the kicking leg.

## Herringbone

This step is most commonly used for steep uphill climbs where the diagonal stride cannot be maintained. It is best accomplished by pivoting the skis down to the inside. This will assure firm footing. The skis should form a 45-degree angle to each other. If the hill is very steep, place the pole grips in the palms of your hands so that the poles act as a brake in case the skis lose sufficient grip. If the hill becomes steeper, separate the tips of the skis even farther.

363

## Modified Sidestep

This technique is used as a means to climb steep slopes as an alternative to the herringbone. It is faster and much easier than the standard sidestep. This technique is demonstrated by the skier on the left who is keeping his skis parallel to one another and stepping uphill with the uphill ski being placed slightly forward each time. This step is especially helpful in deep powder snow.

Fig. 1

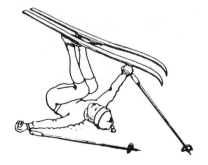

Fig. 2

## Recovering from a Fall

Undoubtedly, the first technique that you will become most proficient in will be how to get up from a fall. Even with a well-groomed track and the best of instruction, the first fall will occur much sooner than you wish. With a little common sense, getting up is not hard or difficult, regardless of how tangled your skis, legs, arms and poles may be.

For a simple fall to the side this technique is not necessary, but when you really take a spill. . . . you must take the weight off your skis and poles before repositioning them will be possible.

Fig. 3

Fig. 4

In figure 1 the skier is shown immediately after a fall. Though the poles are clear of the tangled skis, many times you will not find this the situation.

Figure 2 shows the skier has taken his weight off the back skis by rolling onto his back and raising the skis above his head. This will also free any poles that are tangled.

Next, in figure 3 the skier has brought both skis down next to his body with his feet tucked under him as closely as possible. This is important so that the skis will not slide out from under him when attempting to stand. When falling on a slope, reposition the skis perpendicular to the slope to keep them and you from sliding down the slope before you are ready.

Figure 4 shows the skier using the poles as an aid in getting up on his feet. Though this is not absolutely necessary, if they are used, be sure to grasp them together before putting weight on them, so they will not break.

Regardless of how tangled you may be, if you are in deep snow resist the temptation to remove your skis. They are an excellent flotation device. And remember, how do you expect to get into your bindings if you can't even see them!

## Snowplow

The skier below is executing the most common method of controlling speed. With his skis pivoted inward, to increase resistance, all he has to do to reduce speed is to increase the angle between the skis. Poles can be dragged to increase resistance but this is not usually necessary. To steer when using the snowplow, just shift more weight to the opposite ski in the direction you wish to turn.

## Snowplowing in a Track

When it is necessary to reduce speed in a track, the snowplow can be used, but only one ski at a time. On the straight this will reduce speed substantially without damage to the track or loss of control. The skier above, is controlling speed in a curve by placing the ski on the outside of the curve in the snowplow position. This will assist him in offsetting the outward force that occurs in a curve. With only one ski out of the track at a time, it will be much easier to place it back in the track than if both skis were out simultaneously.

The two skiers below show additional methods for controlling downhill speed, especially in deep powder snow. Poles *must* be put into the positions shown prior to the start of the downhill run. Do not attempt to reposition poles once the downhill run has begun.

365

## Skate Turn

This technique is a very efficient method of turning, since it is very quick, resulting in an increase in speed. To execute this turn, the skier in figure 1 has unweighted the ski in the direction he wishes to turn (right shown here), while pushing off with the left ski that has been slightly pivoted to increase bite. In figure 2 the unweighted ski has been repositioned in the direction of travel, which then is quickly followed by the left ski (not shown). If the turn is large, these steps may have to be repeated in quick succession.

*Fig. 2*

*Fig. 1*

## Crouch or Racing Tuck

This position is used to increase speed (by reducing air resistance) on downhill runs. Keep body weight balanced with legs relaxed and one ski slightly forward to improve stability.

## Parallel Turn

The parallel turn involves weight shift from side to side and up and down and the pivoting of skis to properly execute this downhill technique. Begin by planting the pole that is on the inside of the turn (not shown). The skier then positions himself in a more erect stance to unweight the skis. This will then allow the skis to turn. Once in the turn the skier then weights the outside ski to push against the snow. Now in the new direction, the skier then evenly distributes his weight between both skis.

## Telemark Turn

This is the classic nordic turn that was developed in the province of Telemark, Norway when cross country skis were much larger and more difficult to control. While using poles for balance, figure 1 shows the skier with the inside ski in a position where the tip of the inside ski is even with the boot of the outside ski. At this point, the inside lower leg should be just about parallel with the ski. Continue this position until the new direction is reached. An advantage of this turn is that a change in direction can be executed very easily simply by reversing the relative positions of the skis. This technique requires a great deal of practice to execute properly. But, if done well, it is one of the most enjoyable turns a nordic skier can perform.

With the recent revival of Telemark skiing, several touring centers are now teaching this classical technique.

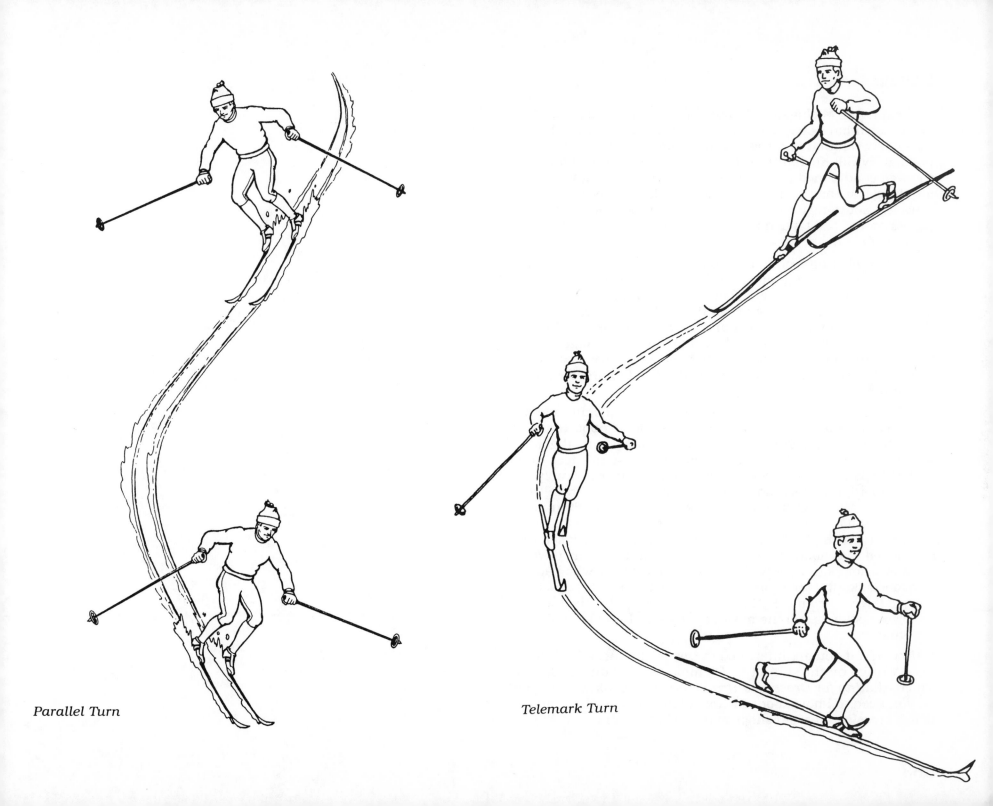

*Parallel Turn*

*Telemark Turn*

## Skating

In exploring Michigan's plethora of beautiful trails, you may on occasion have observed some skiers skating on skis. This is a recent revolution in cross country skiing technique made popular by Bill Koch. It is a revolution but should be limited to the well conditioned serious skier and racer. Skating with anything less than racing equipment could seriously strain muscles, not to mention the significant physical demands placed on the body when using normal light touring equipment.

The new skating technique should only be tried when using light weight racing equipment or better still the specifically designed skating equipment. This equipment includes boots that support the ankle more than the traditional nordic boot, skis that have a stiffer camber and are not designed for kick wax and poles that are as much as a foot or more longer than the standard pole. Some poles even have a grip like a canoe paddle. All this special equipment is designed to provide for maximum thrust.

Its important to realize that skating is a 100% commitment since skating skis have no kick wax. There is no opportunity to fall back on the old standard classic technique when fatigue sets in. That is why I have chosen not to discuss this technique in the chapter. For the general cross-country skier it simply is not an appropriate technique to use. Dennis Hansen travelled throughout Michigan in 1988 and visited more than 80 trails from one end of the state to the other. Although many have developed skating trails, they all have their trails track set. He mentioned that none of the operators intend to convert their trails over for skating only. On the contrary, many who had developed skating lanes are reducing them, since there just is not the interest from the general public. Except for the races, the classic style is still the most popular and I predict it will stay that way.

However, if you are interested in this technique, a book has been written on the subject by Olympic skier Audun Endestad. Titled *Skating for Cross-Country Skiers*, this book will tell you all you need to know about the technique. It is available at better cross country ski shops and touring centers.

# Appendices

# APPENDIX 1

## Ski Trails

Addis Lakes Cross Country Ski Trail
Addison Oaks County Park
Al Quaal Recreation Area
Algonquin Cross Country Ski Trail
Allegan State Game Area
Alligator Hill Trail
Alpine Center Trails
Aman Park
American Adventure/Woods & Waters Resort
Anderson Lake Pathway
Ashford Lake Pathway
Bald Mountain Recreation Area—North Unit
Bald Mountain Recreation Area—South Unit
Bay Valley Hotel & Resort
Bay View Ski Trail
Beechwoods Recreation Center
Bergland Trail
Betsie River Pathway
Bewabic State Park
Big M Cross Country Ski Area
Binder Park Inc.
Bintz Apple Mountain
Black River Pathway
Blueberry Ridge Pathway
Bond Falls Ski Trail
Bowman Lake Foot Travel Area
Boyne Highlands
Boyne Mountain
Brighton Recreation Area
Brock Park
Bruno's Run Trail
Buttles Road Pathway
Cadillac Pathway
Canada Lakes Pathway
Candlestone Inn Inc.

Cannonsburg State Game Area
Carp River Forge Trail
Cedar River Pathway
Cedar Trail
Central Park
Chalet Cross Country
Charlevoix Cross Country Ski Trail
Chassell Classic Ski Trail
Cheboygan State Park
Chippewa Hills Pathway
Cleveland Cross Country Ski Trail
Coldbrook County Park
Cool Ski Area
Copper Harbor Pathway
Corsair Trails
County Farm Park
Craig Lake State Park
Cross Country Ski Headquarters
Cross Country Ski Shop
Crystal Mountain Resort
Days River Pathway
Deerfield County Park
Dr T. K. Lawless Park
Drummond Island Ski Trail
Eagle Run
Egypt Valley Trail
Elizabeth Park
Empire Bluff Trail
Escanaba Cross Country Ski Pathway
Fayette State Park
Fisherman's Island State Park
Fit Strip Ski Trail
Fitzgerald Park
For-Mar Nature Preserve
Forbush Corner

Fort Custer Recreation Area
Fort Wilkins State Park
Fox Park
Freedom Hill County Park
Garland
Ge-Che Trail
Gladstone Cross Country Ski Trail
Glen Oaks Golf Course
Good Harbor Bay Ski Trail
Grand Marais Cross Country Ski & Snowshoe Trail
Grand Mere State Park
Grand River Park
Grand Traverse Resort Village
Grass Lake Natural Area
Green Pine Lake Pathway
Hanson Hills Recreational Park
Harlow Lake Pathway
Hart-Montague Bicycle Trail State Park
Hartwick Pines State Park
Hayo-Went-Ha Nordic Ski Center
Heritage Park
Hickory Hills
Highbanks Trail
Highland Recreation Area
Hinchman Acres Resort
Hoeft State Park
Hoffmaster State Park
Hoist Lakes Foot Travel Area
Holly Recreation Area
Homestead
Howell Nature Center
Hudson-Mills Metropark
Hungerford Trail
Huron Meadows Metropark
Imerman Memorial Park

Independence Oaks County Park
Indian Lake Pathway
Indian Springs Metropark
Indian Trails
Ionia State Recreation Area
Iron Land Ski Trail
Island Lake Recreation Area
Jellystone Park Camp Resort
Johnson's Nordic Trails
Kal-Haven Trail Sesquicentennial State Park
Keehne Environmental Area
Kellogg Forest
Kensington Metropark
Kinsmen Ski Trails  See Star System/Kinsmen Ski
    Trails
Lake Ann Pathway
Lake Erie Metropark
Lake Gogebic State Park
Lake Mary Plains Pathway
Lamoreaux Park
Leelanau State Park
Legg Park
Lost Lake Nature Pathway
Lost Twin Lakes Pathway
Loud Creek Cross Country Ski Trail
Love Creek County Park & Nature Center
Ludington State Park
M.S.U. Cross Country Ski Trails
Maasto Hiihto Ski Trail
MacKenzie National Recreation Trail
Mackinac Island
Madeline Bertrand County Park
Maple Lane Touring Center
Mason Tract Pathway
Maybury State Park
McCormick Experimental Forest
McLain State Park
Mecca Ski Trail
Merriman East Pathway
Metamora-Hadley Recreation Area
Metro Beach Metropark

Michaywe Slopes
Midland to Mackinac Pathway—Mio Section
Missaukee Mountain
Montreal Public Trail
MTU Trail
Muncie Lakes Pathway
Munising Cross Country Ski Trail
Muskegon State Park
National Mine Ski Area
Negaunee Township Touring Trail
Neithercut Woodland
Nokomis Pathway
Norden Hem
Nordhouse Dunes Trails
North Country Trail—Baldwin
North Country Trail—Manistee
North Country Trail—Munising South
North Country Trail—Sturgeon River
North Country Trail—White Cloud
North Country Trail Connector
North Higgins Lake State Park
North Lake Lansing Park
Norway Ridge Pathway
Nub's Nob
Oak Pointe Golf Course
Oakwoods Metropark
Ocqueoc Falls Bicentennial Pathway
Ogemaw Hills Pathway
Old Grade Ski Trail
Old Indian Trail
Ortonville Recreation Area
Owasippe Scout Reservation
Paint Creek Trail
Palmer Park
Pando Ski Area
Paradise Pathway
Park Lyndon
Pentwater Pathway
Petoskey State Park
Pinckney Recreation Area
Pine Baron Pathway

Pine Bowl Pathway
Pine Haven Recreation Area
Pine Mountain Lodge
Pine Valleys Pathway
Pinery Lakes Trail
Platte Plains Trail
Plymouth Orchards and Cider Mill
Ponnistus Athletic Club Ski Trail
Porcupine Mountains Wilderness State Park
Port Crescent State Park
Prairie View Park
Presque Isle Park
Price Nature Center
Proud Lake Recreation Area
Provin Trails Park
Ranch Rudolf
Rapid River Cross Country Ski Trail
Reid Lake Foot Travel Area
Ringwood Forest
River Falls Trail
Rochester-Utica Recreation Area
Rolling Hills County Park
Rose Lake Wildlife Research Area
Russ Forest Park
Sand Dunes Cross Country Ski Trail
Sand Dunes Quiet Area
Saugatuck Dunes State Park
Sauk Valley Farms Resort
Sault Finnish Ski Club  See Star System/Kinsmen
    Ski Trails
Sault Nordic Ski Trail
Sault Ste. Marie Canal
Scenic Drive Cross Country Ski Trail
School Forest Ski Trail
Searchmont
Seidman Park
Seney National Wildlife Refuge
Seven Lakes State Park
Shanty Creek/Schuss Mountain Resorts
Sheep Ranch Pathway
Sherman Park

Shingle Mill Pathway
Shore To Shore Trail—Segment A
Shore To Shore Trail—Segment B
Shore To Shore Trail—Segment C
Silver Creek Trail—Marquette
Silver Mountain Ski Trail
Sinkhole Pathway
Ski Brule/Ski Homestead
Sleeper State Park
Sleepy Hollow State Park
Snowcrest
South Higgins Lake State Park
Spring Brook Pathway
Springfield Oaks Golf Course
St. Ignace Town Trail
St. Patrick's County Park
Star System/Kinsmen Ski Trails
Sterling State Park
Stokely Creek Ski Touring Center
Stony Creek Metropark

Sugar Loaf Resort
Suicide Bowl
Swedetown Ski Trail
Sylvan Glen Municipal Golf Course
Sylvan Resort
Sylvania Recreation Area
Tabor Hill Vineyard
Tahquamenon Falls State Park
Timberlane Nordic Ski Center, Inc
Tisdale Triangle Pathway
Trout Lake Pathway
Tur-Ski-Ree Trails
Twin Lakes State Park
Uller Trail
Valley Spur Ski Trail
Van Riper State Park
Wakeley Lake Non-Motorized Area
Warner Creek Pathway
Warren Dunes State Park
Warren Valley Golf Course

Warren Woods State Park
Waterloo Recreation Area
Waterloo-Pinckney Hiking Trail
Watersmeet Ski Trail
Wells State Park
West Higgins Lake Trail
White Lake Oaks Golf Course
Whitecap Mountains Nordic
Wilderness State Park
Wilderness Valley
Wildwood Hills Pathway
Willow Metropark
Windmill Farms
Windy Moraine Trail
Woldumar Nature Center
Wolverine Ski Trail
Yankee Springs Recreation Area
Young State Park

# APPENDIX 2

## Hiking Trails

Addison Oaks County Park
Algonquin Cross Country Ski Trail
Allegan State Game Area
Alligator Hill Trail
Alpine Center Trails
Aman Park
American Adventure/Woods & Waters Resort
Anderson Lake Pathway
Ashford Lake Pathway
Bald Mountain Recreation Area—North Unit
Bald Mountain Recreation Area—South Unit
Bay De Noc—Grand Island Trail
Bay View Ski Trail
Besser Bell Pathway
Betsie River Pathway
Bewabic State Park
Big Bear Lake Nature Pathway
Binder Park Inc.
Black River Pathway
Blueberry Ridge Pathway
Bowman Lake Foot Travel Area
Boyne Highlands
Boyne Mountain
Brighton Recreation Area
Brock Park
Bruno's Run Trail
Buttles Road Pathway
Cadillac Pathway
Canada Lakes Pathway
Cannonsburg State Game Area
Carp River Forge Trail
Cedar River Pathway
Central Park
Cheboygan State Park
Chippewa Hills Pathway

Clear Lake—Jackson Lake Pathway
Cleveland Cross Country Ski Trail
Coldbrook County Park
Cool Ski Area
Copper Harbor Pathway
Corsair Trails
County Farm Park
Craig Lake State Park
Cross Country Ski Headquarters
Days River Pathway
Deerfield County Park
Dr. T. K. Lawless Park
Dunes Trail
Eagle Run
Egypt Valley Trail
Elizabeth Park
Empire Bluff Trail
Fayette State Park
Fisherman's Island State Park
Fit Strip Ski Trail
Fitzgerald Park
For-Mar Nature Preserve
Fort Custer Recreation Area
Fort Wilkins State Park
Fox Park
Fox River Pathway
Freedom Hill County Park
Ge-Che Trail
Gladstone Cross Country Ski Trail
Gogebic Ridge Hiking Trail
Grand Mere State Park
Grand River Park
Grass Lake Natural Area
Green Pine Lake Pathway
Harlow Lake Pathway

Hart-Montague Bicycle Trail State Park
Hartwick Pines State Park
Heritage Park
Hidden Lake Gardens
High Country Pathway
Highbanks Trail
Highland Recreation Area
Hinchman Acres Resort
Hoeft State Park
Hoffmaster State Park
Hoist Lakes Foot Travel Area
Holly Recreation Area
Howell Nature Center
Hudson-Mills Metropark
Hungerford Trail
Imerman Memorial Park
Independence Lake County Park
Independence Oaks County Park
Indian Lake Pathway
Indian Springs Metropark
Ionia State Recreation Area
Island Lake Recreation Area
Isle Royale National Park
Jordan Valley Pathway
Kal-Haven Trail Sesquicentennial State Park
Keehne Environmental Area
Kellogg Forest
Kensington Metropark
Lake Ann Pathway
Lake Gogebic State Park
Lake Mary Plains Pathway
Lakeshore Trail
Lamoreaux Park
Leelanau State Park
Legg Park

Lost Lake Nature Pathway
Lost Tamarack Pathway
Lost Twin Lakes Pathway
Loud Creek Cross Country Ski Trail
Love Creek County Park & Nature Center
Ludington State Park
MacKenzie National Recreation Trail
Mackinac Island
Madeline Bertrand County Park
Maple Lane Touring Center
Mason Tract Pathway
Maybury State Park
McCormick Experimental Forest
McLain State Park
Merriman East Pathway
Metamora Hadley Recreation Area
Midland to Mackinac Pathway—Mio Section
Montreal Public Trail
Muncie Lakes Pathway
Muskallonge Lake State Park
Muskegon State Park
Neithercut Woodland
Nokomis Pathway
Norden Hem
Nordhouse Dunes Trails
North Country Trail—Baldwin
North Country Trail—Bergland
North Country Trail—Black River
North Country Trail—DNR
North Country Trail—Manistee
North Country Trail—Munising South
North Country Trail—Sault Ste. Marie
North Country Trail—St. Ignace
North Country Trail—Sturgeon River
North Country Trail—White Cloud
North Country Trail Connector
North Higgins Lake State Park
North Lake Lansing Park
North Manitou Island
Norway Ridge Pathway
Oak Pointe Golf Course
Oakwoods Metropark
Ocqueoc Falls Bicentennial Pathway
Old Grade Ski Trail
Old Indian Trail

Ortonville Recreation Area
Owasippe Scout Reservation
Palmer Park
Paint Creek Trail
Paradise Pathway
Park Lyndon
Pentwater Pathway
Petoskey State Park
Pinckney Recreation Area
Pine Baron Pathway
Pine Bowl Pathway
Pine Haven Recreation Area
Pine Valleys Pathway
Platte Plains Trail
Porcupine Mountains Wilderness State Park
Port Crescent State Park
Prairie View Park
Presque Isle Park
Price Nature Center
Proud Lake Recreation Area
Provin Trails Park
Pyramid Point Trail
Ranch Rudolf
Reid Lake Foot Travel Area
Rifle River Recreation Area
Ringwood Forest
Rochester-Utica Recreation Area
Rolling Hills County Park
Rose Lake Wildlife Research Area
Russ Forest Park
Sand Dunes Cross Country Ski Trail
Sand Lakes Quiet Area
Saugatuck Dunes State Park
Sault Ste. Marie Canal
School Forest Ski Trail
Searchmont
Seidman Park
Seney National Wildlife Refuge
Seven Lakes State Park
Shanty Creek/Schuss Mountain Resorts
Sheep Ranch pathway
Sherman Park
Shingle Mill Pathway
Shore to Shore Trail
Shore to Shore Trail—Segment A

Shore to Shore Trail—Segment B
Shore to Shore Trail—Segment C
Silver Creek Trail—Marquette
Silver Mountain Ski Trail
Sinkhole Pathway
Sleeper State Park
Sleepy Hollow State Park
South Higgins Lake State Park
South Manitou Island
Spring Brook Pathway
St. Patrick's County Park
Star System/Kinsmen Ski Trails
Sterling State Park
Stokely Creek Ski Touring Center
Stony Creek Metropark
Sugar Loaf Mountain Pathway
Sugar Loaf Resort
Swedetown Ski Trail
Sylvan Resort
Sylvania Recreation Area
Tabor Hill Vineyard
Tahquamenon Falls State Park
Tisdale Triangle Pathway
Trout Lake Pathway
Twin Lakes State Park
Tyoga Historical Pathway
Uller Trail
Valley Spur Ski Trail
Van Riper State Park
Wakeley Lake Non-Motorized Area
Warner Creek Pathway
Warren Dunes State Park
Warren Woods State Park
Waterloo Recreation Area
Waterloo-Pinckney Hiking Trail
Wells State Park
West Higgins Lake Trail
Wilderness State Park
Wildwood Hills Pathway
Windmill Farms
Windy Moraine Trail
Woldumar Nature Center
Yankee Springs Recreation Area
Young State Park

# Index

# INDEX

# Trail Notes